Answering Queries Using Views

Second Edition

Synthesis Lectures on Data Management

Editor
H.V. Jagadish, *University of Michigan*

Founding Editor
M. Tamer Özsu, *University of Waterloo*

Synthesis Lectures on Data Management is edited by H.V. Jagadish of the University of Michigan. The series publishes 80–150 page publications on topics pertaining to data management. Topics include query languages, database system architectures, transaction management, data warehousing, XML and databases, data stream systems, wide scale data distribution, multimedia data management, data mining, and related subjects.

Answering Queries Using Views, Second Edition
Foto Afrati and Rada Chirkova

ISBN: 978-3-031-00743-9   paperback
ISBN: 978-3-031-01871-8   ebook
ISBN: 978-3-031-00098-0   hardcover

DOI 10.1007/978-3-031-01871-8

A Publication in the Springer series
SYNTHESIS LECTURES ON DATA MANAGEMENT

Lecture #54
Series Editor: H.V. Jagadish, *University of Michigan*
Founding Editor: M. Tamer Özsu, *University of Waterloo*
Series ISSN
Print 2153-5418   Electronic 2153-5426

Answering Queries Using Views

Second Edition

Foto Afrati
National Technical University of Athens

Rada Chirkova
North Carolina State University

SYNTHESIS LECTURES ON DATA MANAGEMENT #54

ABSTRACT

The topic of using views to answer queries has been popular for a few decades now, as it cuts across domains such as query optimization, information integration, data warehousing, website design and, recently, database-as-a-service and data placement in cloud systems.

This book assembles foundational work on answering queries using views in a self-contained manner, with an effort to choose material that constitutes the backbone of the research. It presents efficient algorithms and covers the following problems: query containment; rewriting queries using views in various logical languages; equivalent rewritings and maximally contained rewritings; and computing certain answers in the data-integration and data-exchange settings. Query languages that are considered are fragments of SQL, in particular select-project-join queries, also called conjunctive queries (with or without arithmetic comparisons or negation), and aggregate SQL queries.

This second edition includes two new chapters that refer to tree-like data and respective query languages. Chapter 8 presents the data model for XML documents and the XPath query language, and Chapter 9 provides a theoretical presentation of tree-like data model and query language where the tuples of a relation share a tree-structured schema for that relation and the query language is a dialect of SQL with evaluation techniques appropriately modified to fit the richer schema.

KEYWORDS

conjunctive queries, aggregate queries, arithmetic comparisons, negation, acyclic queries, query containment, query equivalence, equivalent query rewritings, maximally contained query rewritings, tuple-generating dependencies, equality-generating dependencies, the chase algorithm query containment and rewriting under dependencies, data exchange, determinacy, XPath, tree data

Contents

Preface to the First Edition

Views are used in various scenarios; some of the view-based settings have been considered in depth by the research community. The settings that we cover in this book include the following.

1. The problem of rewriting queries using views, where a set of views and a set of queries are given, and we need to find equivalent rewritings (if they exist) of the queries using these views.

2. Sometimes we cannot find equivalent rewritings but can still compute a significant part of the answer to the query. This gives rise to the problems of computing certain answers and of finding maximally contained query rewritings.

3. The picture of finding rewritings changes when we assume that the data satisfy certain constraints (dependencies). We re-examine the problem of finding rewritings for the setting in which the constraints are tuple-generating dependencies and equality-generating dependencies.

4. A closely related topic based on the same theoretical foundations is the data-exchange setting. We define the concept of certain answers and present algorithms to find them.

5. Some theoretical aspects of the more general problem of answering queries using views have also been investigated in more general and abstract settings, such as determining the (query) language fragments for which there are rewritings in the cases where the queries are determined by the views.

In order to solve problems in the above settings, we need technical tools. Thus, we provide detailed treatments of some tools, including conjunctive-query containment (with and without arithmetic comparisons and negation), the chase algorithm for reasoning about dependencies, and going beyond nonrecursive languages to find rewritings, with a discussion of Datalog.

What the book is not about: This book is not about indexes or data structures that implement the techniques considered in the exposition. Instead, this books focuses on the formal-logic perspective on the topic.

The book is written in a linear way, in the sense that each chapter depends on all the previous chapters. We have made every effort for the book to be self-contained, thus there are no substantial prerequisites. A reader familiar with the basics of the theory of database systems and knowledge of logic will move faster through the chapters. Exercises are included. More exercises, including online exercises, and any supplementary material will be found on the website[1] of the book.

Foto Afrati and Rada Chirkova
October 2017

---

[1] bit.ly/2zMYBHf

Preface to the Second Edition

We have added two chapters that refer to tree-like data and respective query languages. Chapter 8 presents the data model for XML documents and the XPath query language and gives query containment tests and query rewriting techniques. However, besides the relational data model and the tree-structured XML data model, many recently developed systems, to manage big data, use data models that combine relational and tree-like features. In terms of defining and using views, these models have not be investigated. However, they are mature enough to be presented in a rigorous way. Thus, Chapter 9 provides a theoretical presentation of such data model and query language as extensions of the relational model and SQL query language. In these data models, the tuples of a relation share a tree-structured schema for that relation and the query language is a dialect of SQL. The query language uses SQL-style syntax but the evaluation techniques have to be modified to fit the richer schema. The conclusions and bibliographical notes for these two chapters are included in the chapters themselves. Chapters 8 and 9 can also be read independently of the rest of the chapters in the book and independently of each other.

In the chapters of the first edition, we have corrected errors.

Foto Afrati and Rada Chirkova
January 2019

Acknowledgments

Rachel Pottinger kindly reviewed this book and provided constructive comments. Jeff Ullman contributed immensely in an elegant and concise way in the improvement of this book. We acknowledge here his many comments that have greatly improved and enhanced the text.

Foto Afrati and Rada Chirkova
October 2017

CHAPTER 1

Queries and Views

In this chapter, we first introduce the topic that we discuss in this book by presenting some application scenarios that hint at the technical issues to which they give rise (Section 1.2). An informal discussion follows about specific technical problems in answering queries using views with concrete examples (Section 1.3). Then, for completeness and consistency of notation, we give formal definitions for the relational data model and query languages (Section 1.4). We conclude the chapter with an outline of the structure of the book.

This is the only chapter of the book that is structured so that it can be read in a nonlinear way. Section 1.4 is the only part of this chapter that is a prerequisite for the rest of the book and is independent of the rest of the sections in this chapter. The other sections offer motivation for studying the topic and a few examples to introduce the main idea of answering queries using views and introduce the notion of "query rewriting." The already motivated reader and those familiar with such concepts can skip those sections. For the readers who first introduce themselves to the topic of views, Section 1.3 can be read before or after Section 1.4 depending on their level of familiarity with the notation. For readers that are not familiar with SQL, they can skip safely the SQL part in Section 1.3 and, depending on their familiarity with the notation of conjunctive query as a rule, they may read Section 1.3 before or after Section 1.4. For readers that are familiar with SQL but not the rule-notation of conjunctive queries, Section 1.3 can also serve as a smooth introduction to how the two notations relate to each other.

1.1 VIEWS

A view is a query on a database. However, what we understand by "view" may not be the same as a query when it comes to its functionality in a database system. For example, a view may not be submitted by a user, hence its output is not necessarily forwarded to a user who requested this information, but is stored for future use. Also, a view may not be physically stored at all, but used to enable users to form simpler queries. In the first case, we refer to it as *materialized view*, and in the second case we say that it is a *virtual view*.

When we use a CREATE statement in SQL, what we actually define can be seen as a virtual view, which, in turn, is treated in queries as if it were a physically stored base table. The database-management system maintains the definition of the view, unless it is explicitly changed. When views are used in a query, then the tuples of the actually physically stored relations are called to compute the output of the views, as per their definition.

Materialized views are physically stored. Thus, they may serve the purpose of speeding up the computation of queries, by providing parts of the query that are already precomputed and stored.

In the next two sections, we present examples of views and how they play a role in some query-answering scenarios. SQL queries use the Datalog rule syntax in this book. This is the only chapter that contains references to SQL queries, for the sake of those readers who want to see how their familiar SQL queries can be expressed in the Datalog-rule syntax that we use throughout the book.

1.2   USING VIEWS IN DATABASE SYSTEMS

We now mention some use cases, invoking application scenarios where views come to be useful, and then we mention some technical problems that arise from these scenarios. In the next section, we will give concrete examples in SQL for the notions we mention here.

1.2.1   VIEWS AND USE CASES

We mention some application scenarios to see the role of views in database systems. Later in this chapter we will also give some concrete examples around these scenarios.

- Query optimization: We can significantly speed up query processing if we have precomputed some part of the query in the form of views. Many queries may share common sub-queries, which, if identified, can be precomputed as views and save a lot of "duplicated" computation (indexed views).

- Data integration: Using views to address data-integration problems is a popular technique. In that, we have two approaches: (a) views describe a set of autonomous heterogenous data sources and are defined over a global mediated schema, over which the query is also defined. This is known as the *local as view* (LAV) approach. In this case, query processing needs to rewrite the query first—as we will be explaining later; (b) views represent the global schema over which the query is defined, while the views themselves are defined over the data sources. This is known as the *global as view* (GAV) approach. In this case, query processing is straightforward.

- Data exchange: When we have heterogenous sources, we often want to transform data structured under a schema into data structured under another schema (they are called *source* and *target* schemas, respectively). The transformation is defined by an expression written in a particular language, pretty much as a view is defined, only more general (therefore it is referred to as the GLAV approach—incorporating both the LAV and GAV approaches). The goal is again to materialize data under the target schema that satisfy the relationship between the schemas, with the purpose of being used to answer queries posed over the target schema. However, only the information in the data of the source schema should be used to provide these answers.

- Data warehousing: A data warehouse stores data for the purpose of reporting and data analysis. Data warehouses are repositories of integrated data that come from various sources (that can be thought of as views). They serve two main types of queries, Online Analytical Processing (OLAP) and Online Transaction Processing (OLTP).

  OLAP is characterized by a relatively low volume of transactions; queries are complex and use aggregation. The OLAP approach is used to analyze multidimensional data (often in star databases) from many sources.

  OLTP is characterized by a large number of short online transactions (INSERT, UP-DATE, DELETE).

1.2.2   VIEWS AND TECHNICAL ISSUES

For the scenarios of Section 1.2.1 to be addressed in a satisfactory way, we need to understand how to compute a query using a set of views (which we either choose or are given), or, more generally, how to produce answers to a query that is defined over a schema different from the schema of the data. Further, we need to understand how to select views with the maximum benefit (e.g., when used to speed up query computation). Here is a list of the main technical problems that this book will present, together with a discussion of how they arise in the above scenarios. We will mention them briefly in this section and then, in Section 1.3, we will give concrete SQL examples, which will enlighten some technical points that we do not mention in any detail below.

- Computing certain answers using views in the LAV setting. The concept of "certain answers" is often used when there are not any equivalent rewritings. Then, intuitively, finding the certain answers is the best we can do. Their high-level definition (which will be made formal in later chapters in the book) is as follows: We are given view definitions for views in $\mathcal{V}$ and a query definition for query Q, with all the definitions over the same database schema. We are also given data in a database $\mathcal{V}(D)$, where $\mathcal{V}(D)$ is the result of computing the views on D. There exists also a database D over the schema of the query and view definitions, but we do not know what D is. All we know is that D is some database such that when we apply the view definitions, we get the local database $\mathcal{V}(D)$ that we can access. Now we want to find as many answers as possible to the query computed on D, but having access only to $\mathcal{V}(D)$. The answers that are desirable to be found this way are called *certain answers*. Certain answers capture the intuition that we want to include in our result those answers that have the following property: No matter what D is, as long as we can construct $\mathcal{V}(D)$ from it using the view definitions, the certain answers will be in $Q(D)$. The application scenarios include data integration and data warehousing (here all the answers are desirable, but if we cannot find them all, then we have to settle for only the certain answers).

- Computing certain answers using views in the data-exchange (GLAV) setting. Here, we are given a data-exchange transformation from the source schema to the target schema. Given any database on the source schema, we want to find a database (possibly incomplete) on the target schema that, for, any query Q, can be used to derive as many answers as possible among those that the query Q would have derived on the source schema. The application scenarios include all applications of data exchange and in general, applications of interoperability in businesses.

- Equivalent rewritings. We are given view definitions and a query definition, all the definitions being over the same database schema. We want to find another query, which now is over the schema of the views (i.e., it uses only the views as the basic database relations), such that the resulting query is equivalent to the given query. The constructed query is called an *equivalent rewriting*. The equivalent rewriting and the original query are equivalent in the following sense: We compute the views over the original database (on the schema of the views and the query) D, to get database $V(D)$. Now equivalence of the rewriting and of the original query means that when we compute the query on D, we get the same set of answers as the answers of the rewriting over $V(D)$; and, of course, we want that to happen for every database D. The application scenarios include query optimization and data warehouses.

- Maximally contained rewritings (MCRs). The setting is the same as that for producing certain answers. However, now we try to find a rewriting that gives the certain answers, or at least most of them. One reason for looking for MCRs is because the complexity of computing a query in one of the common database languages is often lower than the complexity of computing all certain answers.

1.3   ANSWERING QUERIES USING VIEWS

We compute a query Q_V on a database D, and then store (i.e., materialize) the answer $V(D) = Q_V(D)$ for future use. We may not have access to database D after that (for various reasons, e.g., D is too large to access efficiently). Thus, if we have another query Q on the schema of D that requires the data in D to be computed, we want to figure out how we can compute Q using the data in $V(D)$. As an example, suppose D is a directed graph, i.e., its schema is a single binary relation, and suppose Q_V is asking for all paths of length 2 in the graph. Now, if query Q wants to compute all paths of length 4, it can use $V(D)$ to compute all the answers that would have been computed if D were available (no answers are lost). If, however, Q asks for all paths of length either 2 or 3, then only a portion of the answers can be computed using $V(D)$. Thus, we have essentially two problems to look at: either how to produce the same set of answers using the views (i.e., $\mathcal{V}(D)$), or "do our best" and produce a subset of the answers. Let us look at these two problems in a little more detail here. We begin with a motivating example to explain the notions of *certain answers*, equivalent rewritings, and maximally contained rewritings.

In the examples, when we define the queries, we use both the Datalog rule syntax of a conjunctive query that we define formally in the next section, and the equivalent definition in SQL.

Example 1.1 Let us take two conjunctive queries defined as follows:

$$Q_1 : q_1(ename) :- Employee(eID, addr, tel, zip, ename), Dept(`Toy', eID),$$

which is equivalent to the following SQL query: `SELECT ename FROM Employee, Dept WHERE Employee.eID=Dept.eID AND dname='Toy'`. Query Q_1 asks for the names of the employees that work in the Toy department.

$$Q_2 : q_2(ename) :- Employee(eID, addr, tel, zip, ename), Dept(`Toy', eID), zip \neq 94304.$$

This query is equivalent to the following SQL query: `SELECT ename FROM Employee, Dept WHERE Employee.eID=Dept.eID AND dname='Toy' AND zip<>94304`. Query Q_2 asks for the names of the employees that work in the Toy department, except for those whose zip code is 94304.

Now we consider two views defined as follows:

$$V_1 : v_1(ename, eID) :- Employee(eID, addr, tel, zip, ename), zip \neq 94304,$$

which is equivalent to the following SQL query: `SELECT ename, eID FROM Employee WHERE zip<>94304`. View V_1 returns a binary relation that consists of the tuples that associate with each eID the corresponding name of this employee, but only for those employees whose zip$\neq$ 94304.

$$V_2 : v_2(dname, eID) :- Dept(dname, eID),$$

which is equivalent to the following SQL query: `SELECT dname, eID FROM Dept`. View V_2 returns a binary relation that consists of all the tuples of relation Dept.

We are going to argue that the views V_1 and V_2 can be used to produce all the answers to query Q_2, but this is not the case for query Q_1. However, the view answers can still be used to produce some (but not all) answers for query Q_1.

1.3.1 PRODUCING ALL THE ANSWERS—EQUIVALENT REWRITINGS

Creating an equivalent rewriting is a way to produce all the answers to a query.

Definition 1.2 (Equivalent rewritings)
Given a query Q and a set of views $\mathcal{V}$, a query P is an *equivalent rewriting* of the query Q using

$\mathcal{V}$ if P uses only the views in $\mathcal{V}$, and for any database D on the schema of the base relations, we have that $P(\mathcal{V}(D)) = Q(D)$, where $\mathcal{V}(D)$ is the database computed by evaluating the views in $\mathcal{V}$ on D.

Let us see how it works for the views and queries of Example 1.1.

Example 1.3   We refer to the queries and views of Example 1.1. Let us take the following rewriting:

$$R : r(ename) :\text{-} v_1(ename, eID), v_2(dname, eID),$$

which in SQL is:

```
SELECT ename
FROM    v₁, v₂
WHERE   v₁.eID = v₂.eID
```

Now let us consider a concrete database instance, the one shown in Figures 1.1 and 1.2. Let us find answers to the queries on this database instance. In Figures 1.3a, 1.3b, 1.3c, and 1.3d, we find the results of applying the query Q_1, the query Q_2, and the views V_1 and V_2 on the instance of the database in Figures 1.1 and 1.2.

Employee:

eID	addr	tel	zip	ename
13	82 Main St	450	94305	*Andrew*
54	12 Alton Ave	300	94304	*John*
45	14 Main Ave	314	94304	*George*

Figure 1.1: Database instance: relation employee.

Dept:

dname	eID
Toy	13
Toy	54
Books	45

Figure 1.2: Database instance: relation Dept.

Now we apply the rewriting R on the instance of V_1 and V_2 (that are depicted in Figures 1.3c and 1.3d); the result in shown in Figure 1.3e.

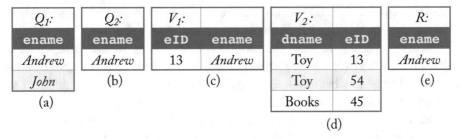

Q_1:
ename
Andrew
John

(a)

Q_2:
ename
Andrew

(b)

V_1:	
eID	ename
13	*Andrew*

(c)

V_2:	
dname	eID
Toy	13
Toy	54
Books	45

(d)

R:
ename
Andrew

(e)

Figure 1.3: Answers to the queries.

The result of R (Figure 1.3e) is the same as the result of Q_2 (Figure 1.3b). We will show in Chapter 3 (the chapter about equivalent rewritings) that this is not a coincidence: It can be proved rigorously using Definition 1.2 that this will be the case for any database instance.

1.3.2 PRODUCING A SUBSET OF THE ANSWERS—CONTAINED REWRITINGS

Example 1.4   We continue with the same query, views, and data as in Example 1.3. In Figure 1.3a we see the result of Q_1 as applied to the database shown in Figures 1.1 and 1.2.

We observe that the rewriting R from the previous example produces a subset of the answers of Q_2. This is no coincidence either: R will always produce a subset of the answers of Q_2. We will discuss such rewritings in Chapter 4, where we call R a contained rewriting. Those among the contained rewritings that produce most of the answers to the query will be called maximally contained rewritings (MCRs) and this is where we focus in Chapter 4.

Thus, the problem that we illustrated in this section is the following: *We are given the definitions of a query and a set of views (e.g., query Q_1 and views V_1 and V_2 in Example 1.3. We are given relations that represent the views (we will call it a "view instance") (e.g., the relations in Figures 1.3c and 1.3d). We are asked to compute answers to the query.*

For contained rewritings, there is a subtlety that does not occur in the case of equivalent rewritings. Contained rewritings are not necessarily computed on $\mathcal{V}(D)$, i.e., a view instance that is produced by computing the views on a certain database instance D. It may be required to be computed on a subset $\mathcal{I}$ of $\mathcal{V}(D)$. In other words, we may have two different ways to obtain a view instance $\mathcal{I}$: (1) either construct it from the relations in D in which case $\mathcal{I} = \mathcal{V}(D)$ (and this is what is the case when we do query optimization) (2) or seeing $\mathcal{I}$ as the source that resulted from $\mathcal{V}(D)$ where D does not consist of a single set of given relations but rather different such sets, even in different locations, thus we assume $\mathcal{I} \subseteq \mathcal{V}(D)$ (and this is the case when $\mathcal{I}$ is a description of what you can expect from a source that in data-integration practical scenarios). In the former case ($\mathcal{I} = \mathcal{V}(D)$), we say that we consider the closed world assumption (CWA), while, in the latter case ($\mathcal{I} \subseteq \mathcal{V}(D)$), we say that we consider the open world assumption (OWA). We will discuss about CWA and OWA in the beginning of Chapter 4.

We discussed one way to solve the problem of answering queries using views which is by finding equivalent and contained rewritings. We will discuss such rewritings and efficient algorithms to find them in Chapters 3, 4, and 5. In Chapter 6, we will take a different approach that we will present below in Section 1.3.3.

Equivalent and contained rewritings depend on the language of the rewriting in addition to the query and views definition and the given input database. There is another concept that we will define formally in Chapter 7 that is not related to any rewriting; this is the concept of "certain answers." Certain answers are not necessarily obtained via rewritings. We will discuss, in Chapter 7, the relationship between the output of a maximally contained rewriting and the set of certain answers.

1.3.3   DATA EXCHANGE

We look at the same problem as the one we described in the end of Section 1.3.2, which we repeat below.

We are given the definitions of a query and a set of views (e.g., query Q_1 and views V_1 and V_2 in Example 1.3. We are given relations that represent the views (we will call it a "view instance") (e.g., the relations in Figures 1.3c and 1.3d). We are asked to compute answers to the query.

The approach we will discuss in this section is to solve this problem by creating a database of the relations used in the query and then apply the query on this database to get the answers to the query. We consider an example.

Example 1.5   We consider queries and views as in Example 1.3. We will use the view instance given in Figures 1.3c and Figures 1.3d to create relations `EmployeeT` and `DeptT` to use in the place of `Employee` and `Dept` to answer the query.

Looking at the database of V_1 (see Figures 1.3c) and the definition of V_1, the maximum we can guess about what tuples the relation `EmployeeT` could have is in Figure 1.4. In other words, we know there is a tuple in `Employee` which has the value 13 in the attribute `eID` and the value *Andrew* in the attribute `ename` but we do not know anything about the values of the attributes `Addr`, `tel`, and `zip`. Thus, we represent their values by Nulls, which we call X, Y, and Z.

EmployeeT:

eID	addr	tel	zip	ename
13	X	Y	Z	*Andrew*

Figure 1.4: Incomplete database instance: relation EmployeeT.

Similarly looking at V_2 we can guess the whole relation Dept because the definition of V_2 is to copy the relation Dept.

Now we apply both query Q_1 on relations Dept and EmployeeT. We get an answer which is the same as what we see in Figure 1.3e. However, if we apply query Q_2 on relations Dept and EmployeeT, we get the empty set as output, because query Q_2 has the additional constraint that the zip must not be equal to 94,304. However, in closer inspection of the information we have, we observe that in the definition of the view V_1 this constraint appears. Thus for the tuple in Figure 1.4, we may add this additional information on the Null Z since it is known. Hence, we can also find the answer to Q_2 to be same as what we see in Figure 1.3e.

This approach is referred to as data exchange. We will discuss this approach to finding answers to queries in Chapter 6.

1.4   RELATIONAL DATABASES AND QUERIES

A *relation* is a named, two-dimensional table of data. Each column of the relation has a distinct name that is called *attribute*; and each row of data (called *tuple*) is a sequence of values of the attributes of the relation, one value for each attribute. The number of the attributes is the *arity* of the relation. A *relation schema* is a signature of the form $r(A_1, A_2, \ldots, A_n)$ defined by the *name* r of the relation, and a sequence of all attributes $(A_1, A_2, \ldots, A_n)$ in the relation. A collection of tuples over a relation schema is a *relation instance*. A (*relational*) *database schema*, $\mathcal{S}$, is a set of relational schemas, whereas a (*relational*) *database instance* (*database*, for short) over schema $\mathcal{S}$ is a set of relation instances, one instance for each relation schema in $\mathcal{S}$. We describe a database instance by listing the tuples appearing in each relation instance of a database, and attaching to each tuple the name of the relation that the tuple belongs to.

A *predicate* is naturally associated with a relation over the same signature, in that predicate $P_r(t)$ is true for tuple t iff t belongs to relation r. In the rest of the book we will refer to relations and predicates interchangeably, often denoting them by the same symbol.

Example 1.6   Let database $D = \{r_1(a, b), r_2(c, d)\}$ contain two tuples; the tuple (a, b) included in the relation r_1, and the tuple (c, d) included in the relation r_2.

Example 1.7   A database T with two relations:

$$\text{Employee(eID, addr, tel, zip, ename);}$$
$$\text{Dept(dname, eID).}$$

The relation Employee contains data on employees such as ID (eID), address (addr), telephone (tel), zip code (zip), employee's name (ename). The table Dept stores information concerning the name of the department (dname) and the ID of each employee (eID). Figure 1.5 shows an instance of the relation/table Employee, and Figure 1.6 shows an instance of the relation/table Dept.

Employee:

eID	addr	tel	zip	ename
13	82 Main St	450	94305	*Andrew*
54	12 Alton Ave	300	94304	*John*
45	14 Main Ave	314	94304	*George*

Figure 1.5: Database instance: relation Employee.

Dept:

dname	eID
Toy	13
Toy	54
Books	45

Figure 1.6: Database instance: relation Dept.

1.4.1   CONJUNCTIVE QUERIES

A *database query* is a mapping from databases to relations. This mapping is usually specified by a logical formula on the schema S of the input database.

A *conjunctive query (CQ* for short) is a database query given by an ordinary select-project-join SQL query with equality comparisons. A *conjunctive query* is definable by a positive existential first-order formula, with conjunctions as its only Boolean connective, i.e., it has the following form that produces a set of value vectors for the vector of variables $\overline{X}$:

$$\{\overline{X} : \exists \overline{Y} \phi(\overline{X}, \overline{Y}), \text{ where } \phi(\overline{X}, \overline{Y}) = \bigwedge_i g_i(\overline{X}_i)\}.$$

Conjunctive queries are usually written as *Datalog rules* of the form:

$$Q : q(\overline{X}) :\text{-} g_1(\overline{X}_1), \ldots, g_n(\overline{X}_n),$$

where $g_1, \ldots, g_n$ are database relation names, $\overline{X}_1, \ldots, \overline{X}_n$ are vectors of variables or constants and $\overline{X}$ is a vector of variables. We say that query Q is defined by a *rule*, where the *atom* $q(\overline{X})$ is the *head* of the rule, while the atoms $g_i(\overline{X}_i)$'s on the right of :- constitute the *body* of the rule. Each $g_i(\overline{X}_i)$ is also called a *subgoal*. The variables in $\overline{X}$ are called *distinguished* or *head variables*, whereas the variables in $\overline{X}_i$ but not in $\overline{X}$ are called *non-distinguished variables*. The query is *Boolean* (i.e., the output is either *true* or *false*) when the head has no variables.

Safe conjunctive queries are those CQs where all the head variables also occur in their body. We only consider safe conjunctive queries.

The result of a CQ, which is also called *answer or output of the CQ*, is given by a database containing a single relation, and is obtained by evaluating the CQ on D. A subgoal $g_i(\overline{X}_i)$

becomes true if after substituting the variables in $\overline{X}_i$ we get a tuple in relation g_i in D. A conjunctive query is *evaluated* on a relational database D by substituting variables in the definition of the query by values in D. If, after this substitution, all the subgoals become true, then the tuple in the head of the definition/rule is added to the *output* of the query.

Example 1.8   The following conjunctive query on the schema of the database of Figure 1.5 asks about the names of the employees with zip code 94303.

$$A(name) :- T(eID, addr, tel, 94304, name).$$

It is equivalent to the following SQL query:

```
SELECT DISTINCT name FROM T WHERE zip=94304
```
The answer to this query is a relation with one attribute in its schema that contains two tuples: (*John*) and (*George*).

Example 1.9   The following query lists all the zip-code information:

$$A(zip) :- T(eID, addr, tel, zip, name).$$

It is equivalent to the following SQL query: `SELECT DISTINCT zip FROM T`. The answer to this query on the database of Figure 1.5 is the table in Figure 1.7.

Answer:

zip
94305
94304

Figure 1.7

Set vs. bag semantics: What we defined as the output of a conjunctive query above is the most common definition that uses the set semantics of CQs. This is what we will use throughout this book, except when we treat aggregate queries, where we need bag semantics or set-bag semantics. We will give their definition in this paragraph.

In set semantics we used variable substitutions to compute a tuple in the output of a query. However, we may have more than one variable substitutions that give the same tuple as output. In this case, we can define bag semantics, for the case where we want to keep count of how many substitutions give a specific tuple.[1]

[1]In evaluating SQL queries in relational database-management systems, all such possible tuples are computed, and then deduplication is performed if the query calls for that.

Here we define those semantics formally. We first define substitution formally: a *substitution* σ is a finite set of the form $\{X_1/Y_1, \ldots, X_n/Y_n\}$, where each Y_i is a variable or a constant, and $X_1, \ldots, X_n$ are distinct variables. When $Y_1, \ldots, Y_n$ are distinct variables, σ is called *renaming*.

Let $\sigma = \{X_1/Y_1, \ldots, X_n/Y_n\}$ be a substitution. Applying σ on the body E of a CQ, denoted as $\sigma(E)$, means that we simultaneously replace each occurrence of X_i in E by Y_i (i.e., $\sigma(X_i) = Y_i$), for all $i = 1, \ldots, n$. (We assume that all the variables of E are in the domain of σ.) Similarly, when applying σ on a CQ Q, denoted as $\sigma(Q)$, we apply σ both on the head and the body of Q.

Given a database instance D (which is either set valued or bag valued), we *evaluate* CQ Q on D as follows: for each substitution σ of the variables in the body of Q we check whether all ground facts (that is, tuples without variables) that result from this substitution are in D. If they are, then this is a *valuation* of Q on D, and the head of Q under σ contributes a tuple to the multiset (bag) of tuples that is the answer to the query. If the evaluation is done under set semantics, then we disregard multiplicities and turn the multiset into a set. From this definition, notice that there might be multiple valuations giving the same tuple in the head of Q. However, in set semantics the number of different valuations giving the same tuple in the head of Q is not reflected in the answer of the query, since the answer to the query is always a set. On the other hand, in both bag-set and bag semantics we take into consideration all the valuations.

The difference between bag-set and set semantics is that under the former, the database instance is set valued, and under the latter it is bag valued. That is, a relation R can be defined either as a set of tuples or a multiset (a.k.a. bag) of tuples. In the second case, each tuple from the *core set* (of the multiset) has associated with it a *multiplicity*, which records the number of times this tuple appears in the multiset. For example, the multiset $\{(1, 2), (1, 2), (2, 3)\}$ has two tuples in the core set: the tuple $(1, 2)$ with multiplicity equal to 2, and the tuple $(2, 3)$ with multiplicity equal to 1. In a *set-valued database*, all stored relations are sets; in a *bag-valued database*, multiset stored relations are allowed. In query evaluation under bag-set semantics, we allow computation of query answers only on set-valued databases, whereas in query evaluation under bag semantics, bag-valued databases are permitted.

Example 1.10 Consider the same query as in Example 1.9 but computed under bag semantics.

$$A(zip) :\text{-} T(eID, addr, tel, zip, name).$$

The equivalent SQL query is as in Example 1.9, except the word DISTINCT is removed:

```
SELECT zip FROM T
```

The answer now, however, gives back a multiset (bag) in Figure 1.8.

That is, every time an answer is computed, we list it in the table, regardless of the fact that it was computed using a different valuation (a different tuple in this simple example). Note that the database instance in this example is a set, which means that the query answer under bag-set semantics will be the same as under bag semantics.

Answer:

zip
94305
94304
94304

Figure 1.8

1.4.2 CONJUNCTIVE QUERIES WITH ARITHMETIC COMPARISONS (CQAC)

CQs with arithmetic comparisons are of the following form:

$$q(\bar{X}) :- g_1(\bar{X}_1), \ldots, g_n(\bar{X}_n), C_1, \ldots, C_m.$$

Now we have two different kinds of subgoals in the body. The set of relational subgoals called *ordinary subgoals* $g_1(\bar{X}_1), \ldots, g_n(\bar{X}_n)$ (as in CQs defined previously), is also known as "regular subgoals," "uninterpreted subgoals," or "ordinary subgoals." (2) The set of arithmetic-comparison subgoals C_i. Each C_i is an arithmetic comparison of the form "$A_1 \ \theta \ A_2$," where A_1 is a variable or a constant, and A_2 is a variable. If they are variables, they appear in the ordinary subgoals. The operator "θ" is $\neq, <, \leq, =, >$, or $\geq$. We use the terms "inequality" and "arithmetic comparison," or simply "comparison," interchangeably to denote either of the above operators. In addition, we make the following assumptions about the arithmetic comparisons.

1. Values for the arguments in the arithmetic comparisons are chosen from an infinite, totally densely ordered set, such as the rationals or reals.

2. The arithmetic comparisons are not contradictory; that is, there exists an instantiation of the variables such that all the arithmetic comparisons are true.

3. All the comparisons are safe, i.e., each variable in the comparisons appears in some ordinary subgoal.

We *evaluate a CQAC* in the same way as we evaluate a CQ, except that we also require that all the arithmetic-comparison subgoals become true after we substitute values/constants for variables.

Example 1.11   We refer again to the database instance of Figure 1.5, and pose the query:

$$A(zip) :- T(eID, addr, tel, zip, name), zip > 94304.$$

This query asks for a list of zip codes that are greater than 94304. The equivalent SQL query is: SELECT zip FROM T WHERE zip > 94304. The answer to this query appears in Figure 1.9.

Answer:

zip
94305

Figure 1.9

Finally, the following example shows that the picture is different if the domain is not densely ordered.

Example 1.12   Consider the following query:

$$Q(x) :\text{-} r(x), x > 5, x < 7, x \neq 6.$$

If the domain is the set of integers, then the output of this query is empty on any database instance. But this is not true if the domain is the set of reals.

1.4.3   CONJUNCTIVE QUERIES WITH NEGATION (CQN)

The general form of a conjunctive query with safe negated subgoals (CQN) is:

$$H :\text{-} G_1 \wedge \ldots \wedge G_n \wedge \neg F_1 \wedge \ldots \wedge \neg F_m,$$

where H is $h(\overline{X})$ and G_i, F_i are of the form $g_i(\overline{X})$, $f_i(\overline{X})$. The G's are called *positive* subgoals, while the F's are called *negative* subgoals. A CQN is *safe* if each variable appearing in a negated subgoal also appears in a positive subgoal. We consider only safe CQNs.

Example 1.13   Suppose we have a database with two binary relations r_1 and r_2, and in the database instance, r_1 has the tuples $\{(1,2),(2,3)\}$ and r_2 has the tuples $\{(2,4),(4,5),(3,2)\}$. Consider the query:

$$A(X,Y) :\text{-} r_1(X,Y), \neg r_2(Y,X).$$

The answer to this query is $\{(1,2)\}$, because for the tuple $(2,3)$ in r_1 there is the tuple $(3,2)$ in r_2, which makes the second subgoal, $\neg r_2(Y,X)$, false. For an equivalent SQL query, we need to use the NOT EXISTS predicate.

1.4.4   UNIONS OF CONJUNCTIVE QUERIES

A union of CQs (or CQACs or CQNs) is defined by a number of CQs (CQACs, CQNs, respectively) and the output is the union (as a set) of the sets of tuples given in the output of each of the CQs (CQACs, CQNs, respectively).

Example 1.14   The union of the following two queries

$$A(zip) :\text{-} T(eID, addr, tel, zip, name), zip > 94304$$

$$A(zip) :\text{-} T(eID, addr, tel, zip, name), zip = 94304,$$

when applied to the database shown in Figure 1.5, gives as output the same as the following query:

$$A(zip) :\text{-} T(eID, addr, tel, zip, name).$$

In general, however, a union of conjunctive queries cannot be equivalently defined by a single conjunctive query.

1.4.5   CONJUNCTIVE QUERIES WITH AGGREGATION (CQA)

Let us denote the body of a conjunctive query by A. An *assignment* (a.k.a. substitution) γ for A is a mapping of the variables appearing in A to constants, and of the constants appearing in A to themselves. Assignments are naturally extended to tuples and atoms.

We assume that the data we want to aggregate are real numbers, $\mathbf{R}$. If S is a set, then $\mathcal{M}(S)$ denotes the set of finite multisets over S. A k-ary aggregate function is a function $\alpha : \mathcal{M}(\mathbf{R}^k) \to \mathbf{R}$ that maps multisets of k-tuples of real numbers to real numbers. An *aggregate term* is an expression built up using variables and aggregate functions. Every aggregate term with k variables gives rise to a k-ary aggregate function in a natural way.

We use $\alpha(y)$ as abstract notation for a unary aggregate term, where y is the variable in the term. Aggregate queries that we consider have (unary or 0-ary) aggregate functions *count*, *count*(∗), *sum*, *max*, and *min*. Note that *count* is over an argument, whereas *count*(∗) is the only function that we consider that takes no argument. (There is a distinction in SQL semantics between *count* and *count*(∗).) In the remainder of this book, we will not refer again to the distinction between *count* and *count*(∗), as our results carry over.

An *aggregate query* is a conjunctive query augmented by an aggregate term in its head. For a query with a k-ary aggregate function α, the syntax is

$$q(\bar{s}, \alpha(\bar{y})) \leftarrow A . \tag{1.1}$$

Here, A is a conjunction of atoms, see definition of conjunctive queries; $\alpha(\bar{y})$ is a k-ary aggregate term; $\bar{s}$ are the *grouping attributes* of q; none of the variables in $\bar{y}$ appears among $\bar{s}$. Finally, q is *safe*, that is, all the variables in $\bar{s}$ and $\bar{y}$ occur in A. We consider queries with unary aggregate functions sum, $count$, max, and min.

Definition 1.15   With each aggregate query q (Eq. (1.1)) we associate its *conjunctive core* $\breve{q}$:

$$\breve{q}(\bar{s}, \bar{y}) \leftarrow A . \tag{1.2}$$

We define the semantics of an aggregate query as follows: Let D be a database and q an aggregate query as in Eq. (1.1). When q is applied on D, it yields a relation $q(D)$ that is defined by the following three steps. First, we compute the core $\breve{q}$ of q on D as a bag B. We then form equivalence classes in B: Two tuples belong to the same equivalence class if they agree on the values of the grouping arguments of q. This is the *grouping* step. The third step is *aggregation*; it associates with each equivalence class a value that is the aggregate function computed on a bag that contains all the values of the input argument(s) of the aggregated attribute(s) in this class. For each class, it returns one tuple, which contains the values of the grouping arguments of q and the computed aggregated value.

Example 1.16 Consider the aggregate query

$$Answer(zip, count) :\text{-} \ T(eID, addr, tel, zip, name),$$

which is equivalent to the following SQL query: `SELECT zip, COUNT FROM T GROUPBY zip` This query first computes a bag, exactly as the query in Example 1.10, because the query in Example 1.10 is the core of the query in this current example. Then the query counts in the resulting relation the tuples with each specific zip code. The final answer appears in Figure 1.10.

Answer:

zip	count
94305	1
94304	2

Figure 1.10

This answer is correct, because in the answer to the query of Example 1.10, there are two tuples with zip code 94304, and one tuple with zip code 94305.

Example 1.17 Consider a database with three relations—relation P that stores transactions, and relations T and W that store information about store branches, all with self-explanatory attribute names:
`P(storeId, product, salePrice, profit, dayOfSale, monthOfSale, yearOfSale);`
`T(storeId, storeChain); W(storeId, storeCity).`
Suppose a user is interested in the answers to query Q, which gives total sales per product per year per city, for all stores. Q can be defined in SQL as follows:
`    SELECT product, yearOfSale, storeCity, SUM(salePrice) FROM P, W WHERE`
`P.storeId = W.storeId GROUP BY product, yearOfSale, storeCity;`
    In Datalog-rule notation:

$$q(Y, M, U, sum(Z)) :\text{-} \ p(X, Y, Z, T, N, L, M), \ w(X, U).$$

1.5   THE STRUCTURE OF THE BOOK

In this book we want to present, formally and rigorously, algorithms and their technical tools that are relevant to solving problems related to the topic of answering queries using views. We focus on presenting efficient algorithms that find good (e.g., minimal) rewritings and find certain answers. In terms of computational complexity of the problems we present, the algorithms we present give upper bounds, for the case of minimization optimization problems. We do not focus on the complexity analyses, concentrating instead on correctness proofs for the algorithms. The lower bounds and other related issues are discussed in the bibliographical notes. We also include exercises, which call for applying the algorithms to concrete inputs, or refer to theoretical results that can be easily solved by the presented techniques.

Algorithms for finding rewritings of queries using views are based on whether two queries give the same answers on any input database, or on whether one gives a subset of the answers of the other query. These are the problems of query containment (one query gives a subset of the answers of the other query) and query equivalence (two queries give the same set of answers). In Chapter 2 we present efficient algorithms that test query containment, using technical tools such as homomorphisms and containment mappings. (These tools are used throughout the book.) We discuss the relationship between the problems of query containment and query evaluation, as both use homomorphisms. The algorithms range from simple to more complex, as we add to CQs extra expressive power by allowing arithmetic comparisons and negation. We introduce the notion of canonical database, and show how it is used in testing query containment. For conjunctive queries with arithmetic comparisons, the "homomorphism property" enables simpler containment tests. Aggregate queries behave differently due to not belonging to core relational algebra. Their evaluation depends on bag semantics: as an intermediate step we compute a CQ, but store the output as a bag. This is the only reason we also discuss bag semantics and bag-set semantics. We do not refer to them outside the scope of aggregate queries. Finally, some queries with special structure have simpler algorithms for query containment and evaluation. We discuss one class of such queries, acyclic queries.

Chapters 3 and 4 discuss efficient algorithms for finding rewritings of queries using sets of views: Chapter 3 discusses equivalent rewritings, and Chapter 4 discusses maximally contained rewritings. The existence of both kinds of rewritings depends on the language of rewritings, as illustrated with examples. In both chapters, we discuss the central notion of expansion of a rewriting and examine its properties, which allow for efficient algorithms for finding rewritings.

Chapter 3 presents efficient algorithms for finding equivalent rewritings for conjunctive queries with or without arithmetic comparisons. We also discuss equivalent rewritings for aggregate queries. For equivalent rewritings, the notion of canonical rewriting is central.

Chapter 4 presents efficient algorithms for finding maximally contained rewritings (MCRs) for CQs and CQACs with the homomorphism property. It also includes Datalog queries, and presents the inverse-rule algorithm for finding MCRs using CQ views. Chapter 4 also discusses cases of nonrecursive queries and views where we need recursion in order to find an MCR. The open-world assumption vs. the closed-world assumption are also discussed in Chapter 4.

Chapter 5 revisits the problems of the previous three chapters in the presence of constraints on the data. These constraints are tuple-generating dependencies and equality-generating dependencies. Here we discuss the chase algorithm, and show how it helps in solving such problems.

Chapter 6 discusses settings where (a) all the answers to a query cannot be derived, and (b) the definitions that derive data from a set of base data (this is what views do when they are computed on base data) are given in more general form than conjunctive queries, specifically in the form of tuple-generating dependencies. We define the notion of certain answers based on possible worlds, and present algorithms that find certain answers. We also present more expressive tuple-generating dependencies that use arithmetic comparisons. We discuss the chase algorithm and study conditions for its termination.

The problem of answering queries using views gives rise to questions of theoretical importance, some of them quite challenging. Chapter 7 considers some of these questions, such as computing certain answers (which is similar to a special case of the data-exchange problem) and its relationship with MCRs and determinacy.

In the second edition, we added two chapters, Chapter 8 and Chapter 9, which refer to tree-like data and respective query languages. Chapter 8 presents the data model for XML documents and the XPath query language and gives query containment tests and query rewriting techniques. However, besides the relational data model and the tree-structured XML data model, many recently developed systems, to manage big data, use data models that combine relational and tree-like features. In terms of defining and using views, these models have not be investigated. However, they are mature enough to be presented in a rigorous way. Thus, Chapter 9 provides a theoretical presentation of such data model and query language as extensions of the relational model and SQL query language. In these data models, the tuples of a relation share a tree-structured schema for that relation and the query language is a dialect of SQL. The query language uses SQL-style syntax but the evaluation techniques have to be modified to fit the richer schema. The conclusions and bibliographical notes for these two chapters are included in the chapters themselves. Chapters 8 and 9 can also be read independently of the rest of the chapters in the book and independently of each other.

Chapter 10 contains bibliographical notes for Chapters 1–7, which in particular point out complexity results for the problems considered in these chapters and this is the chapter that contains citations for the material in Chapters 1–7. In Chapters 1–7 and Chapter 8 we do not present hardness results for the problems being discussed. That is, we offer the algorithms with correctness (and complexity, when necessary) proofs, but we do not delineate complexity in the main text. The reason for this presentation style is that, in the main text, we focus on methods and techniques, as well as on how they are used to discover algorithms.

1.6   EXERCISES

1.1. Consider the queries q_1 and q_2:

$$q_1(X) :- r(X, Y), r(Y, X), r(X, X), s(X).$$
$$q_2(Y) :- r(X, Y), r(Y, X), r(X, X), s(X).$$

Compute each of them on the database:

$$D = \{r(1, 1), s(1), r(2, 2), s(2), r(1, 2), r(2, 1)\}.$$

1.2. Consider the query:

$$q(X_1, X_2, X_3, X_4) :- a(X_1, X_2, X_3, X_4), b(X_1, X_2, X_3), c(X_1, X_2), d(X_1).$$

Compute this query on the following database:

$$D = \{a(1, 2, 3, 4), b(1, 2, 3), c(1, 2), d(1), a(1, 2, 2, 4), b(1, 2, 2), a(1, 2, 2, 1)\}.$$

1.3. Consider the query:

$$q(X_1, X_2, X_3, X_4) :- a(Y, X_3, X_4), b(Y, X_1, X_2), c(Y, X_5), d(Y, X_6), f(Y).$$

Compute this query on the following database:

$$D = \{a(8, 3, 4), b(8, 1, 2), c(8, 5), d(8, 6), f(8), a(8, 4, 4)\}.$$

1.4. Consider the queries q_1 and q_2:

$$q_1(X) :- r(X, Y), r(Y, X), r(X, X), s(X), X < 9.$$
$$q_2(Y) :- r(X, Y), r(Y, X), r(X, X), s(X), X < 1.$$

Compute each of them on the database:

$$D = \{r(1, 1), s(1), r(2, 2), s(2), r(1, 2), r(2, 1)\}.$$

1.5. Consider the query:

$$q(X_1, X_2, X_3, X_4) :- a(X_1, X_2, X_3, X_4), b(X_1, X_2, X_3), c(X_1, X_2), d(X_1), X_3 < 3.$$

Compute this query on the following database:

$$D = \{a(1, 2, 3, 4), b(1, 2, 3), c(1, 2), d(1), a(1, 2, 2, 4), b(1, 2, 2), a(1, 2, 2, 1)\}.$$

1.6. Consider the query:

$$q(X_1, X_2, X_3, X_4) :- a(X_1, X_2, X_3, X_4), b(X_1, X_2, X_3), c(X_1, X_2), d(X_1), X_2 < X_3.$$

Compute this query on the following database:

$$D = \{a(1, 2, 3, 4), b(1, 2, 3), c(1, 2), d(1), a(1, 2, 2, 4), b(1, 2, 2), a(1, 2, 2, 1)\}.$$

CHAPTER 2

Query Containment and Equivalence

The problem of rewriting queries using views is closely related to the problem of checking for query containment or equivalence. For most classes of problems, containment tests enable simple algorithms to rewrite queries using views. Rewriting queries is one of the techniques that is most often used to answer queries using views.

In this chapter we discuss containment tests for conjunctive queries (CQs), conjunctive queries with arithmetic comparisons (CQACs), conjunctive queries with negation (CQNs), and SQL aggregate queries, which will be written in the notation of conjunctive queries supplemented with information about the groupby attributes and the aggregated attribute. We call queries of the latter type *conjunctive queries with aggregation* (CQA queries). We will also present containment tests that are of lower complexity for special cases of these queries.

Definition 2.1   We say that query Q_2 is *contained* in query Q_1, denoted $Q_2 \sqsubseteq Q_1$, iff, for any database D, the set of answers to Q_2 computed on D is a subset of the set of answers to Q_1 computed on D, i.e., $Q_2(D) \subseteq Q_1(D)$.

We say that two queries Q_1 and Q_2 are *equivalent*, denoted $Q_1 \equiv Q_2$, iff each query is contained in the other, i.e., $Q_1 \sqsubseteq Q_2$ and $Q_2 \sqsubseteq Q_1$.

It follows from the definition that $Q_1 \equiv Q_2$ iff for all databases D we have that $Q_1(D) = Q_2(D)$.

As an example, a query Q_2 on a binary relation (that can be thought of as a graph) that computes all paths of length 2 with the path beginning at a node with ID greater than 43 is contained in query Q_1 that computes all paths of length 2. (That is, the query Q_1 does not include the additional restriction that will be represented by the arithmetic comparison > 43—we will see details of such queries later in this chapter.)

2.1   CQ QUERY CONTAINMENT

To present an algorithm for testing CQ containment, we need to introduce some technical notions.

2.1.1   CONTAINMENT MAPPING AND HOMOMORPHISMS: CANONICAL DATABASE

If r is a relation symbol of arity n, and X_i's take values from domain Dom, then $r(X_1, \ldots, X_n)$ is an *atom* over domain Dom. A *relational structure* S is a set of atoms over a *domain* $Dom(S)$ of variables and constants. A relational atom without variables among its arguments is called a *ground atom*. The body of a conjunctive query is a finite relational structure. A database instance (or database) is a finite relational structure with only ground atoms.

Definition 2.2   A *homomorphism* from relational structure S to relational structure S' is a function $h : Dom(S) \to Dom(S')$ such that:

If a_i is a constant, then $h(a_i) = a_i$, and

If $r_i(a_1, \ldots, a_{m_i})$ is an atom in S, then $r_i(h(a_1), \ldots, h(a_{m_i}))$ is an atom in S'.[1]

We say that a homomorphism h is *one-to-one* if, whenever $a_i \neq a_j$, then $h(a_i) \neq h(a_j)$. We say that there is an *isomorphism* between two relational structures iff there is a one-to-one homomorphism from one onto the other and vice versa. In such cases, we say that the two structures are *isomorphic*. If the isomorphism is from a structure to itself, then we call it *automorphism*.

The definition for conjunctive queries is related to a relational structure over the domain of variables and constants that are used in the definition. The relational structure related to a CQ definition can either be the set of all atoms that appear in the definition of the query (both head and body of the query), or just the atoms that appear in the body. We choose what is customary, by relating a CQ to the relational structure that contains the atoms in its body.

Definition 2.3   A *containment mapping* is a homomorphism h from the relational structure of the body of Q_1 to the relational structure of the body of Q_2, which additionally maps the head of Q_1 to the head of Q_2. (That is, if $q_1(X_1, \ldots, X_n)$ is the head of Q_1, then $q_2(h(X_1), \ldots, h(X_n))$ is the head of Q_2.)

We will show that a conjunctive query Q_2 is contained in another conjunctive query Q_1 if and only if there is a *containment mapping* from Q_1 to Q_2. An example follows. In the rules in the example, as in all the rules that we write, the reader can assume that an uppercase letter represents a variable. A lowercase letter can represent a constant (in this case, we usually choose a letter from the beginning of the alphabet) or a predicate name (in this case, we usually choose a letter from the middle of the alphabet) . For the names of rules, we shall use uppercase letters, typically Q or R.

Example 2.4   Consider queries Q_1 and Q_2:

$$Q_1 : q_1(X, Y) \text{ :- } a(X, Z_1), b(Z_1, Z_2), c(Z_2, Y),$$

---

[1] The standard definition of homomorphism does not necessarily require that the relation symbol has to be the same in both structures. For the needs of this book, and as is customary in related literature, this restricted definition of homomorphism is sufficient.

$$Q_2 : q_2(X', Y') :\text{-} a(X', Z_1'), b(Z_1', Z_1'), c(Z_1', Y'), a(X', Y').$$

A containment mapping from Q_1 to Q_2 is defined by giving a mapping μ from the variables of Q_1 to the variables of Q_2. Let us consider the following mapping μ:

$$\{X \rightarrow X', Y \rightarrow Y', Z_1 \rightarrow Z_1', Z_2 \rightarrow Z_1'\}.$$

It is indeed a containment mapping, because the variables in the head of Q_1 are mapped position-wise to the variables in the head of Q_2, and each subgoal of Q_1 is mapped to a subgoal of Q_2 with the same relation symbol. That is, $a(X, Z_1)$ is mapped to $a(X', Z_1')$, $b(Z_1, Z_2)$ is mapped to $b(Z_1', Z_1')$, and $c(Z_2, Y)$ is mapped to $c(Z_1', Y')$. This containment mapping proves that query Q_2 is contained in query Q_1. Notice that the subgoal $a(X', Y')$ of Q_2 is not a target of any subgoal of Q_1, i.e., it is not used to verify the containment mapping μ. In other words, the subgoal $a(X', Y')$ can be deleted from Q_2, and the containment mapping will still be valid.

These queries have an intuitive meaning on labeled graphs, which explains containment in an intuitive level as follows: Think of the atoms as representing arcs with labels, so that Q_1 in this example is any path from node X to node Y of length 3, labeled by sequence a, b, c. Query Q_2 here is a path from node X' to node Y' of length 3, labeled by sequence a, b, c, which contains a loop for arc labeled b, and also has an arc labeled a between nodes X' and Y'. It is not hard to show that whenever the latter happens, then the former also happens.

When we evaluate a query, Q, on a database, i.e., when we replace variables in the definition of the query by values in the database, this is equivalent to finding a homomorphism from the body of the query to the database that maps the head of the query definition to the computed tuple t. We will refer to such homomorphisms as *homomorphism that computes t*. We often need to consider the relational structure of the body of a CQ definition as a database. This database is constructed by replacing all the variables by distinct constants (distinct among themselves and distinct from the constants already in the query definition). We call the resulting structure a *canonical database* of the CQ, and denote it by D_Q. Formally, there are an infinite number of canonical databases, as it all depends on the choice of the constants we use. At the same time, as all these databases are isomorphic, we refer from here on to "the" canonical database of a conjunctive query.

We state and prove the CQ containment-test result in the following theorem.

Theorem 2.5   *A CQ query Q_2 is contained in CQ query Q_1 iff there is a containment mapping from Q_1 to Q_2.*

Proof. For the "if" direction: Suppose there is a containment mapping from Q_1 to Q_2. A containment mapping is a homomorphism. When Q_2 is evaluated on database D producing a tuple t, this tuple is produced because of a homomorphism from the body of Q_2 to the database. This homomorphism can be combined with the homomorphism of the given containment mapping, to produce a homomorphism from the body of Q_1 to the database. The latter homomorphism will produce the tuple t in the result of evaluating Q_1 on the database D. Thus, Q_2 is contained in Q_1.

For the "only-if" direction: Suppose Q_2 is contained in Q_1. Let the database D_{Q_2} be the canonical database of Q_2. Since the tuple in D that corresponds to the head of Q_2 is in the result when we compute Q_2 on D_{Q_2}, this tuple is also in the result when we compute Q_1 on D_{Q_2}. But computing Q_1 on D_{Q_2} means there is a homomorphism from the body of Q_1 to D_{Q_2}. However, D_{Q_2} is isomorphic to the body of Q_2. Hence, this homomorphism is a containment mapping from Q_1 to Q_2.   □

The canonical database is the minimal counterexample if containment is not satisfied. This is stated in the following theorem, which gives an alternative containment test. (We omit the straightforward proof.)

Theorem 2.6   *A CQ query Q_2 is contained in CQ query Q_1 iff Q_1 computes its head atom on the canonical database of Q_2.*

A containment mapping from Q_1 to Q_2 is defined by a mapping μ from the variables of Q_1 to the variables of Q_2. Since it is a homomorphism, a containment mapping defines a unique mapping from all the subgoals of Q_1 to subgoals of Q_2 (but not necessarily all the subgoals of Q_2). We refer to this as the *induced subgoal mapping* of μ. A containment mapping from Q_1 to Q_2 is called *subgoals-onto* if its induced subgoal mapping uses each subgoal of Q_2 as the target of some subgoal of Q_1. The containment mapping in Example 2.4 is not subgoals-onto, because the subgoal $a(X', Y')$ of Q_2 is not a target of any subgoal of Q_1 under this mapping.

2.1.2   QUERY EVALUATION VS. QUERY CONTAINMENT

In Section 2.1.1, we already noticed the relationship between query evaluation and query containment, and saw how they are both based on the existence of homomorphisms. (This is the first hint that conjunctive queries are preserved under homomorphisms.) Actually, the relationship between the two problems is strong, so algorithms for one of the problems can be used for the other. For one direction, we have already seen how CQ query containment can be tested by evaluating the containing query on the canonical database of the contained query. (Here and in the rest of the book wherever clear from the context, we say "contained (containing, respectively) query" to refer to a query that we hypothesize to be contained in (to contain, respectively) the other query.)

We illustrate the other direction with an example.

Example 2.7   Suppose that on a database $D = \{r(1, 2), r(2, 3), r(3, 4)\}$, we would like to know whether the tuple $(1, 3)$ is in $Q_1(D)$, where Q_1 is the following path query:

$$Q_1(X, Y) :\text{-} r(X, Z), r(Z, Y).$$

We form query Q_2 by constructing its subgoals out of the tuples in the database D; the head of Q_2 has the two variables that correspond to $(1, 3)$:

$$Q_2(X_1, X_3) :\text{-} r(X_1, X_2), r(X_2, X_3), r(X_3, X_4).$$

Now, it is easy to check that indeed Q_2 is contained in Q_1, because there is a containment mapping from Q_1 to Q_2. Moreover, since the body of Q_2 and the database D are isomorphic, this containment mapping gives the homomorphism that computes $(1, 3)$ in $Q_1(D)$.

Preservation of CQs under Homomorphisms

Recall that a database instance is a relational structure that uses only constants, rather than variables. For database instances, it is useful to define a slightly different notion of homomorphism, which highlights an interesting property of CQs. (We will not use this definition of homomorphism again in this book, unless very specifically stated with pointers to the definition below. Thus, we do not need to introduce a distinguishing name for it.)

Definition 2.8   A *homomorphism* from database D to database D' is a function $h : dom(D) \to dom(D')$ such that

    if $(a_1, \ldots, a_{m_i}) \in r_i$, then $(h(a_1), \ldots, h(a_{m_i})) \in r_i$.

Notice that this definition does not require constants to map to the same constant as in Definition 2.2.

Definition 2.9   Query Q is *preserved under homomorphisms* if, whenever $\mathcal{D}$ and $\mathcal{D}'$ are two databases and there is a homomorphism h as in Definition 2.8 from D to D', we have that

    if $(a_1, \ldots, a_m) \in Q(\mathcal{D})$, then $(h(a_1), \ldots, h(a_m)) \in Q(\mathcal{D}')$.

We say that $\mathcal{D}'$ is the *homomorphic image* of $\mathcal{D}$ under h, if h is *onto* and, whenever $(a'_1, \ldots, a'_{m_i}) \in r_i$, there exists an $a_1, \ldots, a_{m_i}$ such that $(a_1, \ldots, a_{m_i}) \in r_i$ and $h(a_j) = a'_j, j = 1, \ldots, m_i$.

CQs without constants in their definition are preserved under homomorphisms. The following CQ is not preserved under homomorphisms:

$$q(X) :\text{-} p(X, Y), r(Y, 3).$$

Indeed, consider databases $D = \{p(1, 2), r(2, 3)\}$ and $D' = \{p(1, 2), r(2, 4)\}$. There is a homomorphism from D to D' as in Definition 2.8. At the same time, because of the constant 3 in the definition of the query, this homomorphism does not enable a computation of the atom $q(1)$ in $q(D')$ as it does in $q(D)$.

We now summarize the two algorithms for CQ query containment.

CQ containment test 1:
Given two conjunctive queries Q_1 and Q_2, $Q_2 \sqsubseteq Q_1$ if and only if there is a *containment mapping* from Q_1 to Q_2, such that the mapping maps each constant to the same constant and maps each variable to either a variable or a constant. Under this mapping, the head of Q_1 becomes the head of Q_2, and each subgoal of Q_1 maps to *some* subgoal of Q_2.

CQ containment test 2:
Given two conjunctive queries Q_1 and Q_2, $Q_2 \sqsubseteq Q_1$ if and only if Q_1 computes its head on the canonical database of Q_2.

2.2   CQAC QUERY CONTAINMENT

Recall that we use "CQ" to represent "conjunctive query," "AC" for "arithmetic comparison," and "CQAC" for "conjunctive query with arithmetic comparisons." We write a CQAC as "$Q = Q_0 + \beta$," where "β" denotes the comparisons of Q, and "Q_0" denotes the query obtained by deleting the comparisons from Q. We say that a set of arithmetic comparisons is *consistent* if there is an assignment of values to variables over densely totally ordered domains such that all the comparisons in the set are true.

Whenever we consider CQAC queries in this book, we assume a densely totally ordered domain. Before we proceed, consider the following example, which shows that the picture is different if the domain is not densely totally ordered.

Example 2.10   Consider the following query:

$$Q(X) :\text{-} r(X), X > 5, X < 7, X \neq 6.$$

If the domain is the integers (which is not a densely totally ordered domain), then the output of Q is empty on any database instance. Thus, the query is contained in all queries. However, over the reals (which is a densely totally ordered domain), this is not true.

The following query Q' uses inconsistent arithmetic comparisons. Hence, its output is empty on any database, independently of the domain being densely totally ordered or not.

$$Q'(X) :\text{-} r(X), X > 5, X < 4.$$

Indeed, consider the database instance $D = \{r(6.5)\}$. The output $Q(D)$ of Q on D is $\{(6.5)\}$. The output $Q'(D)$ of Q' on D is empty.

2.2.1   MULTIPLE CONTAINMENT MAPPINGS AND NORMALIZATION: SET OF CANONICAL DATABASES

Definition 2.11   Let Q_1 and Q_2 be two conjunctive queries with arithmetic comparisons (CQACs). We want to test whether $Q_2 \sqsubseteq Q_1$. To do the testing, we first *normalize* each of Q_1 and Q_2 to, respectively, Q_1' and Q_2', as follows.

- For each occurrence of a shared variable X in a normal (i.e., relational) subgoal, except for the first occurrence, replace the occurrence of X by a fresh variable X_i, and add $X = X_i$ to the comparisons of the query; and

- for each constant c in a normal subgoal, replace the constant by a fresh variable Z, and add $Z = c$ to the comparisons of the query.

Theorem 2.12 below says that $Q_2 \sqsubseteq Q_1$ iff the comparisons in the normalized version Q_2' of Q_2 logically imply (denoted by "$\Rightarrow$") the disjunction of the images of the comparisons of the normalized version Q_1' of Q_1 under each containment mapping from the normal subgoals of Q_1' to the normal subgoals of Q_2'.

Theorem 2.12

Let Q_1, Q_2 be CQACs, and $Q_1' = Q_{10}' + \beta_1'$, $Q_2' = Q_{20}' + \beta_2'$ be the respective queries after normalization. Suppose there is at least one containment mapping from Q_{10}' to Q_{20}'. Let $\mu_1, \ldots, \mu_k$ be all the containment mappings from Q_{10}' to Q_{20}'. Then $Q_2 \sqsubseteq Q_1$ if and only if the following logical implication ϕ is true:

$$\phi : \beta_2' \Rightarrow \mu_1(\beta_1') \vee \ldots \vee \mu_k(\beta_1').$$

(We refer to ϕ as the containment entailment throughout this book.)

Proof. For the "if" direction: First observe the following: If the containment entailment holds, then for any assignment of constants to variables in Q_2 that computes a tuple, there is at least one containment mapping μ_i that makes $\mu_i(\beta_1')$ true. (Since we are considering constants, the "OR" in the implication means that one specific clause becomes true.) Now, if a tuple t is computed by query Q_2 on a database D, there is a homomorphism h from Q_{20}' to D that produces t such that β_2' is satisfied, i.e., all the comparisons in $h(\beta_2')$ are true. However, the homomorphism h assigns constants to the variables of the containment entailment that makes β_2' true. Thus, there is a μ_i such that the same assignment makes $\mu_i(\beta_1')$ true. But this assignment is the assignment of constants to the variables of $h \circ \mu_i$. Hence, we can combine μ_i with the homomorphism h from Q_2 to D that produced t, and thus prove that t is computed by the query Q_1 as well.

For the "only-if" direction, suppose Q_2 is contained in Q_1, but the containment entailment is false. We assign constants to the variables that make this implication false. Then for all the containment mappings μ_i (for each of which $\mu_i(\beta_1')$ does not hold), the query containment is false, because we have found a counterexample database. On this counterexample database, Q_2 produces a tuple, but there is no μ_i that will make Q_1 produce the same tuple (because all $\mu_i(\beta_1')$ fail). We need to remember that, using the μ_i's, we can produce *all* homomorphisms from Q_1 to any database where the relational atoms of Q_2 map via a homomorphism. This is because the μ_i's were produced using the normalized version of the queries – and, hence, μ_i's were not constrained by duplication of variables or by constants (recall that, in a homomorphism, a variable is allowed to map to a single target and a constant is allowed to map on the same constant). □

Observe that normalization helps, because we do not miss any containment mappings— see Examples 2.15 and 2.20 to gain intuition. Also, observe that in Theorem 2.12, the "OR" operation "$\vee$" in the implication is critical, since there might not be a single mapping μ_i from $Q_{1,0}$ to $Q_{2,0}$ such that $\beta_2 \Rightarrow \mu_i(\beta_1)$. The following examples shows that to prove containment, we need to consider all possible mappings. We give several examples here to make some points, starting with a simple example.

Example 2.13 Consider the following queries:

$$Q_1() \quad :\text{-} \ r(X, Y, Z), X < Y.$$
$$Q_2() \quad :\text{-} \ r(X, Y, Z), r(Y, Z, W), X \leq Y, X < Z.$$

This example uses no constants. The intuitive explanation that Q_2 is contained in Q_1 is the following: If, in Q_2, $X < Y$ then the single subgoal of Q_1 maps on the first subgoal of Q_2. Otherwise, if $X = Y$, then from $X < Z$ we get that $Y < Z$, hence the single subgoal of Q_1 maps on the second subgoal of Q_2.

Example 2.14 Consider the following queries:

$$Q_1() \quad :\text{-} \ r(X_1, X_2), r(X_2, X_3), r(X_3, X_4), r(X_4, X_5), r(X_5, X_1), X_1 < X_2.$$
$$Q_2() \quad :\text{-} \ r(X_1, X_2), r(X_2, X_3), r(X_3, X_4), r(X_4, X_5), r(X_5, X_1), X_1 < X_3.$$

The two queries have different comparisons, which do not become the same even after applying automorphisms to the variables that preserve the structure of the regular subgoals. (Notice that the two variables in the comparison $X_1 < X_2$ appear in the same subgoal, whereas the two variables in the comparison $X_1 < X_3$ never appear in the same subgoal.) At the same time, rather surprisingly, $Q_1 \equiv Q_2$ holds. To show $Q_1 \sqsubseteq Q_2$, we consider the five mappings from the five ordinary subgoals of Q_2 to the five of Q_1; here, each mapping corresponds to a cyclic shift of the variables. Under these mappings, β_2 becomes $X_1 < X_3$, $X_2 < X_4$, $X_3 < X_5$, $X_4 < X_1$, and $X_5 < X_2$, respectively. We can show the following:

$$(X_1 < X_2) \Rightarrow (X_1 < X_3) \vee (X_2 < X_4) \vee (X_3 < X_5) \vee (X_4 < X_1) \vee (X_5 < X_2).$$

It can be shown that if the right-hand side of the implication is false, then $X_1 = X_2$.

We conclude that $Q_1 \sqsubseteq Q_2$. It can be proved in a similar way that $Q_2 \sqsubseteq Q_1$. Notice that there is no single containment mapping μ_i such that $\beta_2 \Rightarrow \mu_i(\beta_1)$.

Notice that in Example 2.14 we did not need normalization. The following example shows that the containment test of Theorem 2.12 does not go through until we normalize *both* queries; once both queries are normalized, we can find the mappings and check the logical implication.

Example 2.15   Consider the following queries:

$$Q_1() \quad :\text{-} \quad p(A, 4), A < 4.$$
$$Q_2() \quad :\text{-} \quad p(X, 4), p(Y, X), X \leq 4, Y < 4.$$

Q_2 is contained in Q_1. The informal justification is that if the value of the variable X in Q_2 is less than 4, then the subgoal $p(A, 4)$ can be mapped to the subgoal $p(X, 4)$, and if the value of X is 4, then the second subgoal becomes $p(Y, 4)$; in this case, subgoal $p(A, 4)$ maps to $p(Y, 4)$. However, there is only one containment mapping from the ordinary subgoals of Q_1 to Q_2: that mapping sends A to X. But $X \leq 4$ together with $Y < 4$ does not imply $X < 4$. Thus, we would have concluded that the logical entailment is false. Now let us begin by normalizing the queries.

The normalized versions of the two queries are:

$$Q_1'() \quad :\text{-} \quad p(A, B), A < 4, B = 4.$$
$$Q_2'() \quad :\text{-} \quad p(X, Z), p(Y, X_1), X \leq 4, Y < 4, X = X_1, Z = 4.$$

To convince ourselves that normalizing only Q_2 does not suffice, we may want to try to work through the test of Theorem 2.12 on Q_1 and Q_2'. The informal reason that it does not work is that if we are to consider more than one mapping, then we must map subgoal $p(A, 4)$ to $p(Y, X_1)$, but constant 4 in the subgoal requires a constant to map to (specifically, the same constant 4), and X_1 is not a constant. However, when we deal with Q_1', we do not have this problem, because now we have two possible mappings: We map the only subgoal of Q_1' either to the first subgoal of Q_2' or to the second subgoal of Q_2', which amounts to mapping the variable B to either Z or X_1.

After applying the two mappings on the normalized queries, we check the following entailment:

$$X \leq 4 \wedge Y < 4 \wedge X = X_1 \wedge Z = 4 \Rightarrow (X < 4 \wedge Z = 4) \vee (Y < 4 \wedge X_1 = 4).$$

An equivalent rewriting of the entailment provides us with a tautology:

$$X \leq 4 \wedge Y < 4 \wedge X = X_1 \wedge Z = 4 \Rightarrow$$

$$(X < 4 \vee Y < 4) \wedge (X < 4 \vee X_1 = 4) \wedge (Z = 4 \vee Y < 4) \wedge (Z = 4 \vee X_1 = 4).$$

The following example is even simpler, as each query there has only one AC.

Example 2.16   Consider the queries:

$$Q_1() \quad :- \; p(A, 4), A < 4.$$
$$Q_2() \quad :- \; p(X, 4), p(3, X), X \leq 4.$$

The normalized versions of the queries are:

$$Q_1'() \quad :- \; p(A, B), A < 4, B = 4.$$
$$Q_2'() \quad :- \; p(X, Z), p(W, Y), X \leq 4, X = Y, Z = 4, W = 3.$$

There are two containment mappings from the ordinary subgoals of Q_1' to the ordinary subgoals of Q_2'.

In the following example, the contained query has no ACs, and the containing query has only two ACs. Yet the normalization step is needed.

Example 2.17   For the following two queries, without normalization we would never consider the mapping from the second subgoal of Q_1 to the fourth subgoal of Q_2. Yet this mapping is needed to prove the containment of Q_2 in Q_1:

$$Q_1(W) \quad :- \; q(W), p(X, Y, Z, Z', U, U), X < Y, Z > Z'.$$
$$Q_2(W) \quad :- \; q(W), p(X, Y, 2, 1, U, U), p(1, 2, X, Y, U, U), p(1, 2, 2, 1, X, Y).$$

The intuitive explanation of the containment uses the variables X and Y of Q_2: If $X = Y$, then the p-subgoal of Q_1 is mapped to the third p-subgoal of Q_2. Otherwise, in case $X < Y$, the p-subgoal of Q_1 is mapped to the first p-subgoal of Q_2, and if $X > Y$, then the p-subgoal of Q_1 is mapped to the second p-subgoal of Q_2. We have exhausted all the cases.

Another containment test is based on canonical databases, which are defined for CQACs as follows:

Definition 2.18   For a CQAC query Q, the set of its *canonical databases* with respect to another CQAC query Q' is constructed as follows: consider the set of the variables of Q and of the constants of Q and Q'; we partition this set into blocks, with the restriction that two distinct constants do not belong to the same block.

For each partition and for each total ordering of the blocks, we construct a canonical database of Q by: (a) equating the variables in the same block to a distinct constant (or the constant in the block if there is one), so that the total ordering is satisfied; and (b) adding to the canonical database exactly those tuples (ground atoms) that result from replacing the variables in the relational atoms in the body of Q by the constants in their block.

We now test for $Q_2 \sqsubseteq Q_1$, as follows: consider all the canonical databases of Q_2 with respect to Q_1. Then $Q_2 \sqsubseteq Q_1$ iff the following holds on any canonical database D of Q_2: If the head of Q_2 is computed on D, then the head of Q_1 is also computed on D.

Observe that, unlike the case of CQs, not all the canonical databases of a CQAC query Q necessarily produce the head of Q. However, we can prune the number of canonical databases by keeping only those on which Q computes its head (notice that the only reason that Q would not compute its head is that the ACs are not satisfied). If we have deleted the canonical databases that fail to compute the head of Q_2, then we need to only test for the head of Q_1 to test for containment of Q_2 to Q_1.

Theorem 2.19   *Let Q_1 and Q_2 be CQACs. Then $Q_2 \sqsubseteq Q_1$ if and only if Q_1 computes its head on each canonical database of Q_2 with respect to Q_1 when Q_2 computes its head on this canonical database.*

Proof. When Q_2 computes a tuple, it does that by assigning values (constants) to the variables in the body of the query (i.e., by finding a homomorphism). The target of this homomorphism is isomorphic to one of the canonical databases. Thus, if $Q_2 \sqsubseteq Q_1$, then there is a homomorphism from Q_1 to the target (or the corresponding canonical database). For the other direction, observe that if there is a computation of a tuple t of Q_2 on any given database D, then this means that one of the canonical databases of Q_2 is isomorphic with the target of the homomorphism that derives the tuple t. If there is a homomorphism from Q_1 to the corresponding canonical database of Q_2, then there is a homomorphism to the target (of Q_2) in the given database (which is isomorphic to the canonical database). □

The following example tests for containment based on canonical databases. In fact, observe also that in this example, if we do the containment test based on the containment entailment, then normalization is needed.

Example 2.20   Consider the following queries:

$$Q_1() \quad :- \quad p(A), q(A), A < 4.$$
$$Q_2() \quad :- \quad p(X), q(Y), X \leq Y, Y \leq X, Y < 4.$$

Q_2 is contained in Q_1, but there is no containment mapping from the non-normalized body of Q_1 to the non-normalized body of Q_2.

Now let us test for containment based on the canonical databases of Q_2. Q_2 has two variables, X and Y, and one constant, 4. We can construct the following canonical databases.

1. First partition: There are three blocks, each containing one element of the set $\{X, Y, 4\}$. In constructing canonical databases for ordered domains, we use the reals as the representative domain; thus we do not have to point out the order of its elements. Thus, we have the following canonical databases: $\{p(1), q(2)\}$, $\{p(2), q(1)\}$, $\{p(3), q(5)\}$, $\{p(5), q(3)\}$, $\{p(5), q(6)\}$, and $\{p(6), q(5)\}$. Note that we have considered all the total orderings of X and Y with respect to themselves and the constant 4—these are $X < Y < 4$, $Y < X < 4$, $X < 4 < Y$, $Y < 4 < X$, $4 < X < Y$, $4 < Y < X$.

2. Second partition: Now we form two blocks in the following three ways: $(X, Y), 4$; $(X, 4), Y$; and $(Y, 4), X$. We now derive seven more canonical databases: $\{p(3), q(3)\}$, $\{p(4), q(4)\}$, $\{p(5), q(5)\}$, $\{p(4), q(3)\}$, $\{p(4), q(5)\}$, $\{p(3), q(4)\}$, and $\{p(5), q(4)\}$.

3. Third partition: Finally, we have one block with all the items equated; this results in one more canonical database, $\{p(4), q(4)\}$.

Now we can prune the above canonical databases by observing that, e.g., the ACs imply that $X = Y$, hence that excludes all the databases that were constructed by considering three blocks. Moreover, we have that both $X < 4$ and $Y < 4$, hence that leaves us with the database $\{p(3), q(3)\}$ to check against Q_1. Indeed, there is a homomorphism from Q_1 to this database, which satisfies the single AC (since $3 < 4$).

CQAC containment test 1:

Given two normalized conjunctive queries with arithmetic comparisons Q_1 and Q_2, $Q_1 \sqsubseteq Q_2$ if and only if there are *containment mappings* $\mu_1, \dots, \mu_k$ from the relational atoms of Q_1 to the relational atoms of Q_2, such that the following entailment is true:

$$\phi : \beta_2' \Rightarrow \mu_1(\beta_1') \vee \dots \vee \mu_k(\beta_1').$$

where β_1' and β_2' are the arithmetic comparisons in Q_1 and Q_2 respectively.

CQAC containment test 2:

Given two conjunctive queries with arithmetic comparisons Q_1 and Q_2, $Q_1 \sqsubseteq Q_2$ if and only if the following holds: Consider all the canonical databases of Q_2 with respect to Q_1. Then $Q_2 \sqsubseteq Q_1$ iff the following holds on any such canonical database D of Q_2: If the head of Q_2 is computed on D, then the head of Q_1 is also computed on D.

2.2.2   WHEN NORMALIZATION IS NOT NEEDED

Finally, there are cases where we do not need to normalize, as the following theorem shows.

Theorem 2.21   *Consider two CQAC queries, $Q_1 = Q_{10} + \beta_1$ and $Q_2 = Q_{20} + \beta_2$, not necessarily normalized, over densely totally ordered domains. Suppose β_1 contains only $\leq$ and $\geq$, and each of β_1 and β_2 does not imply any "=" restrictions. Then $Q_2 \sqsubseteq Q_1$ if and only if*

$$\phi' : \beta_2 \Rightarrow \gamma_1(\beta_1) \vee \dots \vee \gamma_l(\beta_1),$$

where $\gamma_1, \dots, \gamma_l$ are all the containment mappings from Q_{10} to Q_{20}.

Proof. One of the directions is straightforward: If the containment entailment is true, then in any database that satisfies β_2, one of the $\gamma_i(\beta_1)$ will be satisfied (because we deal with constants), and hence containment is proven.

Now we prove the other direction: Suppose Q_2 is contained in Q_1, and the implication in the statement of the theorem is false. Then there is an assignment σ of values that are constants from a densely ordered domain to the variables that satisfies the left-hand side but not the right-hand side of the implication. This assignment σ can create a counterexample to the claim of the theorem. The critical observation is the following: Suppose, in this assignment σ, there are either two variables that are equal to the same constant or there is a variable that is equal to a constant appearing in the queries. Then there is another assignment σ' where this does not happen with the same property as σ. Indeed, because all the ACs are either $\leq$ or $\geq$, we can create another σ' by making the variables in question different. The domain is dense, so this is feasible without disturbing the truth values of the ACs in the containment entailment. We simply do as follows: Suppose N is the number of variables in the queries. We choose a small value ϵ so that $N\epsilon$ is much smaller than any distance between the constants used in σ and also between the constants in the queries and between constants used in σ and between constants appearing in the queries. We create σ' by a) changing the values of two variables with $X = Y$ in σ to $X = c_1 - \epsilon$ and $Y = c_2 + \epsilon$ if we have the AC $X \leq Y$ in Q_2 and b) changing the value of variable with $X = c$ in σ, where c is a constant from either query to $X = c - \epsilon$ ($X = c + \epsilon$, respectively) if we have the AC $X \leq c$ ($X \leq c$, respectively) in Q_2. Now we turn the relational subgoals of Q_2 into a database D by assigning the values in σ' to variables. Since Q_2 is contained in Q_1, there must be a homomorphism h from the relational subgoals of Q_1 to D such that the ACs in Q_1 are satisfied. Now, remember, that the ACs in either query do not imply "=" restrictions. Hence, any homomorphism h from the relational subgoals of Q_1 to D that satisfies the ACs of Q_1 derives one of the homomorphisms γ_i if we simply replace the targets of h with the corresponding variables. This means that the assignment σ' makes one of the $\gamma_i(\beta_1)$'s true. Hence, we arrive at a contradiction.   □

2.2.3 WHEN SINGLE MAPPING SUFFICES—THE HOMOMORPHISM PROPERTY: AC-CANONICAL DATABASES

In this section we present some observations concerning those special cases where the containment test for CQACs can be simplified. These cases are those where the test for containment is simpler, in that a single containment mapping suffices. We state in Theorems 2.22 and 2.54 two such cases. Theorem 2.22 concerns the case where the ACs in the contained query induce a total ordering on its variables together with the constants in both queries. For example, if the contained query Q_2 has only variables X and Y and also uses constants 4 and 15, and the containing query Q_1 uses constant 20, then, $X < Y$ is not sufficient, because we also need to know how X and Y compare with all the constants, i.e., 4, 15, and 20. At the same time, the following is a total ordering: $4 < X < 15 < Y < 20$. The following is also a total ordering: $X < 4 < 15 < 20 = Y$.

Theorem 2.22   *Let $Q_1 = Q_{10} + \beta_1$ and $Q_2 = Q_{20} + \beta_2$ be CQAC queries. If β_2 is a total ordering of all the variables in $Q_{2,0}$ and of all the constants in both Q_1 and Q_2, then $Q_2 \sqsubseteq Q_1$ iff there is a single containment mapping μ from $Q_{1,0}$ to $Q_{2,0}$ such that $\beta_2 \Rightarrow \mu(\beta_1)$.*

Proof. In this case, there is a single canonical database of Q_2 up to isomorphism, on which Q_2 computes its head.   □

A query is called *left semi-interval (LSI) query* if all its comparisons are *left semi-interval (LSI) comparisons*, i.e., are all of the form $X < c$ or $X \leq c$, where X is a variable and c is a constant. A *right semi-interval (RSI) query* and a *right semi-interval (RSI) comparison* are defined similarly, i.e., the comparisons are all of the form $X > c$ or $X \geq c$, where X is a variable and c is a constant. We use the notation SI ("semi-interval") to refer to the queries and sets of comparisons that contain both LSI and RSI comparisons. When we say that an arithmetic comparison is *open*, we mean that its operator is either $<$ or $>$; when we say that an arithmetic comparison is *closed*, we mean that its operator is either $\leq$ or $\geq$. We refer analogously to open LSI or RSI and closed LSI and RSI. The same result as Theorem 2.23, below, holds for CRSI comparisons in the containing query, since this is a symmetric case.

Theorem 2.23   *Let Q_1 be a conjunctive query with closed left semi-interval arithmetic-comparison subgoals (CLSIs), and Q_2 a conjunctive query that uses only $\leq$ or $\geq$ comparisons in β_2, and β_2 does not imply "=" restrictions. Then $Q_2 \sqsubseteq Q_1$ iff there is a single containment mapping μ from $Q_{1,0}$ to $Q_{2,0}$ such that $\beta_2 \Rightarrow \mu(\beta_1)$.*

Proof. Suppose Q_2 is contained in Q_1. First, we notice that, according to Theorem 2.21, normalization is not needed. (Indeed, if there are equalities, we can "absorb" them by having all the variables (or variables and constants) that are equated replaced by the same variable or constant in the normal (relational) subgoals, up until the point where there are no more equalities in the arithmetic-comparison subgoals.) Thus, the right-hand side of the containment entailment (as defined in the containment test, see Theorem 2.12) contains only CLSIs.

We consider now the containment entailment, and turn its right-hand side into a conjunction of disjunctions. Let us say that one of the conjuncts is $d_1 \vee d_2 \vee \ldots$. Then the containment entailment is equivalent to several entailments, each coming from one conjunct of the right-hand side, as follows: the left-hand side is the same as in the original entailment, and the right-hand side is this conjunct. Thus, for the above conjunct the right-hand side is $d_1 \vee d_2 \vee \ldots$. Each conjunct being a disjunction of CLSIs makes the entailment simpler to reason about: It is not hard to prove that such an entailment holds iff there is one disjunct, d_i, on the right-hand side, such that the left-hand side implies this disjunct d_i. In other words, d_i is directly implied by the left-hand side of the original entailment.

However, now going back to the original entailment (and before we have turned the right-hand side into a conjunction), we notice that d_i occurs in one of the disjuncts. Thus, we can delete this d_i from the original entailment, which results in an entailment to satisfy with strictly fewer arithmetic comparisons. We proceed with this new entailment in a similar manner, and continue to argue in the same fashion, producing a sequence of entailments up until the point where one of the disjuncts, $e_j = \mu(\beta_1)$, of the original entailment is such that all its conjuncts are directly implied by the left-hand side of the original entailment. This e_j gives the single homomorphism, μ, which proves the desired query containment. $\qquad\square$

We say that two classes of queries have the homomorphism property iff, in order to check containment for a query belonging to one class in a query belonging to another class, the existence of a single homomorphism suffices, for which the following is true: $\beta_2 \Rightarrow \mu(\beta_1)$. Since the homomorphism property is a general property that concerns homomorphisms between relational structures, we define it below for any relational structure. First, we define a *relational structure with arithmetic comparisons* to be a set of relational atoms over variables and constants, together with a set of arithmetic comparisons that use variables that appear in relational atoms.

Definition 2.24   (Homomorphism property)
For two relational structures with arithmetic comparisons, K_1 and K_2, we say that *the homomorphism property holds* from K_1 to K_2 if the following two statements are equivalent.

1. We normalize $K_1 = K_{10} + \beta_1$ and $K_2 = K_{20} + \beta_2$ to $K'_{10} + \beta'_1$ and $K'_{20} + \beta'_2$, respectively (see Definition 2.11 for normalization). Let $\mu_1, \ldots, \mu_k$ be all the homomorphisms from K'_{10} to K'_{20}. Then the following is true:

$$\beta'_2 \Rightarrow \mu_1(\beta'_1) \vee \ldots \vee \mu_k(\beta'_1).$$

2. There is a homomorphism μ from K_{10} to K_{20}, such that the following is true:

$$\beta_2 \Rightarrow \mu(\beta_1).$$

We say that a pair of sets of arithmetic comparisons $(\mathcal{B}_1, \mathcal{B}_2)$ *enables the homomorphism property under condition C* if the homomorphism property holds from K_1 to K_2, where K_1 is a relational structure with ACs from $\mathcal{B}_1$, and K_2 is a relational structure with ACs from $\mathcal{B}_2$ and condition C holds[2].

Thus, if we denote by $\mathcal{B}_1$ the set of closed left semi-interval arithmetic comparisons, and $\mathcal{B}_2$ is the set of $\leq$ or $\geq$ comparisons, then Theorem 2.23 says that the pair $(\mathcal{B}_1, \mathcal{B}_2)$ enables the homomorphism property under the condition that the ACs in the queries do not imply "=" restrictions.

---

[2]Condition C is usually a simple condition or empty, so, here, we do not specify further how we express it.

> **CQAC containment test—homomorphism property:** Given two conjunctive queries with arithmetic comparisons Q_1 and Q_2, $Q_1 \sqsubseteq Q_2$ if and only if there is a *containment mapping* from Q_2 to Q_1, such that the mapping maps a constant to the same constant, and maps a variable to either a variable or a constant. Under this mapping, the head of Q_2 becomes the head of Q_1, each subgoal of Q_2 becomes a subgoal in Q_1, and the image of each arithmetic comparison in Q_1 is implied by the arithmetic comparisons in Q_2.

We now define canonical databases a bit differently: They now have variables instead of constants, and include ACs over these variables.

Definition 2.25 Let Q be a CQAC query. An *AC-canonical database* of this query is a canonical database of the regular (relational) subgoals of Q, which is modified by using variables instead of constants and by adding the AC subgoals (comparisons) of Q on these variables.

The following theorem shows the usefulness of the AC-canonical database.

Theorem 2.26 *Let $(\mathcal{B}_1, \mathcal{B}_2)$ be a pair of sets of arithmetic comparisons that enables the homomorphism property. Let Q be a query with ACs from $\mathcal{B}_1$, and Q' a query with ACs from $\mathcal{B}_2$. Then the following is true: If there is a homomorphism from Q to the AC-canonical database of Q' such that the ACs in Q' imply the image of the ACs in Q, then there is a homomorphism from Q to any canonical database of Q' that satisfies the ACs in Q.*

The following example shows how to use this result.

Example 2.27

$$Q_1() \quad :\text{-} \ r(X,Y), r(Y,Z), Z \leq 8, X \leq 3.$$
$$Q_2() \quad :\text{-} \ r(X,Y), r(Y,Y), s(W), Y \leq W, W \leq 5, X \leq 2.$$

We will show that Q_2 is contained in Q_1. First we use the general containment test for CQACs. Then observe that the homomorphism property holds, because the ACs in the containing query are all CLSIs, and the ACs in the contained query use only $\leq$. Hence we can apply Theorem 2.26.

There are two containment mappings from the relational subgoals of Q_1 to the relational subgoals of Q_2: The mapping μ_1 that maps X to X, Y to Y, and Z to Y, and the mapping μ_2 that maps all the variables to Y. We form the containment entailment (as used in Theorem 2.12):

$$Y \leq W \wedge W \leq 5 \wedge X \leq 2 \Rightarrow \mu_1(Z \leq 8 \wedge X \leq 3) \vee \mu_2(Z \leq 8 \wedge X \leq 3),$$

which becomes:

$$Y \leq W \wedge W \leq 5 \wedge X \leq 2 \Rightarrow (Y \leq 8 \wedge X \leq 3) \vee (Y \leq 8 \wedge Y \leq 3).$$

We can see that this entailment is true, because the following is true:

$$Y \leq W \wedge W \leq 5 \wedge X \leq 2 \Rightarrow (Y \leq 8 \wedge X \leq 3),$$

which means that the mapping μ_1 was sufficient to prove the containment.

The containment test can be now simplified by using Theorem 2.26. The AC-canonical database of Q_2 is: $\{r(X, Y), r(Y, Y), s(W), Y \leq W, W \leq 5, X \leq 2\}$. Now, we compute the query Q_1 on this AC-canonical database. In order to do that, we use the μ_1 from Q_1 to this AC-canonical database. This proves the containment, because the ACs in Q_2 imply the images of the ACs in Q_1, i.e.,

$$Y \leq W \wedge W \leq 5 \wedge X \leq 2 \Rightarrow (Y \leq 8 \wedge X \leq 3),$$

which is the same implication that was observed in the reasoning above. Theorem 2.26 guarantees that if we could not find a single containment mapping to satisfy the requirement about ACs, then The query Q_2 would not be contained in Q_1.

2.3   CQN QUERY CONTAINMENT

The containment test for CQNs is based on canonical databases, whose construction begins in the same way as for CQACs, but then proceeds differently.

2.3.1   SET OF CANONICAL DATABASES

We construct a set of canonical databases as follows. The first stage is the same as that for CQACs: We consider only the positive query subgoals, and enumerate all the possible partitions of their variables into blocks. We then assign a distinct constant to each block. (We do not have to worry about taking these constants from a totally ordered domain, because in case of CQNs ordering does not matter.) The result of this stage is the basic canonical databases.

In the second stage, we check whether we can compute the head of the query on each of the basic canonical databases. The ones that pass this test comprise the canonical databases of the query.

In the third and final stage, from the canonical databases formed in the second stage we construct more canonical databases, as follows. For each canonical database formed in the second stage, we form a number of databases from the tuples of the relations mentioned in the query, with all possible ways of using the available constants. (We do not use any additional constants.) For each of those databases, we check whether the head of the query can be computed: For each database for which the answer is positive, the database becomes another canonical database of the query.

Example 2.28   Consider the following queries:

$$Q_1() \quad :\text{-} \ r(X,Y), s(Y,Z), r(X,Z), \neg r(X,X).$$
$$Q_2() \quad :\text{-} \ r(X,Y), s(Y,Z), r(X,Z), \neg r(X,X), \neg s(Z,Z).$$

Let us show that Q_2 is contained in Q_1. Indeed, the basic canonical databases of Q_2 are the canonical databases of the following five CQs:

$$Q_a() \quad :\text{-} \ r(X,Y), s(Y,Z), r(X,Z).$$
$$Q_b() \quad :\text{-} \ r(X,X), s(X,Z), r(X,Z).$$
$$Q_c() \quad :\text{-} \ r(X,Y), s(Y,Y), r(X,Y).$$
$$Q_d() \quad :\text{-} \ r(X,Y), s(Y,X), r(X,X).$$
$$Q_e() \quad :\text{-} \ r(X,X), s(X,X).$$

These five CQs are all the homomorphic images of the body of Q_a:

$$Q_a() \quad :\text{-} \ r(X,Y), s(Y,Z), r(X,Z).$$

Now we check whether we can compute the head of Q_2 on those basic canonical databases. This check is passed only by the canonical database of Q_a. To see why, let us take one of the other four CQs, say Q_b. Its canonical database is $D = \{r(1,1), s(1,2), r(1,2)\}$. There is only one homomorphism from the positive subgoals of Q_2 to D. Under this homomorphism, the negated subgoals of Q_2 are not satisfied, in particular the first one, $\neg r(X,X)$, because of the presence of $r(1,1)$. Hence the head of Q_2 is computed on D.

Now we proceed with the canonical database D' of Q_a, $D' = \{r(1,2), s(2,3), r(1,3)\}$. Remember that D' is still a basic canonical database for Q_2. Now we form a number of databases, by adding more facts to D' using in all possible ways its constants 1, 2, and 3. Among the resulting databases, the ones that qualify as canonical databases for Q_2 are the ones on which the head of Q_2 is computed. Thus, e.g., $D'_1 = \{r(1,2), s(2,3), r(1,3), r(1,1)\}$ does not qualify, because the negated subgoal $\neg r(X,X)$ is not true. (All the other instances that come from $D' = \{r(1,2), s(2,3), r(1,3)\}$ and do not contain $r(1,1)$, qualify as canonical databases.) E.g., if we take $D'_2 = \{r(1,2), s(2,3), r(1,3), r(2,1), r(3,3), s(2,2)\}$, this qualifies as a canonical database of Q_2.

Now that we have formed the canonical databases of Q_2, we check for each of them whether it can be used to derive the head of Q_1. As an example, let us see what Q_1 computes when applied on D'. Q_1 computes to true on D', because of the homomorphism $X \to 1, Y \to 2$, $Z \to 3$, which makes the non-negated subgoals true. In addition, the negated subgoal becomes true, because D' does not include the fact $r(1,1)$. This test works for all the canonical databases of Q_2, hence $Q_2 \sqsubseteq Q_1$.

If, however, we had another query for Q_1, say Q'_1:

$$Q_1() \quad :\text{-} \ r(X,Y), s(Y,Z), r(X,Z), \neg r(Y,Y),$$

then $Q_2 \sqsubseteq Q'_1$ would not hold. To prove this, we only need one canonical database of Q_2 to use as a counterexample. Indeed, on $D'' = \{r(1,2), s(2,3), r(1,3), r(2,2)\}$, the head of Q_2 is computed, but the head of Q'_1 is not.

Theorem 2.29   *Let Q_1 and Q_2 be CQN queries. Then $Q_1 \sqsubseteq Q_2$ iff the procedure given in Figure 2.1 outputs "yes."*

Containment of CQNs (checking whether $Q_2 \sqsubseteq Q_1$):

1. Construct the set of basic canonical databases that correspond to all the partitions of the set of variables of Q_2.

   a. For each partition, assign a unique constant to each block of the partition.

   b. Create basic canonical database DB by replacing each variable in the body of Q_2 by the constant of its block, and treat the resulting subgoals as the only tuples in the database (i.e., *freeze* the body of Q_2). The basic canonical DB is the set of the resulting *positive* subgoals.

2. For each basic canonical DB D constructed in step (1), check that if $Q_2(D)$ contains the frozen head of Q_2, then so does $Q_1(D)$.

3. If the above check is successful, then we must also consider the larger set of (*extended*) canonical DB's D', formed by adding to D other tuples, which are formed from the same symbols as D, but not using any of the tuples among the negated subgoals of Q_2. Check that $Q_1(D')$ contains the frozen head of Q_2.

4. If the above condition holds for all the D', then $Q_2 \sqsubseteq Q_1$ holds; if not, then $Q_2 \sqsubseteq Q_1$ does not hold.

Figure 2.1: Containment test for CQNs.

Proof. ($\Leftarrow$) Let D be any database, and t be a tuple in the set of answers to the query Q_1 on D, i.e., t is in $Q_1(D)$. The mapping from Q_1 to D that produces t equates some variables of Q_1; let Q_1^i be Q_1 with those variables merged. There is a homomorphism from the positive subgoals in the body of Q_1^i to D that maps the head of Q_1^i to t. The image of this homomorphism is isomorphic to a canonical database D_j that makes the body of Q_1^i true. That is, t is in $Q_2(D)$. Therefore, $Q_1 \sqsubseteq Q_2$.
($\Rightarrow$) Suppose $Q_1 \sqsubseteq Q_2$. If the test is not successful, then one of the canonical databases of Q_2 is a counterexample database that proves that containment does not hold.   □

> **CQN containment test:**
> Given two conjunctive queries with negation Q_1 and Q_2, $Q_2 \sqsubseteq Q_1$ if and only if the following holds: Consider all the canonical databases of Q_2 with respect to Q_1. Then $Q_2 \sqsubseteq Q_1$ iff the following holds on any canonical database D of Q_2: If the head of Q_2 is computed on D, then the head of Q_1 is also computed on D.

2.4   CQA QUERY CONTAINMENT AND EQUIVALENCE

One categorization of aggregate operators considers those that are *duplicate insensitive*, and those that are *duplicate sensitive*. An aggregate operator is *duplicate insensitive* if, when it is computed on a bag, the result does not depend on the multiplicities, otherwise it is *duplicate sensitive*. *Max* and *min* are in the first category, and *sum* and *count* are in the second category.

For duplicate-insensitive queries, we provide a detailed analysis with examples, by focusing on *max* queries. (*Min* queries are "symmetical" to *max*, so the analysis is similar.) For duplicate-sensitive queries, the analysis is analogous. We then introduce a more general category of *expandable queries*; this category contains the aggregate operators *max*, *min*, *sum*, and *count*.

Recall that to evaluate aggregate queries, we form bags of tuples. In this context, the following theorem is relevant and useful.

Before we state the theorem, let us clarify that under set semantics, a conjunctive query with duplicate subgoals is equivalent to the same query with the duplicate subgoals removed. Thus, we never assume that we have duplicate subgoals in conjunctive queries. Theorem 2.30, below, says that under bag-set semantics, duplicate subgoals can be removed as well.

Theorem 2.30   *(1) Two conjunctive queries are bag equivalent iff they are isomorphic. (2) Two conjunctive queries are bag-set equivalent iff they are isomorphic after the duplicate subgoals are removed.*

2.4.1   MAX QUERIES

To gain intuition, we begin with an example of a *max* query.

Example 2.31   Consider queries

$$q_1(X, \max(Y)) \leftarrow r(X, Z), s(Z, Y),$$

$$q_2(X, \max(Y)) \leftarrow r(X, Z), s(Z, Y), s(Z', Y),$$

$$q_3(X, \max(Y)) \leftarrow r(X, Z), s(Z, Y), t(W, Y).$$

The following database is a counterexample to the containment of q_3 in q_1:

$$D = \{r(1, 2), s(2, 5), t(6, 5), s(2, 7)\}.$$

On this database, q_3 computes one tuple, $(1, 7)$, because there are two appropriate homomorphisms from the body of the query to the database, which compute the set $\{(1, 5), (1, 7)\}$. However, there is only one appropriate homomorphism from the body of q_1 to the database, which computes the set $\{(1, 5)\}$. Hence the output of q_1 on D is $\{(1, 5)\}$. This is proof that q_3 is not contained in q_1, although there is a homomorphism from the body of q_3 to the body of q_1 that maps both the grouping (i.e., x) and aggregate (i.e., y) attributes to themselves.

At the same time, the queries q_1 and q_2 are equivalent, although their bodies are not isomorphic up to duplicate-subgoal elimination.[3] Later, we will prove a theorem that says that for *max* queries with only one grouping attribute in each, query containment reduces to query equivalence.

When we talk about *appropriate* homomorphisms between subgoals of aggregate queries, we refer to homomorphisms that map all the head attributes of one query to the same attributes of the other query.

Theorem 2.32 *Two max queries q_1 and q_2 with single aggregation are equivalent if and only if their conjunctive cores (see Definition 1.15 for conjunctive core of an aggregate query) $\breve{q}_1$ and $\breve{q}_2$ are set equivalent.*

The proof of this result is based on the observation that if the conjunctive cores are not set equivalent, then one value for the aggregated attribute can appear in the result of applying the conjunctive core on a database for one query and not for the other. This value could be the maximum, and this will give different results.

Theorem 2.33 *For two max queries with only one grouping attribute in each, one is contained in the other iff these queries are equivalent.*

Proof. For one of the directions, the proof is straightforward. For the other direction, suppose the queries are not equivalent. Then we can construct a counterexample database. We have two cases: If there is no homomorphism from the body of Q_1 to the body of Q_2, then we can construct a counterexample database the same way as we did for CQs. Suppose there is a homomorphism from the body of Q_1 to the body of Q_2, but there is no homomorphism from the body of Q_2 to the body of Q_1. Then we can construct a counterexample database D so that there is an extra homomorphism from the body of Q_1 to some part of the database. We make sure that this part has the maximum value for the aggregated attribute, say value v_1, whereas for

---

[3]We assume that a CQ may have duplicate subgoals only under bag semantics. For set semantics, this does not make any difference, so, for the rest of the book, duplicate subgoals do not appear.

the homomorphisms of Q_2, the maximum value is lower, say $v_2 < v_1$ (for the same grouping attribute value a_x). Then, in the output of Q_2 we have the tuple (a_x, v_1), whereas in Q_1 we have the tuple (a_x, v_2).

Now, in detail, we construct the counterexample database D as follows. We place in D all the facts of the canonical database of the conjunctive core of Q_1. Here, assume that a_x is the value of the grouping attribute, and v_1 is the value of the aggregated attribute. Then we use a fresh constant v_2 (not used so far in the facts we added in D), and add more facts in D: We add all facts of the canonical database of the conjunctive core of Q_2, where the value of the grouping attribute is a_x and the value of all the other attributes is v_2. Finally, we choose v_2 so that $v_2 < v_1$. □

When there is more than one grouping attribute, then for *max* queries, containment may hold without the queries being equivalent.

Example 2.34   Consider queries

$$q_1(X, X', \max(Y)) \leftarrow r(X, Z), s(Z, Y), r'(X, X'),$$

$$q_2(X, X', \max(Y)) \leftarrow r(X, Z), s(Z, Y), s(Z', Y), r'(X, X'), s'(X, X').$$

The bodies of q_1 and q_2 are not such that there is an appropriate homomorphism both ways, therefore the queries are not equivalent (it is easy to build a counterexample database), but q_2 is contained in q_1. The reason is that q_2 may miss (wrto q_1) certain tuples with a specific list of values of the grouping attributes. At the same time, in those cases where q_2 does not miss a grouping-attribute value, whenever there is a homomorphism from the body of q_2 to the database, then there is a homomorphism from the body of q_1 to the same tuples of the database. To see this, consider the database

$$D = \{r(1, 2), s(2, 5), s(2, 7), r'(1, 9), r'(1, 8), s'(1, 8)\}.$$

The result of the query q_2 on D is $\{(1, 8, 7)\}$, whereas the result of the query q_1 on D is $\{(1, 8, 7), (1, 9, 7)\}$.

The reason that q_2 is contained in q_1 is a little more subtle: In the query definitions in this example, we can see that the subgoals in the body of the query that do not allow homomorphisms among the bodies both ways are the primed subgoals (with relation symbols s' and r'). However, these subgoals contain only grouping attributes. Hence, when we compute either query on a database, those subgoals either generate homomorphisms with a specific value-list of grouping attributes, or they do not. When such homomorphisms are generated by q_2, they are also generated by q_1. (Note that this does not hold the other way around, hence there is containment but not equivalence in this case.) Since the rest of the subgoals in both queries have homomorphisms both ways, both queries generate the same homomorphisms on the database. The following theorem proves this point.

For an aggregate query Q, we say that a subgoal is a *grouping subgoal* if it only contains grouping attributes. We call all the other subgoals *non-grouping subgoals*. When we check query containment or equivalence, we think of the grouping attributes in the head of both queries as having the same names.

Theorem 2.35   *For max queries Q_1 and Q_2 with minimized cores, Q_2 is contained in Q_1 iff the following is true: (a) the set of grouping subgoals of Q_1 is a subset of the set of grouping subgoals of Q_2 and (b) between the non-grouping subgoals of the two queries there are containment mappings both ways.*

Proof. When the conditions (a) and (b) do not hold, we have two cases. (i) The first of the two conditions holds, but the second does not; then there is a counterexample database that is constructed along the lines of the counterexample database in the proof of Theorem 2.33. (ii) The first of the two conditions does not hold; then a counterexample database can be constructed so that it produces a list of values of the grouping attributes for Q_2 but not for Q_1. This counterexample database is constructed as follows: suppose Q_1 has a grouping subgoal g, and Q_2 does not have g. We construct the canonical database D of the core of Q_2. Since the core of Q_1 is minimized (i.e., before we decide that g is not in Q_2), g does not map to any fact in D (otherwise the core of Q_1 would not have been minimized). Thus, Q_2 produces a nonempty result on D, but Q_1 produces an empty result. Actually, this proof shows that it is sufficient to minimize the set of grouping subgoals, i.e., to delete any grouping subgoal that homomorphically maps to another grouping subgoal.

For the other direction, suppose both conditions (a) and (b) hold. Then if the grouping subgoals of Q_2 can be mapped to a database, then a "same-value" mapping can be used for the grouping subgoals of Q_1 and the same database, so that a tuple with these grouping values is formed on the database for both queries. Because the non-grouping subgoals have homomorphisms both ways between them, the same homomorphisms on the database can be found for both queries. Hence for any assignment of values to the grouping attributes, the aggregate operator provides the same value in both queries. □

Note: Theorem 2.33 assumes that there are no unary relations on the grouping attribute.

2.4.2   SUM QUERIES

The analysis here is analogous to that of Section 2.4.1, and the proofs of the following two theorems are analogous to their previous-section counterparts as well.

Theorem 2.36   *Two sum queries are equivalent iff their cores are bag-set equivalent.*

Theorem 2.37   *For two sum queries with only one grouping attribute in each, containment holds iff the queries are equivalent.*

In the following theorem, we assume that conjunctive queries may have duplicate subgoals. This assumption does not make a difference in the case of set semantics, and the only place in this book where this assumption makes a difference is when we discuss aggregate queries. By minimizing the set of grouping subgoals in a query definition, we mean deleting any grouping subgoal that homomorphically maps to another grouping subgoal.

Theorem 2.38   *For sum queries Q_1 and Q_2 with minimized sets of grouping subgoals, containment of Q_2 in Q_1 holds iff the following is true: (a) the set of all the grouping subgoals of Q_1 is a subset of the set of all the grouping subgoals of Q_2 and (b) the non-grouping subgoals of the two queries are isomorphic after duplicate-subgoals elimination.*

CQA containment test:
Given two CQA queries Q_1 and Q_2, $Q_2 \sqsubseteq Q_1$ if and only if the following holds.
The set of all the grouping subgoals of Q_1 is a subset of the set of all the grouping subgoals of Q_2, and the following additional conditions hold:
(a) for *min* and *max*: the non-grouping subgoals of Q_2 and Q_1 have appropriate homomorphisms from one to the other; and
(b) for *sum* and *count*: the non-grouping subgoals of Q_2 and Q_1 are isomorphic after duplicate-subgoal elimination.

2.4.3   MORE GENERAL AGGREGATE OPERATORS

We now turn to an exploration of the problems of containment and equivalence of compatible queries:

Definition 2.39   (Compatible queries)
Two queries are *compatible* if the tuples of arguments in their heads are identical.

An aggregate function γ is *expandable* if equality, as computed on two different multisets, implies equality as computed on two other multi-sets, each of which comes from the respective original multiset by multiplying all the multiplicities by the same number. In other words, if $\gamma(B) = \gamma(B')$ and B_1 comes from B by multiplying all the multiplicities by integer k, and B_1' comes from B' by multiplying all the multiplicities by the same integer k, then $\gamma(B_1) = \gamma(B_1')$. The aggregation functions *max*, *min*, *cntd*, *count*, *sum*, *avg*, and *topK* are expandable.

For expandable functions, testing query containment is reduced to testing query equivalence, as follows. The inspiration comes from the following theorem for CQs (the proof is straightforward using methods that have been explained in this chapter).

Theorem 2.40   *Suppose Q_1, Q_2, and Q_3 are compatible queries. Given CQs Q_1 and Q_2, let query Q_3 have the same head as those of Q_1 and Q_2, and have a body that contains all the subgoals of Q_1 and Q_2 and has no other subgoals. Then Q_2 is contained in Q_1 iff Q_2 and Q_3 are equivalent.*

To check containment for aggregate expandable queries Q and Q', we need to define two new queries. Each new query has the same head as Q and Q'. Further, the body of Q_1 comprises the subgoals of Q' twice, and the body of Q_2 comprises all the subgoals of Q and all the subgoals of Q' (and has no other subgoals).

Theorem 2.41   *Let Q and Q' be compatible aggregate queries with expandable aggregate operators. Then Q' is contained in Q iff Q_1 and Q_2 as constructed above are equivalent.*

The proof of this result is based on the material provided in this section and is left as an exercise to the reader.

2.5   ACYCLIC CQS

As we have discussed, testing for query containment and query evaluation for CQs both use checking for the existence of a homomorphism as a subroutine. When the queries are "acyclic CQs," then we can find a homomorphism more efficiently—which, intuitively, is not surprising, because we expect to be able to take advantage of the tree-like structures (hence lack of cycles) in the query definitions. In this section, we define acyclic CQs, and then present these efficient algorithms.

2.5.1   DEFINITION OF ACYCLIC QUERIES AND SPECIAL CASES

A hypergraph extends the definition of a graph in that it contains edges, each edge including more than two nodes and is formally defined as follows: a *hypergraph* is a pair (V, E), where V is a set of nodes and E is a set of hyperedges, each hyperedge containing a subset of the nodes. Figure 2.2 shows a hypergraph with $V = \{A, B, C, D, E, F, G, H, I, J, K\}$ and with six hyperedges, each hyperedge being indicated by an ellipse in the figure. Thus, e.g., the leftmost hyperedge in the figure contains the nodes K and G, while the highest hyperedge contains the nodes A, H, D, and E. A conjunctive query can be viewed as corresponding to a hypergraph: the attributes of the query are the nodes of the hypergraph, and there is a hyperedge for each subgoal in the body of the query, which includes exactly the attributes/nodes that are in the schema of this relation.

A hypergraph is *acyclic* if the "GYO-elimination" procedure results in a single hyperedge. (The name GYO comes from the first letter of three authors of a related paper—see Chapter 8 for

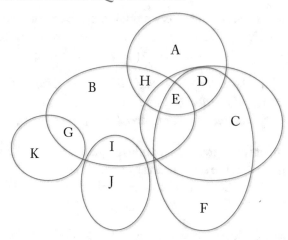

Figure 2.2: Hypergraph for the query of Example 2.43. This hypergraph is acyclic.

more details.) The GYO-elimination procedure eliminates a hyperedge e_1 from the hypergraph if this hyperedge is *consumed* by another hyperedge e_2. Hyperedge e_1 is *consumed* by hyperedge e_2 if the attributes of e_2 can be partitioned into two sets, the set of attributes that belong only to e_1 and no other hyperedges, and the set of attributes that belong to both e_1 and e_2. The elimination procedure creates a parse tree, where edge e_1 is a child of the edge e_2 when e_1 is eliminated due to being consumed by e_2. The nodes of this tree are the hyperedges of the hypergraph.

Definition 2.42   A CQ query is *acyclic* if its corresponding hypergraph is acyclic.

Example 2.43   Consider a CQ with the following relations in the body:

$$r_1(A, H, D, E), r_2(B, H, E, G, I), r_3(E, D, C), r_4(K, G), r_5(I, J), r_1(E, D, C, F).$$

Figure 2.2 shows the hypergraph that corresponds to this query. We will show that this is an acyclic query, because its corresponding hypergraph is acyclic.

We apply GYO elimination to the hypergraph of Figure 2.2. We observe that the hyperedge $\{K, G\}$ is consumed by hyperedge $\{B, H, E, G, I\}$, because K only belongs to the former hyperedge and G to the latter. Thus, we start by eliminating the hyperedge $\{K, G\}$, and begin building the parse tree in Figure 2.3 by connecting hyperedge $\{K, G\}$ to its parent hyperedge $\{B, H, E, G, I\}$. Now, hyperedge $\{F, D, C, E\}$ is consumed by hyperedge $\{D, C, E\}$, thus we proceed with building the parse tree by making $\{D, C, E\}$ the parent of $\{F, D, C, E\}$. Observe that the hyperedge $\{A, H, D, E\}$ does not consume $\{F, D, C, E\}$, because F is the only node of $\{F, D, C, E\}$ that does not belong to any other hyperedge, and the rest of its nodes need to belong to the *same* hyperedge to enable the conclusion that it is consumed by this hyperedge.

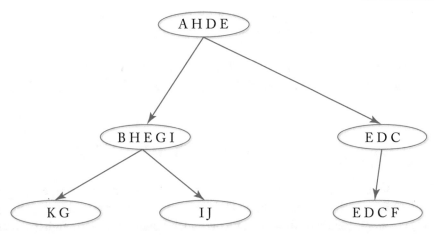

Figure 2.3: The parse tree of the hypergraph for the query of Example 2.43.

Below, we define chain queries and path queries, which we will use in this book in several different contexts. Queries in both classes are acyclic and have parse trees that are simple paths.

Definition 2.44   A CQ query is a *chain query* if it is defined over binary predicates, and the following also holds: The set of subgoals of the query, when viewed as a labeled graph, forms a directed path, whose start and end nodes are the only arguments in the head. (For example, the following query is a chain query: $q(X, Y) :\!- a(X, Z_1), b(Z_1, Z_2), c(Z_2, Y)$.)

Path queries are chain queries over a single binary relation. Path queries can be fully defined by the length of the path in the body (i.e., the number of subgoals in the body). Hence, we denote by P_k the path query of length k. We denote the language of all chain queries by CQ_{chain}, and the language of all path queries by CQ_{path}.

We will also work with the class of *Boolean path queries*, denoted P_k^b and with the meaning that the body of P_k^b is the same as P_k, but the head contains no variables. In other words, a Boolean path query returns the value true or false, depending on whether its variables are instantiated to nodes along a path in the graph that represents the database.

Chain queries have parse trees that are simple paths; that is, each node in the parse tree has only one child. Notice that, in general, hypergraphs (and corresponding CQs) do not have unique parse trees. Other classes of acyclic queries that have been studied for their special properties include (a) *tall* queries (informally defined as a series of relational subgoals, each relation having a subset of the attributes of the previous one—a parse tree is a simple path), and (b) *star* queries (informally defined as having a subgoal that can be the parent in a parse tree of all other subgoals, i.e., it contains all the attributes appearing in each subgoal which are not unique to the subgoal). Tall queries have the property that (unlike chain queries), when attributes or even whole relations are deleted, they remain connected and are still tall queries. Moreover, in tall queries, there is an attribute (or attributes) of a relation that appear in all the other relations. The following are examples of tall queries and star queries:

Tall query: $q(X_1, X_2, X_3, X_4) :- a(X_1, X_2, X_3, X_4), b(X_1, X_2, X_3), c(X_1, X_2), d(X_1)$.
Star query: $q(X_1, X_2, X_3, X_4) :- a(Y, X_3, X_4), b(Y, X_1, X_2), c(Y, X_5), d(Y, X_6), f(Y)$.

2.5.2 EFFICIENT ALGORITHM FOR CHECKING QUERY CONTAINMENT

Now let Q_1 be a Boolean path query on binary relation e, so its schema is a single binary relation. Let Q_2 be a CQ for which we would like to check whether it is contained in Q_1. Suppose the schema of Q_2 is a single binary relation; so data over such schema can be thought of as a directed graph. How do we check containment?

We can prove that containment holds iff the canonical database of Q_2 (which includes a graph on relation e) contains a path labeled e (not necessarily simple) of length that is the same as the path of Q_1. There is a polynomial algorithm (in the size of Q_2 and Q_1) to check this: In the first stage, look for paths of length 1. In the second stage of the algorithm, check whether those paths can be extended to paths of length 2, and so on. In the i-th stage, check whether the paths of length $i - 1$ can be extended to paths of length i. In order to implement each stage, all that is needed is to keep a table of nodes by lengths up to length $i - 1$, and all that is needed to record for each node N in the current stage is whether there is a path of length i from any node to node N. For that, the algorithm checks whether there is an adjacent edge that can extend the path.

To see that the runtime of the algorithm is polynomial, notice that the number of its stages is at most equal to the length of the path in Q_1. Also, in each stage we visit all the edges of the graph for the query Q_2, to determine whether they can form a longer path. This checking is bounded from above by the size of the query Q_2. Thus, the total time is proportional to $O(size(Q_1) \times size(Q_2))$.

When the containing query is an acyclic CQ and the contained query is any CQ, then the following algorithm checks for containment efficiently.

The algorithm follows one of the parse trees of Q_1. In each step, the algorithm considers a subgoal s_i of Q_1, such that all the children of s_i in the parse tree were processed in earlier steps of the algorithm. For each partial mapping μ from s_i to the subgoals of Q_2, the algorithm checks whether μ is "successful;" it is successful if μ, together with the partial mappings from the children of s_i, can be assembled into a ("larger") partial mapping from s_i and its children to some set of subgoals of Q_2.

We now provide a formal description of the algorithm. Let Q_1 and Q_2 be two CQ queries, such that Q_1 is acyclic; we would like to check whether Q_2 is contained in Q_1. Let T be a parse tree for the query Q_1, such that each node, i, in T corresponds to subgoal s_i of the query.

For each node i of T, the algorithm maintains a set of tuples; each tuple consists of the same number of variables of Q_2. For example, for the parse tree of Figure 2.3, if the node (B, H, E, G, I) is node 2, then the relation is $M_2(H, E)$, because the parent of this node is the root, and (H, E) are the attributes in the intersection of the nodes (B, H, E, G, I) and (A, H, D, E).

Algorithm Acyclic Containment:

1. Initialize all sets of leaves as follows. For each leaf i in T, corresponding to subgoal g_i of Q_1, consider all homomorphisms from g_i to any subgoal of Q_2; for each such homomorphism h, add $h(t)$ to the relation M_i for leaf i, where t are the shared variables between g_i and its parent. All the leaves are labeled "processed."

2.   For each subgoal g such that all its children are processed, do:

3.   For each homomorphism h_g from g to the subgoals of Q_2, do:

4.   For each child g_i of g in the parse tree, do: check whether $h(t_i)$ is in M_i
            where t_i is the tuple of variables from g that are shared with g_i.
            If it is not, abort h_g.

5.   Put $h_g(t)$ into the relation $M_{i(g)}$,
            where $i(g)$ is the name of the node of the parse tree for the subgoal g,
            and t are the variables that g shares with its parent (or all its variables
            if g is the root of the entire tree) in the parse tree.

6.   Label subgoal g "processed."

7. If the list for the root of the entire tree is nonempty, then return "Q_2 is contained in Q_1"; otherwise, return "Q_2 is not contained in Q_1."

Example 2.45   We will apply the algorithm to check for containment of the query Q_2, which has the following subgoals:

$$r_1(A, H, D, E), r_2(P', H, E, P, P), r_3(E, D, P), r_4(P, P), r_5(P, P), r_1(E, D, P, P),$$

in the query Q_1, which is the acyclic query

$$r_1(A, H, D, E), r_2(B, H, E, G, I), r_3(E, D, C), r_4(K, G), r_5(I, J), r_1(E, D, C, F),$$

whose hypergraph is shown in Figure 2.2. We will use the parse tree shown in Figure 2.3. Let us call the leaves in Figure 2.3 node 1, node 2, and node 3 (corresponding to (K, G), (I, J), and (E, D, C, F), respectively). We call node 4 the parent of nodes 1 and 2, we call node 5 the parent of node 3, and call node 6 the root of the tree. Thus, the algorithm maintains the relations: $M_1(G), M_2(I), M_3(E, D, C), M_4(H, E), M_5(E, D), M_6(A, H, E, D)$. Running the algorithm is easy in this example, because from each subgoal of the query Q_1 there is only one homomorphism to the subgoals of query Q_2, except for the subgoal with relation r_1, which has two homomorphisms. Now, for the leaves the relations M_i will be:

$$M_1(G) = \{P\}, M_2(I) = \{P\}, M_3(E, D, C) = \{(E, D, P), (A, H, D)\}.$$

For node 4, we find the homomorphism h that maps B to P', H to H, E to E, G to P, and I to P. Since $h(G) = P$, we need to check whether P is in $M_1(G)$. Since $h(I) = P$, we also need to check whether P is in $M_2(I)$. Since both are true, we put (H, E) in $M_4(H, E)$. We proceed in the same fashion, and conclude that Q_2 is contained in Q_1.

Theorem 2.46 *Given CQ queries Q_1 and Q_2, such that Q_1 is acyclic. Then Q_1 contains Q_2 iff algorithm AcyclicContainment returns "Q_2 is contained in Q_1."*

Proof. For the "if" direction, assume the algorithm returns "Q_2 is contained in Q_1." Then it is easy to prove that there is a homomorphism from Q_1 to Q_2, which proves the containment. For the other direction, we prove the following inductive hypothesis for the subtrees of the parse tree T_0 of the query Q_1.

Inductive hypothesis: If there is a homomorphism h from the subgoals of the subtree T of Q_1 to the subgoals of Q_2, and T has at most n subgoals, then $h(t)$ is in the relation M_i, where i is the node at the root of subtree T.

Now, let h be any homomorphism from the subgoals of subtree T of Q_1 to the subgoals of Q_2, and let T have $n + 1$ subgoals. Then any subtree rooted at a child i_j of node i has at most n subgoals, therefore the inductive hypothesis holds, and $h(t_{i_j})$ is in the relation M_{i_j}, where t_{i_j} are the shared variables between the subgoal g_i of node i and the subgoal g_{i_j} of node i_j. Hence, when the algorithm considers homomorphism h_g from subgoal g (that is at node i in the parse tree) to the subgoals of Q_2, where h_g is h restricted to g, the algorithm will find for each child $i_j, j = 1, 2, \ldots$ of i, that $h_g(t_{i_j})$ belongs in the relation M_{i_j}. Hence, the algorithm will put $h(t)$ in the relation M_i, where t are the shared variables between g and its parent. □

Time complexity: In each iteration and for each subgoal in the containing query, we keep account of the subgoals in the contained query that satisfy, in the bottom-up fashion, the partial containment mapping. This number is at most equal to the number of subgoals in the contained query, times the number of subgoals in the containing query.

> **CQ containment test—when the containing query is acyclic:**
> Polynomial-time algorithm: The algorithm finds homomorphisms from the acyclic query to the contained query by following the parse tree of the former query in a bottom up fashion.

2.5.3   EFFICIENT ALGORITHM FOR QUERY EVALUATION

As explained in Section 2.1.2, CQ query containment is related to CQ query evaluation, since both are based on finding homomorphisms from one relational structure to another. This is one reason to discuss the algorithm of lower complexity than the general case that computes an acyclic CQ. Another reason is that later, when we present algorithms for finding rewritings, part of the algorithm is to compute the views on the canonical database of the query. Thus, when the views are acyclic queries, this part of the algorithm is of lower complexity.

For query evaluation, we will give an algorithm whose runtime is polynomial both in the size of the query and in the size of the data, as well as in the size of the output. Shortly we will illustrate with examples that sometimes a query output may be empty, but in some cases the query output can be exponential in the size of the input relations and the size of the query, even if the CQ is acyclic.

The following is an example where the output of a conjunctive query is exponential in the size of the input relations.

Example 2.47   Consider a query

$$q(X_1, \ldots, X_n) :\text{-} R_1(X_1, X_2), \ldots, R_{n-1}(X_{n-1}, X_n).$$

For the relations mentioned in the query, let each attribute of each such relation accept values from the domain $\{1, 2, 3, 4\}$. Let each relation consist of all the eight tuples that can be formed using this domain, such that one component of each tuple is odd, and the other is even. Then the output of the query consists of all the tuples that alternate odd and even components, with the total of 2^{n+1} tuples. Yet the sum of the sizes of the $n - 1$ input relations is only $8(n - 1)$.

The semijoin algorithm, described below, has been developed to address the challenge of handling intermediate query answers of size that could be exponential in the size of the input and output data. When we say that we compute a *semijoin* of two relations r_1 and r_2, the meaning is that we compute the query $q(\bar{X}) : -r_1(\bar{X}), r_2(\bar{Y})$ (we use the notation $\bar{X}$ for a vector of variables), and then replace r_1 with the result.

In the algorithm, the intent of the **semijoin phase** is to eliminate all the *dangling tuples*, i.e., those tuples that will not contribute to the final output; this is done by computing a series of semijoin operations on the input relations. Then in the **join phase**, the algorithm performs a series of joins on the semijoined relations. The dangling-tuple elimination in the semijoin phase guarantees that the sizes of all the intermediate join outputs during the join phase are smaller than or equal to the size of the final output. We now discuss each phase in detail.

Semijoin Phase

Consider a parse tree T induced by the GYO-elimination of an acyclic query. The semijoin phase of the semijoin algorithm operates as follows. The semijoin phase has two stages: the bottom-up stage and the top-down stage. That is, one stage works from the leaves up on the parse tree, and the other phase works from the root down toward the leaves.

Bottom-up stage: If the tree has more than one node, pick a leaf representing relation R, and let S be the relation represented by the parent of this leaf.

1. Replace S by the semijoin of S with R, that is, by the answer to the following query:

$$q(\bar{Y}) :\text{-} R(\bar{X}), S(\bar{Y}).$$

2. Remove the leaf for R from the tree.

3. Recursively process the resulting tree.

The top-down stage takes as input the relations computed during the bottom-up stage and the parse tree of the join.

Top-down stage: If the tree has more than one node, begin with the root (say it represents relation R), and let $S_1, \ldots, S_i, \ldots$ be the relations represented by all the children of R.

1. For each child S of R, replace S by the semijoin of S with R, i.e., by

$$q(\bar{X}) :\text{-} R(\bar{X}), S(\bar{Y}).$$

2. Mark S "finished" and mark R "discarded."

3. Recursively process the resulting tree starting downward from those nodes/relations that are marked "finished" but are not marked "discarded."

In total, this algorithm performs $2(n-1)$ semijoin operations.

Join Phase

In this phase, the algorithm performs a series of $(n-1)$ joins, in any bottom-up order on the parse tree. We call a database instance *locally consistent with respect to a CQ* if the instance does not have "locally dangling tuples." This means that for any two subgoals of the query, all the tuples in the corresponding relations are joined together—that is, there are no tuples that cannot find a match in the other relation. We can use the algorithm presented above to make a database instance locally consistent with respect to an acyclic CQ. We call a database instance *globally consistent with respect to a CQ* if every tuple of every relation participates in the join of all the relations. For acyclic queries, the following holds: when a database instance is locally consistent, then it is globally consistent. Thus, we can use this algorithm to compute an acyclic CQ in time that is polynomial in the size of the query, of the database instance, and of the output of the query on this database instance.

> **Evaluating a CQ acyclic query:** The runtime of the algorithm is polynomial in the number of subgoals in the query, the number of facts in the database, and the number of facts in the answer to the query. The algorithm follows the parse tree of the query and has two phases: (a) the semijoin phase, which traverses the parse tree first bottom up and then top down, and makes the database instances locally consistent by computing locally semijoins both ways (i.e., both up and down the parse tree) and (b) the join phase, which traverses the parse tree bottom up and computes the final query answer.

2.6   QUERY EQUIVALENCE

Query equivalence can be checked by checking query containment both ways. In this section we discuss an interesting property of CQ queries that are equivalent.

A CQ query Q is *minimized* if by deleting any subgoal we obtain a query that is not equivalent to Q. We say then that a minimized query is a *core* of the given query. The following result states that the core is unique in a precise sense.

Theorem 2.48   *The core of a CQ query is unique up to isomorphism.*

Proof. Suppose there are two different cores. Then, since the cores are equivalent, there is a containment mapping from one to the other, i.e., two containment mappings h_{12} and h_{21}. The composition of these two containment mappings produces a containment mapping, h_1, of one of the cores, call it c, to itself. This mapping h_1 has to be an automorphism, otherwise c is not a core (because an application of h_1 would generate a proper subset of the alleged core with the same properties). Thus, the containment mappings h_{12} and h_{21} (between the allegedly different cores) are one to one (otherwise h_1 cannot be an automorphism). Thus, each of h_{12} and h_{21} is an isomorphism. □

Example 2.49   Consider queries q and q':

$$q() :- r(X, Y), r(Y, X), r(X, X).$$

$$q'(X, Y) :- r(X, Y), r(Y, X), r(X, X).$$

The core of q is

$$q() :- r(X, X),$$

and the core of q' is

$$q'(X, Y) :- r(X, Y), r(Y, X), r(X, X).$$

The reason is, we cannot map X to Y in q' as in q, due to the distinguished variables in the head of q'. (Recall that distinguished variables are the variables in the query definition that appear in the head of the definition.)

Consider now queries q_1 and q_2:

$$q_1(X) :- r(X, Y), r(Y, X), r(X, X), s(X).$$

$$q_2(Y) :- r(X, Y), r(Y, X), r(X, X), s(X).$$

The core of q_1 is

$$q_1(X) :- r(X, X), s(X),$$

and the core of q_2 is

$$q_2(Y) :- r(X, Y), r(Y, X), r(X, X), s(X).$$

The following algorithm minimizes a CQ, taking advantage of the uniqueness of the core: Delete query subgoals, until no more subgoals can be deleted without compromising equivalence with the original query. The proof is straightforward: it does not matter in which order subgoals are deleted, because either subgoals not belonging to the core are deleted, hence equivalence is not compromised, or subgoals belonging to the core are deleted, hence equivalence is compromised.

2.7   CONTAINMENT AND EQUIVALENCE FOR UNIONS OF QUERIES

Suppose we have queries belonging to the classes of unions of: CQ, or CQAC, or CQN queries. In these cases, the problem of checking containment, for query Q_2 in query Q_1, reduces to the problem of finding tests in which Q_1 is a trivial union (i.e., a union with just one disjunct that is a conjunctive query, possibly with ACs or negation). One can show that to prove containment, it suffices to prove that each disjunct of the contained query is contained in the containing query. The argument is that if there is a disjunct d of Q_2 that is not contained in Q_1, then a counterexample database for containment of d in Q_1 can be used as a counterexample database for the containment of the entire Q_2 in Q_1.

Moreover, for the general case of Q_1 belonging to the class of unions of CQs (i.e., without arithmetic comparisons or negation), the following theorem holds:

Theorem 2.50 *Let Q_1 and Q_2 be two queries in the language of unions of CQs. Query Q_2 is contained in query Q_1 if and only if for each CQ in Q_2, there is a CQ in Q_1 that contains it.*

Now, if we use the containment test with entailment for CQAC (Theorem 2.12), we add to the entailment the OR of all the mappings from all the queries in the containing query to the contained query, and also add the $\mu_i(\beta_j)$, where μ_i is a mapping from CQAC Q_j, and β_j is the arithmetic comparisons of Q_j. In particular, we have the following result.

Theorem 2.51 *Let Q_1 and Q_2 be queries in the language of unions of CQACs. Let $Q'_{i1} = Q'_{i10} + \beta'_{i1}, i = 1, 2, \ldots$, and $Q'_{j2} = Q'_{j20} + \beta'_{j2}, j = 1, 2, \ldots$ be the CQAC queries in Q_1 and Q_2, respectively, after normalization. Then Q_2 is contained in Q_1 if and only if the following holds for each Q'_{j2}.*

For each Q'_{i10}, let $\mu_{i1j}, \ldots, \mu_{ik(i,j)j}$ be all the containment mappings from Q'_{i10} to Q'_{j20} (assuming there is at least one such containment mapping). Then the following is true:

$$\phi : \beta'_{j2} \Rightarrow \bigvee_i \mu_{ik(i,j)j}(\beta'_{i1}).$$

The following example shows that, in contrast with the case of CQs, when checking containment of query Q_2 in Q_1 in those cases where both queries are unions of CQACs, it may be necessary for Q_2 to be contained in two or more disjuncts of Q_1, rather than in a single disjunct of Q_1. Even if the contained query is a single CQAC, the containing query may need two or more CQACs for the containment to hold.

Example 2.52 Consider query Q_1 with disjuncts q_{11} and q_{12}:

$$q_{11}() :- r(x), x < 1, \qquad q_{12}() :- r(x), x = 1.$$

Let query Q_2 be a CQAC query with a single disjunct:

$$Q_2 : q_2() :- r(x), x \leq 1.$$

It can be shown that, while q_2 is not contained in either q_{11} or q_{12}, it is contained in their union.

Consider another example, in which Q_2 is a CQ query.

Example 2.53 Consider query Q_1 with disjuncts q_{11} and q_{12}:

$$q_{11}() :- r(x), x \leq 1, \qquad q_{12}() :- r(x), x > 1.$$

Let query Q_2 be a CQ query with a single disjunct:

$$q_2() :\text{-} r(x).$$

It can be shown that q_2 is not contained in either q_{11} or q_{12}, but is contained in their union.

The tests that use canonical databases for CQACs and CQNs can be extended to the case where the contained query is a union of CQACs or CQNs, respectively. We again form the canonical databases of the contained query, and check whether the head of the containing query can be computed.

2.8   EXERCISES

2.1.   Theorem 2.21 presents a case where normalization is not needed. Examine the following cases and prove or disprove that normalization is not needed.

    (a) The case where there are no constants in the relational subgoals of the containing query.

    (b) The case where the contained query has only open arithmetic comparisons.

2.2.   Prove the following result.

    Theorem 2.54   *Let $Q_1 = Q_{1,0} + \beta_1$ and $Q_2 = Q_{2,0} + \beta_2$ be two left–semi–interval (right–semi–interval, respectively) queries. Suppose that either (i) β_2 does not contain a closed arithmetic comparison, or (ii) β_1 does not contain an open arithmetic comparison. Then $Q_2 \sqsubseteq Q_1$ if and only if there is a* single *containment mapping μ from $Q_{1,0}$ to $Q_{2,0}$, such that $\beta_2 \Rightarrow \mu(\beta_1)$.*

2.3.   Prove the following result.

    Theorem 2.55   *Let Q_1 be a conjunctive query with left semi–interval arithmetic-comparison subgoals, and Q_2 a conjunctive query with any arithmetic-comparison subgoals. If Q_1 and Q_2 do not use constants, then the homomorphism property holds.*

2.4.   Define canonical databases to be used in a query-containment test for the case where the given conjunctive query contains both negation and arithmetic comparisons.

2.5.   Prove Theorem 2.30.

2.6.   Consider the following relational structures:

$S_1 : \{r(X_1, X_2, X_3), p(X_3, X_4)\};$

$S_1' : \{p(Y, Y)\};$

$S_2 : \{r(Y_1, Y_2, Y_2), p(Y_2, Y_3), s(Z, Y_3), p(Y_2, Y_3')\}.$

There are two homomorphisms from S_1 to S_2, h_1 and h_2:

$h_1 : X_1 \rightarrow Y_1, X_2 \rightarrow Y_2, X_3 \rightarrow Y_2, X_4 \rightarrow Y_3;$

$h_2 : X_1 \rightarrow Y_1, X_2 \rightarrow Y_2, X_3 \rightarrow Y_2, X_4 \rightarrow Y_3'.$

The homomorphism h_1 maps the atom $p(X_3, X_4)$ to $p(Y_2, Y_3)$, while h_2 maps the atom $p(X_3, X_4)$ to $p(Y_2, Y_3')$.

(a) Check and explain why these two are homomorphisms. Are there any other homomorphisms from S_1 to S_2?

(b) How many homomorphisms are there from S_1' to S_2?

2.7. Prove or disprove that for the following two CQs it is true that Q_2 is contained in Q_1 under set semantics.

(1) $Q_1() \:\text{:-}\: p(A, B, C), r(B, C, D), r(F, C, B).$

$\quad Q_2() \:\text{:-}\: p(X, Y, Z), r(Y, Z, Y).$

(2) $Q_1() \:\text{:-}\: p(A, B, C), r(B, C, A), r(A, C, B).$

$\quad Q_2() \:\text{:-}\: p(X, Y, Z), r(Y, Z, Y).$

(3) $Q_1() \:\text{:-}\: p(X, Y, Z), r(Y, Z, Y).$

$\quad Q_2() \:\text{:-}\: p(A, A, C), r(A, C, C), s(A, C, A).$

(4) $Q_1() \:\text{:-}\: p(X, Y, Z), r(Z, Z, Y).$

$\quad Q_2() \:\text{:-}\: p(A, A, C), r(A, C, A), r(A, C, C).$

2.8. Give an argument that would prove or disprove that for the following two CQs it is true that Q_2 is contained in Q_1 under bag semantics.

(1) $Q_1() \:\text{:-}\: p(X, Y).$

$\quad Q_2() \:\text{:-}\: p(A, B), p(A, B).$

(2) $Q_1() \:\text{:-}\: p(X, Y), p(X, Z).$

$\quad Q_2() \:\text{:-}\: p(A, B), p(A, B).$

(3) $Q_1() \:\text{:-}\: p(X, Y).$

$\quad Q_2() \:\text{:-}\: p(A, B), s(A, C).$

2.9. Prove or disprove that for the following two CQAs it is true that Q_2 is contained in Q_1 (as we mentioned before, when we do not specify in particular whether it is set or bag or bag-set semantics, then we consider by default set semantics).

(1) $Q_1() \:\text{:-}\: r(X, Y), X < 7.$

$Q_2()$:- $r(9,7), r(A, B), A \leq B$.

(2) $Q_1()$:- $r(X, Y), X \leq 7$.

$Q_2()$:- $r(6,7), r(A, B), A \leq B, B < 4$.

(3) $Q_1()$:- $p(X, Y), X > Y$.

$Q_2()$:- $p(A, 3), p(4, B), A \geq B, B > 3$.

(4) $Q_1()$:- $p(X, Y), X > Y$.

$Q_2()$:- $p(A, 3), p(7, B), A \geq B, B > 3$.

2.10. In the setting of Example 2.43, let the contents of the relations be as follows: $R_1 = \{$ $(a, h, d, e), (b, c, d, e), (e, d, c, f), (e, d, c, m)$ $\}$; $R_2 = \{$ $(b, h, e, g, i), (f, g, h, i,$ $k)$ $\}$; $R_3 = \{$ $(e, d, c), (l, d, c)$ $\}$; $R_4 = \{$ $(k, g), (k, p)$ $\}$; and $R_5 = \{$ $(i, j), (i, l)$ $\}$. For these relations, compute the join of Example 2.43 by applying the algorithm from Section 2.5.3 Show the detailed computations through all the stages of the algorithm.

2.11. Redo Exercise 2.10 with the following contents of the five relations: $R_1 = \{$ $(a, d, h,$ $e), (b, c, d, e), (e, d, c, f), (e, d, c, m)$ $\}$; $R_2 = \{$ $(b, h, e, g, i), (f, g, h, i, k)$ $\}$; $R_3 =$ $\{$ $(e, d, c), (l, d, c)$ $\}$; $R_4 = \{$ $(k, g), (k, p)$ $\}$; and $R_5 = \{$ $(i, j), (i, l)$ $\}$.

2.12. Prove or disprove that for the following two UCQ queries it is true that Q_2 is contained in Q_1.

(1) $Q_1()$:- $p(A, B, C), r(B, C, D), r(F, C, B)$.

$Q_1()$:- $p(X, Y, Z), r(Y, Z, Y)$.

$Q_2()$:- $p(X, Y, Z), r(Y, Z, Y)$.

$Q_2()$:- $p(A, A, C), r(A, C, C), s(A, C, A)$.

(2) $Q_1()$:- $p(A, B, C), r(B, C, D), r(F, C, B)$.

$Q_1()$:- $p(A, B, C), r(B, C, A), r(A, C, B)$.

$Q_2()$:- $p(X, Y, Z), r(Y, Z, Y)$.

2.13. What are the cores of the following queries?

$Q_1(A, B, C)$:- $p(A, B, C), r(B, C, D), r(C, C, B)$.

$Q_2(A, B, C)$:- $p(A, B, C), r(B, C, D), r(C, C, B), r(F, C, B)$.

2.14. Consider bag semantics. Prove that the following queries are not equivalent:

$Q_1(A, B, C)$:- $p(A, B, C), r(B, C, D), r(C, C, B)$.

$Q_2(A, B, C)$:- $p(A, B, C), r(B, C, D), r(C, C, B), r(F, C, B)$.

2.15. Prove or disprove that the following queries are acyclic. For the ones they are acyclic, draw the parse tree that proves it.

(1) $Q_1() \; :- \; p(A, B, C), r(B, C, D), s(F, C, B)$.

(2) $Q_2() \; :- \; p(A, B, C), r(B, C, A), s(A, C, B)$.

(3) $Q_3() \; :- \; p(A, C), r(C, D), s(D, A)$.

(4) $Q_4() \; :- \; p(A, C), r(C, D), s(D, E), q(E, A)$.

(5) $Q_1() \; :- \; p(A, B, C), r(B, C, D), s(F, C, B), q(A, D)$.

(6) $Q_1() \; :- \; p(A, B, C), r(B, C, D), s(F, C, B), q(A, D), p(A, D, B, C)$.

(7) $Q_3() \; :- \; p(A, C), r(C, D), s(D, E)$.

2.16. Decide whether you need one or more mappings to prove that the query Q_2 is contained in the query Q_1 in the following cases. Can you apply Theorem 2.23 to any of them to decide that the homomorphism property holds?

(1) $Q_1() \; :- \; r(X, Y), X < 7$.

$\quad Q_2() \; :- \; r(9, 7), r(A, B), A \leq B$.

(2) $Q_1() \; :- \; r(X, Y), X \leq 7$.

$\quad Q_2() \; :- \; r(6, 7), r(A, B), A \leq B, B < 4$.

(3) $Q_1() \; :- \; p(X, Y), X > Y$.

$\quad Q_2() \; :- \; p(A, 3), p(4, B), A \geq B, B > 3$.

(4) $Q_1() \; :- \; p(X, Y), X > Y$.

$\quad Q_2() \; :- \; p(A, 3), p(7, B), A \geq B, B > 3$.

(5) $Q_1() \; :- \; r(X, Y), X \leq 7$.

$\quad Q_2() \; :- \; r(X, Y), r(A, B), A \leq B, X \geq Y$.

Finding Equivalent Rewritings

In this chapter, we use query-containment and query-equivalence tests to find equivalent rewritings of queries using sets of views. We cover the cases of CQ, CQAC, and CQN queries and views, as well as aggregate queries. We generally restrict the discussion to the cases where we are looking for a rewriting in the language of conjunctive queries, with or without ACs and negation. Furthermore, in the case of aggregate queries we restrict our consideration to the fragment of the language of conjunctive queries with aggregation that is called "central rewritings." Our focus will be on finding (minimal) equivalent rewritings in an efficient way. Other languages for rewritings will be discussed in other parts of the book.

We begin by defining the notions of expansion and canonical rewriting; for aggregate queries, we will define a related notion of unfolding.

3.1   PRELIMINARIES

For a set $\mathcal{V}$ of views defined on schema $\mathcal{S}$, we denote by $\mathcal{V}(D)$ the result of computing the views in $\mathcal{V}$ on database D of schema $\mathcal{S}$. That is, $\mathcal{V}(D) = \bigcup_{V \in \mathcal{V}} V(D)$, where $V(D)$ contains the atom $v(t)$ for each answer t to the view definition V on the database D.

Definition 3.1   Let Q be a query defined on schema $\mathcal{S}$, and $\mathcal{V}$ a set of views defined on $\mathcal{S}$. Let R be a query formulated in terms of the view relations in the set $\mathcal{V}$. We say that R is an *equivalent rewriting of Q using the views $\mathcal{V}$* iff for any database D on the schema $\mathcal{S}$:

$$R(\mathcal{V}(D)) = Q(D).$$

The following example shows that the existence of an equivalent rewriting depends on the language of the rewriting.

Example 3.2   Consider a query and views that are path queries. (Recall that P_i is the query that asks for pairs of nodes on a graph connected by a path of length i—see also Definition 2.44 for path queries.) Let viewset $\mathcal{V}$ comprise two views defined by the path queries P_3 and P_4. This means that $P_3(X, Y)$ is a query over a schema of a single binary relation; on the graph represented by that relation, the query finds pairs of nodes (X, Y) that are connected by a path (not necessarily simple) of length 3. Similarly, $P_4(X, Y)$ finds pairs of nodes that are connected by a path of length 4. Let query Q be P_7. Then the following query R is an equivalent CQ rewriting of Q in terms of the two views:

$$R(X, Y) :\text{-} P_3(X, Z), P_4(Z, Y).$$

Consider now a query Q' defined as P_5. We will show in this chapter that there is no equivalent *CQ* rewriting of Q' using the views P_3 and P_4. However, there is an equivalent *first-order* rewriting R' of Q' in terms of these views:

$$R'(X, Y) :\text{-} \exists Z \, [\, P_4(X, Z) \wedge \forall W \, ((P_3(W, Z) \rightarrow P_4(W, Y)) \,].$$

Later in the book we will formally prove that R' is an equivalent rewriting of Q'. Here is some intuition: Consider the first node on a path of length 4 from X to Z; call that node W. The second condition says that there is a path of length 4 from W to Y. Since there is also an edge from X to W, there is a path of length 5 from X to Y.

In the remainder of the chapter, we will explore ways to formally prove that the rewritings in the above examples are actually equivalent to the respective queries, and how to prove for the query Q' of Example 3.2 that there is no equivalent rewriting of the query in terms of the given views, either in the language of CQ or in the language of unions of CQs.

Assumption: We assume that view definitions do not have repeated variables in their head. We will discuss this restriction and ways to lift it in other chapters of the book. This assumption holds in the rest of this book, except for those parts where it is lifted explicitly.

3.1.1   EXPANSION OF A REWRITING

The definition of equivalent rewriting does not depend on the languages of the queries, views, or rewritings. When the given query and views are in the language CQACs, we can use the *expansion* of the rewriting to show that the rewriting is equivalent to the query (or contained in the query, as we will discuss shortly). First we define the notion of expansion for the case of CQ queries, views, and rewritings.

Definition 3.3   (Expansion of a rewriting)
Suppose the given views and query are in the language of CQs, and the rewriting R is also a CQ query. To construct the expansion R^{exp} of R, we replace each view subgoal g_i of R, as follows.

- Suppose v_j is the relation symbol of g_i.

- We find the mapping μ_i from the variables in the head of the definition of the view v_j to the variables of g_i that maps the variable in each position to the variable in the corresponding position. (Such a mapping always exists and is unique due to the above assumption about non-repetition of variables in view heads.)

- We use the mapping μ_i to find the set of subgoals that will replace g_i in R to produce the expansion R^{exp} of R.

  - Apply μ_i to the body of the definition of the view v_j, replacing each distinguished variable X in the atoms of the body by $\mu_i(X)$.

  - Replace each nondistinguished variable in the definition of v_j by a fresh distinct variable. (This means that we maintain a set of fresh variables, to be used throughout for all subgoals in the rewriting, of sufficiently large cardinality—i.e., we assume have an infinite supply of fresh variables. Each nondistinguished variable Y is replaced by a variable, say Z, from this set. Z is then removed from the set and is never reused in the expansion.)

  - We then replace g_i in R with the resulting conjunction of subgoals from the body of the definition of v_j.

For CQAC queries, views, and rewriting, the definition of expansion is as follows. First consider only the regular subgoals (together with the head of the definitions), and find the expansion according to Definition 3.3. Then for each subgoal in the rewriting add the ACs that appear in their view definition, as each AC is a subgoal in the definition. Finally, the ACs in the rewriting are kept in the expansion.

Example 3.4   Consider query q and views v_1 and v_2:

$$q(X, Y) :\text{-}\ r(X, Z), r(Z, Y), r(X, Z'), r(Z', Y), Z > 5, Z' < 5.$$

$$v_1(X, Y) :\text{-}\ r(X, Z), r(Z, Y), Z > 5.$$

$$v_2(X, Y) :\text{-}\ r(X, Z), r(Z, Y), Z < 5.$$

The following query R is an equivalent CQ rewriting of q in terms of the views v_1 and v_2:

$$R(X, Y) :\text{-}\ v_1(X, Y), v_2(X, Y).$$

The expansion of the rewriting R is:

$$R^{exp}(X, Y) :\text{-}\ r(X, Z''), r(Z'', Y), Z'' > 5, r(X, Z'), r(Z', Y), Z' < 5.$$

Here, the first three subgoals (two ordinary subgoals and an AC subgoal) come from expanding the view subgoal $v_1(X, Y)$ in the rewriting R, and the last three subgoals come from expanding the view subgoal $v_2(X, Y)$ in R. Notice that we have replaced the nondistinguished variable in the body of the definition of $v_1(X, Y)$ with a fresh variable Z'', and used another fresh variable, Z', in the body of the definition of $v_2(X, Y)$.

Let us construct the above expansion, by following the steps in Definition 3.1.1. The first subgoal g_1 of R is $v_1(X, Y)$, its view symbol is v_1, so we consider the definition for view v_1, which is

$$v_1(X, Y) :\text{-} r(X, Z), r(Z, Y), Z > 5.$$

The mapping μ_1 from the variables in the head of this definition, $v_1(X, Y)$, to the variables of the subgoal $g_1 = v_1(X, Y)$ is $\mu_1 : \{X \to X, Y \to Y\}$. We use the set $\{Z', Z''\}$ of fresh variables. Then for the nondistinguished variable Z of v_1 we have $Z'' = \mu_1(Z)$. Thus, $v_1(X, Y)$ in R is replaced with

$$\{r(\mu_1(X), \mu_1(Z)), r(\mu_1(Z), \mu_1(Y)), \mu_1(Z) > 5\} = \{r(X, Z''), r(Z'', Y), Z'' > 5\}.$$

For the other subgoal of R, g_2, we consider the view definition

$$v_2(X, Y) :\text{-} r(X, Z), r(Z, Y), Z < 5.$$

We then find mapping μ_2 and proceed similarly to the case of g_1.

Theorem 3.5   *Suppose query Q, views V, and rewriting R all belong to the language of CQACs. Then R is an equivalent rewriting of Q using the views V iff $R^{exp} \equiv Q$.*

Proof. Let D be any database, and suppose $R(V(D)) = Q(D)$. On D, we compute $V(D)$ by using appropriate homomorphisms from the view definitions to D. Then on the instance $V(D)$, we compute R, by using homomorphisms from the definition of R to $V(D)$. Now, any homomorphism h that computed a tuple t in $R(V(D))$ can be combined with the homomorphisms that computed the view tuples that h used in $V(D)$; thus, we have a homomorphism that computes tuple t in $R^{exp}(D)$. We conclude that $R^{exp}(D) = R(V(D))$, thus by transitivity of equality we obtain $R^{exp}(D) = Q(D)$.

For the other direction, suppose that $R^{exp} \equiv Q$ is true. Let D be any database. By construction of R^{exp}, the homomorphism that computes a tuple t in $R^{exp}(D)$ can be decomposed into a set of homomorphisms that compute tuples t_i in $V(D)$ and a homomorphism that computes t in $R(V(D))$, using the tuples t_i. Thus, $R(V(D)) = R^{exp}(D)$, hence $R(V(D)) = Q(D)$. □

3.1.2   CONTAINED REWRITINGS

In the next chapter, we present a detailed discussion of contained rewritings. At the same time, as an equivalent rewriting is also a contained rewriting (see Definition 3.6 below), we comment on contained rewritings in this chapter as well.

Definition 3.6   (Contained rewriting)
Let Q be a query defined on schema S, and V a set of views defined on S. Let R be a query

formulated in terms of the view relations in the set $\mathcal{V}$. We say that R is a *contained rewriting of Q using the views $\mathcal{V}$* iff for any database D it holds that $R(\mathcal{V}(D)) \subseteq Q(D)$.

Theorem 3.7   *Suppose query Q, views $\mathcal{V}$, and rewriting R all belong to the language of CQACs. Then R is a contained rewriting of Q using views $\mathcal{V}$ iff $R^{exp} \sqsubseteq Q$.*

The proof of this result is similar to that of Theorem 3.5.

Notice that when we use the term "rewriting," we refer to a query (in some query language) that is defined on the schema of the view relations. Thus, a rewriting always has an expansion, but is not necessarily associated with a specific query it is "supposed" to rewrite.

> **CQAC query and views, CQAC rewriting—expansion of a rewriting:**
> R is an equivalent rewriting of the given query iff the expansion of the rewriting is equivalent to the query.
> R is a contained rewriting of the given query iff the expansion of the rewriting is contained in the query.

3.2   CQ QUERIES AND VIEWS

In this section we consider the case of rewriting CQ queries using CQ views. That is, we consider the case of queries and views without arithmetic comparisons and without negation. Recall that, unlike the case of CQAC queries, for CQ queries the containment test only needs one homomorphism to go through. This property allows for efficient algorithms for finding an equivalent rewriting, which is a conjunctive query in case such an equivalent rewriting exists. (If there is no equivalent *CQ* rewriting of a CQ query in terms of CQ views, then no equivalent rewriting can be found in the language of unions of CQs, for either infinite or finite unions.)

3.2.1   CANONICAL REWRITINGS AND THE NAIVE ALGORITHM

Canonical Rewriting. Let D_Q be the canonical database of Q. By computing the views on D_Q, we obtain view instance $\mathcal{V}(D_Q)$. We construct the *canonical rewriting R_{can}* as follows. The body of R_{can} contains as subgoals exactly all the view tuples in $\mathcal{V}(D_Q)$, after we have replaced each constant by the variable originally in the respective positions, and the tuple in the head of R_{can} is the same as the tuple in the head of the query Q. Conveniently, we use, throughout the book, the upper-case-to-lower-case change in the variables to represent the replacement of variables by constants. Consider an example that illustrates the construction.

Example 3.8   Let query Q be $Q : q(X, Y) :- a(X, Z_1), a(Z_1, Z_2), b(Z_2, Y)$, and let the views $\mathcal{V}$ be defined as: $V_1 : v_1(X, Z_2) :- a(X, Z_1), a(Z_1, Z_2)$ and $V_2 : v_2(X, Y) :- b(X, Y)$. Then D_Q contains the tuples $\{a(x, z_1), a(z_1, z_2), b(z_2, y)\}$, and $\mathcal{V}(D_Q)$ contains the tuples $\{v_1(x, z_2),$

$v_2(z_2, y)$}. The canonical rewriting R_{can} in this case is $R_{can}(X, Y) :- v_1(X, Z_2), v_2(Z_2, Y)$; it happens to be equivalent to the query Q.

The following result can be used in those cases where we would like to show that there is no equivalent CQ rewriting of a CQ query using a set of CQ views.

Proposition 3.9   *Let Q be a CQ query, and V be a set of conjunctive views. Let R_{can} be the canonical rewriting. If there exists a conjunctive query that is an equivalent rewriting of Q using V, then R_{can} is such a rewriting.*

Proof. Suppose there is an equivalent CQ rewriting R of Q using V. First observe that, by construction of R_{can}, there is a containment mapping from its expansion R_{can}^{exp} to Q. We will show that there is also a containment mapping from Q to R_{can}^{exp}.

Since R is an equivalent rewriting of Q, there is a homomorphism from R^{exp} to Q. This homomorphism can be decomposed to compute the view tuples in D_Q; hence, all the subgoals in R are also subgoals in R_{can}. It follows that there is a homomorphism from Q to R_{can}^{exp}, because of the homomorphism from Q to R^{exp}.   □

Example 3.10   We build here on the setting of Example 3.2. Recall that the set of views given in Example 3.2 comprises two views, which are path queries P_3 and P_4. First consider query Q, which is the path query P_7. A canonical database of the query $Q = P_7$ is

$$D_Q = \{(1, 2), (2, 3), (3, 4), (4, 5), (5, 6), (6, 7), (7, 8)\}.$$

If we compute the two views on D_Q, we obtain a set with the elements

$$P_3(1, 4), P_3(2, 5), P_3(3, 6), P_3(4, 7), P_3(5, 8), P_4(1, 5), P_4(2, 6), P_4(3, 7), P_4(4, 8).$$

From this collection, we derive a rewriting that consists of nine subgoals, corresponding to the above nine atoms. Consider the following rewriting:

$$R(X_1, X_8) :- P_3(X_1, X_4), P_4(X_4, X_8).$$

This rewriting can be obtained from the canonical rewriting after deleting some subgoals. Specifically, it is obtained by replacing each integer i in the canonical database D_Q by X_i in the rewriting. It can be shown that the expansion of this rewriting is contained in P_7. Hence, the rewriting is an equivalent rewriting of P_7 using the views P_3 and P_4. (In Section 3.2.3 we will discuss how such a minimal rewriting can be obtained systematically.) This is the rewriting mentioned in Example 3.2.

Now consider the query Q' of Example 3.2; recall that it is the path query P_5. We now prove that there is no equivalent CQ rewriting of Q' using the views P_3 and

P_4. Let us compute the above views on the canonical database $D_{Q'}$ of $Q' = P_5$: $D_{Q'} = \{1, 2), (2, 3), (3, 4), (4, 5), (5, 6)\}$. The result of the computation is the collection

$$\{P_3(1, 4), P_3(2, 5), P_3(3, 6), P_4(1, 5), P_4(2, 6)\}.$$

The canonical rewriting has five subgoals:

$$R_{can}(X_1, X_6) :\text{-} P_3(X_1, X_4), P_3(X_2, X_5), P_3(X_3, X_6), P_4(X_1, X_5), P_4(X_2, X_6).$$

The expansion of the rewriting R_{can} is

$$R_{can}^{exp}(X_1, X_6) :\text{-} r(X_1, Z_2), r(Z_2, Z_3), r(Z_3, X_4),$$

$$r(X_2, Z_2'), r(Z_2', Z_3'), r(Z_3', X_5), r(X_3, Z_2''), r(Z_2'', Z_3''), r(Z_3'', X_6),$$

$$r(X_1, W_1), r(W_1, W_2), r(W_2, W_3), r(W_3, X_5), r(X_2, W_1'), r(W_1', W_2'), r(W_2', W_3'), r(W_3', X_6).$$

It is straightforward to check that there is no containment mapping from P_5 to R_{can}^{exp}. It follows that R_{can} is not an equivalent rewriting of P_5. Thus, according to Proposition 3.9, there is no equivalent rewriting of P_5 in the language of CQ rewritings using the views P_3 and P_4.

Proposition 3.9 gives rise to the following sound and complete *naive* algorithm for finding a CQ equivalent rewriting for CQ query and views, in case such a rewriting exists.

1. Compute all the views on the canonical database of the query.

2. Form the canonical rewriting.

3. Check whether there is a containment mapping from Q to the expansion of the rewriting; if so, return the canonical rewriting as an equivalent rewriting. Otherwise, return "no equivalent CQ rewriting exists."

For an equivalent CQ rewriting R of query Q in terms of a given viewset, R is *minimal* if deleting any subgoal from R results in a rewriting that is not equivalent to Q. We can minimize a rewriting by deleting views, as long as we still have a containment mapping from the query to the expansion of the rewriting. In particular, we can do the following: For each containment mapping from Q to the expansion, to obtain a candidate rewriting, delete all the views that do not participate as targets in the containment mapping. We repeat the procedure for each candidate rewriting, until all the containment mappings use the expansions of all the views as targets. The result is the set of all the minimal rewritings.

As we will discuss in Section 3.2.3, we can do better than this algorithm, as for some individual views it is easy to tell just from their definitions whether they can participate in any equivalent CQ rewriting.

> **CQ query and views—equivalent rewriting:** There is an equivalent rewriting of the given query in the language of CQs iff the canonical rewriting is such a rewriting.

3.2.2   PROPERTIES OF THE EXPANSION

Because of the way an expansion is constructed, it has certain properties that can be exploited to obtain more efficient algorithms for finding both minimal equivalent rewritings and contained rewritings. Given an expansion R^{exp} of a rewriting R of query Q in terms of views in set $\{V_1, \ldots, V_i, \ldots\}$, we can partition the variables in R^{exp} into two classes.

- The variables that come from replacing nondistinguished variables of some view definition with a fresh variable. We call those variables *non-exported* variables; the intuition is that they cannot "communicate" with other variables outside the particular view.

- The rest of the variables are called *exported* variables. Among them are all the variables that appear in the head of the expansion.

We can further partition the non-exported variables to s *view-classes*, where s is the number of subgoals in the rewriting, one class for each subgoal in the rewriting. Thus, a non-exported variable belongs to *view-class* TC_i if it has been created from expanding the ith subgoal in the rewriting, according to its view definition.

We call a subgoal of R^{exp} *non-exported* if it contains at least one non-exported variable. All other subgoals are called *exported* subgoals.

Example 3.11   In Example 3.10, we provided the expansion $R^{exp}_{can}(X_1, X_6)$ of the path query P_5 using the views that are path queries P_3 and P_4. We reproduce R^{exp}_{can} below:

$$R^{exp}_{can}(X_1, X_6) :- r(X_1, Z_2), r(Z_2, Z_3), r(Z_3, X_4),$$

$$r(X_2, Z'_2), r(Z'_2, Z'_3), r(Z'_3, X_5), r(X_3, Z''_2), r(Z''_2, Z''_3), r(Z''_3, X_6),$$

$$r(X_1, W_1), r(W_1, W_2), r(W_2, W_3), r(W_3, X_5), r(X_2, W'_1), r(W'_1, W'_2), r(W'_2, W'_3), r(W'_3, X_6).$$

This expansion has 6 exported variables (they are the X_i's) and 12 non-exported variables (these are all the other variables in the expansion).

The non-exported variables of the expansion can be partitioned into five view-classes, as follows. The first three subgoals in $R^{exp}_{can}(X_1, X_6)$ come from replacing the first subgoal $P_3(X_1, X_4)$ of $R_{can}(X_1, X_6)$ using the view definition for view P_3—recall that this view definition is $P_3(X, Y) :- r(X, A), r(A, B), r(B, Y)$. The first three subgoals of the expansion use two non-exported variables, Z_2 (to represent A in the view defintion) and Z_3 (to represent B in the view defintion); thus, these two variables belong to the view class TC_1.

Similarly, for the second subgoal in the rewriting, we have that the variables Z'_2 and Z'_3 belong to view-class TC_2. Then, for the third subgoal in the rewriting we have that variables Z''_2 and Z''_3 belong to view-class TC_3. Similarly, the variables W_i belong to view-class TC_4, and the variables W'_i belong to view-class TC_5.

All the subgoals in this rewriting are non-exported.

Note that the rewriting R in this example is not a contained rewriting of query P_5.

Suppose R is a contained rewriting of Q using a set of views. Then any containment mapping μ from Q to the expansion R^{exp} of R has the following property: μ can be decomposed into *partial containment mappings*, one mapping μ_i for each subgoal g_i^R in R. In particular, $\mu_i(X) = \mu(X)$ if $\mu(X)$ is a variable in the expansion of subgoal g_i^R in R. These partial containment mappings have an important property, the shared-variable property, which is useful in finding rewritings efficiently. This property is defined as follows.

Definition 3.12   (Shared-variable property)
Let queries Q and Q' be CQs. Consider the relational structure S of all the atoms that are subgoals in the body of CQ Q, and let S' be any substructure, i.e., subset, of S. Let h be a homomorphism from the substructure S' to the relational structure that comprises the subgoals of Q'. We say that the triple (S, S', h) has the *shared-variable property* if the following is true for each nondistinguished variable Y of Q' that is a target of h: Suppose X is a variable that appears in an atom in S' for which $h(X) = Y$. Then all the atoms of S that contain X are in S'.

If the triple (S, S', h) has the shared-variable property, we say that (S, S', h) **covers** the query subgoals in S'.

Example 3.13   To illustrate the shared-variable property, we consider the following two queries and two views. (Recall that when there are no variables in the head of the query, the query is called Boolean query, i.e., its output is "true" or "false.")

$$Q_1() \text{ :- } a(A, B), c(B, C).$$

$$Q_2() \text{ :- } a(A, B).$$

$$V_1(X, Y) \text{ :- } a(X, Z), b(Z, Y).$$

$$V_2(X, Y, Z) \text{ :- } a(X, Z), b(Z, Y).$$

For the query Q_1 and view V_1, we take the homomorphism h_1: A to X and B to Z. We take $a(A, B), c(B, C)$ for S and only one atom $a(A, B)$ for S'. Then the triple (S, S', h_1) does not have the shared-variable property, because Z is a nondistinguished variable in the definition of V_1, and B (which maps to Z according to h_1) also appears in the subgoal $c(B, C)$ of Q_1, which (subgoal) is not in S'. However, if we take the query Q_1 and view V_2, then the triple (S, S', h_1) has the shared-variable property, because now Z appears in the head of V_2, hence it is a distinguished variable in the definition of V_2.

For the query Q_2 and view V_1, the triple (S, S', h_1) has the shared-variable property, because the variable B in Q_2 does not appear in any other subgoal of Q_2.

In both theorems that follow, we use the phrase "homomorphism (or containment mapping) μ can be decomposed." By "decomposed" we mean that we can find one or more homomorphisms μ_i that are restrictions of μ, such that all variables that appear in μ appear in at least one of the μ_is. The shared-variable property is useful because of the following theorem:

Theorem 3.14 *Suppose R is a contained CQ rewriting of a CQ query Q using a set of CQ views. Let R^{exp} be the expansion of the rewriting R. Then any containment mapping μ from the query to R^{exp} can be decomposed into a number of homomorphisms, one homomorphism μ_i for each subgoal in the rewriting R, as follows.*

- *Let S' be the set of those subgoals in Q that map to those subgoals of R^{exp} that come from expanding the i-th subgoal of the rewriting R, and*

- *let μ_i be defined as the restriction of μ to those variables that appear in S'.*

Let S be all the atoms in the body of Q. Then the triple (S, S', μ_i) has the shared-variable property.

Proof. A containment mapping is a homomorphism from the data structure of the query subgoals to the data structure of the subgoals in the expansion. Consider in the body of the expansion only those atoms in the set S_i that come from expanding a certain subgoal of the rewriting, say subgoal g_i. Now g_i uses a view definition, say for view v_i. Restrict μ to those atoms S_i, and from there to those atoms in the body of Q that map (according to μ) to S_i. Let Y' be a nondistinguished variable of the definition of v_i, and let Y be the fresh variable that replaced Y' to form the expansion. Then consider the variable X of Q such that $Y = \mu(X)$. Suppose there is a subgoal g of Q that contains X, such that g does not map to an atom in S_i. This means that there is another atom, g_a, which has arisen from expanding a view subgoal of the rewriting that (subgoal) was not g_i, and that μ maps g to g_a. Since μ is a homomorphism, $Y = \mu(X)$, and g contains X, g_a should contain Y. This is, however, impossible by construction of the expansion, because Y is a non-exported variable of the expansion. ☐

In those cases where the rewriting is an equivalent rewriting, the result of Theorem 3.14 can be strengthened.

Theorem 3.15 *Suppose R is an equivalent CQ rewriting of a CQ query Q using a set of CQ views. Suppose the view and query definitions are minimized, and the rewriting is minimal.*

  Let R^{exp} be the expansion of the rewriting R. Then any one-to-one containment mapping, μ, from the query to R^{exp} can be decomposed into a number of one-to-one mappings, one mapping μ_i for each subgoal in the rewriting R, as follows.

- *Let S' be the set of the subgoals of Q that map to the subgoals of R^{exp} coming from expanding the i-th subgoal of the rewriting R, and*

- *let μ_i be defined as the restriction of μ to those variables that appear in S'.*

Let S be all the atoms in the body of Q. Then the triple (S, S', μ_i) has the shared-variable property.

We will use Theorem 3.14 in the next chapter, to construct maximally contained rewritings. Here we use Theorem 3.15 to describe an efficient algorithm to find equivalent CQ rewritings for CQ queries and views. The interesting observation from Theorem 3.15 is that if a view tuple from the canonical rewriting participates in any minimal equivalent rewriting, then we can find, for each view independently, a one-to-one containment mapping μ_v from some query subgoals S' to its subgoals, such that the shared-variable property holds. The sense in which the shared-variable property holds is that the triple (S, S', μ_v), where S is the set of all subgoals of the query, has the shared-variable property. Thus, there exists a maximal S' for which we can find a one-to-one containment mapping μ_v. We call this maximal S' the *tuple core* of the view tuple (i.e., of the subgoal from the canonical rewriting).

Algorithm CoreCover of the next section is based on Theorem 3.15; the algorithm works by finding those tuple cores that cover all the subgoals of the query.

> **CQ query and views—property of the expansion:** The rewriting expansion has the shared-variable property. This enables each homomorphism from the query to the expansion to be decomposable into rewriting-independent sub-homomorphisms. This enables algorithm CoreCover to find efficiently an equivalent rewriting, without necessarily having to consider all the views (as when we use the canonical rewriting). There are more benefits of this algorithm; for instance, whenever a view is found to not contribute to the rewriting, it can be removed from further consideration.

3.2.3 ALGORITHM CORECOVER

We now introduce algorithm CoreCover based on Theorem 3.15. Recall that in Example 3.10 we noticed that if the canonical rewriting is an equivalent rewriting, in general we can still delete some of its subgoals and get an equivalent CQ rewriting with fewer subgoals. Algorithm CoreCover does that systematically. We say that a query subgoal *is covered* by a certain tuple core if it belongs to the subset from which the containment mapping is considered.

1. For each subgoal in the canonical rewriting, find its tuple core.

2. Construct candidate equivalent rewritings, by taking those subgoals of the canonical rewriting that cover all the subgoals of the query.

3. Check each resulting candidate rewriting for containment in the query.

A tuple core can be empty, in which case we ignore this view tuple in the rewriting, since it cannot contribute to the containment mapping from the query to the expansion of the rewriting. Consider an example:

Example 3.16   Let view V_1 and query Q be as follows:

$$V_1(X, Y) :\text{-} r(X, Z), r(Z, Y),$$

$$Q(A) :\text{-} r(A, A), s(A, Z'), s(Z', Y').$$

The canonical rewriting $R_{can}^{(V_1)}$ using only the view V_1 is $R_{can}^{(V_1)}(A) :\text{-} V_1(A, A)$. The expansion of the single subgoal, $V_1(A, A)$, of the canonical rewriting is $r(A, B), r(B, A)$. There is no one-to-one partial containment mapping from subgoals of Q to the atoms $r(A, B), r(B, A)$. (Actually, there is no containment mapping at all.) Hence, the tuple core of $V_1(A, A)$ is empty, and V_1 will not be used for any equivalent rewriting, even if more views were available in the given viewset.

Now consider the following view V_2:

$$V_2(X, Y) :\text{-} s(X, Z), s(Z, Y).$$

The canonical rewriting in terms of this view is $R_{can}^{(V_2)}(A) :\text{-} V_2(A, Y')$. The expansion of the single subgoal, $V_2(A, Y')$, of the canonical rewriting is $s(A, Z'), s(Z', Y')$. There is a one-to-one mapping from the last two subgoals of the query Q to $s(A, Z'), s(Z', Y')$—the mapping maps each variable to its same-name counterpart. Hence, the tuple core of $V_2(A, Y')$ is $s(A, Z'), s(Z', Y')$. Thus, view V_2 may be used in an equivalent rewriting if more views were available in the viewset, e.g., if we also had a view

$$V_3(A) :\text{-} r(A, A).$$

Indeed, the view V_3 has the tuple core $r(A, A)$, and we can use it and V_2 to form the following equivalent rewriting of the query Q:

$$R(A) :\text{-} V_3(A,), V_2(A, Y').$$

The algorithm CoreCover ensures a minimal number of subgoals in rewritings. It can also be modified for use with other objectives. For instance, if we have many views, and it is impractical to consider all of the them, then we can stop considering views (i.e., can stop computing view tuples on the canonical database of the query) when the CoreCover algorithm has covered all the subgoals of the query. This is much more efficient than considering the canonical rewriting, which will contain a large number of subgoals in such cases (i.e., when we have a large number of views).

3.3   ACYCLIC CQ VIEWS

We now consider the case where the available views belong to the language of acyclic CQs. We have already seen in Section 2.1.2 how CQ query evaluation and query containment are related. Thus, we can use the efficient algorithm for acyclic-CQ query containment to evaluate the views on the canonical database of the query. The computation of the views will take time polynomial in the size of query and in the maximum size of any view definition, multiplied by the number of views.

3.4   CQAC QUERIES AND VIEWS

Consider the case where the query, views, and rewriting belong to the language CQAC. In the case of conjunctive queries without arithmetic comparisons, if an equivalent rewriting exists in the language of unions of conjunctive queries, then there exists one that is a single conjunctive query. However, for conjunctive queries with arithmetic comparisons this property does not hold. Indeed, even for very simple cases of conjunctive queries and views with arithmetic comparisons, it is often not possible to find equivalent rewritings in the form of a single conjunctive query with arithmetic comparisons. Still, it may be possible to find equivalent rewritings in the form of unions of conjunctive queries with arithmetic comparisons, as the following example illustrates.

Example 3.17   A CQAC equivalent rewriting of a query may not exist even when the input query has no ACs. At the same time, a union-of-CQAC equivalent rewriting may exist.
    Consider query Q and views V_1 and V_2:

$$Q : q() \; :\text{-} \; p(X).$$

$$V_1 : v_1() \; :\text{-} \; p(X), X \geq 0.$$

$$V_2 : v_2() \; :\text{-} \; p(X), X < 0.$$

We can show that there is no conjunctive query that is an equivalent rewriting of Q using V_1 and V_2. Instead, the following union of conjunctive queries is an equivalent rewriting:

$$r_0() \; :\text{-} \; v_1().$$

$$r_0() \; :\text{-} \; v_2().$$

The following example illustrates a different challenge.

Example 3.18   Consider query Q and views V_1 and V_2:

$$Q : q(X, X) \; :\text{-} \; a(X, X), b(X), X < 7.$$

$$V_1 : \ v_1(T,U) \ :- \ a(S,T), b(U), T \le S, S \le U.$$

$$V_2 : \ v_2(T,U) \ :- \ a(S,T), b(U), T \le S, S < U.$$

The query $R : \ q(A,A) \ :- \ v_1(A,A), A < 7$ is an equivalent rewriting of Q using V_1. To see why, suppose that we expand R by replacing the view subgoal $v_1(A,A)$ by its definition; we obtain the expansion $R^{exp} : \ q(A,A) \ :- \ a(S,A), b(A), A \le S, S \le A, A < 7$. By equating S and A, which is permissible due to $S \le A$ and $A \le S$, we see that the AC $A < 7$ also applies, resulting in $S < 7$. Hence, the expansion is equivalent to Q. Notice that the definitions of the views V_1 and V_2 differ only in their respective second inequalities. However, V_2 cannot be used to answer Q. Thus, it is the comparison subgoal that affects the existence of the rewriting.

3.4.1   ALGORITHMS FOR FINDING EQUIVALENT REWRITINGS FOR QUERIES AND VIEWS WITH ACS

For the general case of CQAC queries and views, there is an algorithm for finding a CQAC equivalent rewriting, and there is an algorithm to find a union-of-CQAC equivalent rewriting, if such a rewriting exists. The following two results establish these facts, by showing that if there is such a rewriting, then there is a short one, i.e., with a number of subgoals in its definition that is bounded by a function of the number of subgoals in the query and in the view definitions.

Theorem 3.19   **(CQAC Equivalent Rewriting)** *For a query Q and views in the language of conjunctive queries with arithmetic comparisons, there is an algorithm for finding an equivalent rewriting in the language CQAC, if such a rewriting exists.*

Proof. Suppose that for query Q, there exists an equivalent CQAC rewriting R. Let R^{exp} be its expansion. We will show that there is an equivalent rewriting R', whose size is bounded by a function of the size of the query and views definitions. We consider homomorphisms from the expansion R^{exp} to query Q after imposing total orderings on the variables of Q. We consider all the total orderings of the variables and constants of Q that satisfy the arithmetic comparisons in Q. For each total ordering, there must be a homomorphism from R^{exp} to Q that satisfies the arithmetic comparisons in R^{exp}. For each variable of R^{exp} we construct a list of the variables of Q, such that each of these homomorphisms sends the variable of R^{exp} to that variable. We say that two variables of R^{exp} are "equivalent" if their lists are the same. Since the lists are of bounded length, and each entry on the list has one of the values from the variables of Q only, there is a bounded number of equivalence classes.

We now construct from R a new rewriting R' that equates all the "equivalent" variables. The expansion R'^{exp} of R' is contained in R^{exp}, since all we did was equate variables, thus restricting each of R and R^{exp}. Moreover, R'^{exp} has containment mappings to Q for all the orderings, since all we did was equate variables that always went to the same variable of Q anyway. Thus, Q is contained in R'. Since Q contains R^{exp}, which contains R'^{exp}, it is also true that R'^{exp} is contained in Q. Thus, R' is another equivalent rewriting of Q. It follows that there is a bound on the number of subgoals in R'. Thus, in order to find an equivalent rewriting of Q in terms of the input views, we need to look only at a bounded number of solutions.   □

Theorem 3.20   **(Union-of-CQAC Equivalent Rewriting)** *For a query Q and views in the language of conjunctive queries with arithmetic comparisons, there is an algorithm to find an equivalent rewriting in the language of unions of CQACs, if such a rewriting exists.*

Proof. We extend the proof of Theorem 3.19 to the case where an equivalent rewriting is a union of CQACs. Let R be a union of CQACs that is an equivalent rewriting of Q. Similarly to the proof of Theorem 3.19, we consider all orderings of the variables in Q that satisfy the arithmetic comparisons in Q. Now, however, for each ordering, there must be a containment mapping from the expansion of one of the CQACs of R to Q that preserves the ordering. Then, for each CQAC in R, we argue as in the proof of Theorem 3.19 to show that we need to look only at solutions of bounded size for each CQAC of R.   □

> **CQAC queries and views—finding equivalent rewritings:** There are algorithms for finding equivalent rewritings in the language of CQAC and in the language of unions of CQACs—if such rewritings exist. The algorithms are not efficient, in that they consider exhaustively all the combinations of view subgoals, up to a certain number of subgoals.

3.4.2   WHEN THE HOMOMORPHISM PROPERTY HOLDS

The crux of the problem of rewriting conjunctive queries using views lies in ensuring that the expansion of the rewritten query is contained in the original query. Testing for containment of conjunctive queries with arithmetic comparisons can be done more efficiently when the *homomorphism property* holds. Definition 2.25 in Chapter 2 defines AC-canonical databases of a CQAC query; in those cases where the homomorphism property holds, such databases have the good property pointed out in Theorem 2.26. This justifies the following definition of AC-canonical rewritings.

Definition 3.21   For a CQAC query Q and a set of CQAC views $\mathcal{V}$, an *AC-canonical rewriting* of Q using $\mathcal{V}$ is a rewriting that uses the view tuples computed on the AC-canonical database (see Definition 2.25), in the following sense: A tuple t is in the AC-canonical rewriting if and only if the homomorphism that computes t is such that the ACs of the AC-canonical database imply the image of the ACs in the view definition.

We use Theorem 2.26 to prove the following.

Theorem 3.22   *Let $(\mathcal{B}_1, \mathcal{B}_2)$ be a pair of sets of arithmetic comparisons that enables the homomorphism property. Let $\mathcal{V}$ be a set of CQAC views with all the ACs in their definitions belonging to the class $\mathcal{B}_1$, and Q be a CQAC query whose all ACs belong to $\mathcal{B}_2$. Then, if there is a CQAC equivalent rewriting of Q using $\mathcal{V}$, the AC-canonical rewriting with possibly additional ACs is such a rewriting. The additional ACs need only consider constants that already appear in the query Q.*

Consider the following query and views.

Example 3.23

$$
\begin{aligned}
Q : q() \quad &:\!- \ r(X, Y), r(Y, Y), s(W, Y), Y \le W, W \le 5, X \le 2. \\
V_1 : v_1(Y) \quad &:\!- \ r(X, Y), r(Y, Z), Z \le 8, X \le 3. \\
V_2 : v_2(Y) \quad &:\!- \ s(W, Y), Y \le W, W \le 5. \\
V_3 : v_3(Y) \quad &:\!- \ s(W, Y), W \le 15. \\
V_4 : v_4(Y) \quad &:\!- \ s(W, Y), W \le 1.
\end{aligned}
$$

The AC-canonical database of Q is $D = \{r(x, y), r(y, y), s(w, y), y \le w, w \le 5, x \le 2\}$. Now we evaluate the four views on this AC-canonical database. The result is the following view instance on D: $D_V = \{v_1(y), v_2(y), v_3(y)\}$. Notice that for the view V_4, there are no tuples in D_V, because the homomorphism h from the subgoals of V_4 to D does not satisfy the ACs.

Now the canonical rewriting is

$$R() :\!- v_1(Y), v_2(Y), v_3(Y).$$

The expansion of this rewriting is

$$R^{exp}() :\!- r(X, Y), r(Y, Z), Z \le 8, X \le 3, s(W, Y), Y \le W, W \le 5, v_3(Y), s(W, Y), W \le 15.$$

Now, if R^{exp} is equivalent to Q, then there is an equivalent CQAC rewriting of Q using the four given views; this rewriting is the canonical rewriting. If R^{exp} is not equivalent to Q, then there is no equivalent CQAC rewriting of Q using the given views.

> **CQAC query and views—the homomorphism property:** When the homomorphism property holds, i.e., one homomorphism from the expansion of the rewriting to the query suffices to prove the containment of the query in the expansion, then the canonical rewriting can be defined and be useful: If there is an equivalent rewriting in the language CQAC, then the canonical rewriting, possibly with arithmetic comparisons added, is such a rewriting.

3.5   REWRITING CQN QUERIES USING CQN VIEWS

We consider queries and views that are CQs with safe negation, and further restrict our consideration to the cases in which all the variables in view definitions are distinguished, i.e., are all used in the heads of the view definitions. Recall that we have defined CQNs with safe negation to be those queries in which the variables in the negated subgoals also appear in some non-negated subgoal.

As in the case of CQAC queries and views, here we may also have an equivalent rewriting in the language of unions of CQNs, but not in the language CQN. Consider an example.

Example 3.24   Consider CQ query Q and CQN views V_1 and V_2:

$$Q : q(X, Y) :\text{-} \ a(X, Y).$$

$$V_1 : v_1(X, Y) :\text{-} \ a(X, Y), b(Y).$$

$$V_2 : v_2(X, Y) :\text{-} \ a(X, Y), \neg b(Y).$$

The following union of CQ queries is an equivalent rewriting of Q using V_1 and V_2:

$$q(X, Y) :\text{-} \ v_1(X, Y),$$

$$q(X, Y) :\text{-} \ v_2(X, Y).$$

Note that there is no equivalent *CQ* rewriting of Q using V_1 and V_2.

Before we give a formal definition of a notion whose functionality is the same as the notion of *expansion* for CQAC queries and views (and prove a result that is analogous to Theorem 3.5), we discuss the issue using an example:

Example 3.25   In this example, in the bodies of the queries we use $\wedge$ instead of comma, to emphasize the fact that it is a logical expression that is a conjunction of atoms. We consider rewriting R and views V, and discuss the intuition for defining an expansion R^{exp} such that, for any database D, we have $R(V(D)) = R^{exp}(D)$. Consider the following rewriting R and views V_1 and V_2.

$$R(X, Y, Z) :\text{-} \ \neg v_1(X, Y, Z) \wedge v_2(X, Y, Z).$$

$$V_1 : v_1(X, Y, Z) :\text{-} \ a(X, Y) \wedge \neg a(Y, Z).$$

$$V_2 : v_2(X, Y, Z) :\text{-} \ b(X, Y) \wedge b(Y, Z).$$

Intuitively, we can get the expansion of the rewriting by replacing the view subgoals with the view definitions, while maintaining the notation with logical operators:

$$R^{exp}(X, Y, Z) :\text{-} \ \neg\Big(a(X, Y) \wedge \neg a(Y, Z)\Big) \wedge \Big(b(X, Y) \wedge b(Y, Z)\Big).$$

That is:

$$R^{exp}(X, Y, Z) \;:\!-\; \Big(\neg a(X, Y) \wedge b(X, Y) \wedge b(Y, Z)\Big) \vee \Big(a(Y, Z) \wedge b(X, Y) \wedge b(Y, Z)\Big).$$

If we write the disjunction as a union, then R^{exp} is in the language of unions of CQNs:

$$R^{exp}(X, Y, Z) \;:\!-\; \neg a(X, Y) \wedge b(X, Y) \wedge b(Y, Z),$$

$$R^{exp}(X, Y, Z) \;:\!-\; a(Y, Z) \wedge b(X, Y) \wedge b(Y, Z).$$

Indeed, for this definition of expansion, we have, for all D, $R(V(D)) = R^{exp}(D)$.

We now formalize the concept of *expansion* of a rewriting for CQN queries and views.

Definition 3.26   Let Q be a CQN query, V a set of CQN views, and R a CQN equivalent rewriting of Q using V. The *expansion* of R, denoted R^{exp}, is obtained as follows: replace each view atom in R with the body of the corresponding view definition, with each nondistinguished variable replaced by a fresh variable. The body of R is thus a logical expression that may no longer be representable as a conjunction of literals (see Example 3.25). We put this logical expression into the disjunctive normal form. Now each disjunct is used to form a CQN. R^{exp} then becomes a union of CQNs, as follows: each disjunct of the logical expression is a CQN in the union, and the head of R^{exp} is the same as the head of R.

Theorem 3.27   *Suppose query Q, views V, and rewriting R all belong to the language of CQNs. Suppose the views have no nondistinguished (a.k.a. existential) variables in their definition. Then R is an equivalent rewriting of Q using the views V iff $R^{exp} \equiv Q$.*

Proof.   We show that $R^{exp}(D) = R(V(D))$ for every D; this suffices to prove the result. We will first show that $R(V(D))$ is contained in $R^{exp}(D)$ for every D.

We say that a subgoal of a query, view, or rewriting is *negative* if it has the negation symbol $\neg$ on its atom, otherwise we say it is positive. To compute $V(D)$, we consider homomorphisms from the positive subgoals of the view definitions, such that the negated subgoals in these definitions are not in D. To compute $R(V(D))$, we consider homomorphisms from the body of R on $V(D)$, such that the negated view subgoals in R are not in $V(D)$.

Tuple t is in $R(V(D))$ because (i) of homomorphisms μ_i from the positive subgoals of the view definitions to D, which compute tuples $v_j(\mu_i(\bar{X}))$, and homomorphism μ from positive subgoals of R to $V(D)$ that uses the view tuples computed by μ_i's to compute t; and (ii) of the lack of any homomorphisms μ_i that computes a $\mu(t_i)$ for any negative subgoal $v_j(t_i)$ in R. In particular, (ii) means that either there is no homomorphism from the positive subgoals of v_j to produce $v_j(t_i)$, or that for any homomorphism μ_i, there is a negative subgoal $\neg a(\bar{X})$ in the definition of v_j, such that $a(\mu_i(\bar{X}))$ is in D.

Now we compose the homomorphisms μ_i from the positive view subgoals in R with the homomorphism μ, and call the resulting homomorphism h. We claim that there is a CQN, R_i^{exp}, in R^{exp} such that t is in $R_i^{exp}(D)$ due to the homomorphism h. Observe that h makes all the subgoals in all the CQNs in R^{exp} true, as long as these subgoals come from expanding positive view subgoals in R.

Now consider any negative view subgoal g_n in R. Since we only consider safe queries, all the variables of g_n are instantiated by μ. In addition, the view definitions have no nondistinguished variables. Hence, this instantiation passes on to the subgoals of the corresponding view definitions. Since g_n is a negative subgoal, this instantiation should make false at least one subgoal of the corresponding view definition. If this false subgoal is positive in the view definition, it will pass as negative to some of the CQNs of R^{exp}, hence these CQNs would become candidates for computing t. If a false subgoal is negative in the view definition, it will pass as positive to some of the CQNs of R^{exp}, hence these CQNs would become candidates for computing t. However, by construction of R^{exp}, each subgoal in the expansion of a negative view subgoal in R meets in a CQN of R^{exp} with each subgoal in the expansion of any other negative view subgoal in R. Hence, we continue the same reasoning to argue that one of the candidates will remain a candidate after processing the second negative view subgoal in R, all the way until we are done with processing all the negative view subgoals in R. The CQN that remains a candidate until the end is the one that will compute t.

So far we have shown that $R(\mathcal{V}(D))$ is contained in $R^{exp}(D)$ for every D. Now we show that $R^{exp}(D)$ is contained in $R(\mathcal{V}(D))$ for every D. Suppose tuple t is not in $R(\mathcal{V}(D))$ and is in $R^{exp}(D)$. Since t is in $R^{exp}(D)$, there is a CQN R_i^{exp} of R^{exp}, such that t is in $R_i^{exp}(D)$. The subgoals of R_i^{exp} are formed by taking one subgoal from each view expansion in R for negative view subgoals in R, and taking all the subgoals of a view expansion for positive view subgoals in R. Let h be the homomorphism that produces t in $R_i^{exp}(D)$. We can decompose h to produce appropriate tuples for the positive view subgoals in R. We can also decompose h to show that all appropriate negative view subgoals in R are not in $\mathcal{V}(D)$, hence we can compute t in $R(\mathcal{V}(D))$.

$\square$

> **Expansion of a rewriting for CQN rewriting:** For CQN queries and views, where all the views have no nondistinguished (a.k.a. existential) variables in their definition, the rewriting expansion can be a union of CQNs. Similarly t the CQAC case, a rewriting is equivalent to the query iff its expansion is equivalent to the query.

Example 3.28 is more elaborate than Example 3.24. We use it to show how one could use Theorem 3.27 and the containment test for CQNs to prove equivalence of a rewriting to the given query.

Example 3.28   Consider query Q and views V_1, V_2, and V_3:

$$Q : q() :- a(X,Y), \neg a(X,X).$$

$$V_1 : v_1(X,Y) :- a(X,Y), \neg a(Y,X), \neg a(X,X).$$

$$V_2 : v_2(X,Y) :- a(X,Y), a(Y,X), \neg a(X,X), \neg a(Y,Y).$$

$$V_3 : v_3(X,Y) :- a(X,Y), a(Y,X), \neg a(X,X), a(Y,Y).$$

An equivalent rewriting of Q is the following union:

$$q() :- v_1(X,Y), \qquad q() :- v_2(X,Y), \qquad q() :- v_3(X,Y).$$

Note that there is no rewriting in the form of a single CQN. The four canonical databases of Q are (i) $\{a(X,Y)\}$; (ii) $\{a(X,Y), a(Y,Y)\}$; (iii) $\{a(X,Y), a(Y,X)\}$; and (iv) $\{a(X,Y), a(Y,X), a(Y,Y)\}$. The canonical databases (i) and (ii) are covered by the view V_1; the canonical database (iii) is covered by V_2; and the canonical database (iv) is covered by V_3.

3.6   CQA QUERIES

In this section we discuss CQA queries. As usual, when discussing aggregate queries, we refer to bags as well as sets. (Throughout this book, the only place we refer to bags/multisets is when we discuss aggregate queries.) We say that a view V is *set valued* if V is computed and stored to be accessed as a set, and that V is *bag valued* if V is computed and stored to be accessed as a bag. In rewritings, a bag-valued view V is denoted by an adornment, as V^b. When there is no adornment, we assume that it is easily deduced from the context.

Example 3.29   Consider the following queries, views, and rewritings:

$$
\begin{aligned}
Q_1 &: q_1(S, Y, max(T)) &:- \; & p(X, Y, Z, T, N, L, 2005), \; t(X, S).\\
Q_2 &: q_2(Y, M, U, sum(Z)) &:- \; & p(X, Y, Z, T, N, L, M), \; w(X, U).\\
V_1 &: v_1(X, Y, M, max(T)) &:- \; & p(X, Y, Z, T, N, L, M).\\
V_2 &: v_2(X, Y, M, sum(Z)) &:- \; & p(X, Y, Z, T, N, L, M).\\
V_3 &: v_3(X, S) &:- \; & t(X, S).\\
V_4 &: v_4(X, U) &:- \; & w(X, U).\\
R_1 &: r_1(S, Y, max(K)) &:- \; & v_1(X, Y, 2005, F, K), \; v_3(X, S).\\
R_2 &: r_2(Y, M, U, sum(J)) &:- \; & v_2(X, Y, M, J, K), \; v_4(X, U).
\end{aligned}
$$

In each rewriting, the view V_1 or V_2 is the only subgoal that contributes to the computation of the aggregation; we call this view *central view*. Thus, in rewriting R_1, the central view is V_1 and, in rewriting R_2, the central view is V_2. Observe that the other views in the rewritings (V_3 or V_4) can be either set valued or bag valued. The view V_3 can be either set or bag valued, and the rewriting R_1 will still be equivalent to query Q_1. However, the view V_4 should be bag valued for the rewriting R_2 to be equivalent to query Q_2. We will discuss how to prove this formally in this section.

We now define *central rewritings*.

Definition 3.30   A *central rewriting* consists of the following template R:

$$r(\bar{X}, \alpha(Y)) \leftarrow v_0(\bar{X}_0, Y), v_1(\bar{X}_1, Y_1), \ldots, v_k(\bar{X}_k, Y_k),$$

where α is either a nontrivial aggregate operator or identity (in which case the head is $r(\bar{X}, Y)$) and the variable Y does not appear in any other place in the rewriting, except the two places shown. View v_0, which contains the variable Y, is called the *central view* of the rewriting. We refer to Y as the *special variable of the rewriting*.

We use the notation CQA/CQ to say that the central view is CQA and the rewriting is CQ, the notation CQ/CQA to say that the central view is CQ and the rewriting is CQA, and the notation CQA/CQA when both the central view and the rewriting are CQA.

3.6.1   UNFOLDINGS OF REWRITINGS

In case of aggregate queries, the definition of unfoldings of rewritings is analogous to the definition (and use) of the notion of expansion for CQ rewritings. A different name is used to alert the reader to the complexities introduced by aggregation. (Note that aggregate queries are not relational-algebra queries.)

Definition 3.31   The *unfolding* R^u of R is obtained by (a) considering the core CQ for each view, (b) considering also the core CQ of the rewriting, forming its expansion (as if it were a CQ query with CQ views), and (c) supplying an aggregate operator γ to the special variable Y of the rewriting in the head of R^u, as follows: γ is the aggregate operator of the central view v_0 of R when v_0 is aggregated, or else is the aggregate operator in the head of R.

3.6.2   EQUIVALENCE OF UNFOLDINGS AND REWRITINGS

Unfoldings may lack equivalence to the respective rewritings. We provide examples that make several points.

CQ/CQA: A Non-central View has Aggregation:

Example 3.32   Consider a CQ/CQA rewriting R in terms of views V and W; R^u is the unfolding of R:

$$
\begin{array}{ll}
r(B, C, sum(A)) & :\text{-} \ v(A, B), \ w(B, C, F). \\
v(A, B) & :\text{-} \ p(A, B). \\
w(B, C, count(D)) & :\text{-} \ s(B, C, D), \ t(C, G). \\
r^u(B, C, sum(A)) & :\text{-} \ p(A, B), \ s(B, C, D), \ t(C, G).
\end{array}
$$

The *sum*-rewriting R is not equivalent to its unfolding R^u, because the noncentral view W of R has aggregation. To show the nonequivalence, we let the third (aggregated) argument D in the head of the view W be the marked argument. We can construct a database $\mathcal{D}$ that has four tuples: $\mathcal{D} = \{ p(1,4), \ s(4,5,2), \ s(4,5,3), \ t(5,6) \}$. (Note that the tuples $s(4,5,2)$ and $s(4,5,3)$ differ in the values of the marked variable D in R^u.) We can show that on this database $\mathcal{D}$, the answer to R is $\{(4,5,1)\}$, whereas the answer to R^u is $\{(4,5,2)\}$. Thus, $\mathcal{D}$ serves as a counterexample database in checking the equivalence of R and R^u. The multiplicity 2, which is introduced by the two tuples in relation s, is captured by the view w but not by the view v. At the same time, in the rewriting R the view V is the central view that provides the values to compute the aggregated attribute $sum(A)$.

CQA/CQ: For Duplicate-insensitive Aggregation, Set-valued Computation is Needed

If *bag* projection is used as the last step of evaluating R on a database $\mathcal{D}_V$, then $R(\mathcal{D}_V)$ may be a nontrivial bag and thus cannot be the same *bag* as $R^u(\mathcal{D})$, which is a set on any database. Consider an example.

Example 3.33   Consider the following views V and W:

$$v(B, max(A)) \quad :\text{-} \ \ p(A, B).$$
$$w(B, C, D) \quad\quad :\text{-} \ \ s(B, C, D), t(C, G).$$

We use the views to construct the following rewriting R and its unfolding R^u (note that R has a nondistinguished argument D):

$$r(B, C, H) \quad\quad\quad :\text{-} \ \ v(B, H), w(B, C, D).$$
$$r^u(B, C, max(A)) \quad :\text{-} \ \ p(A, B), s(B, C, D), t(C, G).$$

On the *set-valued* database $\mathcal{D} = \{p(6,1), \ \ s(1,2,3), \ \ s(1,2,5), \ \ t(2,4)\}, \ \ R(\mathcal{D}_V) = \{(1,2,6), (1,2,6)\}$ is a nontrivial bag if bag projection is used as the last step of computing R on $\mathcal{D}_V$. On the other hand, $R^u(\mathcal{D})$ is a set $\{(1,2,6)\}$.

CQA/CQ: Non-central Views Should not have Nondistinguished Variables in Their Definition

If non-central views have nondistinguished variables in their definition, then there is a database D such that $R(V(D)) \neq R^u(D)$, as is demonstrated in the following example.

Example 3.34   Consider the following setting, with views v and w, rewriting R and its unfolding, and database instance D:

$$v(X, Y) :\text{-} \ p(X, Y, W).$$

$$w(X, sum(Z)) :\text{-} \ r(X, Z).$$

$$R(X, Y, S) :\text{-} \ v(X, Y), w(X, S).$$

$$R^u(X, Y, S) :\text{-}\ p(X, Y, W), r(X, Z).$$

$$D = \{p(1, 2, 3),\ p(1, 2, 4),\ r(1, 3)\}.$$

If we compute the two views V and W on D, we get the following $\mathcal{V}(D)$:

$$v(D) : (1, 2), (1, 2)$$

and

$$w(D) : (1, 3).$$

If we compute R on $\mathcal{V}(D)$, we get the following $R(\mathcal{V}(D))$:

$$R : (1, 2, 3), (1, 2, 3).$$

However, if we compute R^u on D, we get the following $R^u(D)$:

$$R^u : (1, 2, 6).$$

CQA/CQA: The Case where Non-central Views have Aggregation or are Set Valued

If a *sum* or *count* rewriting R has non-central views that are set valued or have aggregation, it could be that R is not equivalent to its unfolding R^u.

Example 3.35   Consider a *sum* rewriting R and its unfolding R^u:

$$
\begin{aligned}
r(B, sum(W)) \quad &:\text{-}\ v_1(C, W),\ v_2(B, C).\\
r^u(B, count(*)) \quad &:\text{-}\ s(B, C, D),\ t(C, G).\\
v_1(C, count(*)) \quad &:\text{-}\ t(C, G).\\
v_2(B, C) \quad &:\text{-}\ s(B, C, D).
\end{aligned}
$$

If the relation for the noncentral view V_2 is computed as a set, R and its unfolding R^u are not equivalent, as evidenced by the database $D = \{s(1, 2, 3),\ s(1, 2, 4),\ t(2, 5)\}$.

Now consider a *sum* rewriting R' that has a noncentral view with aggregation; R' is the result of slightly modifying in R the noncentral view V_2:

$$
\begin{aligned}
v_2'(B, C, count(*)) \quad &:\text{-}\ s(B, C, D).\\
r'(B, sum(W)) \quad &:\text{-}\ v_1(C, W),\ v_2'(B, C, count(*)).
\end{aligned}
$$

The rewriting R' is not equivalent to its unfolding R^u, as evidenced by the same database D.

The techniques illustrated in these examples show various cases in which the unfolding is not equivalent to the given rewriting. It turns out that these are the only exceptions, and in all the other cases we have equivalence. These observations are captured in the following results.

Theorem 3.36   *Let R be a CQA rewriting with the max or min operator. Then $R \equiv R^u$ in the following cases:*

- *CQ/CQA;*

- *CQA/CQ, with R is computed as set; and*

- *CQA/CQA.*

Theorem 3.37   *Let R be a CQA rewriting with the max or min operator. Then $R \equiv R^u$ in the following cases:*

- *CQ/CQA, where all the views are conjunctive without aggregation and are bag valued;*

- *CQA/CQ, where all the grouping attributes in the central view are also grouping attributes in the rewriting, all the noncentral views are conjunctive without aggregation, and there are no nondistinguished variables in their definitions; and*

- *CQA/CQA, where all the noncentral views are conjunctive without aggregation and are bag valued.*

3.6.3   CONSTRUCTING CENTRAL REWRITINGS

The algorithm for constructing central rewritings is based on the following proposition, which uses the results from Section 3.6.2.

Proposition 3.38   *The following results hold for the three types of central rewritings.*

- *In a CQA/CQ rewriting, the set of all grouping attributes of the central view is a subset of the set of all grouping attributes of the rewriting. (We call this central view grouping complete.)*

- *In a CQA/CQA rewriting, the set of the grouping attributes of the rewriting is a union of subsets of the grouping attributes in the central view and of the non-aggregated attributes in noncentral views. (We call this central view grouping incomplete.)*

- *In a CQ/CQA rewriting, the set of the grouping attributes of the rewriting is a union of subsets of the attributes in the central view and of the non-aggregated attributes in noncentral views.*

Suppose we are given a query Q, a set of views $\mathcal{V}$, and a rewriting R of the query using the views. We now discuss how to construct the *reduced-core query*, the *reduced-core viewset*, and the *reduced-core rewriting with respect to the viewset* $\mathcal{V}$. Given an aggregate view V, we define its *reduced-core view* V^r as the view whose body is the body of V and whose head is a new predicate name V^r; the arguments in the head of V^r are all the grouping attributes of V. We construct the *reduced-core query* in a similar way. For the rewriting R, its *reduced-core rewriting with respect to the viewset* $\mathcal{V}$ is a conjunctive rewriting R^r whose head attributes are R's grouping attributes only, and whose body is the same as the body of R, with the view subgoals of R replaced by the corresponding reduced-core views. The reduced-core rewriting is a conjunctive query that can be viewed as a rewriting of the reduced-core query using the reduced-core views. The proposition that follows shows that if R is an equivalent rewriting of Q using $\mathcal{V}$, then the reduced-core rewriting of R wrto $\mathcal{V}$ is also an equivalent rewriting of Q using $\mathcal{V}$.

Proposition 3.39   *Given a query Q and views $\mathcal{V}$, suppose that there exists a central rewriting R that uses $\mathcal{V}$, including a CQA central view, such that R is equivalent to the query. Then the following holds: Let $\mathcal{V}'$ be the reduced-core views of $\mathcal{V}$, R^r be the reduced-core rewriting of R with respect to $\mathcal{V}$, and Q' be the reduced-core query of Q. Then R^r is an equivalent rewriting of Q' using $\mathcal{V}'$.*

Proof. The proof is a direct consequence of Definition 3.30 and of the results of Section 3.6.2. In particular, it is a consequence of the following observations. (a) If R is a rewriting of the query, then its unfolding is equivalent to the query. (b) All the subgoals that contain the aggregated attribute in the unfolding of the rewriting are subgoals of the central view. (This follows from the definition of central rewritings.) Hence by dropping the aggregated attribute from the head of the view definition, we still have a mapping to ensure that the reduced rewriting and the reduced query are equivalent.   □

We now describe an algorithm that, given a query and a set of views, constructs all the central rewritings that are equivalent to the query. We reduce this problem to the problem of obtaining rewritings for purely conjunctive queries. First we describe the case for *max* and *min* queries.

In the following algorithm, Q^r and V^r are the reduced-core queries of a query Q and of the views, respectively. We use the algorithm described previously in this book to find equivalent rewritings of CQ views and queries.

Procedure *Find-R.* Input: query Q, set of views V
Consider Q^r, V^r.
Find all the rewritings of Q^r using V^r.
  For each rewriting R^r do:
  Consider the expansion R^{r-exp}
    For each containment mapping from Q^r to R^{r-exp} do:
      If there is a view in the rewriting R^r such that all its subgoals containing its aggregated attribute are exactly the subgoals containing the aggregated attribute in the query, then all this view the central view.
      If the central view is grouping incomplete, then construct CQA/CQA rewriting.
      If the central view is grouping complete, then construct CQA/CQ rewriting.
      If there is a conjunctive view in the rewriting R^r such that all the subgoals of the query containing the aggregated attribute are exactly the subgoals of the view that contain

in the same predicate position an attribute B, then do:
Call this the central view and B the aggregated attribute,
and construct a CQ/CQA rewriting.
  end
 end
end

> **CQA queries and views—finding equivalent rewritings:** We focus on *central rewritings*, i.e., those rewritings that have only one view subgoal, called the central view subgoal, which contains the attribute aggregated in the head of the rewriting. Unfoldings of rewritings are used to reason about the equivalence of the rewriting to the query. In the case of aggregate queries, for rewritings R and unfoldings R^u, views $\mathcal{V}$, and database D, the results $R^u(D)$ of unfoldings are not always equal to $R(\mathcal{V}(D))$ (as was the case of, e.g., CQs and expansions of CQ rewritings).

3.6.4   NON-CENTRAL REWRITINGS

If we allow in the rewriting aggregate operators beyond sum, avg, count, max, and min, then we may obtain richer rewritings, such as the one in the following example.

Example 3.40 Consider query q, views v_1 and v_2, and query r over the views:

$$q(X, sum(Y)) \text{ :- } a(X, Y, U), b(Y, W).$$

$$v_1(X, Y, count) \text{ :- } a(X, Y, U).$$

$$v_2(Y, count) \text{ :- } b(Y, W).$$

$$r(X, sum(Y, Z_1 Z_2)) \text{ :- } v_1(X, Y, Z_1), v_2(Y, Z_2).$$

Here, $sum(Y, Z_1 Z_2)$ is a new aggregate operator, which computes the sum, over all the values y_i of Y, of the products $z_1 \times z_2 \times y_j$.

 For each pair of values for X and Y, the view v_1 counts the number of tuples with a certain value in U. For each value of Y, the view v_2 counts the number of tuples with a certain value in W. Thus, for each value of Y, from the result of the view v_2 we know in how many tuples in the relation b this value occurs. Similarly (albeit in a little more involved manner), from the result of the view v_2 we know for each value of Y, as it is paired with a value of X, in how many tuples of the relation a this pair appears. By using basic calculations, we can obtain that the following would give us the result of the query. For each value x_j of x we do: for each value y_i of Y, multiply the result of count in v_1 for the tuple (x_j, y_i, z_1), by the result of count in v_2 for the tuple (x_j, z_2), then multiply the outcome by the value y_j. As a result, we have the sum as required in the query for the specific value y_j (i.e., if we consider only the tuples that contain y_j, and ignore the others). To finish up, we do this for all the values of Y, and sum up the partial results.

3.7   EXERCISES

3.1. Prove the following: If an equivalent rewriting of a CQ query in terms of CQ views does not exist in the language of CQs, then there is no such rewriting in the language of unions (infinite or finite) of CQs.

3.2. Prove Theorem 3.15.

3.3. Prove Theorem 3.36.

3.4. Prove Theorem 3.37.

3.5. Find all possible equivalent rewritings of the given query Q using the given set of views $\mathcal{V} = \{\, U, V, W, T, M \,\}$.

(1) $Q(X, Y) :- p(X, Z, N), s(N, R, Y)$.

$U(A, B) :- p(A, C, B)$.

$V(A, B) :- p(A, B, C)$.

$W(A, B) :- s(A, C, B)$.

$T(A, B, C) :- p(A, D, F), S(F, C, B)$.

$M(A, B, C, D) :- p(A, F, C), s(D, H, B)$.

3.6. Use algorithm CoreCover to find all possible equivalent rewritings of the given query Q using the given set of views $\mathcal{V} = \{\, U, V, W, M \,\}$.

(1) $Q(X, Y) :- p(X, N), s(N, Z), t(N, Y)$.

$U(A, B) :- p(A, C), s(C, B)$.

$V(A, B, C) :- p(A, C), s(C, B)$.

$W(A, B, C, D) :- p(A, C), t(D, B)$.

$M(A, B, C) :- s(A, B), t(A, C)$.

3.7. Use algorithm CoreCover to find all possible equivalent rewritings of the given query Q using the given set of views $\mathcal{V} = \{\, U, V, W, M \,\}$.

(1) $Q(A) :- p(A, B), s(B, C), t(C, B)$.

$U(X, Y) :- p(X, Z), s(Z, Y)$.

$$V(X,Y) :- s(X,Z), t(Z,Y).$$

$$W(X,Y) :- t(X,Y), s(U,X).$$

$$M(X,Y,Z) :- s(X,Z), t(Z,Y).$$

3.8. Find all possible equivalent rewritings of the given query Q using the given set of views $\mathcal{V} = \{ U, V, W, T \}$.

(1) $Q(X) :- p(X), s(X,Y), X \geq 5, X < 10, Y > 8.$

$\quad U(X) :- p(X), X \geq 5.$

$\quad V(X) :- s(X,Y), Y > 8.$

$\quad W(X) :- s(Y,X), Y > 8.$

$\quad T(X,Y) :- p(X), s(X,Y), Y > 9.$

3.9. Find all possible equivalent rewritings of the given query Q using the given set of views $\mathcal{V} = \{ U, V, W \}$.

(1) $Q(Y) :- p(X,Z), s(Z,Y), Z > Y, X > 3.$

$\quad U(X,Y) :- p(X,Y), X > 3.$

$\quad V(X,Y) :- p(X,Z), s(Z,Y), X > 3.$

$\quad W(Z,N,Y) :- p(X,Z), s(N,Y).$

CHAPTER 4

Maximally Contained Rewritings (MCRs)

We may obtain a view instance $\mathcal{I}$ in either of the following two ways.

- Under the Closed World Assumption (CWA), $\mathcal{I}$ is such that there is D with $\mathcal{I} = \mathcal{V}(D)$.

- Under the Open World Assumption (OWA), $\mathcal{I}$ is such that there is D with $\mathcal{I} \subseteq \mathcal{V}(D)$.

In Chapter 3, we only considered the CWA, as it was proper for equivalent rewritings. For contained rewritings, however, we may have the following two different definitions.

Definition 4.1   Given a query Q and a set of view definitions $\mathcal{V}$, we define contained rewritings under the CWA and under the OWA.

- *Under the Closed World Assumption (CWA). R is a contained rewriting of Q using $\mathcal{V}$ under the CWA if and only if for every view instance $\mathcal{I}$ the following is true: for any database D such that $\mathcal{I} = \mathcal{V}(D)$, we have that $R(\mathcal{I}) \subseteq Q(D)$.*

- *Under the Open World Assumption (OWA). R is a contained rewriting of Q using $\mathcal{V}$ under the OWA if and only if for every view instance $\mathcal{I}$ the following is true: for any database D such that $\mathcal{I} \subseteq \mathcal{V}(D)$, we have that $R(\mathcal{I}) \subseteq Q(D)$.*

Definition 3.6 is equivalent to the above definition under the CWA. The way in which the two definitions are related is expressed by the following two results.

Proposition 4.2   *Given a query Q and a set of view definitions $\mathcal{V}$, R is a contained rewriting under the OWA if it is a contained rewriting under the CWA.*

Proof. If R is a contained rewriting of Q under the OWA, then for any $\mathcal{I}$ it holds that for any database D such that $\mathcal{I} \subseteq \mathcal{V}(D)$, we have that $R(\mathcal{I}) \subseteq Q(D)$. This means that this is true for any database D such that $\mathcal{I} = \mathcal{V}(D)$. Thus R is also a contained rewriting of Q under the CWA. □

For the other result, we need to define monotone queries.

Definition 4.3   A query Q is *monotone* if the following is true: if $D \subseteq D'$, then $Q(D) \subseteq Q(D')$.

Proposition 4.4   *Assume monotone queries, views, and rewritings. Given a query Q and a set of view definitions $\mathcal{V}$, let R be a monotone query. Then R is a contained rewriting of Q under the CWA if it is a contained rewriting of Q under the OWA.*

Proof. If R is a contained rewriting of Q under the CWA, then for any $\mathcal{I}$ it holds that for any database D such that $\mathcal{I} = \mathcal{V}(D)$, we have that $R(\mathcal{I}) \subseteq Q(D)$. Consider, for a certain D such that $\mathcal{I} = \mathcal{V}(D)$, any $\mathcal{I}'$ such that $\mathcal{I}' \subseteq \mathcal{V}(D)$. Since R is monotone, we have that $R(\mathcal{I}') \subseteq R(\mathcal{V}(D))$. Thus R is also a contained rewriting of Q under the OWA.   □

Thus, the two definitions coincide for monotone rewritings. CQs and CQACs are monotone queries. In this chapter, we consider the OWA for contained queries; this reflects in the definition of maximally contained rewritings given in the next section. In the rest of this chapter, we present the following.

1. For CQ queries and views: An efficient algorithm to find maximally contained rewritings (MCRs) in the language of unions of CQs.

2. For CQAC queries and views: In cases where the homomorphism property holds, the results are analogous to the case of CQ queries and views. Otherwise, the general case is more involved. At the same time, we show that in certain cases recursion, such as in Datalog, is sufficient to find MCRs. Thus, we proceed as follows.

3. For the case where the queries are in Datalog and the views are CQs, we provide an algorithm for finding MCRs in the language of Datalog.

4. We illustrate cases where the queries and views are defined by unions of CQs or by CQACs, but recursion is needed to find MCRs.

4.1   PRELIMINARIES

Informally, we define maximally contained rewritings (MCRs) to be those rewritings in a certain language that produce all the answers that would be returned by any contained rewriting of the query under the OWA. The formal definition is as follows.

Definition 4.5   A rewriting R is called a *maximally contained rewriting (MCR)* of query Q using views $\mathcal{V}$ with respect to query language $\mathcal{L}$ if (1) R is a contained rewriting of Q using $\mathcal{V}$ in $\mathcal{L}$, and (2) every contained rewriting of Q using $\mathcal{V}$ in language $\mathcal{L}$ is contained in R.

The following example demonstrates that an equivalent rewriting under the CWA (which is also a contained rewriting under the CWA) may not even be a contained rewriting under the OWA.

Example 4.6   Recall that in Example 3.2 we considered query Q' defined as path query P_5. (P_i is the query that asks for pairs of nodes on a graph connected by a path of length i—

see Definition 2.44.) We proved that there is no equivalent *CQ* rewriting of Q' using views P_3 and P_4. However, there is an equivalent *first-order* rewriting R' of Q' in terms of these views, as given in Example 3.2. The rewriting R' is equivalent to P_5 only if we have access to all the data computed by the views. On the other hand, if we have access to only some of the data, then this rewriting is not equivalent to P_5. To see this, suppose we have the view instance $\mathcal{I} = \{P_4(1, 2), P_3(3, 2), P_4(3, 4)\}$. $\mathcal{I}$ is a subset of the views P_3 and P_4 computed on

$$D = \{e(1, 11), e(11, 12), e(12, 14), e(14, 4), e(3, 31), e(31, 32), e(32, 2), e(3, 34),$$

$$e(34, 35), e(35, 36), e(36, 4)\}.$$

We observe that $(1, 4)$ is in $R'(\mathcal{I})$. Thus, under the OWA, $(1, 4)$ should be in $Q(D)$ too. If $(1, 4)$ is in $Q(D)$, then there should exist a path of length five from node 1 to node 4 in D. However, there is no such path in D, hence $(1, 4)$ is an incorrect answer under the OWA. Hence, R' is not a contained rewriting of Q' using the views P_3 and P_4.

We now provide intuition on how to use Definition 4.5 to find MCRs in the following example.

Example 4.7   Consider a CQ query Q

$$q(X, Y) :\text{-} a(X, Z), b(Z, W), c(W, Y)$$

and views

$\quad V_1 :\quad v_1(X, W) :\text{-} a(X, Z), b(Z, W),$
$\quad V_2 :\quad v_2(W, Y) :\text{-} c(W, Y),$
$\quad V_3 :\quad v_3(Z, Y) :\text{-} b(Z, W), c(W, Y),$
$\quad V_4 :\quad v_4(X, Z) :\text{-} a(X, Z),$
$\quad V_5 :\quad v_5(X, Y) :\text{-} a(X, Z), b(Z, Z), c(Z, Y).$

Let the language of rewritings be unions of CQs (UCQs). The following rewriting, which consists of three CQs R_1, R_2 and R_3, is the MCR of the query Q for the language UCQ:

$\quad R_1 : q(X, Y) :\text{-} v_1(X, Z), v_2(Z, Y).$
$\quad R_2 : q(X, Y) :\text{-} v_3(X, Z), v_4(Z, Y).$
$\quad R_3 : q(X, Y) :\text{-} v_5(X, Y).$

Observe that R_1 is an equivalent rewriting of the query Q using the given views; the same holds for R_2. However, we need both R_1 and R_2 in a UCQ rewriting to construct an MCR. To see why, observe that R_1 is not contained in R_2 (as queries), although R_1^{exp} and R_2^{exp} are equivalent. Moreover, we need rewriting R_3, which is a contained but not equivalent rewriting.

The purpose of the following example is to show how to prove that a UCQ rewriting is an MCR of a CQ query using CQ views.

Example 4.8   Consider query Q, views V_1 and V_2, and rewriting R, as follows:

$$(X, Y) :\text{-} p(X), s(Y).$$

$$V_1(X) :\text{-} p(X).$$

$$V_2(X) :\text{-} s(X).$$

$$R(X,Y) :\text{-} V_1(X), V_2(Y).$$

Here R is an MCR of Q. Indeed, suppose R' is a contained rewriting of Q using the two views. Then there is a containment mapping μ from Q to the expansion of R'. The mapping μ maps subgoal $p(X)$ of the query to some subgoal g of the expansion. However, g can be produced in the expansion only by expanding the view V_1. Hence, R' has a subgoal $V_1(X)$. For similar reasons, R' has a subgoal $V_2(Y)$. Hence, there is a containment mapping from R to R'.

4.1.1   CQAC QUERIES AND VIEWS

The problem of finding MCRs gets considerably more involved in presence of arithmetic comparisons. We begin by showing that, unlike the CQ case, we need recursion to find an MCR, even if all the ACs are semi-interval comparisons (see Example 4.9). Then we develop a new notion of AC-containment, motivated by the following observation: Unlike CQ queries and views, for CQAC queries and views we may have two contained rewritings R_1 and R_2, such that for any view instance $\mathcal{I}$ we have $R_2(\mathcal{I}) \subseteq R_1(\mathcal{I})$, but R_2 is not contained in R_1 (see Example 4.10).

Language of Rewritings
The following example shows the importance of the language of maximally contained rewritings.

Example 4.9   Let the query and views be as follows:

$$
\begin{aligned}
Q_1() \quad &:\text{-} e(X,Z), e(Z,Y), X \geq 5, Y \leq 8. \\
V_1(X,Y) \quad &:\text{-} e(X,Z), e(Z,Y), Z \geq 5. \\
V_2(X,Y) \quad &:\text{-} e(X,Z), e(Z,Y), Z \leq 8. \\
V_3(X,Y) \quad &:\text{-} e(X,Z_1), e(Z_1,Z_2), e(Z_2,Z_3), e(Z_3,Y).
\end{aligned}
$$

To see the intuition in this example, we begin with a simple contained rewriting:

$$P_2 \quad :\text{-} V_1(X,Z_1), V_2(Z_1,Y).$$

To see that P_2 is a contained rewriting of Q_1, let us consider its expansion:

$$P_1^{exp} \quad :\text{-} e(X,Z), e(Z,Z_1), Z \geq 5, e(Z_1,Z'), e(Z',Y), Z' \leq 8.$$

The query asks for a path of length two with two ends, the start end with value no less than five, and the other end with value no greater than eight. Looking at P_1^{exp}, this path is the $e(Z,Z_1), e(Z_1,Z')$.

Now we argue that there is no maximally contained rewriting of this query using these views in the language of unions of conjunctive queries with arithmetic comparisons. We can show that for any positive integer $k > 0$, the query P_k is a contained rewriting of Q_1:

$$P_k \;:\text{-}\; V_1(X, Z_1), V_3(Z_1, Z_2), V_3(Z_2, Z_3), \ldots, V_3(Z_{k-1}, Z_k), V_2(Z_k, Y).$$

This example shows that to find a maximally contained rewriting, we may need a language that

is more expressive than the language of the query or view definitions.

We now present an important feature of contained rewritings in the case of CQACs. This feature has to be incorporated in the theory of finding MCRs with a bounded number of subgoals. This feature leads to the introduction of AC-containment between rewritings as queries.

Containment of Rewritings—AC-containment

Unlike CQ queries and views, in the case of CQAC query and views arithmetic comparisons introduce a challenge for defining MCRs.

- We may have two contained rewritings R_1 and R_2 of a query, such that for any view instance $\mathcal{I}$, $R_2(\mathcal{I}) \subseteq R_1(\mathcal{I})$ but R_2 is not contained in R_1.

An example follows.

Example 4.10 Consider query Q and view V_2:

$$
\begin{aligned}
Q(A) \quad &:\text{-}\; p(A), A < 4. \\
V_2(Y, Z) \quad &:\text{-}\; p(X), s(Y, Z), Y \leq X, X \leq Z.
\end{aligned}
$$

The following rewriting is a contained rewriting of the query in terms of the view in the language CQAC:

$$R(Y_1) \;:\text{-}\; V_2(Y_1, Z_1), V_2(Y_2, Z_2), Z_1 \leq Y_2, Y_1 \geq Z_2, Y_1 < 4.$$

Now consider the following contained rewriting:

$$R'(X) \;:\text{-}\; V_2(X, X), X < 4.$$

This rewriting uses only one copy of the view. We can show that R is not contained in R' and that R' is not contained in R.

At the same time, we can show that for any view instance $\mathcal{I}$, $R(\mathcal{I}) = R'(\mathcal{I})$ holds. The reason is the following: if there is a tuple (y, z) in $\mathcal{I}$, then we deduce from the view definition that $y \leq z$. Thus, we can append to the definition of the rewriting R this AC, since it is always true. If we do that for both atoms in the definition of R, we obtain the ACs $Z_1 \leq Y_2, Y_1 \geq Z_2, Y_1 \leq Z_1$, and $Y_2 \leq Z_2$, which imply that $Y_1 = Z_1 = Y_2 = Z_2$. Thus, $R(\mathcal{I}) = R'(\mathcal{I})$.

Example 4.10 shows that a rewriting may have many semantically equivalent yet syntactically different variants, whose size is not necessarily a-priori bounded. It turns out that the "minimized" versions do have bounded size. In order to obtain such a "minimized" version of the rewriting, it does not suffice to simply remove subgoals, which is done in known minimization techniques, such as CQ minimization. In addition, one may have to also add comparisons. This is the reason AC-extensions are of interest. Example 4.10 motivates the following definitions and formal result.

Definition 4.11   (AC-extension of a rewriting)
Given a CQAC query, CQAC views, and CQAC contained rewriting R of the query, we define the *AC-extension R^{ext}* of R to be R with ACs added as follows: consider the expansion R^{exp} of R and the set Ext of all those ACs implied by the ACs in R^{exp} that contain only variables appearing in R. (Recall that in order to form R^{exp}, we also use fresh variables that are not included in R.) From Ext, we keep those ACs that are either semi-interval or whose both variables also appear together in the same view subgoal. We form R^{ext} by adding those ACs to R.

Definition 4.12   Let R_1 and R_2 be contained rewritings of query Q using views $\mathcal{V}$. We say that R_2 is *AC-contained* in R_1 if R_2^{ext} is contained in R_1^{ext}.

Theorem 4.13   *Suppose query Q and views $\mathcal{V}$ are CQACs. Let R be a contained rewriting of Q in the language CQAC. For every database $\mathcal{I}$ on the schema of the views (i.e., $\mathcal{I}$ is a view instance) such that there exists a database D defined on the schema of the view definitions and such that $\mathcal{I} \subseteq \mathcal{V}(D)$, tuple t is in $R(\mathcal{I})$ iff it is in $R^{ext}(\mathcal{I})$.*

Proof. The "if" direction is straightforward. For the "only-if" direction, suppose t is in $R(\mathcal{I})$. The computation of t must have used those tuples/facts in $\mathcal{I}$ that were computed when we applied the definition of some view on some database D' on the schema of the query and view definitions. Thus, the additional ACs that appear in $R^{ext}(\mathcal{I})$ already hold. (Notice that the ACs in $R^{ext}(D)$ come from each view definition separately, rather than being "cross-view" ACs.) Hence, R^{ext} can use the same tuples/facts that R used to compute t. □

You may find it interesting to observe that AC-containment does not change things in Example 4.9, because the ACs in the view definitions do not imply any ACs on their distinguished variables.

For the rest of the book, whenever we refer to rewritings containing each other as queries, we mean they are AC-contained unless otherwise mentioned.

The structure of the rest of this chapter is as follows. First, for the setting of CQ queries and views we provide an efficient algorithm, called the MS algorithm, to find a maximally contained rewriting (MCR) in the language of unions of CQs. Then, for CQAC queries and views, we extend the MS algorithm to the subclass of CQACs for which the homomorphism property holds.

In Section 4.4 we move to a more expressive language, Datalog. We describe the inverse-rule algorithm that finds an MCR for the case of Datalog queries and CQ views. Sections 4.4.2 and 4.4.4 illustrate cases where the queries and views are nonrecursive, but there is no MCR in the language of unions of CQs or CQACs. At the same time, we show that MCRs in the language of Datalog can be found.

4.2   FINDING MCRS FOR CQ QUERIES AND VIEWS: THE MS ALGORITHM

In the case of CQ queries and views, there always exists an MCR in the language of unions of CQs, due to the following result.

Theorem 4.14   *Suppose query Q and views V are CQs. For every contained rewriting R, there is a contained rewriting R' with no more subgoals than Q and such that R is contained in R'.*

Proof. Let R^{exp} be the expansion of R. There is a homomorphism h from Q to R^{exp} that uses as targets no more subgoals than the number of subgoals in Q. These target subgoals in R^{exp} came from expanding some subgoals in R. We construct R' by keeping those subgoals in R that provided the targets for h, and by deleting the rest of the subgoals of R. Now, h can still provide proof that R'^{exp} is contained in Q, Moreover, there is an obvious homomorphism from the subgoals of R' to the subgoals of R, which proves that R is contained in R'.   □

In this section, we present the algorithm called *MiniCon/Shared-Variable algorithm (MS)*; the name comes from two algorithms that were developed independently. For CQ inputs, the algorithm constructs efficiently MCRs in the language of unions of CQs. We start with an example to make some of the key points of this algorithm. In particular, we illustrate Theorem 3.14 of Section 3.2.2, and observe that it can be refined/strengthened. Of Q (Section 3.2.2) and observe that it can be refined/strengthened.

Example 4.15   Consider the following query:

$$Q : q_1(S, C) :\!- a(M, D), b(D, C), c(S, M, C)$$

and views:

$$V_1: \quad v_1(M_1, D_1, C_1) \quad :\!- a(M_1, D_1), b(D_1, C_1).$$
$$V_2: \quad v_2(S_2, M_2, C_2) \quad :\!- c(S_2, M_2, C_2).$$

Consider the contained rewriting R_1 of the query:

$$R_1: \quad q_1(S, C) \quad :\!- v_1(M, D, C), v_2(S, M, C).$$

The expansion of R_1 is

$$R_1^{exp}: \quad q_1(S,C) \quad :\text{-} \; a(M,D), b(D,C), c(S,M,C).$$

Theorem 3.14 tells us that any homomorphism from Q to this expansion can be decomposed into two partial homomorphisms, one for each view subgoal in the rewriting R_1. Let us take the first subgoal of R_1. Then, if we define $S = \{a(M,D), b(D,C), c(S,M,C)\}$, $S' = \{a(M,D), b(D,C)\}$, and homomorphism h_1 from the subgoals of Q to the subgoals of R_1^{exp} that maps M to M, C to C, and D to D, we have that (S, S', h_1) has the shared-variable property (see Definition 3.12). Observe, however, that S' is not minimal with respect to the shared-variable property. That is, there is a subset of S', $S_1' = \{a(M,D)\}$, such that (S, S_1', h) has the shared-variable property, where h maps M to M and D to D. Motivated by this example, we define such minimal triples as MCDs (MCD stands for MiniConstruction Description which is the name that was adopted in the description of the MiniCon algorithm), and refine/strengthen Theorem 3.14 to Theorem 4.18.

The following are key observations about the MS algorithm.

- We can find minimal triples even if we do not know the rewriting and its expansion, simply by considering partial mappings from the query subgoals to the subgoals of the view definitions.

- We can put together such minimal triples to construct a contained rewriting.

  We use only the view definitions to find minimal triples with the shared-variable property.

- The first triple is the (S, S_1', h) that we defined above. Since we use the view definitions, the homomorphism h is from the subgoals of the query to the subgoals of the definition for the view V_1; it maps M to M_1 and D to D_1.

- The second triple is (S, S_2', h'), where $S_2' = \{b(D,C)\}$, and h' maps D to D_1 and C to C_1.

- The third triple, which refers to the view subgoal for the view V_2, is (S, S'', h''), where $S'' = \{c(S,M,C)\}$ and h'' maps C to C_2, M to M_2, and S to S_2.

Each triple has the shared variable property; together they cover all the query subgoals. Hence, we can put them together to construct the contained rewriting R_1 of the query. The way we put them together comes from the homomorphisms h, h', and h''. First we put together the view subgoals $v_1(M_1, D_1, C_1)$ and $v_2(S_2, M_2, C_2)$ as the only subgoals in the body of the rewriting with head $q_1(S,C)$. Then we observe that variable M from the query maps (via either of the three homomorphisms h, h', and h'') to each of M_1 and M_2, hence we should have $M_1 = M_2$. Similarly, we obtain that $C_1 = C_2$. Hence, the rewriting is $q_1(S,C) :\text{-} v_1(M_1, D_1, C), v_2(S, M_1, C)$, which is syntactically isomorphic to the rewriting R_1.

Thus, we have constructed a contained rewriting in which the first and second triples correspond to the view subgoal $v_1(M,D,C)$, and the third triple—to the view subgoal $v_2(S,M,C)$ in the rewriting. However, if we do this, we miss the fact that the first two triples are "independent," meaning that we can use the subgoal $v_1(M,D,C_1)$ for the first triple, because h puts no restriction on the third variable in the head of the view definition for V_1. Hence, we introduce and use a fresh variable C_1. For the same reason we use subgoal $v_1(M_1, D, C)$, for the second triple. For the third triple we have to use subgoal $v_2(S, M, C)$. Thus, now we have constructed the contained rewriting:

$$R_2: \quad q_1(S, C) \quad :\text{-} \quad v_1(M, D, C_1), v_1(M_1', D, C), v_2(S, M, C).$$

Observe that R_1 is contained in R_2, hence R_1 does not need to be included in an MCR. We will define the rewriting R_2 as the most relaxed rewriting that comes from combining these three triples. The MS algorithm constructs such most relaxed rewritings, as we now explain formally.

4.2.1   FINDING MCDS

The discussion in the previous section hints that we may search for candidate view subgoals for a contained rewriting by considering each view definition and finding all the partial mappings from a subset of the query subgoals to the subgoals of the view definition, making sure that the shared-variable property holds. (See Definition 3.12 for the shared-variable property.) However, we do not know yet the format of the head arguments for this view in the rewriting. That is, we may have a view definition with head of the form $V(X, Y, Z)$, but the view may appear in the rewriting as subgoal $V(X, X, Z)$, or $V(Z, Y, Z)$, or $V(X, X, X)$, or $V(X, Y, Y)$. Thus, we will be looking specifically for partial containment mappings, in which we have relaxed the requirement that each query variable must map to exactly one variable in the view definition.

The requirement still holds when a query variable maps to a nondistinguished variable of a view. At the same time, a query variable is allowed to map to several distinct distinguished variables of the view. Our allowing this non-function behavior for the mappings will be reconciled at a later step of the algorithm. For now we provide the intuition: Suppose a query variable W has been mapped to variables X and Y in $V(X, Y, Z)$. Then we form a subgoal in the rewriting for this view, with head $V(X, X, Z)$, which "restores" the correctness of the mapping.

These mappings also tell us which subgoals in the rewriting share variables, and which variables are the shared variables. For example, if query variable W maps to variable X in view $V(X, Y, Z)$ and to variable Z' in $V(X', Y', Z')$, this means that $X = Z'$ in the rewriting, i.e., the rewriting will have view subgoals $V(X, Y, Z)$ and $V(X', Y', X)$, with the shared variable X.

Finally, we apply transitivity of equality to identify more variables, e.g., if we deduce from the above that $X = Y$ and $Y = Z$, we must replace these three variables with a single variable.

Definition 4.16 (MiniConstruction Description (MCD))
Let query Q and view V be CQs. Consider the relational structure S of all the atoms that are subgoals in the body of Q; let S' be any substructure, i.e., subset, of S. We will allow the homomorphism h, below, to map a variable of the query to multiple variables in the view, as long

as they are all distinguished variables in the view definition.[1] Let h be a homomorphism from the substructure S' to the relational structure comprised from the subgoals of V. We say that the triple (S, S', h) is an *MCD for view V in a rewriting of Q* (or simply an MCD when confusion does not arise) if (S, S', h) has the shared-variable property and is minimal with respect to this property, i.e., there is no S'' that is a proper subset of S' such that there exists an h' for which (S, S'', h') has the shared-variable property.

The following example illustrates the part of Definition 4.16 that says that the triple should have the shared-variable property.

Example 4.17   We revisit Example 3.13 to illustrate the shared-variable property. Consider the following two queries and views:

$$Q_1() :\text{-} a(A, B), c(B, C).$$

$$Q_2() :\text{-} a(A, B).$$

$$V_1(X, Y) :\text{-} a(X, Z), b(Z, Y).$$

$$V_2(X, Y, Z) :\text{-} a(X, Z), b(Z, Y).$$

We begin by defining sets of subgoals and homomorphism, so we may refer to them. Let set S have atoms $a(A, B), c(B, C)$, and let set S' comprise atom $a(A, B)$. These sets may refer to subgoals of either of the two queries, as determined by the context. Consider the homomorphism h_1 that maps A to X and B to Z; it may refer to variables of either query or view. Let us discuss what MCDs we can form and why.

MCD for view V_2 in a rewriting of Q_1: The triple (S, S', h_1) has the shared-variable property, as explained in Example 3.13. Moreover, there is no non-empty subset S'' of S' such that (S, S'', h_1) is an MCD. We conclude that (S, S', h_1) is an MCD.

MCD for view V_1 in a rewriting of Q_2: The triple (S', S', h_1) is an MCD.

No MCD for the view V_1 in a rewriting of Q_1: The triple (S, S', h_1) is not an MCD, because Q_1 has two subgoals, which share a variable. This prevents (S, S', h_1) from having the shared-variable property, because the shared variable B maps to Z, which is not distinguished in the definition of V_1. Interestingly, the same triple works for the view V_2, because in its definition Z is a distinguished variable.

These are all the MCDs that we can find.

---

[1]Technically, h is not a homomorphism, but we still use this term, since we will turn h into a homomorphism when considering the expansion of the assembled contained rewriting.

4.2.2   PROPERTY OF MCDS

Having defined MCD, we can now restate and strengthen Theorem 3.14 of Section 3.2.2.

Theorem 4.18   *Let R be a CQ contained rewriting of a CQ query Q using a set of CQ views V, and let E be the expansion of the rewriting R. Then any containment mapping μ from the query Q to E can be decomposed into mappings, with at least one mapping for each subgoal in the rewriting R, such that the mappings can be used to form MCDs and have the following properties: Any two MCDs that participate in this decomposition have an empty intersection (i.e., the query subgoals they cover do not overlap), and all the MCDs cover all the query subgoals.*

Proof.   We first show how to define MCDs from the given mapping μ. For each variable X of the query, if $\mu(X)$ is a non-exported variable that comes from expanding subgoal g_i^R of R, then we set $\mu_i(X) = \mu(X)$ and make μ_i the only partial mapping that X participates in. Otherwise, X may participate in two or more partial mappings, as follows: Suppose that subgoal g_i^Q of Q that contains X maps to a subgoal $\mu(g_i^Q)$ of the expansion E. (By slightly abusing the notation, we keep the same name μ for the mapping that is induced by μ on the subgoals.) Suppose subgoal $\mu(g_i^Q)$ comes from expanding subgoal g_j^R in R. Then $\mu_j(X) = \mu(X)$. However, X may occur in more than one subgoal of Q; thus, we may also have $\mu_k(X) = \mu(X)$ for some $k \neq j$. (The multiple occurrences of X in partial mappings will help later in the construction of the rewriting, by determining which variables of the view subgoals used in the rewriting should be equated to each other.) The mappings μ_i do not define MCDs yet, because they are not minimal with respect to the shared-variable property. To find the minimal mappings, we further decompose each μ_j in the finest way possible, while retaining the property that each part of the decomposition still preserves the shared-variable property. The outcome is a collection of mappings μ_{jk} for subgoal g_j^R in R.

Now we show that the MCDs thus decomposed are disjoint. A MCD either has a single exported query subgoal (i.e., it contains only exported variables), or has zero exported query subgoals. Thus, if two MCDs from the same view subgoal of the rewriting (i.e., coming from two partial mappings μ_{jk1} and μ_{jk2}) have an overlap, they have at least one non-exported subgoal g in their intersection. If subgoal g belongs in the intersection and shares a variable X with subgoal g', then it must be that either (a) X is an exported variable in both MCDs (because both have the same set of exported variables), or (b) X is a non-exported variable in both MCDs. In the latter case, g' belongs in the intersection too. The reason is, whenever two subgoals share a non-exported variable and one of the subgoals is in both MCDs, then the other has to be in each MCD due to the shared-variable property, hence the second subgoal has to be in the intersection too. Hence, the intersection has the shared-variable property, hence it is an MCD.

Thus, the MCDs of the same view subgoal of the rewriting do not overlap with each other. We finish the proof by recalling that MCDs from different view subgoals of the rewriting do not overlap by construction of the expansion.   □

4.2.3   COMBINING MCDS—MOST RELAXED REWRITING

In Section 4.2.1, as we were discussing the definition of MCD, we also showed informally how to use them, i.e., how to combine them to find the most relaxed contained rewriting of the given query. We now formalize the process in Procedure *FindMostRelaxedRewriting* (Figure 4.1). The procedure provides a systematic way to find all the CQs whose union constitutes an MCR in the language of unions of CQs.

Input: a set of MCDs.
Output: The most relaxed rewriting for the input set based on the classes of variables to
      be equated.
Method:
      For each query variable/constant X, do:
         Form a class that contains all the view variables/constants that are images of X;
      While the classes are not disjoint, do:
         Merge those classes that share an element;
      Return (the classes) or fail if there is a class containing two distinct constants.

Figure 4.1: Procedure FindMostRelaxedRewriting.

The following result says that all the rewritings found by Procedure *FindMostRelaxedRewriting* are actually contained rewritings of the given query.

Theorem 4.19   *For a set of non-overlapping MCDs that cover all the subgoals of the input query, the rewriting that is found by combining these MCDs as in Procedure* **FindMostRelaxedRewriting** *is a contained rewriting in the query.*

Now given a set of MCDs that cover all the query subgoals, we can construct more than one contained rewriting. The following result establishes the semi-lattice structure of all such contained rewritings. As a result, we can include in the MCR only the top element of the semi-lattice.

Theorem 4.20   *Let $\mathcal{R}$ be the set of all the contained rewritings of query Q using a given minimal set of MCDs that covers all the query subgoals. Then, for any pair (R_1, R_2) of rewritings in $\mathcal{R}$, there exists an R in $\mathcal{R}$ such that (a) R contains both R_1 and R_2; and (b) if there exists a rewriting R' in $\mathcal{R}$ such that R' contains both R_1 and R_2, then R' contains R as well.*

Proof.   We construct R as follows: The variables of R will be taken from the set of pairs of variables, where each pair has as its first component a variable of R_1, and has as its second component a variable of R_2. Atom $V((X_1, X_2), (Y_1, Y_2), \ldots)$ is a subgoal of R iff (a) atom $V(X_1, Y_1), \ldots)$ is a subgoal of R_1, and (b) atom $V(X_2, Y_2), \ldots)$ is a subgoal of R_2. The head of R is a sequence of the following pairs: (first variable of head of R_1, first variable of head of R_2), (second variable of head of R_1, second variable of head of R_2), and so on.

For the R thus constructed, proving part (a) in the statement of the theorem is straightforward. To prove part (b), let R' be a minimal rewriting that contains both R_1 and R_2. Therefore, there exist two containment mappings, h_1 from R' to R_1 and h_2 from R' to R_2. We create a containment mapping h from R' to R by mapping variable X of R' to the pair $(h_1(X), h_2(X))$.

□

We now summarize the algorithm MS.

1. The input is CQ query Q and set of CQ views $\mathcal{V}$.

2. Find all MCDs for each V in $\mathcal{V}$ for a rewriting of Q.

3. For each minimal set of MCDs that cover all query subgoals do:

4.   Find and output the most relaxed rewriting.

5. The resulting MCR is the union of all the most relaxed rewritings in the output.

MS algorithm
CQ query and views; finding MCRs for UCQ
The input is a CQ query and a set of CQ views.
The output is an MCR in the language of union of CQs.
For each given view, find all MCDs.
Find minimal sets of MCDs that cover all the query subgoals and do not overlap.
For each minimal set of MCDs discovered, construct the most relaxed rewriting using Procedure FindMostRelaxedRewriting.

CQ query and views: There is always an MCR in the language of union of CQs. However, an MCR in the language of CQs may not exist.

Algorithm MS is sound and complete. Theorem 4.18 says that any contained rewriting has the property of being decomposable into MCDs, hence the algorithm is complete in the sense that by using MCDs we do not miss any contained rewriting. Theorem 4.20 says that, for any combination of MCDs, if we take only the top rewriting in the semi-lattice, then all other rewritings are contained in it as queries. Thus, we do not miss any CQ contained rewriting when we form the MCR. Soundness, i.e., the fact that all the rewritings that we find are actually contained in the query, follows from Theorem 4.19.

The algorithm MS has the advantage of not considering views that do not offer the possibility of a partial mapping. In addition, the algorithm does not consider contained rewritings that are not necessary, in the sense that they are already contained in another contained rewriting.

Discussion of the Algorithms MS and CoreCover

The two algorithms, MS for finding MCRs in the language of unions of CQs and CoreCover for finding equivalent rewritings in the language of CQs, are based on the same intuition. We now discuss the differences between them, and show by examples why these differences are necessary.

The following example shows that the requirement that the MCDs be non-overlapping is necessary for the algorithm MS to be sound.

Example 4.21 Consider a query that is the path query P_7, and the view be the path query P_4. We name the subgoals of P_7 $g_1, \ldots, g_7$, in the order in which they appear along the path. Then, among others, we have two MCDs, one that covers the subgoals $g_1, \ldots, g_4$, and the other that covers the subgoals $g_4, \ldots, g_7$. The two MCDs overlap and together cover all the query subgoals. However, we can show that $R(X, Y) :- P_4(X, X_4), P_4(X_3, Y)$ is not a contained rewriting of P_7.

The following example shows that, in the CoreCover algorithm, the requirement that the tuple cores not overlap cannot be added. The reason is that adding the requirement would cause the algorithm to become incomplete.

Example 4.22 Consider query $q(X, Y) :- a(X, Y), b(X, Y), c(X, Y)$ and two views, $V_1(X, Y)$ $:- a(X, Y), b(X, Y)$ and $V_2(X, Y) :- b(X, Y), c(X, Y)$. We can show that $R(X, Y) :- V_1(X, Y), V_2(X, Y)$ is an equivalent rewriting of the query. However, the tuple core for each view tuple is the same as its body. The two tuple cores overlap, but both need to be included in the rewriting.

4.3 CQACS, THE HOMOMORPHISM PROPERTY, EXTENDING ALGORITHM MS

In this section we extend the MS algorithm to find MCRs for CQAC queries and views for the cases where the homomorphism property holds.

When looking for equivalent rewritings in Chapter 3, we would use the homomorphism property for the direction of finding homomorphisms that satisfy the ACs, from view definitions to the query canonical databases (see Theorem 3.22). This means that we were using the homomorphism property for the direction of testing whether a query is contained in a rewriting. Now we use the homomorphism property for the direction of testing whether a rewriting is contained in a query.

Definition 4.23 Let $(\mathcal{B}_1, \mathcal{B}_2)$ be a pair of sets of arithmetic comparisons that enables the homomorphism property. Let $\mathcal{V}$ be a set of CQAC views with ACs, such that all the ACs in V are in B_2, and let Q be a CQAC query whose all ACs are in B_1. Then we say that the homomorphism property holds for finding MCRs.

For queries and views in the language of CQAC, we have that when the homomorphism property holds, there always exists an MCR in the language of unions of CQACs.

Theorem 4.24 *Let Q be a query and V a set of views, such that the homomorphism property holds for finding MCRs. Then for any contained rewriting R of Q using V there exists a contained rewriting R_1 that AC-contains R, and such that the number of subgoals in R_1 is at most equal to the number of subgoals in the query.*

Proof. Consider the AC-extension R_e of R and its expansion R_e^{exp}. Since the homomorphism property holds, there is a containment mapping μ that maps all the ordinary and comparison subgoals of Q to subgoals in R_e^{exp}. The key observation here is that there are no two variables in R_e that are equated in R_e^{exp}—the reason is that all the ACs that would contribute to such an equation are already exported in R_e by definition. Thus, all the variables that are targets of μ in R_e^{exp} appear in at most n subgoals in R_e, where n is the number of subgoals in the query. Hence, we construct a rewriting R_1 by keeping those subgoals, both relational and arithmetic comparison, of R_e that contain target variables. We can show that R_1 is a contained rewriting that also contains R_e, and hence AC-contains R.   □

When the homomorphism property holds, we can use the intuition from the CQ case. When the homomorphism property does not hold, the setting is considerably more involved. The following example shows that finding an equivalent rewriting for the case of CQAC queries and views does not follow the intuition that comes from the CQ case. (As each equivalent rewriting is also a contained rewriting, this case is of interest in this chapter, whose focus is on finding maximally contained rewritings.) While the following example does not give formal evidence of the complexities of the general case, it is a simple illustration that offers a hint.

Example 4.25 Consider the query Q_1 from Example 2.14, which we also repeat here:

$$Q_1() \;:\text{-}\; r(X_1, X_2), r(X_2, X_3), r(X_3, X_4), r(X_4, X_5), r(X_5, X_1), X_1 < X_2,$$

as well as two views:

$$V_1(X_1, X_3) \quad :\text{-}\; p(X_1, X_2), p(X_2, X_3), X_1 < X_3.$$
$$V_2(X_1, X_3) \quad :\text{-}\; p(X_3, X_4), p(X_4, X_5), p(X_5, X_1).$$

The following is an equivalent rewriting of Q_1 using the views:

$$R_1() \;:\text{-}\; V_1(X_1, X_3), V_2(X_1, X_3).$$

Now consider view V_3:

$$V_3(X_1, X_3) \quad \text{:-} \quad p(X_1, X_2), p(X_2, X_3), X_1 < X_2.$$

The following rewriting R_2 is an equivalent rewriting of Q_1 using the views V_3 and V_2:

$$R_2() \text{ :- } V_3(X_1, X_3), V_2(X_1, X_3).$$

Notice that the bodies of the two rewritings are the same, with the exception that the first relation symbol is different (i.e., it is V_1 for R_1 and V_3 for R_2). However, the definitions of V_1 and V_3 are very different.

Now we turn to the cases in which the homomorphism property holds. As in the case without arithmetic comparisons, the extended MS algorithm has two parts. In the first part, we construct MCDs by finding partial mappings from the query subgoals to the view subgoals. In the second part, we combine these mappings to construct a maximally-contained rewriting. However, there are two major differences that we will explain next.

4.3.1   EXPORTABLE AND DISTINGUISHABLE VARIABLES OF AN EXPANSION

We classify the variables in the expansion of a rewriting depending on their potential to enforce ACs in other variables in the expansion of the rewriting, with the exception of the variables appearing in the heads of the view definitions. Thus, each variable in an expansion belongs to one of the following categories: exported, exportable, distinguishable, and non-exported variables. We start with examples to offer intuition for the definitions that will follow.

Exportable Variables

The following example shows that some variables behave like exported variables. This class of variables was defined in Section 3.2.2, in which we were discussing the properties of the expansion of a rewriting. We can use this example as a justification of the definition of exportable variables in the next section.

Example 4.26   We illustrate that arithmetic comparisons could "export" nondistinguished variables. Consider the following query Q_1 and views V_1 and V_2:

$$
\begin{aligned}
Q_1(A) \quad &\text{:-} \quad p(A), A \le 4. \\
V_1(Y, Z) \quad &\text{:-} \quad p(X), s(Y, Z), Y \le X, X \le Z. \\
V_2(Y, Z) \quad &\text{:-} \quad p(X), s(Y, Z), Y \le X, X < Z.
\end{aligned}
$$

The following query R is a contained rewriting of the query Q_1 using V_1:

$$R(A) \text{ :- } V_1(A, A), A \le 4.$$

To see that the containment holds, suppose we expand this query by replacing the view subgoal $V_1(A, A)$ by its definition:

$$R^{exp}(A) \text{ :- } p(X), s(A, A), A \le X, X \le A, A \le 4.$$

The arithmetic comparisons in R^{exp} imply $X = A$. (X is exported, and hence arithmetic comparisons can be added on X in the rewriting—this is done by adding $A \leq 4$ in the rewriting.) Thus, the expansion is contained in Q_1. Notice how the presence of the arithmetic comparisons helps in finding a rewriting. Indeed, consider how the two views differ. Although V_1 and V_2 differ only in their second inequalities, V_2 cannot be used to answer Q_1. The reason is that the variable X of $p(X)$ in V_2 does not appear in the head, and thus cannot be equated with another view variable appearing in the head using arithmetic comparisons. Therefore, the condition $A \leq 4$ in the query cannot be enforced on V_2. However, in V_1 the variable X of $p(X)$ was "exported" as distinguished, with the help of the proper inequalities.

Distinguishable Variables

Some variables are not necessarily exportable, but may still have some connection (via ACs) with exported or exportable variables. Hence, one can control them in rewritings by adding ACs.

Example 4.27   Consider the same views as in Example 4.26. To build on the observation of that example, consider query

$$Q'() \; :- \; p(A), A < 4.$$

Let the rewriting be as follows:

$$R'() \; :- \; V_2(Y, Z), Z < 4.$$

The constraint "< 4" is imposed on the argument Z of R' indirectly, because it is implied in the expansion of the rewriting by the two inequalities $Z < 4$ in the rewriting and $X < Z$ in the definition of the view.

Now that we presented the intuition with examples, we are ready to define the four kinds of variables.

– *Exported variables* are the variables in rewritings that occur in the head of the view subgoals.

– *Exportable variables:* A variable X is *exportable* if there are two exported variables Y and Z, such that the ACs in the view definition imply $Y \leq X$ and $X \leq Z$. We call the variables Y and Z *anchors* of X, specifically the *left anchors* and the *right anchors,* respectively. (There can be more than one left or right anchors for a given variable.) The intuition for variables of this type is that the ACs in the view definition give us the option of making these variables equal to two exported variables. As a result, we can treat variables of this type as exported.

– *Disinguishable variables:* A variable X is *distinguishable* if there is an exported variable Y such that $X\theta Y$, where θ is a comparison operator in $\{<, >, \leq, \geq, \neq\}$. If there is no other exported variable Z such that $X\theta Z\theta Y$, then Y is called an *enabling* variable of X. (There can be more than one enabling variable for a given variable.) The intuition is that we can impose certain kinds of ACs on variables of this type, due to the presence of ACs in the view definition.

– *Non-exported variables* are the rest of the variables.

4.3.2 AC-MCDS

In the case of CQAC queries and views, when the homomorphism property holds for finding MCRs, then the components of the algorithm are the same as in the CQ case. We still need to figure out how to add ACs. First, we define a seemingly straightforward replacement of an MCD, called AC-MCD. However, we add an example to show that we still need to use MCDs, because AC-MCDs as defined do not cover all the cases.

Definition 4.28 (AC-MCD)
Let query Q and view V be CQACs. Consider the relational structure S of all the relational atoms that are subgoals in the body of Q; let S' be any substructure, i.e., subset, of S. We will allow the homomorphism h, below, to map a variable of the query to multiple variables in the view, as long as they are all distinguished or exportable variables in the view definition.[2] Consider the following.

- Let h be a homomorphism from the substructure S' to the relational structure that is comprised from the subgoals of V.

- Let AC_V be a set of ACs on the head variables of the view definition, such that the following is true: The ACs in the view definition, together with the ACs in AC_V, imply the image under h of the ACs in S'.

- Suppose that the triple (S, S', h) has the shared-variable property and is minimal with respect to this property.

    Then the quadruple (S, S', h, AC_V) is an *AC-MCD for view V for rewriting Q*.

Cross-View ACs

Example 4.29 Consider the following query and views:

$$Q() :\text{-} a(X, Y), b(X', Z), Y \leq Z.$$

$$V_1 : v_1(X) :\text{-} a(X, Y), Y \leq X.$$

$$V_2 : v_2(X) :\text{-} b(X, Y), X \leq Y.$$

Compare the two rewritings of Q:

$$R_1() :\text{-} v_1(X), v_2(X').$$

$$R_2() :\text{-} v_1(X), v_2(X).$$

---

[2]Technically, h is not a homomorphism, but we still use this term, since we will turn h into a homomorphism when considering the expansion of the assembled contained rewriting.

While R_2 is contained in the query Q, R_1 is not. This example illustrates how the most relaxed rewriting is not necessarily a contained rewriting.

Now consider removing the ACs from the query Q; the result is the following query:

$$Q'() :\!\!- a(X, Y), b(X', Z).$$

Each of R_1 and R_2 is contained in Q'.

Let us provide some details. Consider the expansions of $R_1()$ and $R_2()$:

$$R_1^{exp}() :\!\!- a(X, Y), Y \leq X, b(X', Y'), X' \leq Y'.$$

$$R_2^{exp}() :\!\!- a(X, Y), Y \leq X, b(X, Y'), X \leq Y'.$$

In R_2^{exp}, we have the ACs $Y \leq X$ and $X \leq Y'$. As these ACs imply $Y \leq Y'$, there is a containment mapping from Q to R_2^{exp} such that the ACs in R_2^{exp} imply the image of the AC in Q. Observe that this is not possible for R_1^{exp}.

This example shows that AC-MCDs are not sufficient for providing contained rewritings for an MCR. Another point illustrated by the example is that the most relaxed rewriting may not work, but there could be another rewriting that works. Hence, we need to consider in the algorithm not just AC-MCDs, but also MCDs, which are formed by ignoring the ACs in the query and views. We designate the most relaxed rewriting as MCR only when all the ACs of the query are implied by the images of the ACs in the AC-MCDs; otherwise, we test for containment in the query all the rewritings formed by using MCDs and AC-MCDs. In the next section we discuss how to add the necessary ACs to a rewriting formed by using MCDs and AC-MCDs.

4.3.3   COMBINING AC-MCDS AND MCDS, AND ADDING ACS

Overall, the procedure for constructing MCRs is similar to the one for the CQ case, except that now the final step involves (a) adding the appropriate ACs and (b) combine the newly added ACs with the ACs that are already present in the expansion of the rewriting. If we are not able to add ACs in such a way that the ACs in the expansion of the rewriting imply the image of the ACs in the query, then we discard the current CQAC rewriting candidate. We now provide the details.

The original MS algorithm applies to CQ queries and views without arithmetic comparisons, and combines MCDs by finding equivalence classes of variables in the heads of view definitions. Recall that in the CQ case, when defining a containment mapping we define equivalence classes explicitly, understanding an equivalence class as a set of variables that are equated.

In the CQAC case, there is an implicit way to put variables into classes. Whenever two variables belong to the same class and there is a third variable that is connected to both by comparisons, these comparisons together with the equation of the two variables (implied by the fact that they belong to the same equivalence class) may imply that the third variable is also equal to the two others, and hence should be put into the same class. For example, suppose that variables X and Y are in the same class, and there are two comparisons, $X \leq Z$ and $Y \geq Z$. The fact that X and Y are in the same equivalence class would imply that $X = Y$; this equation, together with $X \leq Z$ and $Y \geq Z$, would then imply that $Z = X$. Hence, Z belongs to the same class as X and Y.

In the second step of the algorithm, we consider combinations of views for covering all the query subgoals. Each combination represents a candidate rewriting, and we add comparison predicates to satisfy the comparison predicates in the query. Let $X \; \theta \; c$, with θ being one of $<$ and $\leq$, be an arithmetic comparison in the query, and suppose that X is mapped to a view variable Y in a partial mapping. The expansion of a rewriting must imply the image of this restriction, i.e., $Y \; \theta \; c$. If Y is distinguished, we can just add "$Y \; \theta \; c$" to the rewriting. If Y is nondistinguished, we cannot add any arithmetic comparison using Y directly to the rewriting, since Y does not appear in the rewriting at all. However, there are two ways to satisfy this restriction even in the case where Y is nondistinguished.

- Case I: The conjunction of the arithmetic comparisons in the definition of view V implies "$Y \; \theta \; c$."

- Case II: The conjunction of the arithmetic comparisons in the definition of view V implies an AC between a non-distinguished variable Y and a distinguished variable Z; that is the AC makes Y distinguishable. In this case, we can add to the rewriting an arithmetic comparison "$Z < c$" or "$Z \leq c$," as appropriate, to satisfy "$Y \; \theta \; c$."

> **CQAC MS algorithm—the homomorphism property:** When the homomorphism property holds, in the sense that a single homomorphism from the query to the expansion of the rewriting suffices to show the containment of the expansion to the query, then the algorithm MS can be extended to find an MCR in the language of unions of CQACs.

> **CQAC existence of MCR in unions of CQs—the homomorphism property:** When the homomorphism property holds, in the sense that a single homomorphism from the query to the expansion of the rewriting suffices to show the containment of the expansion to the query, then there is always an MCR in the language of unions of CQACs.

We now summarize the algorithm Extended-MS.

1. The input is a CQAC query Q and set of CQAC views V.

2. For each set of exportable variables do:

3. Find all MCDs and AC-MCDs.

4. For each minimal set of MCDs and AC-MCDS that cover all the query subgoals, do:

5. Combine the MCDs and AC-MCDs in the set to form a candidate rewriting R.

6. Consider rewriting R and all the containment mappings from Q to R^{exp}. For each containment mapping, do:

7. Add ACs to the variables of R^{exp} that are also variables of R, so that the ACs in the thus enhanced R^{exp} imply the image (under the considered containment mapping) of the ACs in Q.

8. Return R', which is R enhanced with the ACs added in Step 7.

9. The MCR of Q using V is the union of all the returned rewritings.

Theorem 4.30 *The algorithm Extended-MS finds an MCR in the language of unions of CQACs in the cases where the homomorphism property holds for finding MCRs.*

Proof. Let R be a contained rewriting of the given query, and let R^{exp} be the expansion of R in which we the variables have been equated in such a way that the ACs in R^{exp} do not imply equalities. This means that exportable variables are exported. Notice that this is the only way that variables other than exported variables may be included among the variables that it is possible to equate to other variables or values. Thus, the assumption that equalities are not implied by the ACs in R^{exp} covers the part of considering all sets of exportable variables in the algorithm.

Let h be a mapping from the given query Q to R^{exp} such that h proves containment of R^{exp} in Q. The mapping h can be seen as a containment mapping from the query with its ACs removed to the expansion with its ACs removed. Thus, the decomposition into MCDs is the same as in the case without ACs. Since the algorithm does not consider most relaxed rewritings, there is nothing else to prove. The introduction of AC-MCDs is thus just an optimization step, as the algorithm is already correct without considering them.   □

Example 4.31   Consider the following query and views:

$$
\begin{aligned}
Q() \quad &\text{:-} \quad t(A), A < 3. \\
V_1() \quad &\text{:-} \quad t(X_1), X_1 < 3. \\
V_2(X_3) \quad &\text{:-} \quad t(X_1), p(X_2, X_3), X_2 \le X_1, X_1 \le X_3. \\
V_3(X_2, X_3) \quad &\text{:-} \quad t(X_1), p(X_2, X_3, X_4), X_2 \le X_1, X_3 \le X_1, X_1 \le X_4.
\end{aligned}
$$

By mapping the query subgoal $t(A)$ to the subgoal $t(X_1)$ of the view V_1, we obtain a partial mapping μ that maps the variable A to X_1. This forms the MCD $(\{t(A)\}, \{t(A)\}, \mu, \emptyset)$. For a rewriting of the query Q that uses this view, the expansion of the rewriting should entail $\mu(A < 3)$, i.e., $X_1 < 3$.

Now consider view V_2; since V_2 has a comparison predicate $X_1 \le X_3$ and X_3 is distinguished, we can add $X_3 < 3$ to satisfy the inequality $X_1 < 3$. Thus, if we take μ' as the mapping from the variable of Q to the variable X_1 of V_2, we obtain the MCD $(\{t(A)\}, \{t(A)\}, \mu', \{X_1 < 3\})$. The comparison predicate in V_1 belongs to Case I, since its comparison predicate $X_1 < 3$ can satisfy this inequality. The comparison predicates in V_2 belong to Case II.

The comparison predicates in V_3 do not belong to either case, thus V_3 cannot be used to cover the query subgoal. Thus, V_3 cannot be used to form a subgoal in any contained rewriting. As a result, we obtain two CQACs each of which is a contained rewriting of Q; their union is an MCR for Q:

$$
R_1() \text{:-} \ V_1(). \qquad R_2() \text{:-} \ V_2(X_3), X_3 < 3.
$$

4.4   DATALOG

As discussed earlier, the language of MCR is a critical differentiator for whether an MCR exists for the given query and views. In this section, we move to a more expressive language, Datalog, which has recursion. After defining Datalog, in Section 4.4.2 we provide an example with a CQ query and UCQ views, to illustrate that recursion may sometimes be necessary in finding MCRs. (In this book, we will not elaborate further on the case of UCQ views.) In Section 4.4.3 we provide an algorithm for finding MCRs for the case of Datalog queries and CQ views. In Section 4.4.4 we illustrate with an example another case in which Datalog is needed to obtain an MCR for the inputs in the language of CQACs.

4.4.1 DEFINITION OF THE DATALOG LANGUAGE

We have already defined Datalog rules in Chapter 2, where we used the notion to define conjunctive queries. A *Datalog program* is a set of Datalog rules. The predicates that appear in the heads of the rules are called *Intensional Database (IDB)* predicates; the predicates that appear only in the bodies of the rules are called *Extensional Database (EDB)* predicates. We evaluate a query given by a Datalog program on a database that consists of relations that correspond to the EDB predicates. (That is, the EDB predicates represent the relations in the database.) The evaluation is done by evaluating the rules on the database until no more facts are added to the set of the derived IDB predicates. (That is, the evaluation follows the fixpoint, or minimal model, semantics.) The *answer to a Datalog program on a database* is a set of facts derived on the database for a designated IDB predicate, which is called the *query predicate* of the program.

A *partial expansion* of a Datalog program is a conjunctive query that results from unfolding the rules one or more times; the partial expansion may contain IDB predicates. An *expansion* of a Datalog program is a partial expansion that contains only EDB predicates. To avoid confusion with the expansion of a rewriting, when it is not clear from the context, we will use the term *program-expansion* to refer to an expansion of a Datalog program. A Datalog program is, in general, equivalent to an infinite set of conjunctive queries, with one such query for each expansion. A *derivation tree* of a fact computed by a Datalog program on an EDB database comes from the way we unfold the rules to obtain the fact. The *tree of a partial expansion* is similar to the derivation tree, with the exception that each node contains atoms of IDB and EDB predicates. The leaves of the tree contain either EDBs or IDBs that are not unfolded.

We now provide an illustration for derivation trees, as well as for trees for partial expansions and expansions.

Example 4.32 Consider a Datalog program that computes the transitive closure on a graph given as binary EDB relation e.

$$q(X, Y) :- e(X, Y).$$

$$q(X, Y) :- q(X, Z), e(Z, Y).$$

This program has one nonrecursive rule, the first rule above, and one recursive rule—the second rule.

One partial expansion is as follows:

$$q(X, Y) :- q(X, Z), e(Z, Y'), e(Y', Y).$$

This partial expansion was created by unfolding the atom with predicate q in the recursive rule using the same rule. The tree of this partial expansion is shown in Figure 4.2. We construct this tree as follows: Start with the root $q(X, Y)$; use the recursive rule to unfold, which results in the two children of the root, $q(X, Y')$ and $e(Y', Y)$. (We use Y' to replace Z in the recursive rule.) Then unfold $q(X, Y')$, to obtain the two children $q(X, Z)$ and $e(Z, Y')$. (In the recursive rule, we replace X with X, Y with Y', and Z with Z.)

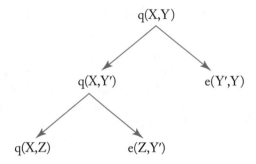

Figure 4.2: The tree for partial expansion $q(X, Y) :- q(X, Z), e(Z, Y'), e(Y', Y)$.

One expansion is as follows:

$$q(X, Y) :- e(X, Z), e(Z, Y'), e(Y', Y).$$

This expansion is obtained from the above partial expansion by unfolding $q(X, Z)$ using the nonrecursive rule. The corresponding tree is shown in Figure 4.3. Comparing Figure 4.2 with Figure 4.3, we observe that the tree for the partial expansion has a leaf that corresponds to the IDB-predicate atom, while in the expansion tree, all the leaves are EDB atoms.

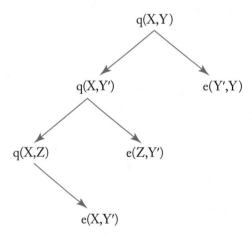

Figure 4.3: The tree for expansion $q(X, Y) :- e(X, Z), e(Z, Y'), e(Y', Y)$.

Now consider a database instance D for predicate e: $D = \{(a, b), (b, c), (c, d)\}$. Let us compute $q(a, d)$, illustrating the computation with the derivation tree of Figure 4.4. We use the nonrecursive rule to compute $q(a, b)$, by replacing X with a and Y with b. This is illustrated at the lowest level of Figure 4.4, where $q(a, b)$ has the only child $e(a, b)$. We then use the recursive rule to compute the fact $q(a, c)$, by replacing X with a, Y with c, and Z with b. This is illustrated in the part of the tree in Figure 4.4 that shows the two children, $q(a, b)$ and $e(b, c)$, of the node $q(a, c)$. We then use the recursive rule again, to compute the root $q(a, d)$, whose children are the facts are used for its computation. This step completes the computation process.

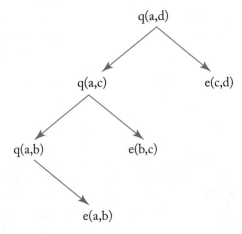

Figure 4.4: Derivation tree that corresponds to the expansion of Figure 4.3.

Observe that the trees of Figure 4.3 and Figure 4.4 are the same, with the exception that the variables of Figure 4.3 are replaced by constants in Figure 4.4. This is no coincidence, because the expansion $q(X, Y) :- e(X, Z), e(Z, Y'), e(Y', Y)$ was used as a conjunctive query to compute $q(a, d)$. The way this expansion tree was constructed was a top-down construction of the derivation tree in Figure 4.4, which was in turn constructed in the bottom-up fashion.

For more details on the Datalog language, see textbooks mentioned in the bibliographical notes in the end of this book.

4.4.2 VIEWS THAT ARE UNIONS OF CQS

In this section we consider views that are unions of CQs, also referred to as "disjunctive views." This section provides a single example, which illustrates that for views in this language, Datalog could be used to find an MCR of a CQ query.

Example 4.33 Consider query Q and views V_1 through V_3:

$$Q() :- c(X, Y), a(Z', Y), b(Y, Z).$$

$$v_1(Y) :- a(X, Y).$$

The view V_2 is a disjunctive view with two rules:

$$v_2(X, Y, Z) :- c(X, Y), b(Y, Z), c(X', Z).$$

$$v_2(X, Y, Z) :- c(X, Y), a(Y, Z), c(X', Z).$$

The view V_3 is as follows:

$$v_3(X) :- b(X, Y).$$

To find a contained rewriting of Q using these three views, we have to use the view V_2, as it is the only view that has an occurrence of an atom with relational symbol c. Thus, a contained rewriting is the following:

$$R_0() :- v_1(X), v_2(Z, X, W_1), v_3(W_1).$$

Its expansion is

$$R_0^{exp}() :- a(W, X), c(Z, X), d_{ab}(X, W_1), c(X_1', W_1), b(W_1, W').$$

Here, we use the symbol d_{ab} to denote that the relational atom $d_{ab}(X, W_1)$ is either $a(X, W_1)$ or $b(X, W_1)$, according to the definition of view V_2. If $d_{ab}(X, W_1)$ is $b(X, W_1)$, then the containment mapping that proves the containment of this expansion in the query maps X to Z, Y to X, Z' to W, and Z to W_1. If, on the other hand, $d_{ab}(X, W_1)$ is $a(X, W_1)$, then the containment mapping that proves the containment of this expansion in the query maps X to X_1', Y to W_1, Z' to X, and Z to W'.

We can build many contained rewritings of Q by using any number of occurrences of the view V_2. In fact, for any natural number i, the following is a contained rewriting in Q using the given views:

$$R() :- v_1(X), v_2(Z, X, W_1), v_2(Z, W_1, W_2), v_2(Z, W_2, W_3), \ldots v_2(Z, W_i, W_{i+1}), v_3(W_{i+1}).$$

Since there are infinitely many contained rewritings, Datalog may be a language in which we can find an MCR for this case.

4.4.3 REWRITING DATALOG QUERIES—THE INVERSE-RULE ALGORITHM

Consider a setting in which the query definition is a Datalog program, and the view definitions are conjunctive queries.

Definition 4.34 For each rule $\mathcal{R}$ that defines a view, we construct a number of *inverse rules*, one inverse rule $\mathcal{R}_i$ for each subgoal of the rule $\mathcal{R}$, as follows. Suppose $\mathcal{R}$ is defined as

$$q(\overline{X}) :- g_1(\overline{X}_1), \ldots, g_n(\overline{X}_n).$$

Then for each subgoal $g_i(\overline{X}_i)$ in $\mathcal{R}$ we construct the inverse rule $\mathcal{R}_i$:

$$g_i(\overline{Y}_i) :- q(\overline{X}).$$

Here, the variable X in $\overline{Y}_i$ is the same as in $\overline{X}_i$ if X appears in $\overline{X}$ (and in the same position of $\overline{Y}_i$ as in $\overline{X}_i$), otherwise X is replaced by $f^X(\overline{X})$ in the same position. Here, f^X is a function symbol that is different for each non-distinguished variable X of the view.

Construction of the inverse-rule program: Suppose we are given a Datalog query Q and set $\mathcal{V}$ of CQ views. The *inverse-rule program* π_Q of Q with respect to the view set $\mathcal{V}$ is constructed as follows. The program consists of the rules of the query Q, together with the inverse rules obtained from the views in $\mathcal{V}$. The *function-free output of the inverse-rule program* comprises those output tuples of this program that do not contain function symbols.

Consider an illustration of the construction.

Example 4.35 Consider a query Q defined by the following Datalog program:

$$q(X,Y) :\text{-} e(X,Y).$$

$$q(X,Y) :\text{-} q(X,Z), e(Z,Y).$$

Let the view V be defined as

$$V(X,Y) :\text{-} e(X,Z), e(Z,Y).$$

For this view, we obtain two inverse rules:

$$e(X, f(X,Y)) :\text{-} V(X,Y).$$

$$e(f(X,Y), Y) :\text{-} V(X,Y).$$

Here, $f(X,Y)$ intuitively represents the value of Z in the view definition, because Z appears in the subgoal but not in the head. The function f is the same in each of the inverse rules created from the view definition. The reason is, while we don't know the value of Z that is needed for making the body of this rule true for a given X and Y, we do know that it has to be the same Z in each of the subgoals of the view V.

The following is the inverse-rule program π_Q of the query Q using the view V:

$$q(X,Y) :\text{-} e(X,Y).$$

$$q(X,Y) :\text{-} q(X,Z), e(Z,Y).$$

$$e(X, f(X,Y)) :\text{-} V(X,Y).$$

$$e(f(X,Y), Y) :\text{-} V(X,Y).$$

The program has one EDB predicate, V, and is constructed as follows: the first two rules are copied from the definition of q, and the remaining rules are the inverse rules.

Now we show that the inverse-rule program π_Q with respect to view set $\mathcal{V}$ is an MCR of Q using $\mathcal{V}$ in the language of Datalog.

Theorem 4.36 *The function-free output of the inverse-rule program π_Q of Q with respect to $\mathcal{V}$ is contained in Q.*

Proof. We prove first that the computation of the inverse-rule program terminates, i.e., that any finite-size relations for the views in $\mathcal{V}$ produce a finite number of tuples for the predicate q. We argue as follows: Observe that there is a finite set of values that can appear in tuples in the heads of the rules of the inverse-rule program. (Some of these values are of the form $f^X(\overline{c})$, that is, they use a function symbol with $\overline{c}$ being a vector of values from the input view relations.) Since there are only a finite set of tuples that could ever be deduced for an IDB relation, then the Datalog program will terminate.

Observe that every bottom-up evaluation of this program progresses in two stages: the recursive stage, which uses the program of the query, and then the non-recursive stage, which uses the inverse rules. Thus, the evaluation terminates whenever the Datalog program of the query terminates.

We now prove the containment. Consider the bottom-up evaluation of π_Q, and take the derivation tree T that is constructed during the computation. The leaves of this tree T are view facts, but their parents are EDB predicates of the Datalog program that computes Q, and the rest of the tree is the same as a derivation tree T' of the Datalog program that computes Q. The derivation trees T and T' correspond to program-expansions E and E'. Viewing E as a rewriting, we prove now that it is a contained rewriting in Q. Consider any leaf in the derivation tree T. This leaf is some view fact $V_i(t)$, whose parent, say $e_j(t')$, came from the construction of an inverse rule (and is the head of this inverse rule), hence it appears in the body of the view definition of V_i. Thus, an atom $e_j(t'')$ instantiated according to the definition of view V_i appears in E^{exp} as well. It is easy to check that there is a mapping from E' to E^{exp} that maps $e_j(t')$ to $e_j(t'')$. This proves containment in E' of the expansion E^{exp} of E. □

Theorem 4.37 *The funcion-free output of the inverse-rule program of Q with respect to $\mathcal{V}$ is equal to the output of an MCR of Q using views in $\mathcal{V}$.*

Proof. Since a Datalog program is equivalent to an infinite union of CQs, it suffices to prove that any CQ rewriting R that is contained in Q is also contained in the function-free output of the inverse-rule program of Q with respect to $\mathcal{V}$. Since R is a contained rewriting of Q, its expansion R^{exp} is contained in Q. The homomorphism from a program-expansion of Q to R^{exp} yields a homomorphism h from the program-expansion of the inverse-rule program of Q using views $\mathcal{V}$ to R^{exp}. To show that, we follow the argument used in the proof of Theorem 4.36. □

Datalog queries, CQ views, MCR inverse-rule program
Constructing the inverse-rule program:

- Use view definitions to obtain inverse rules that use function symbols.

- Construct the inverse-rule program from the Datalog program defining the query and from the inverse rules.

- The output of the inverse-rule program is the tuples computed in the query predicate of the Datalog program that do not contain function symbols among their values.

Eliminating the function symbols: We can produce a program without function symbols; it would yield the function-free output of the inverse-rule program. We do that by *predicate splitting*. The intuition for predicate splitting is that we partition the output of a specific IDB predicate according to which function symbols occur among its arguments, and in which argument positions these function symbols occur. For example, if a predicate p has arity three and we use two function symbols, we will split p into 3^{2+1} new predicates, which we denote using adornments as $p^{*,*,*}$ (for the outputs without function symbols), $p^{*,f_1(*,*...,*),*}$ (for the outputs with function symbol f_1 in the second place only), $p^{*,f_2(*,*...,*),*}$ (for the outputs with function symbol f_2 in the second place only), etc. The number of new predicates is $(2+1)^3$, because we also count the case in which a constant appears without function symbols.

For instance, in working with the IDB predicate q of Example 4.35, we would split it into four new predicates, denoted as $q^{*,*}$, $q^{f(*,*),*}$, $q^{*,f(*,*)}$, and $q^{f(*,*),f(*,*)}$. Now, since we would prefer to work with notation that does not use function symbols, the arity of the adorned predicates would change appropriately. That is, $q^{*,*}$ has arity two, $q^{f(*,*),*}$ and $q^{*,f(*,*)}$ each have arity three, and $q^{f(*,*),f(*,*)}$ has arity four.

The general procedure for eliminating function symbols is as follows: We define an adornment of a predicate p to be a vector with one component for each argument of p, and each argument can be either $*$ (meaning no function symbol) or a function symbol. For each function symbol in the adornment, we do not have to state its arity by using $*$; we still do that, because this makes the arity of the predicate explicit—and thus improves readability. We consider all possible adornments for p, proceeding as follows. For each rule with head predicate p, produce from the rule one or more rules, according to the number of possible adornments of p. For each particular adornment α, we proceed as follows to produce the rules with head p^α. For convenience, we have a preliminary stage where we keep the function symbols in the arguments of p^α in a way that is consistent with α. For example, for $\alpha = *, f(*, *)$, we have $p^\alpha(X, f(Y, Z))$. Then we propagate the variables or functions of variables to the body of the rule, i.e., if the second argument of p appears in a position in some subgoal, we replace the variable in this position with $f(Y, Z)$. Now, if there are no non-distinguished variables in the body, all that remains to be done is to add adornments to the predicates in the body of the rule that follow the pattern in the arguments. For example, if the arguments are $X, Y, f(X, W, W'), Z$, we add the adornment $*, *, f(*, *, *), *$. On the other hand, if there are non-distinguished variables in some arguments in the body, then we construct more than one rule, considering all combinations of those arguments being either $*$ or one of the function symbols used in the inverse rules. In the end, we drop the function symbols in the arguments of the predicates, by simply deleting them and listing the variables as they appear. Notice that this means, e.g., that predicate $p^{*,*}$ will have two arguments, but predicate $p^{f(*,*,*),*}$ will have four arguments. The output of this function-free program is the tuples in the query predicate with adornments $*, *, * \ldots$. A detailed example follows.

Example 4.38   In Example 4.35, we obtained for the predicate q four adorned predicates, $q^{*,*}$, $q^{f(*,*),*}, q^{*,f(*,*)}$, and $q^{f(*,*),f(*,*)}$. Now for the IDBs in the head of each inverse rule, we have trivially only one adorned predicate. This way, we obtain a new program as shown below. Here, we use a broken line to separate the rules in accordance with which rules of the MCR provided in Example 4.35 generate each of these new rules. In other words, the first four rules below originate from the first rule for the MCR of Example 4.35, the next eight rules originate from the second rule, and the last two rules originate from the third and fourth rules, respectively.

$q^{*,*}(X, Y) :- e^{*,*}(X, Y)$. It is easy to see that this rule will never be used.
$q^{*,f(*,*)}(X, W, Y) :- e^{*,f(*,*)}(X, W, Y)$. This rule will be used only when $W = X$.
$q^{f(*,*),*}(X, W, Y) :- e^{f(*,*),*}(X, W, Y)$. This rule will be used only when $W = Y$.
$q^{f(*,*),f(*,*)}(X, Y, Y) :- e^{f(*,*),f(*,*)}(X, Y, Y)$. This rule will never be used.

$q^{*,*}(X, Y) :- q^{*,f(*,*)}(X, Z, Y'), e^{f(*,*),*}(Z, Y', Y)$.
$q^{*,*}(X, Y) :- q^{*,*}(X, Z,), e^{*,*}(Z, Y)$. This rule will never be used.
$q^{f(*,*),*}(X, Y, Z) :- q^{f(*,*),f(*,*)}(X, Y, X', Y'), e^{f(*,*),*}(X', Y', Z)$.
$q^{f(*,*),*}(X, Y, Z) :- q^{f(*,*),*}(X, Y, X'), e^{*,*}(X', Z)$. This rule will never be used.
$q^{*,f(*,*)}(X, Y, Z) :- q^{*,f(*,*)}(X, X', Y'), e^{f(*,*),f(*,*)}(X', Y', Y, Z)$. This rule will never be used.
$q^{*,f(*,*)}(X, Y, Z) :- q^{*,*}(X, X'), e^{*,f(*,*)}(X', Y, Z)$.
$q^{f(*,*),f(*,*)}(X, Y, Z, W) :- q^{f(*,*),*}(X, Y, Z'), e^{*,f(*,*)}(Z', Z, W)$.
$q^{f(*,*),f(*,*)}(X, Y, Z, W) :- q^{f(*,*),f(*,*)}(X, Y, X', Y'), e^{f(*,*),f(*,*)}(X', Y', Z, W)$. This rule will never be used.

$e^{*,f(*,*)}(X, X, Y) :- V(X, Y)$.

$e^{f(*,*),*}(X, Y, Y) :- V(X, Y)$.
The output of the program will be the tuples in predicate $q^{*,*}$.

We have mechanically listed all the rules. It is not hard to see that some of the rules are useless (see the comments above). The reason is that, e.g., predicate $e^{*,*}$ will never have any tuples, because the two inverse rules (the two last rules in the program) provide tuples only for predicates $e^{*,f(*,*)}$ and $e^{f(*,*),*}$, and these are the only rules that provide tuples for predicate e with any adornment.

To see how we do the bookkeeping of which variables to use in the adorned predicates, we use a preliminary stage. For instance, to get the rule

$$q^{f(*,*),*}(X,Y,Z) :\text{-} q^{f(*,*),f(*,*)}(X,Y(X',Y'), e^{f(*,*),*}(X',Y',Z),$$

as explained in the general procedure of function-symbol elimination, we write first the more intuitive rule $q^{f(*,*),*}(f(X,Y),Z) :\text{-} q^{f(*,*),f(*,*)}(f(X,Y),f(X',Y')), e^{f(*,*),*}(f(X',Y'),Z)$, and then drop the function symbols.

Now we are going to derive a more compact (i.e., with fewer rules) equivalent program by making the following observations.

- The only useful rule with head $q^{*,*}$ is the first rule in the second group of rules.

- This rule uses $q^{*,f(*,*)}$ as the only recursive predicate; the only useful rules with head $q^{*,f(*,*)}$ are (a) the second rule in the first group of rules, and (b) the sixth rule in the second group of rules.

- It turns out that these three rules are the only rules apart from the two inverse rules that will be used to provide tuples in $p^{*,*}$. We show below how this is done.

Consider the first rule of the second group; we unfold its first subgoal using the sixth rule of the second group. After the unfolding, this yields

$$q^{*,*}(X,Y) :\text{-} q^{*,*}(X,X'), e^{*,f(*,*)}(X',Z,Y'), e^{f(*,*),*}(Z,Y',Y).$$

We have already seen that we only have tuples in $e^{*,f(*,*)}$ if its first two arguments are equal, and that we only have tuples for $e^{f(*,*),*}$ if its last two arguments are equal. For this reason, we can use the above rule only if $X' = Z$ and $Y' = Y$. Thus, we rewrite the rule after replacing Z with X' and Y' with Y:

$$q^{*,*}(X,Y) :\text{-} q^{*,*}(X,X'), e^{*,f(*,*)}(X',X',Y), e^{f(*,*),*}(X',Y,Y).$$

Using the first inverse rule, we replace $e^{*,f(*,*)}(X',X',Y)$ with $V(X',Y)$; using the other inverse rule, we replace $e^{f(*,*),*}$ with $V(X',Y)$. This yields the rule

$$q^{*,*}(X,Y) :\text{-} q^{*,*}(X,X'), V(X',Y).$$

With similar reasoning, we also obtain the base rule

$$q^{*,*}(X,Y) :\text{-} V(X,Y).$$

These are the two rules of a compact equivalent program.

Note that the equivalence of the program with function symbols to the program without function symbols is straightforward. Indeed, by doing function-symbol elimination, we simply "hide" the function symbols in the adornments of the predicates; hence, they become implicit rather than explicit.

Function-symbol elimination of the inverse-rule program

- Introduce adornments for predicate symbols.

- For each predicate symbol, introduce their adorned version.

- From each rule of the inverse-rule program, construct a collection of rules using the adorned versions of the predicates.

The procedure of function-symbol elimination may result in the empty query. Consider an example.

Example 4.39   Let query Q be given by the following Datalog program:
$q(X, Y) :- e_1(X, Z), e_2(Z, Y).$
　　$q(X, Y) :- q(X, Z), e_1(Z, Z'), e_2(Z', Y).$
Suppose we are also given two views, defined as follows: $V_1(X, Y) :- e_1(X, Z), e_1(Z, Y).$
　　$V_2(X, Y) :- e_2(X, Z), e_2(Z, Y).$
The Datalog query q computes all those paths in a labeled graph whose arcs are labeled $e_1 e_2 e_1 e_2 \cdots$. It turns out that the given views cannot be combined into a contained rewriting of q in the language of CQ. Indeed, one of the views returns paths labeled $e_1 e_1$, and the other view returns paths labeled $e_2 e_2$. We construct now the inverse-rule program to verify this intuition.

The following is the inverse-rule program π_Q of the query Q using the views V_1 and V_2:
$q(X, Y) :- e_1(X, Z), e_2(Z, Y).$
　　$q(X, Y) :- q(X, Z), e_1(Z, Z'), e_2(Z', Y).$
　　$e_1(X, f_1(X, Y)) :- V_1(X, Y).$
　　$e_1(f_1(X, Y), Y) :- V_1(X, Y).$
　　$e_2(X, f_2(X, Y)) :- V_2(X, Y).$
　　$e_2(f_2(X, Y), Y) :- V_2(X, Y).$
The first rule of this program will not produce any outputs that would not contain function symbols, for any view instance. Indeed, the first rule can only be applied to the outputs of the last four inverse rules. Thus, $e_1(X, Z)$ can be replaced either by $e_1(x, f_1(x, y))$ or by $e_1(f_1(x, y), y)$, for some constants x and y. In the first case, the second atom $e_2(Z, Y)$ should be such that Z is replaced by $f_1(x, y)$. But there is no atom of the form $e_2(f_1(x, y), y)$ derived from the last two rules. Hence, this case will not derive any atom in the output of q. The second case is possible

and will derive an atom of the form $q(f_1(x, y), f_2(x, y))$. If we substitute such an output into the second, recursive, rule, we will need an atom of the form $e_1(f_2(x, y), Z')$, which cannot be derived from the two rules with head e_1. Hence, the function-symbol-free output of the above program will be empty for any view instance. In fact, the recursive rule (the second rule above) will never be used.

We now discuss function-symbol elimination. Using the reasoning from Example 4.38, we can obtain the rule

$$q^{*,*}(X, Y) :- q^{*,*}(X, X'),$$
$$e_1^{*,f_1(*,*)}(X', W, W')e_2^{f_1(*,*),f_1(*,*)}(W, W'Z, Y'),$$
$$e_1^{f_1(*,*),f_1(*,*)}(Z, Y', W_1, W_2), e_2^{f_1(*,*),*}(W_1, W_2, Y).$$

This rule will never be used, because there is no predicate $e_2^{f_1(*,*),f_1(*,*)}$. In general, unfolding will yield either predicates $e_i^{*,*}$, or predicates e_1 with adornment containing function symbol f_2, or predicates e_2 with adornment containing function symbol f_1. Since there are no such predicates in the rules of the inverse-rule program, the output of the program is always empty.

4.4.4 CQAC-SI QUERIES AND VIEWS

We now present an example with CQAC query and views whose all comparisons are semi-interval (CQAC-SI) comparisons. We show that there is no MCR in the language of unions of CQs for this example. We also show that a Datalog rewriting is a contained rewriting.

Example 4.40 We revisit Example 4.9. Consider query Q_1 and views V_1, V_2, and V_3, defined as follows:

$$
\begin{aligned}
Q_1() \quad &:- \ e(X, Z), e(Z, Y), X \geq 5, Y \leq 8. \\
V_1(X, Y) \quad &:- \ e(X, Z), e(Z, Y), Z \geq 5. \\
V_2(X, Y) \quad &:- \ e(X, Z), e(Z, Y), Z \leq 8. \\
V_3(X, Y) \quad &:- \ e(X, Z_1), e(Z_1, Z_2), e(Z_2, Z_3), e(Z_3, Y).
\end{aligned}
$$

The following Datalog program is a contained rewriting of the input query Q_1 using the views $V_1(X, Y)$, $V_2(X, Y)$, and $V_3(X, Y)$:

$$
\begin{aligned}
R() \quad &:- \ V_1(X, W), T(W, Z), V_2(Z, Y). \\
T(W, W) \quad &:- \ . \\
T(W, Z) \quad &:- \ T(W, U), V_3(U, Z).
\end{aligned}
$$

To prove that this is a contained rewriting, we need to prove that each program-expansion is a contained rewriting. We provide an argument for one of the expansions; the reasoning is similar for the other expansions.

We focus on the following program expansion:
$$E() :- V_1(X, W), V_3(Z_1, Z_2)V_2(Z_2, Y).$$

Consider the expansion E^{exp} of E:

$$E^{exp}() :\!- e(X, Z), e(Z, W), Z \geq 5, e(W, Z_1'), e(Z_1', Z_2'), e(Z_2', Z_3'), e(Z_3', Z_1), e(Z_1, Z_1''),$$
$$e(Z_1'', Z_2''), e(Z_2'', Z_3''), e(Z_3'', Z_2), e(Z_2, Z_4), e(Z_4, Y), Z_4 \leq 8.$$

To show that E^{exp} is contained in Q_1, we argue informally as follows: Either there is a mapping that satisfies the ACs from the subgoals of Q_1 to the second and fourth subgoals of E^{exp}, which means that $Z_1' \leq 8$, or $Z_1' > 8$, which means $Z_1' \geq 5$. If the latter is true, then either there is a mapping from the subgoals of Q_1 to the fifth and sixth subgoals of E^{exp}, which means that $Z_3' \leq 8$, or $Z_3' > 8$, which means $Z_3' \geq 5$. The argument goes on in a similar way, until we either find a mapping that satisfies the ACs, or we have arrived in the end of E^{exp} without finding such a mapping. We thus derive that $Z_3'' \geq 5$. Thus, also taking into account that $Z_4 \leq 8$, we conclude that there is a mapping that satisfies the ACs on the subgoals $e(Z_3'', Z_2)$ and $e(Z_2, Z_4)$ of E^{exp}.

4.5   EXERCISES

4.1.   Consider query

$$Q : q_1(S, C) :\!- a(M, D), b(D, C), c(S, M, C).$$

and views

$$
\begin{array}{lll}
V_1: & v_1(M_1, D_1, C_1) & :\!- a(M_1, D_1), b(D_1, C_1). \\
V_2: & v_2(S_2, M_2, C_2) & :\!- c(S_2, M_2, C_2). \\
V_3: & v_3(M_3, D_3, C_3) & :\!- a(M_3, D_3), b(D_3, C_3).
\end{array}
$$

Find an MCR in the language of unions of CQs.

4.2.   In the following Example 4.41, prove that the suggested rewriting is an MCR in the language of unions of CQs.

Example 4.41   Consider a CQ query Q that is the path query P_7, and CQ views that are path queries P_2 and P_3 (recall the definition of path queries in Definition 2.44). Let the language of rewritings be unions of CQs (UCQ). The following rewriting, which consists of CQs R_1, R_2, and R_3, is the MCR for the language UCQ:

$R_1 : q(X, Y) :\!- P_2(X, Z), P_3(Z, Z'), P_2(Z', Y).$

$R_2 : q(X, Y) :\!- P_2(X, Z), P_2(Z, Z'), P_3(Z', Y).$

$R_3 : q(X, Y) :\!- P_3(X, Z), P_2(Z, Z'), P_2(Z', Y).$

Each of R_1, R_2, and R_3 individually happens to be an equivalent rewriting of the query Q using the given views. However, we need them all in a union-of-CQs rewriting to construct an MCR. To see why, observe that, for instance, R_1 is not contained in R_2 (as queries), although R_1^{exp} and R_2^{exp} are equivalent.

4.3. Modify the CoreCover algorithm so that the containment test would not be needed. Hint: decompose the tuple cores into MCDs.

4.4. Consider query Q that is a path query P_9; let the three views be path queries P_3, P_6, and P_7. Find an MCR of Q using the views in the language of unions of CQs.

4.5. Consider the query and views of Example 4.9. Prove that, for any positive integer $k > 0$, the following is a contained rewriting of the query using the views:

$$R_k \; :\!\!- \; V_1(X, Z_1), V_3(Z_1, Z_2), V_3(Z_2, Z_3), \ldots, V_3(Z_{k-1}, Z_k), V_2(Z_k, Y).$$

4.6. Consider query Q and view V:

$$Q() :\!\!- p(X, Y), p(Y, Z), s(X, Z), p(Z, Y'), p(Y', Z'), s(Z, Z'), t(Z).$$

$$V(Z, W) :\!\!- p(X, Y), p(Y, Z), s(X, Z''), p(Z, Y'), p(Y', Z'), s(Z'', Z'), t(W),$$

$$Z \leq Z'' \leq W.$$

Prove that the homomorphism property holds for finding MCRs. Find an MCR in the language of unions of CQACs.

4.7. Consider query Q and view V:

$$Q() :\!\!- p(X, Y), p(Y, Z), s(X, Z), p(Z, Y'), p(Y', Z'), s(Z, Z'), t(Z).$$

$$V(Z, W) :\!\!- p(X, Y), p(Y, Z), s(X, Z''), p(Z, Y'), p(Y', Z'), s(Z'', Z').$$

Prove that the homomorphism property holds for finding MCRs. Find an MCR in the language of unions of CQs.

4.8. Consider queries Q and Q', as well as view V.

$$Q() :\!\!- p(X, Y), p(Y, Z), s(X, Z), p(Z, Y'), p(Y', Z'), s(Z, Z'), t(Z).$$

$$Q'() :\!\!- p(X, Y), p(Y, Z), s(X, Z''), p(Z, Y'), p(Y', Z'), s(Z'', Z'), t(W), Z'' \leq 5.$$

$$V(Z, W) :\!\!- p(X, Y), p(Y, Z), s(X, Z''), p(Z, Y'), p(Y', Z'), s(Z'', Z'), t(W), Z'' \leq W.$$

Prove that the homomorphism property holds for finding MCRs. Find an MCR in the language of unions of CQACs for Q using the view and an MCR for Q'. Why there is a difference in the MCR found?

4.9. Let query Q and view V be as follows:

$$Q(X, Z) \;:\!-\; a(X, Y), a(Y, Z).$$

$$V(X, Z, A, B) \;:\!-\; a(X, Y), a(Y, Z), b(A, B), A \leq Y, Y \leq B.$$

Prove that the homomorphism property holds for finding MCRs. Find an MCR of Q using V in the language of unions of CQACs. Hint: think on the dual role of exportable variables.

4.10. Consider the following query Q and view V:

$$
\begin{aligned}
Q(A) \quad &:\!-\quad p(A, A).\\
V(X_1, X_2, X_3, X_6, X_7, X_8) \quad &:\!-\quad p(X_4, X_5), s(X_1, X_2, X_3, X_6, X_7, X_8),\\
&\qquad X_3 \leq X_5, X_5 \leq X_7,\\
&\qquad X_1 \leq X_4, X_8 \leq X_2, X_2 \leq X_4, X_4 \leq X_6.
\end{aligned}
$$

Prove that the homomorphism property holds for finding MCRs, and find an MCR for the query using the view in the language of unions of CQACs.

4.11. Consider the following query and views:

$$
\begin{aligned}
Q \quad &:\!-\; t(A), p(A).\\
V_1(X) \quad &:\!-\; p(X).\\
V_2(X, Z) \quad &:\!-\; t(X), p(Y), s(Y, Z), X \leq Y, Y \leq Z.
\end{aligned}
$$

Prove that the homomorphism property holds for finding MCRs. Construct an MCR in the language of unions of CQACs for the query using the views.

4.12. In Example 4.38, remove the unnecessary rules, and unfold the remaining rules appropriately, to show that the resulting MCR is equivalent to

$R(X, Y) :\!- V(X, Y).$

$R(X, Y) :\!- R(X, Z), V(Z, Y).$

CHAPTER 5

Answering Queries in Presence of Dependencies

In this chapter we revisit the problems of query containment and of finding equivalent and maximally contained rewritings for the case where we are interested in applying the results only on those database instances that satisfy certain dependencies.

5.1 PRELIMINARIES

We consider dependencies that are tuple-generating dependencies (tgds) and equality-generating dependencies (egds), with the definitions to follow. In the definitions, for notational consistency with the literature on the topic, we switch the notation to denoting variables using lowercase letters instead of uppercase, and to denoting vectors of variables in boldface instead of bar.

Definition 5.1   (tgds-egds)
Let **D** be a database schema.
– A *tuple-generating dependency* (*tgd*) is a first-order formula of the form

$$\forall \mathbf{x} \big(\phi(\mathbf{x}) \rightarrow \exists \mathbf{y} \; \psi(\mathbf{x}, \mathbf{y}) \big).$$

– An *equality-generating dependency* (*egd*) is a first-order formula of the form

$$\forall \mathbf{x} \big(\phi(\mathbf{x}) \rightarrow (x_1 = x_2) \big).$$

In the above formulas, $\phi(\mathbf{x})$ is a conjunction of atoms over **D** with variables in **x**, such that each variable in **x** occurs in at least one atom in $\phi(\mathbf{x})$; x_1 and x_2 are variables from **x**. In addition, $\psi(\mathbf{x}, \mathbf{y})$ is a conjunction of atoms with variables in **x** and **y**, such that each variable in **y** occurs in at least one atom in $\psi(\mathbf{x}, \mathbf{y})$.

In what follows we will drop the quantifiers and write tgds using the format

$$\phi(\mathbf{x}) \rightarrow \psi(\mathbf{x}, \mathbf{y}),$$

and will write egds using the format

$$\phi(\mathbf{x}) \rightarrow (x_1 = x_2).$$

Observe the relationship of Definition 5.1 with the definition of conjunctive queries, which are expressions of the form $Q(\mathbf{x})$:- $\exists \mathbf{y} \phi(\mathbf{x}, \mathbf{y})$, with $\phi(\mathbf{x}, \mathbf{y})$ a conjunction of atoms that we call subgoals of the query.

Definition 5.2 Let $d : \phi(\mathbf{x}) \rightarrow \psi(\mathbf{x}, \mathbf{y})$ be a tgd and D a database instance. We say that D *satisfies* d if whenever there is a homomorphism h from $\phi(\mathbf{x})$ to D, there exists an extension h' of h such that h' is a homomorphism from the conjunction $\phi(\mathbf{x}) \wedge \psi(\mathbf{x}, \mathbf{y})$ to D. We say that D satisfies an egd $\phi(\mathbf{x}) \rightarrow x_1 = x_2$ if for each homomorphism h from $\phi(\mathbf{x})$ to D, we have that $h(x_1) = h(x_2)$.

5.1.1 THE CHASE

The chase algorithm is the main tool for reasoning about dependencies. It is applied on a database instance with a given set Σ of dependencies, and the result after termination is guaranteed to satisfy Σ. In this section we describe the chase algorithm, give conditions that guarantee termination of the chase on any database instance, and provide a formal result that describes a property of the chase that we use in the rest of this chapter and in Chapter 6. Then in Section 5.3 we use the chase to develop algorithms for checking CQ query containment and for finding equivalent rewritings of CQ queries using CQ views under dependencies.

In this chapter and in Chapter 6, by *database instance* we understand a set of atoms that are not necessarily ground atoms (i.e., atoms whose all values are constants). The main reason is the definition of the chase procedure, which may be unnecessarily involved otherwise. When we describe the chase procedure, we call the variables *labeled nulls*. In many settings (e.g., in the data-exchange setting, which we present in the next chapter), this term is more suitable, as these variables play the role of nulls. That is, we form database instances in which we know that a tuple t belongs in the instance, but we may not know the exact values in all the fields (argument positions) in this tuple. For example, an instance may have a tuple $t = (5, x, 7, y)$, which means that there is a tuple whose value in the first field equals 5, and whose value in the third field equals 7; at the same time, we do not know the exact values in the two other fields in the tuple t. To represent such information in database instances, we assume an infinite domain of constants <u>Const</u>, as well as an infinite set <u>Var</u> of variables, called *labeled nulls*, such that <u>Const</u> $\cap$ <u>Var</u> $= \emptyset$. A *fact* is a relational atom over constants from <u>Const</u> and labeled nulls from <u>Var</u>. We define an *instance* to be a set of facts. For an instance K, we use <u>Const</u>(K) and <u>Var</u>(K) to denote the set of constants and the set of labeled nulls in K, respectively. A *ground instance* is an instance K with <u>Var</u>$(K) = \emptyset$.

The chase procedure is used extensively for dealing with problems related to satisfaction of tgds and egds. The definition is as follows.

Definition 5.3 (Chase step)
Let K be a database instance and Σ a set of tgds and egds. We distinguish between tgds and egds.

(tgd) Let d be a tgd in Σ of the form $\phi(\mathbf{x}) \to \psi(\mathbf{x}, \mathbf{y})$. Let h be a homomorphism from $\phi(\mathbf{x})$ to K such that there is no extension h' of h that maps $\phi(\mathbf{x}) \wedge \psi(\mathbf{x}, \mathbf{y})$ to K. We say that d can be applied to K with homomorphism h. Let K' be the union of K with the set of facts obtained by:

(i) extending h to h' such that each variable in $\mathbf{y}$ is assigned a fresh labeled null, followed by

(ii) taking the image of the atoms of ψ under h'.

We say that the result of applying d to K with h is K', and write $K \xrightarrow{d,h} K'$ to denote the *chase step* on K with the tgd d.

(egd) Let d be an egd in Σ of the form $\phi(\mathbf{x}) \to (x_1 = x_2)$. Let h be a homomorphism from $\phi(\mathbf{x})$ to K such that $h(x_1) \neq h(x_2)$. We say that d can be applied to K with homomorphism h. We distinguish between two cases.

(a) If $h(x_1)$ and $h(x_2)$ are distinct constants, we say that the result of applying d to K with h is *failure*, and write $K \xrightarrow{d,h} \perp$ to denote the *chase step* on K with the egd d.

(b) Otherwise, let K' be K in which we identify $h(x_1)$ and $h(x_2)$ as follows. If one is a constant and the other is a labeled null, then the labeled null is globally replaced by the constant; if both are labeled nulls, then one is replaced globally by the other. We say that the result of applying d to K with h is K', and write $K \xrightarrow{d,h} K'$ to denote the *chase step* on K with the egd d.

We continue with the definition of the chase.

Definition 5.4   (Chase)
Let Σ be a set of tgds and egds, and K be a database instance.

• A *chase sequence* of K with Σ is a sequence (finite or infinite) of chase steps $K_i \xrightarrow{d,h} K'_{i+1}$, with $i = 0, 1, \ldots$, $K = K_0$, and d a dependency in Σ.

• A *finite chase* of K with Σ is a finite chase sequence $K_i \xrightarrow{d,h} K'_{i+1}$, $0 \leq i < m$ with $K = K_0$, where either *(a)* $K_m = \perp$, or *(b)* there is no dependency d of Σ and there is no homomorphism h such that d can be applied to K_m with h. We say that K_m is the result of the finite chase. We refer to case *(a)* as a *failing* finite chase, and to case *(b)* as a *successful* finite chase.

5.1.2   WEAKLY ACYCLIC SETS OF TGDS

On some database instances, chase may never terminate; thus, it is of interest to identify conditions under which there is a finite chase on all database instances. The notion of *weak acyclicity* guarantees the termination of chase. A characteristic example of weakly acyclic tgds is the class of *full* tgds, i.e., tgds with no existentially quantified variables. The following definition formalizes the concept of weak acyclicity for a set of tgds.

Definition 5.5   (Weakly acyclic set of tgds)
Let Σ be a set of tgds and egds over a database schema. We construct a directed graph (called the *dependency graph*), as follows. (1) There is a node for every pair (R, A) with a relation symbol R of the schema and an attribute A of R. We call such a pair (R, A) a *position*. (2) Add edges as follows: for each tgd $\phi(\mathbf{x}) \rightarrow \psi(\mathbf{x}, \mathbf{y})$ in Σ and for each x in $\mathbf{x}$ that occurs in $\psi(\mathbf{x}, \mathbf{y})$, we call x a *propagated variable*. For a propagated variable x, for each occurrence of x in $\phi(\mathbf{x})$ in position (R, A_i), do the following:

   (i) for each occurrence of x in $\psi(\mathbf{x}, \mathbf{y})$ in position (S, B_j), add an edge $(R, A_i) \rightarrow (S, B_j)$ (if it does not already exist); and

   (ii) for each existentially quantified variable y in $\mathbf{y}$ and for each occurrence of y in $\psi(\mathbf{x}, \mathbf{y})$ in position (T, C_k), add a *special edge* $(R, A_i) \rightarrow (T, C_k)$ (if it does not already exist).

   We say that the set Σ is *weakly acyclic* if the dependency graph has no cycle going through a special edge.

Theorem 5.6   *If a set Σ of tgds and egds is weakly acyclic, then chase with Σ terminates on every instance.*

Proof. The proof is by induction on the maximum number of special edges along any path in the dependency graph. If there are no special edges, then no new variables are introduced during any chase sequence. Thus, there is a finite number of facts of each relevant arity that can be added by the chase steps. As a result, the chase will terminate.

   Before we continue with the proof, let us make a general observation about the structure of the dependency graph. If an atom $U(x_1, \dots,)$ appears on the left-hand side of a tgd that has an existentially quantified variable at position (T, B) in its right-hand side, then the following is true: For *every* position (U, X_i), where X_i is an attribute in U, there is a special edge to (T, B) in the dependency graph. In other words, for a specific U, either there are special edges from *every* position (U, X_i) to a certain other position, or there are no special edges at all from any position $(U, X_i), i = 1, \dots$. Thus, the dependency graph, as defined, can be used to state the following: If the dependency graph has no paths with special edges from a certain position (U, X_i), then U participates on the left-hand side of only those tgds that have no existentially quantified variables, or does not participate on the left-hand side of tgds at all.

   Suppose that there is only one special edge along any path in the dependency graph. The following observation is useful in supporting our argument that the number of the fresh variables introduced by the special edge will be limited. Consider an atom $U(x_1, \dots,)$ in the database K_i created at some step i of chase, such that a fresh variable is introduced in $U(x_1, \dots,)$. This means that there is some special edge in the dependency graph to some position (U, X_j). According to the general observation above about the dependency graph, an atom with relational symbol U either appears on the left-hand side of only those tgds that have no existentially quantified variables, or it does not appear in any tgds. Thus, the number of the new variables that will be introduced equals the number of homomorphisms that exist from the left-hand side of a tgd to the input database instance, times the maximum number of existentially quantified variables in each tgd. Moreover, no other variables will be introduced, because the atoms in the instance K_i that contain newly introduced variables will not participate in the next chase step that could introduce new variables. We conclude that the chase will terminate after a finite number of steps.

The argument for the general case is the same as above. The inductive hypothesis is that the chase will terminate after a finite number of steps in those cases where there are at most $i - 1$ special edges along any path in the dependency graph. If there are at most i special edges, then we repeat the above argument for the ith special edge along the paths. $\square$

5.1.3 PROPERTY OF THE CHASE

We now present the main result that makes the chase algorithm useful in many situations. (Some of the scenarios will be presented in this and the next chapters.)

Theorem 5.7   *Let Σ be a set of tgds and egds, and D a database instance that satisfies the dependencies in Σ. Suppose K is a database instance, such that there exists a homomorphism h from K to D. Let K_Σ be the result of a successful finite chase on K with the set of dependencies Σ. Then the homomorphism h can be extended to a homomoprhism h' from K_Σ to D.*

Proof. The proof is by induction on the number of chase steps. Suppose that the chase of K with Σ terminates after n steps, with chase sequence $K = K_1, K_2, \ldots, K_n = K_\Sigma$, where $K_i \xrightarrow{d_i, g_i} K_{i+1}$ for $d_i \in \Sigma$. We show for each $i = 1, 2, \ldots, n - 1$ that, whenever there exists a homomorphism $h_i : K_i \to D$, then there exists an extension of h_i to a homomorphism $h_{i+1} : K_{i+1} \to D$.

Suppose that $K_i \xrightarrow{d, g_i} K_{i+1}$ with $d \in \Sigma$. Consider the following two cases.

1. d is a tgd $\phi(\mathbf{x}) \to \psi(\mathbf{x}, \mathbf{y})$. By Definition 5.3 of the chase step, there is a homomorphism $g_i : \phi(\mathbf{x}) \to K_i$. Thus, $h_i \circ g_i : \phi(\mathbf{x}) \to D$ is also a homomorphism and, due to D satisfying d, $h_i \circ g_i$ can be extended to a homomorphism $h' : \phi(\mathbf{x}) \wedge \psi(\mathbf{x}, \mathbf{y}) \to D$.

   We now construct h_{i+1}. For each variable y in $\mathbf{y}$, denote by z_y the fresh variable that replaces y in the chase step $K_i \xrightarrow{d, g_i} K_{i+1}$. Let x be a variable of K_{i+1}. If x is among the variables of K_i, then $h_{i+1}(x) = h_i(x)$. If, however, x does not appear in K_i, then x is a fresh variable (that is used to extend the homomorphism h_i to h' during the chase step), and we have that $h_{i+1}(x) = h'(x')$ for an appropriate x'. (Such an x'exists, since the dependencies are satisfied in D.) Thus, h_{i+1} maps all the variables of K_{i+1} to constants in D.

Now h_{i+1} is a homomorphism for the following reasons.

(a) For each fact f in K_{i+1} such that all the variables of f are involved in the homomorphism h_i, by the inductive step we have that h_{i+1} maps f appropriately to a fact of D; and

(b) The rest of the facts originated in K_{i+1} from an application of this chase step; hence these facts are images of the atoms in the conjunction ψ of some tgd in Σ; this means that the homomorphism h' used to define h_{i+1}, when viewed as a mapping from K_{i+1} to D, maps each new atom in K_{i+1} to an atom in D.

2. d is an egd $\phi(\mathbf{x}) \to (x_1 = x_2)$. As in the previous case, by the Definition 5.3 of the chase step, there is a homomorphism $g_i : \phi(\mathbf{x}) \to K_i$, and we have that $h_i \circ g_i : \phi(\mathbf{x}) \to D$ is a homomorphism. Because the instance D satisfies the egd d, we have that $h_i(x_1) = h_i(x_2)$. We now construct $h_{i+1} : K_{i+1} \to D$, such that $h_{i+1}(x) = h_i(x)$. After this step, the only difference between K_{i+1} and K_i is in that two variables in K_i are equated. We argue as in the case of tgd to show these variables are already mapped by h_i to the same element in D, because D satisfies the dependencies.

$\square$

The chase

In this section:

We defined chase applied to a database instance K using a set Σ of tgds and egds.

We observed that chase does not always terminate, but does terminate on all instances for weakly acyclic sets of tgds and egds; and

We stated an important property of the chase.

The following is an interesting observation (that also happens to be easy to prove). Because of this result we can say that computing the canonical rewriting can be done by chasing the canonical database of the given query with a set of tgds.

Theorem 5.8   *Let Σ be a set of tgds, such that each tgd in Σ (i) has no existential variables, and (ii) has one atom on the right-hand side. Let Q be a set of CQ queries where each query Q in Q is constructed from a tgd in Σ by the following process: (a) the head of Q is the same as the right-hand side of the selected tgd, and (b) the body of Q is the same as the left-hand side of the tgd. Then for any database instance K, the result of applying the chase to K with Σ produces the answers to the corresponding CQs in Q, and vice versa.*

5.2 QUERY CONTAINMENT UNDER DEPENDENCIES

We now define query containment under dependencies.

Definition 5.9 Let Σ be a set of tdgs and egds, and Q_1, Q_2 be two conjunctive queries. We say that Q_1 *is contained in* Q_2 *under the dependencies* Σ, denoted $Q_1 \sqsubseteq_\Sigma Q_2$, if for all databases D that satisfy Σ we have that $Q_1(D) \subseteq Q_2(D)$.

Example 5.10 Suppose the database schema is a single binary relation. Let d be the egd $a(X,Y), a(X,Z) \to Y = Z$. Consider a CQ Q:

$$q() :\text{-} a(X,Y), a(X,Z), a(Y,Z).$$

This query is equivalent to the following query Q'

$$q'() :\text{-} a(X,Y), a(Y,Y)$$

on all the database instances that satisfy the egd d.

Containment test when chase terminates: Consider a set Σ of tgds and egds such that chase with Σ terminates (e.g., Σ is weakly acyclic). Then a conjunctive query Q_2 is contained in conjunctive query Q_1 iff there is a containment mapping from Q_1 to the chased body Q_1^{chase} of Q_1. We obtain the chased body of Q_1 by regarding the body of Q_1 as a relational structure, and by applying to it the chase steps until termination. The labeled nulls used in the definition of chase become fresh variables in the query. The outcome of the chase procedure becomes the set of subgoals of the resulting query Q_1^{chase}.

The following result formally states this containment test; the proof is based on Theorem 5.7.

Theorem 5.11 *If chase of conjunctive query Q with set of dependencies Σ terminates with outcome Q_Σ, then for any conjunctive query Q', the following is true:*
$Q \sqsubseteq_\Sigma Q'$ *iff there is a containment mapping from Q' to Q_Σ.*

Proof. By Theorem 5.7, for any database D that satisfies Σ we have the following: If a tuple t is computed by a homomorphism h_t from the subgoals of Q to D, then there is a homomorphism h'_t from Q_Σ to D that computes t. Hence, Q_Σ computes all the tuples computed by Q on D. In addition, Q computes all the tuples computed by Q_Σ on D, because there is a containment mapping from Q to Q_Σ. Thus, Q and Q_Σ are equivalent on D. We conclude that whenever there is a containment mapping from Q' to Q_Σ, this means that Q' contains Q under Σ.

For the other direction, suppose Q' contains Q under Σ. Consider the canonical database I of Q_Σ. Q' computes on I the head of Q_Σ. Hence, there is a containment mapping from Q' to Q_Σ. □

Example 5.12 Consider the query Q and egd d of Example 5.10, repeated here for convenience: $d : a(X, Y), a(X, Z) \rightarrow Y = Z$, and Q is

$$q() :\text{-} a(X, Y), a(X, Z), a(Y, Z).$$

In chase of the atoms in the body of Q with egd d, there is only one applicable chase step. The first two subgoals of Q are targets of a homomorphism from the left-hand side of d. Thus, we enforce on the variables of Q the equality $Y = Z$. The chase yields a query Q' that is equivalent to Q under d:

$$q'() :\text{-} a(X, Y), a(X, Y), a(Y, Y).$$

The minimized version of Q' is

$$q'() :\text{-} a(X, Y), a(Y, Y).$$

Query-containment test for CQs under dependencies

In this section:

We defined query containment under dependencies on the input database instance.

We observed that the chase (when it terminates) can be used to decide CQ query containment.

5.3 EQUIVALENT REWRITINGS

In the following, we define rewritings that are equivalent to queries for the case where we are interested only in those database instances that satisfy a set of dependencies. In this case, an overall equivalent rewriting is still an equivalent rewriting, but if we are not careful, then we may miss an equivalent rewriting. This means that a rewriting could be equivalent to the query on all the database instances satisfying the specific dependencies, but not necessarily on *all* database instances.

Definition 5.13 For a query Q, set $\mathcal{V}$ of views, and set Σ of dependencies, an *equivalent rewriting of Q using $\mathcal{V}$ in presence of Σ* is a query R over the schema of the views such that, for all the databases D that satisfy Σ, $R(\mathcal{V}(D)) = Q(D)$ holds.

Example 5.14 Suppose the database schema is a single binary relation; let edg d be $a(X, Y), a(X, Z) \rightarrow Y = Z$. Consider CQ query Q:

$$q() :\text{-} a(X, Y), a(X, Z), a(Y, Z)$$

and CQ view V:

$$v() :\text{-} a(X, Y), a(Y, Y).$$

Then the following rewriting R

$$R() :\text{-} v()$$

is equivalent to Q under the egd d. The expansion of the rewriting R is

$$R^{exp}() :\text{-} a(X, Y), a(Y, Y).$$

As discussed in Example 5.10, while R^{exp} is equivalent to Q under d, it is not equivalent to Q in general (i.e., without any dependencies assumed).

5.3.1 ALGORITHM FOR CQ QUERIES, VIEWS, AND REWRITINGS

In the case of CQ queries and views, in order to prove that a rewriting R is equivalent to the given query, we can still use the expansion of the rewriting. At the same time, we now need to prove that the expansion is equivalent to the query under the specific dependencies. That is, we need to use the chased bodies of both the query and the expansion in checking for equivalence by containment mappings. (We have already noted this when discussing query containment under dependencies.)

Theorem 5.15   *Let Q be a CQ query, V a set of CQ views, and Σ a set of tgds and egds such that the chase sequence of Q with Σ terminates. Let Q_Σ be the result of chasing Q with Σ (i.e., $Q \xrightarrow{\Sigma} Q_\Sigma$.) Let R^Σ_{can} be the canonical rewriting of Q_Σ using V.*

Then there is an equivalent CQ rewriting of Q using V in presence of Σ iff R^Σ_{can} is an equivalent rewriting of Q in presence of Σ.

The proof of this result is based on Theorem 5.7. Theorem 5.15 gives rise to an algorithm that is similar to the algorithm based on canonical rewritings, which we introduced in Chapter 3. The difference is that now we need to chase the query before constructing the canonical rewriting.

Example 5.16   Consider the setting of Example 5.14. In order to apply Theorem 5.15, we chase the query with d, to obtain Q_Σ:

$$q_\Sigma() :\text{-} a(X, Y), a(Y, Y).$$

Computing the view V on the canonical database of Q_Σ results in a single tuple $v()$. Thus, the canonical rewriting is

$$R() :\text{-} v().$$

We argued in Example 5.14 that this is an equivalent rewriting of the query Q under the dependency d.

> **Equivalent CQ rewritings under dependencies for CQ queries and views**
> We defined equivalent rewritings of queries under dependencies.
> We observed that the chase (when it terminates) can be used to find an equivalent CQ rewriting, in case there is one.

5.3.2 FINDING EQUIVALENT REWRITINGS FOR WEAKLY ACYCLIC LAV DEPENDENCIES

In Chapter 3 we discussed an efficient algorithm, CoreCover, for finding equivalent CQ rewritings for CQ queries and views. Unfortunately, this algorithm does not carry over to the case in which we would like to find equivalent rewritings in presence of dependencies. The reason is that this algorithm treats separately the contribution of each view subgoal to the rewriting, with respect to the containment mapping from the query to the expansion. However, in presence of dependencies we need to chase the expansion first and to then look for the existence of a containment mapping from the query to the expansion. A chase step, however, may consider more that one view subgoal (in their expanded form), because the left-hand side of a tgd or egd may have more than one atom. We can still extend the algorithm CoreCover to the case of dependencies, provided that all the given tgds and egds each have one atom on the left-hand side. We call such dependencies Local As Views (LAV).

In this section we present an algorithm that finds equivalent rewritings in presence of weakly-acyclic LAV dependencies, such that each rewriting has the minimum number of subgoals. The algorithm, $CoreCover\Sigma$, is an extension of CoreCover. We now present $CoreCover\Sigma$:

1. The input is a CQ query Q, set $\mathcal{V}$ of CQ views, and a set of weakly acyclic LAV dependencies Σ.

2. Chase query Q with Σ to obtain Q_Σ.

3. Minimize Q_Σ to obtain Q_m, the minimal equivalent of Q_Σ.

4. Construct the canonical database D'_Q of Q_m; use D'_Q to compute the canonical rewriting by applying the view definitions on D'_Q.

5. For each subgoal in the canonical rewriting, take its expansion according to the view definition, and compute the chased expansion. Compute the tuple core of this view subgoal with respect to its chased expansion and Q_m.

6. Use the nonempty tuple cores to cover all the query subgoals in Q_m with the minimum number of tuple cores. For each cover, construct a candidate rewriting by combining the corresponding view tuples, then check for equivalence with Q_m.

The relationship between $\mathsf{CoreCover}\Sigma$ and the algorithm $\mathsf{CoreCover}$ of Chapter 3 is the following: $\mathsf{CoreCover}\Sigma$ is a slight modification of $\mathsf{CoreCover}$ in that $\mathsf{CoreCover}\Sigma$ uses the minimal chased query and the chased view tuples; thus, "chased" tuple cores are constructed to contribute to equivalent rewritings. The proof techniques for the correctness of $\mathsf{CoreCover}\Sigma$ are largely along the lines of the proof of correctness of $\mathsf{CoreCover}$.

We now give an example to demonstrate how $\mathsf{CoreCover}\Sigma$ works.

Example 5.17   Consider a view set $\mathcal{V}$ that contains the following four views:

$$V_1(X_1, X_2) :\!\!- a(X_1, Z_4), b(Z_4, X_2).$$
$$V_2(X_1, X_2) :\!\!- b(X_1, Z_5), c(Z_5, X_2).$$
$$V_3(X_1, X_2, X_3) :\!\!- b(X_1, X_2), c(X_2, X_3).$$
$$V_4(X_1) :\!\!- a(X_1, X_1), d(X_1, X_1).$$

Consider a query

$$Q(X, Y) :\!\!- a(X, Z_2), b(Z_2, Z_3), c(Z_3, Y), a(Y, Z_1), a(Z_1, Y), d(Y, Y),$$

and tgd $t : d(X, Y) \rightarrow a(X, Y)$.

The result of chasing Q with t is

$$\begin{aligned} Q_\Sigma(X, Y) :\!\!-\ & a(X, Z_2), b(Z_2, Z_3), c(Z_3, Y), \\ & a(Y, Z_1), a(Z_1, Y), a(Y, Y), \\ & d(Y, Y). \end{aligned}$$

Minimizing Q_Σ yields the following query Q_m:

$$\begin{aligned} Q_m(X, Y) :\!\!-\ & a(X, Z_2), b(Z_2, Z_3), c(Z_3, Y), \\ & a(Y, Y), d(Y, Y). \end{aligned}$$

The canonical database is $D'_Q = \{a(x, z_2), b(z_2, z_3), c(z_3, y), a(y, y), d(y, y)\}$, and computing the canonical rewriting on D'_Q yields the following view sugoals in this rewriting: $\mathcal{T}(Q, \mathcal{V}, \Sigma) = \{V_1(X_1, Z_3), V_2(Z_2, Y), V_3(Z_2, Z_3, Y), V_4(Y)\}$. We next compute the "chased" tuple cores for each view subgoal in the canonical rewriting.

- $V_1(X_1, Z_3)$: We have that $(V_1^{exp})'(X_1, Z_3) :\!\!- a(X_1, Z'_4), b(Z'_4, Z_3)$; thus, the chased tuple core is the set $\{a(X, Z_2), b(Z_2, Z_3)\}$.

- $V_2(Z_2, Y)$: We have that $(V_2^{exp})'(Z_2, Y) :\!\!- b(Z_2, Z'_5), c(Z'_5, Y)$; thus, the chased tuple core is the set $\{b(Z_2, Z_3), c(Z_3, Y)\}$.

- $V_3(Z_2, Z_3, Y)$: We have that $(V_3^{exp})'(Z_2, Z_3, Y)$:- $b(Z_2, Z_3), c(Z_3, Y)$; thus, the chased tuple core is the set $\{b(Z_2, Z_3), c(Z_3, Y)\}$.

- $V_4(Y)$: We have that $(V_4^{exp})'(Y)$:- $a(Y, Y), d(Y, Y)$; thus, the chased tuple core is the set $\{a(Y, Y), d(Y, Y)\}$.

In the last step, $\mathsf{CoreCover}\Sigma$ finds a minimum number of view subgoals to cover the Q_m's subgoals, and constructs a rewriting by combining the corresponding view tuples. In our example, $\mathsf{CoreCover}\Sigma$ will find only one equivalent rewriting, which is $R(X, Y)$:- $V_1(X_1, Z_3), V_3(Z_2, Z_3, Y), V_4(Y)$. We can verify that R is an equivalent rewriting of Q using containment mappings between Q_m and R_Σ^{exp}:

$$Q_m(X, Y) \text{ :- } a(X, Z_2), b(Z_2, Z_3), c(Z_3, Y),$$
$$a(Y, Y), d(Y, Y).$$
$$R_\Sigma^{exp}(X, Y) \text{ :- } a(X_1, Z_4'), b(Z_4', Z_3),$$
$$b(Z_2, Z_3), c(Z_3, Y), a(Y, Y),$$
$$d(Y, Y).$$

For example, if $h(X) = X$, $h(Z_2) = Z_4'$, $h(Z_3) = Z_3$, and $h(Y) = Y$, then h is a containment mapping $h : Q_m \to R_\Sigma^{exp}$, which means that $Q_m \sqsubseteq R_\Sigma^{exp}$. The other direction is similar.

Notice that if we had not performed the minimization step in Q_Σ, i.e., if we had considered Q_Σ instead of Q_m, then the canonical database D_Q', the set of chased view subgoals, and the chased tuple cores would be the same, since the two subgoals $a(Y, Z_1), a(Z_1, Y)$ could not be part of any chased tuple core. Indeed, the only view subgoal for which this could happen is $V_4(Y)$; if we include them in $V_4(X_1)_\Sigma$, it is not hard to see that the mapping $\mu : \{a(Y, Z_1), a(Z_1, Y), a(Y, Y), d(Y, Y)\} \to \{a(Y, Y), d(Y, Y)\}$ is not one to one, as is required by the definition of the tuple core. This means that $a(Y, Z_1), a(Z_1, Y)$ would not be covered by the tuple core of any view, and thus $\mathsf{CoreCover}\Sigma$ would not find any equivalent rewriting.

> **Equivalent CQ rewritings under dependencies for CQ queries and views.**
> For LAV dependencies, there is an efficient algorithm to find equivalent rewritings under dependencies.

5.4 MCRS

In this section we first show that for CQ queries and views and for a set of egds, we may need recursion to find an MCR in the language of unions of CQs. Specifically, we show an example in which there is no MCR that is a finite union of CQs. We then present a variant of the inverse-rule algorithm that finds a Datalog MCR for CQ queries and views in the presence of egds.

5.4.1   FUNCTIONAL DEPENDENCIES NEED RECURSION

In presence of dependencies, maximally contained rewritings of a query could exist in Datalog only, as shown in the following example.

Example 5.18   Suppose that we have a database schema that contains relation schedule (Airline, Flight_no, Date, Pilot, Aircraft). The set of views $\mathcal{V}$ contains one view

$$V(D, P, C) :\text{-}\ schedule(A, N, D, P, C),$$

and we have a set $\Sigma = \{d_1, d_2\}$ of two egds:

$$d_1 : schedule(A, N, D, P, C) \wedge schedule(A', N', D', P, C') \to A = A'.$$
$$d_2 : schedule(A, N, D, P, C) \wedge schedule(A', N', D', P', C) \to A = A'.$$

These dependencies say that each pilot works for only one airline, and each aircraft is owned by only one airline. Consider the query

$$Q(P) :\text{-}\ schedule(A, N, D, mike, C), schedule(A, N', D', P, C'),$$

which asks for pilots working for the same airline as Mike. Because of the dependencies, these pilots fly aircraft of the same airline.

For each n, the following query Q_n is a CQ rewriting contained in Q, assuming the dependencies in Σ hold:

$$\begin{aligned} Q_n(P) :\text{-}\ & V(D_1, mike, C_1), V(D_2, P_2, C_1), V(D_3, P_2, C_2), \\ & V(D_4, P_3, C_2), V(D_5, P_3, C_3), V(D_6, P_4, C_3), \dots, \\ & V(D_{2n-2}, P_n, C_{n-1}), V(D_{2n-1}, P_n, C_n), V(D_{2n}, P, C_n). \end{aligned}$$

The intuition behind this contained rewriting is as follows. Each use of a view subgoal introduces either a pilot that works for the same airline as Mike, or an aircraft owned by Mike's airline. Thus, in particular, the first two view subgoals above introduce pilot P_2 who works for aircraft C_1, which is owned by Mike's airline. The second and third subgoals give C_2, which is an aircraft for which P_2 works, and hence (because of the dependency) owned by Mike's airline.

In the real world, conditions could hold that would prevent us from getting all the answers to the query Q. Suppose Mike's airline has both Boeing and Airbus planes, but Mike only knows how to fly Boeing, and there are other pilots who only know how to fly Airbus. Then if we start from Mike, we will never reach an Airbus pilot for the same airline, no matter how large n is in Q_n. Moreover, Q_n needs to be arbitrarily long to capture all the answers that can be derived by a contained CQ rewriting, because we may have an arbitrarily long chain of pilots and aircraft that respectively work for and are owned by Mike's airline. Such answers could only be reached by the number of subgoals in Q_n that is equal to the length of this chain.

Consider a contained rewriting, $\mathcal{P}$, of the query Q using views $\mathcal{V}$ in Example 5.18, such that $\mathcal{P}$ is a finite union of CQs. We now show formally that for any such rewriting $\mathcal{P}$, there is a CQ contained rewriting of Q using $\mathcal{V}$ that is not contained in $\mathcal{P}$.

Suppose each CQ in $\mathcal{P}$ has at most s subgoals. Suppose $s \leq m$. Consider the contained rewriting Q_{m+1}:

$$Q_{m+1}(P_{m+2}) :\text{-}\ V(D_1, mike, C_1), V(D_2, P_2, C_1), V(D_3, P_2, C_2),$$
$$V(D_4, P_3, C_2), V(D_5, P_3, C_3), V(D_6, P_4, C_3), \ldots,$$
$$V(D_{2m}, P_{m+1}, C_m), V(D_{2m+1}, P_{m+1}, C_{m+1}), V(D_{2m+2}, P_{m+2}, C_{m+1}).$$

We now construct a view instance V_{m+1} by replacing the variables in the subgoals in the body of Q_{m+1} with distinct constants, as shown below:

$$V_{m+1} = \{V(d_1, mike, c_1), V(d_2, p_2, c_1), V(d_3, p_2, c_2),$$
$$V(d_4, p_3, c_2), V(d_5, p_3, c_3), V(d_6, p_4, c_3), \ldots,$$
$$V(d_{2m}, p_{m+1}, c_m), V(d_{2m+1}, p_{m+1}, c_{m+1}), V(d_{2m+2}, p_{m+2}, c_{m+1})\}.$$

It is easy to see that $Q_{m+1}(V_{m+1}) = \{mike, p_2, \ldots, p_{m+2}\}$. Since Q_{m+1} is contained in $\mathcal{P}$ by our assumption, there exists a CQ rewriting $R \in \mathcal{P}$, such that $Q_{m+1} \sqsubseteq R$. We will prove that $p_{m+2} \in R(V_{m+1})$ does not hold, thus proving that Q_{m+1} is not contained in $\mathcal{P}$. (Our argument will be based on the fact that R has $s \leq m$ subgoals.)

Assume that $p_{m+2} \in R(V_{m+1})$. By definition, if P is the (only) variable in the head of R, there is a homomorphism $h : Var(R) \to Const(V_{m+1})$ such that $h(P) = p_{m+2}$. If $R_i(\mathbf{y})$ is a subgoal in the body of R, then $R_i(h(\mathbf{y})) \in V_{m+1}$. We now consider the view instance $V_s = \{R_i(h(\mathbf{y})) : R_i(\mathbf{y}) \in Body(R)\}$, where we denote by $Body(R)$ the subgoals in the definition of R. That is, V_s contains only the s tuples from V_{m+1} that were used to produce the answer $\{p_{m+2}\}$, i.e., $R(V_s) = \{p_{m+2}\}$. Since V_{m+1} contains $2m + 2 > m \geq s$ subgoals, at least one of the tuples in V_{m+1} is not present in V_s. Let $V(d', p_i, c')$, $2 \leq i \leq m + 2$, be one such tuple. We now construct a database D' from V_s by replacing the tuples in V_s with their expansions, as shown below:

$$D' = \{schedule(a_1, n_1, d_1, mike, c_1), schedule(a_2, n_2, d_2, p_2, c_1),$$
$$schedule(a_3, n_3, d_3, p_2, c_2), \ldots, schedule(a_{2i-2}, n_{2i-2}, d_{2i-2}, p_{i-1}, c_{i-1}),$$
$$schedule(a_{2i+2}, n_{2i+2}, d_{2i+2}, p_{i+1}, c_{i+1}), \ldots,$$
$$schedule(a_{2m}, n_{2m}, d_{2m}, p_{m+1}, c_m), schedule(a_{2m+1}, n_{2m+1}, d_{2m+1}, p_{m+1}, c_{m+1})$$
$$schedule(a_{2m+2}, n_{2m+2}, d_{2m+2}, p_{m+2}, c_{m+1})\}.$$

Since D' must satisfy the two given functional dependencies, we have that $a_1 = a_2 = \cdots = a_{i-1}$ and $a_{i+1} = a_{i+2} = \cdots = a_{m+2}$ hold, but $a_{i-1} = a_{i+1}$ does not necessarily hold. Thus, it is clear that $p_{m+2} \notin Q(D')$, which is a contradiction, because R is a contained rewriting of Q, which means that $R(V_s)$ includes the fact p_{m+2}.

5.4.2 INVERSE-RULE ALGORITHM FOR FINDING MCRS IN PRESENCE OF EGDS

We now show how to use the inverse-rule algorithm to find MCRs in the language of Datalog for CQ queries and views in presence of egd dependencies.

We introduce a binary predicate e, which will stand for equality, i.e., $e(X, Y)$ means $X = Y$. We construct inverse rules for the views and also for the egds. That is, for each egd $A \to X_1 = X_2$ we introduce a rule whose head is $e(X_1, X_2)$ and whose body comprises the normalized version of the atoms in A. (Recall that Definition 2.11 introduced normalization for checking for containment of CQAC queries.) Before writing the inverse rules, we also normalize the view definitions. Finally, to enforce transitivity on e, we add the rule $e(X, Y) :\text{-} e(X, Z), e(Z, Y)$. We do not need to enforce symmetry of e, because it comes from the symmetry of equality. To illustrate, we now continue with Example 5.18.

Example 5.19   The normalized query rule is one of the rules of the inverse-rule program:

rule 1: $Q(P) :\text{-} schedule(A, N, D, M, C), schedule(A_1, N', D', P_1, C'),$
$e(P, P_1), e(A, A_1), e(M, Mike).$

The next rule is the inverse rule for the single view in the view set:

rule 2: $schedule(f_1(D, P, C), f_2(D, P, C), D, P, C) :\text{-} V(D, P, C).$

The egd: $d_1 : schedule(A, N, D, P, C) \wedge schedule(A', N', D', P, C') \to A = A'$ creates the inverse rule:

rule 3: $e(A, A') :\text{-} schedule(A_1, N, D, P, C), schedule(A'_1, N', D', P_1, C'),$
$e(P, P_1), e(A, A_1), e(A', A'_1).$

For the egd $d_2 : schedule(A, N, D, P, C) \wedge schedule(A', N', D', P', C) \to A = A'$, we have the inverse rule:

rule 4: $e(A, A') :\text{-} schedule(A_1, N, D, P, C), schedule(A'_1, N', D', P', C_1),$
$e(C, C_1), e(A, A_1), e(A', A'_1).$

We add also a rule to enforce transitivity of the equality predicate e:

rule 5: $e(X, Y) :\text{-} e(X, Z), e(Z, Y).$

To make sure that the relation e is reflexive, when we apply the rules we have that $e(X, X)$ is true for any value of X.

Let us see how this works on the following database instance:

$$D' = \{schedule(a_1, n_1, d_1, mike, c_1), schedule(a_2, n_2, d_2, p_2, c_1),$$
$$schedule(a_3, n_3, d_3, p_2, c_2), \ldots,$$
$$schedule(a_{2n+2}, n_{2n+2}, d_{2n+2}, p_{n+2}, c_{n+1})\}.$$

On D', we have the view instance
$$V(D') = \{v(d_1, mike, c_1), v(d_2, p_2, c_1), v(d_3, p_2, c_2), v(d_4, p_3, c_2), \ldots,$$
$v(d_{2n+2}, p_{n+1}, c_{n+1})\}.$

We apply rule 2 to derive from the v facts $schedule$ facts, e.g., $schedule(f_1(d_1, mike, c_1), f_2(d_1, mike, c_1), d_1, mike, c_1)$, $schedule(f_1(d_2, p_2, c_1), f_2(d_2, p_2, c_1), d_2, p_2, c_1)$, and so on. Then we apply rules 3 and 4 as appropriate, to obtain the e facts

$$e\Big(f_1(d_1, mike, c_1), f_1(d_2, p_2, c_1)\Big), \quad e\Big(f_1(d_2, p_2, c_1), f_1(d_3, p_2, c_2)\Big),$$

$$e\Big(f_1(d_3, p_2, c_2), f_1(d_4, p_3, c_2)\Big).$$

Then we use the last (fifth) rule, to perform essentially transitive closure on e, which yields all facts of the form

$$e\Big(f_1(d_3, p_2, c_2), f_1(d_m, p_{m-1}, c_{m-2})\Big).$$

Finally, we use these facts and rule 1 to compute the answer

$$\{P(p_1), P(p_2), P(p_3), \ldots\}.$$

MCRs for CQ queries and views under dependencies.
There is no MCR in the language of unions of CQs.
A variant of the inverse-rule algorithm finds an MCR in the language of
Datalog in the presence of egds dependencies.

5.5 EXERCISES

5.1. Prove Theorem 5.11.

5.2. Prove Theorem 5.15.

5.3. Consider Example 5.19. Prove that the following program is a Datalog MCR of Q:

$$relevantPilot(mike).$$
$$relevantAirCraft(C) :\text{-} \ V(D, mike, C).$$
$$relevantAirCraft(C) :\text{-} \ V(D, P, C), relevantPilot(P).$$
$$relevantPilot(P) :\text{-} \ relevantPilot(P_1), relevantAirCraft(C),$$
$$v(D_1, P_1, C), v(D_2, P, C).$$

This program results from the procedure described in Example 5.19 after function-symbol elimination and renaming of IDB predicates.

5.4. Prove or disprove that for the following two CQs it is true that Q_2 is contained in Q_1 under set semantics, in presence of dependencies $p(A, B, C) \rightarrow r(B, C, A)$ and $r(B, C, A), r(B, C, D) \rightarrow A = D$.

(1) $Q_1() :\text{-} \ p(A, B, C), r(B, C, A), r(B, C, D).$

   $Q_2() :\text{-} \ p(X, Y, Z), r(Z, Y, W), s(W, Y).$

(2) $Q_1() :\text{-} \ p(A, B, C), r(B, C, D).$

   $Q_2() :\text{-} \ p(X, Y, Z).$

(3) $Q_1() :\text{-} \ p(X, Y, Z), r(Y, Z, Y).$

   $Q_2() :\text{-} \ p(Y, Y, Z), r(Y, Z, Y), s(Y, Y).$

(4) $Q_1() :\text{-} \ p(X, Y, Z), r(Z, Z, Y).$

   $Q_2() :\text{-} \ p(A, A, C), r(A, C, A), r(A, C, C).$

5.5. Find all possible equivalent rewritings of the given query Q using the given set of views $\mathcal{V} = \{ U, V, W, M \}$ in presence of dependencies $p(X, Y), p(X, Z) \rightarrow Y = Z$ and $p(X, Y) \rightarrow s(Y, Y)$.

(1) $Q(X, Y) :\text{-} \ p(X, N), p(X, R), t(N, Y).$

   $U(A, B) :\text{-} \ p(A, B).$

   $V(A, B, C) :\text{-} \ p(A, C), s(C, B).$

   $W(A, B, C, D) :\text{-} \ p(A, C), t(D, B).$

   $M(A, B, C) :\text{-} \ s(A, B), t(A, C).$

5.6. Use algorithm CoreCoverΣ to find all possible equivalent rewritings of the given query Q using the given set of views $\mathcal{V} = \{ U, V, W, M \}$ in presence of weakly acyclic LAV dependencies $p(X, Y) \rightarrow X = Y$ and $p(X, Y) \rightarrow t(Y, Y)$.

(1) $Q(A) :\text{-} \ p(A, B), s(B, C), t(C, B).$

   $U(X, Y) :\text{-} \ p(X, Z), s(Z, Y).$

$$V(X, Y) \;:\text{-}\; s(X, Z), t(Z, Y).$$
$$W(X, Y) \;:\text{-}\; t(X, Y), s(U, X).$$
$$M(X, Y, Z) \;:\text{-}\; s(X, Z), t(Z, Y).$$

CHAPTER 6

Answering Queries in Data Exchange

So far, we have worked with the setting in which we would like to compute answers to query Q on database D, without having direct access to D. That is, for a set of views $\mathcal{V}$ defined on the schema of D, we are given an instance I, which is either the set of all tuples in $\mathcal{V}(D)$ or its subset. So, being unable to compute Q directly on D, we have to find techniques for answering Q on the instance I whose schema is that of the view relations. The approach we adopted in Chapters 3 and 4 was to find equivalent or maximally contained rewritings of Q using the views in $\mathcal{V}$, and to then answer Q by computing the rewritings on I. An alternative approach would be to use the view definitions to transform I into an instance D' on the schema of the query, and to then compute Q on D'. However, such a transformation is not at all straightforward. We will begin formalizing an approach to doing this after studying an introductory example.

Example 6.1 Let query Q be the path query P_4. (Recall that a path query P_n computes on a graph pairs of nodes that are separated by a connected path of length n, see Definition 2.44.) Let the single available view V be path query P_2. That is, the schema of the database has a binary relation r, hence we can view each instance as a graph on which the query defines paths of length four, and the view defines paths of length two. Clearly, $R(X, Y) :- V(X, Z), V(Z, Y)$ is an equivalent rewriting of Q in terms of V. Thus, on an instance $I = \{(1, 2), (2, 3)\}$ we would compute the set $R(I) = \{(1, 3)\}$, which would be returned correctly as $Q(D)$.

We can also take a different approach, to be considered in this chapter. Informally, we can guess that I comes from a database $D = \{(1, a), (a, 2), (2, b), (b, 3)\}$, where a and b are used as nulls, i.e., we know that these values exist, but do not have access to them.

This instance D yields $Q(D) = \{(1, 3)\}$. To provide some details, we turn the view definition into a tgd d:

$$v(X, Y) \rightarrow r(X, Z), r(Z, Y),$$

and then apply on I the chase with the set of dependencies $\Sigma = \{d\}$. It is not hard to check that the result is the above guessed database $J = D_{\Sigma} = \{(1, a), (a, 2), (2, b), (b, 3)\}$. In the formal description of this approach in this chapter, we will refer to a and b as *labeled nulls*.

We have started out by considering the specific problem of answering queries using views from a different angle. It turns out that the above approach of using tgds enables us to consider a more general setting, as long as we use tgds whose right-hand side may have more than one atom. We can also introduce additional requirements on the setting, such as dependencies on the database that we called D, whose schema "fits" the given query. Let us revisit Example 6.1 to illustrate.

Example 6.2   Let us add to the setting of Example 6.1 another tgd, d':

$$r(X, Z), r(Z, Y) \rightarrow r(Z, Z).$$

Unlike the tgd d of Example 6.1 whose left-hand side was defined using the schema of the instance I, d' uses the schema of D on both sides.

Applying on I the chase using both tgds, that is, the set $\Sigma = \{d, d'\}$, yields the instance $J = D_\Sigma = \{(1, a), (a, 2), (2, b), (b, 3), (a, a), (2, 2), (b, b)\}$. In J, a and b are labeled nulls. When computing the answers to the query Q by applying it on J, we restrict ourselves to tuples that do not contain nulls. Under this condition, compared to the setting of Example 6.1 we can find additional answers, $(2, 2)$, $(1, 2)$, and $(2, 3)$.

In this chapter we define a new problem, the *data-exchange problem*, as follows. Suppose we are given a source instance I and a set of dependencies, which are of two kinds: *source-to-target* dependencies and *target dependencies*; the former are tgds from the schema of the *source* I to the schema of the *target instance*, which is the same as the schema of the query Q that we would like to evaluate. For this setting, in Section 6.1 we will define formally *certain answers to* Q, and will show how to find certain answers using the chase.

In Example 6.1 we turned a view definition into a tgd, to illustrate how conjunctive queries can be translated into tgds. The next step that we take is to introduce into tgds arithmetic comparisons, to yield *tgd-ACs*, similarly to our defining earlier CQACs by introducing arithmetic comparisons into CQs. In Section 6.2 we consider the problem of data exchange in presence of arithmetic comparisons. Then we consider in Section 6.3 the data-exchange setting for the cases in which the given source instance is incomplete. For the problems considered in Sections 6.1 and 6.3 we use the chase defined in Chapter 5, and for the data-exchange setting with arithmetic comparisons we introduce a chase procedure that can handles arithmetic comparisons.

6.1   COMPLETE DATA EXCHANGE

Let $\mathbf{S} = \{S_1, \ldots, S_n\}$ and $\mathbf{T} = \{T_1, \ldots, T_m\}$ be two disjoint schemas, with each element of $\mathbf{S} \cup \mathbf{T}$ being a relation schema. We refer to $\mathbf{S}$ as *the source schema* and to $\mathbf{T}$ as the *target schema*. Instances over $\mathbf{S}$ are called *source instances*, whereas instances over $\mathbf{T}$ are called *target instances*. Target instances may contain values, called *labeled nulls*, that appear in the target instance but not in the source instance ("fresh" values). These unknown values are represented by variables.

A *source-to-target dependency* is a tgd of the form $\forall \mathbf{x}(\phi_{\mathbf{S}}(\mathbf{x}) \rightarrow \exists \mathbf{y} \; \psi_{\mathbf{T}}(\mathbf{x}, \mathbf{y}))$. A *target dependency* is either a tgd of the form $\forall \mathbf{x}(\phi_{\mathbf{T}}(\mathbf{x}) \rightarrow \exists \mathbf{y} \; \psi_{\mathbf{T}}(\mathbf{x}, \mathbf{y}))$, or an egd of the form $\forall \mathbf{x}(\phi_{\mathbf{T}}(\mathbf{x}) \rightarrow (x_i = x_j))$. In all dependencies, $\phi_{\mathbf{S}}(\mathbf{x})$, $\psi_{\mathbf{T}}(\mathbf{x}, \mathbf{y})$, and $\phi_{\mathbf{T}}(\mathbf{x})$ are each a conjunction of relational atoms over $\mathbf{S}$ or $\mathbf{T}$, respectively, and x_i, x_j are among variables in $\mathbf{x}$. Formally, we assume an infinite domain of constants $\underline{\texttt{Const}}$ and an infinite set $\underline{\texttt{Var}}$ of variables, called *labeled nulls*, such that $\underline{\texttt{Const}}$ and $\underline{\texttt{Var}}$ are disjoint. A source instance is a set of facts over $\underline{\texttt{Const}}$, and a target instance is a set of facts over $\underline{\texttt{Const}}$ and $\underline{\texttt{Var}}$.

We will refer to this setting as the *complete*[1] *(CDE) data-exchange setting.* The following definition summarizes a complete data-exchange setting.

Definition 6.3   (Complete data-exchange setting)
A *complete data-exchange setting (CDE)* is a quadruple $\mathbf{M} = (\mathbf{S}, \mathbf{T}, \Sigma_{st}, \Sigma_t)$, such that:
- $\mathbf{S}$ is the source schema and $\mathbf{T}$ is the target schema;
- Σ_{st} is a finite set of source-to-target tgds; and
- Σ_t is a finite set of target tgds and target egds.

We denote by Σ the union of Σ_{st} and Σ_t. In CDE settings, we do not aconsider source-to-target egds, because they are in essence source egds.

We consider query answering for conjunctive queries posed over the target schema. The semantics adopted for query answering is that of *certain answers*. Definition 6.4 defines certain answers in CDE settings. Given a CDE setting $\mathbf{M}$ and a source instance I, a target instance J is called a *solution for I under* $\mathbf{M}$ if $I \cup J$ satisfies Σ_{st} and J satisfies Σ_t. A *universal solution* is a solution such that for each solution K, there is a homomorphism that maps the universal solution into K.

Definition 6.4   (Certain answers in CDE settings)
Let $\mathbf{M} = (\mathbf{S}, \mathbf{T}, \Sigma_{st}, \Sigma_t)$ be a CDE setting, q be a union of conjunctive queries posed over the target schema $\mathbf{T}$, and I be a source instance. The *set of certain answers of q with respect to I and* $\mathbf{M}$, denoted by *certain*$_M(q, I)$, is defined as

$$certain_M(q, I) = \cap\{q(K) \mid K \in SOL(M, I)\},$$

where $SOL(M, I)$ is the set of solutions for I, and $q(K)$ denotes the result of applying q to instance K.

An infinite set of solutions may exist in a CDE setting. It then follows from Definition 6.4 that computing the set of certain answers may involve checking an infinite space of solutions. We will show that for a CDE setting $\mathbf{M}$ and source instance I, we can use the chase to produce a universal solution J for I under $\mathbf{M}$. A universal solution is used to compute the set of certain answers to queries in the language of unions of conjunctive queries.

Theorem 6.5   *Given a CDE setting* $\mathbf{M} = (\mathbf{S}, \mathbf{T}, \Sigma_{st}, \Sigma_t)$ *with source instance I, the chase on I with dependencies $\Sigma_{st} \cup \Sigma_t$ yields a universal solution for I under* $\mathbf{M}$.

---

[1]The intent of the word "complete" in this context will be apparent in Section 6.3.

The proof of Theorem 6.5 is a straightforward consequence of the property of the chase stated in Theorem 5.7.

Theorem 6.6   *For the CDE setting* $M = (S, T, \Sigma_{st}, \Sigma_t)$, *suppose* J *is a universal solution for source instance* I. *Then we can use* J *to compute certain answers to queries in the language of unions of conjunctive queries:*

$$certain_M(q, I) = q(J)_\downarrow,$$

where $q(J)_\downarrow$ *is the set of all the "null-free" tuples in* $q(J)$, *i.e., the st of all the tuples* t *in* $q(J)$ *such that each value in* t *is a constant.*

In Examples 6.1 and 6.2 we computed the certain answers of the given queries. Notice that the results presented in this section work only for unions of CQs, that is, for queries without arithmetic comparisons or negation. We will need the results of the next section to find certain answers to CQAC queries in presence of dependencies that are tgds and egds. These upcoming results are also more general, in that they consider a (more general) class of dependencies with arithmetic comparisons permitted in the definitions.

CDE setting: $M = (S, T, \Sigma_{st}, \Sigma_t)$
Σ_{st}: set of tgds
Σ_t : set of tgds and egds.
Universal solution is computed by applying the **chase** on the input I, which is an instance of the source schema S.

Let q be a query in the language of unions of conjunctive queries posed over the target schema T, and let I be a source instance. The **certain answers** of q for the input I and setting M, denoted by $certain_M(q, I)$, are computed by evaluating q on any single universal solution.

6.2   DATA EXCHANGE WITH ARITHMETIC COMPARISONS

In this section we define the setting of data exchange with arithmetic comparisons (DEAC), and show how to define and compute certain answers using a variant of the chase called the AC-chase. The DEAC setting extends the CDE setting by using arithmetic comparisons.[2] We begin by defining a new class of dependencies.

---

[2]CDEAC would be a more consistent name for DEAC; at the same time, the already-reserved word "complete" in CDE is used for the sake of ease of presentation in Section 6.3.

6.2.1 DEPENDENCIES WITH ARITHMETIC COMPARISONS

We define two new classes of dependencies, the class of tuple-generating dependencies with arithmetic comparisons, which extends the class of tuple-generating dependencies, and the class of arithmetic-comparison-generating dependencies, which extends the class of equality-generating dependencies.

Recall that an *arithmetic comparison* is of the form "$A\theta B$," where A is a variable, B is a variable or a constant, and θ is in $\{\leq, \geq, <, >, \neq, =\}$. The arithmetic comparisons that we consider are interpreted over densely totally ordered domains.

An *instance with arithmetic comparisons* (to which we will refer as "instance" whenever clear from context) is denoted in this chapter by $F(x) = F_0(x) + \beta_{F(x)}$, where $F_0(x)$ is a set of relational atoms and $\beta_{F(x)}$ is a conjunction of arithmetic comparisons. (We could also use the symbol K instead of F, to write $K(x) = K_0(x) + \beta_K(x)$.) An instance with arithmetic comparisons is in *compact form* if its conjunction of arithmetic comparisons β_F does not imply nontrivial equalities. For each instance with arithmetic comparisons, there is always an instance in compact form that represents the same ground instances, in the sense that we would obtain the same set of ground instances by replacing variables with constants so that the ACs are satisfied.

Example 6.7 Let $F = \{H(2, z_1), H(4, z_2), (z_1 = z_2) \wedge (z_2 < 2)\}$ be an instance with arithmetic comparisons. Clearly, F is not compact because of the equality $z_1 = z_2$. A compact instance obtained from F is $F' = \{H(2, z_1), H(4, z_1), z_1 < 2\}$.

We now introduce the class of *tuple-generating dependencies with arithmetic comparisons (tgd-ACs)*, which extends the class of tuple-generating dependencies (tgds), and also the class of *arithmetic-comparison-generating dependencies (in short acgds)*, which extends the class of equality-generating dependencies (egds).

Definition 6.8 (tgd-AC and acgd)
Let **R** be a database schema.
– A *tuple-generating dependency with arithmetic comparisons (tgd-AC)* is a first-order formula of the form

$$\forall x\big(\phi(x) \wedge \beta_\phi(x) \rightarrow \exists y\, \psi(x, y) \wedge \beta_\psi(x, y)\big).$$

– An *arithmetic comparison generating dependency (acgd)* is a first-order formula of the form

$$\forall x\big(\phi(x) \wedge \beta_\phi(x) \rightarrow (x_1\, \theta\, x_2)\big).$$

In the above formulas, $\phi(x)$ is a conjunction of atoms over **R** with variables in x, with each variable in x occurring in at least one atom in $\phi(x)$. In addition, $\psi(x, y)$ is a conjunction of relational atoms with variables in x and y, such that each variable in y occurs in at least one atom in $\psi(x, y)$. Furthermore, x_1 is a variable from x and x_2 is either a variable from x or a constant; $\beta_\phi(x)$ and $\beta_\psi(x, y)$ are each a conjunction of arithmetic comparisons with variables from x and x, y, respectively.

In some cases, we will drop the universal and existential quantifiers in tgd-ACs and acgds, implicitly assuming such quantification. We will use the abbreviation *rhs*, *lhs*, respectively, to refer to the right-hand side, left-hand side, respectively, of a tgd-AC or an acgd. A tgd-AC with no existentially quantified variables is called *full* tgd-AC.

Let $d : \forall \mathbf{x}\big(\phi(\mathbf{x}) \wedge \beta_\phi(\mathbf{x}) \rightarrow \exists \mathbf{y}\ \psi(\mathbf{x}, \mathbf{y}) \wedge \beta_\psi(\mathbf{x}, \mathbf{y})\big)$ be a tgd-AC and D a database instance. We say that D *satisfies* d if whenever there is a homomorphism h from $\phi(\mathbf{x})$ to D such that $\beta_\phi(h(\mathbf{x}))$ is true, there exists an *extension* h' of h such that h' is a homomorphism from the conjunction $\phi(\mathbf{x}) \wedge \psi(\mathbf{x}, \mathbf{y})$ to D with $\beta_\psi(h'(\mathbf{x}, \mathbf{y}))$ evaluating to true. While for tgds and egds, there is always a non-empty database on which the dependency is satisfied, this property does not hold for tgd-ACs and acgds. We call a tgd-AC (or an acgd) d *consistent* if its arithmetic comparisons are not inconsistent. Notice that if the given arithmetic comparisons d are inconsistent, there does not exist a non-empty database instance on which d would be satisfied.

For dependencies with arithmetic comparisons, the input should be a set of relational atoms over a totally ordered domain. While ground instances satisfy this requirement, for the purposes of DEAC data-exchange settings (to be defined in the next section) and of computing certain answers on them, we need to consider instances that use variables alongside constants. For this purpose, we define a *t-instance* to be a set of relational atoms over a totally ordered domain that contains both constants and variables. For instance, if we have constants 3 and 4 and variables X and Y, two possible total orders on them are $3 < X = Y < 4$ and $3 < 4 < X < Y$. We will use the term *t-homomorphism* to refer to a homomorphism from a relational structure K with arithmetic comparisons to a t-instance K_t such that the homomorphism makes the dependencies of K true on K_t.

Recall that in the CDE setting that was defined in Section 6.1, we did not use egds in the set of source-to-target dependencies, because such egds would essentially impose dependencies on the source data, where they are not needed. For the same reason, we do not use acgds in the set of source-to-target dependencies in DEAC settings, and also require that the tgd-ACs in this set have ACs that contain at least one existential variable. The reason is that if a tgd-AC involves ACs defined over non-existential variables only, then the tgd-AC is equivalent to a set comprising both acgds and tgd-ACs whose ACs contain at least one existential variable. The following example illustrates how to produce such an equivalent set of dependencies.

Example 6.9   Consider the following target tgd-AC:
$$d : a(X, Y), b(Y, W) \rightarrow c(X, Y), X < Y.$$
The arithmetic comparison $X < Y$ does not contain an existentially quantified variable (i.e., a variable that only appears on the right-hand side of the tgd-AC). Thus, d is equivalent to a set of dependencies consisting of a tgd d_1 and acgd d_2, defined as follows:
$$d_1 : a(X, Y), b(Y, W) \rightarrow c(X, Y),$$
$$d_2 : a(X, Y), b(Y, W) \rightarrow X < Y.$$

6.2.2 THE AC-CHASE

To be able to discuss the DEAC setting further, we need to develop a new technical tool, which we call AC-chase. A property of the AC-chase is that it is not linear, in the sense that its chase step can produce from an instance a set of instances, each of which is then chased further. We now provide the details.

AC-chase

While using the same main idea as the chase procedure, *AC-chase* it produces a tree rather than a sequence. The reason is that the result of an AC-chase step on a t-instance may not always be a t-instance. Instead, it could be an instance containing a partial, rather than a total, order. We say that a t-instance K^t *is induced* by instance K if K^t is constructed from K by adding ACs in such a way that all the variables and constants appearing in the relational atoms in K^t now have a total ordering, which is imposed on them by the ACs. If K is the instance resulting from an AC-chase step, before proceeding to the next AC-chase step we might need to consider all the t-instances induced by K. The result of applying AC-chase is a set of instances found on the leaves of the AC-chase tree.

Definition 6.10 (AC-chase step)
Let $K = K_0 \wedge \beta_K$ be a t-instance. An *AC-chase step* consists of three stages.
Stage I: Construct an instance K' by adding to K relational facts and arithmetic comparisons.

(a) **(tgd-AC):** Let $d : \phi(\mathbf{x}) \wedge \beta_\phi(\mathbf{x}) \rightarrow \psi(\mathbf{x}, \mathbf{y}) \wedge \beta_\psi(\mathbf{x}, \mathbf{y})$ be a tgd-AC. Let h be a t-homomorphism from $\phi(\mathbf{x}) \wedge \beta_\phi(\mathbf{x})$ to K, such that there is no extension of h to a t-homomorphism from $\phi(\mathbf{x}) \wedge \beta_\phi(\mathbf{x}) \wedge \psi(\mathbf{x}, \mathbf{y}) \wedge \beta_\psi(\mathbf{x}, \mathbf{y})$ to K. We then say that d can be applied to K with t-homomorphism h. Let h_0 be the underlying homomorphism of h, and let K'_0 be the union of K_0 with the set of facts obtained by:

  (i) extending h_0 to a homomorphism h'_0 in such a way that every variable in $\mathbf{y}$ is assigned a fresh labeled null, followed by

  (ii) taking the image of the atoms in the rhs of d under h'_0.

  For each arithmetic comparison $x_1 \theta x_2$ in $\beta_\psi(\mathbf{x})$, we add $h'_0(x_1 \theta x_2)$ to K'_0, and output K' in compact form.

(b) **(acgd):** Let d be an acgd $\phi(\mathbf{x}) \wedge \beta_\phi(\mathbf{x}) \rightarrow (x_1 \theta x_2)$. Let h be a t-homomorphism from $\phi(\mathbf{x}) \wedge \beta_\phi(\mathbf{x})$ to K, such that $h(x_1 \theta x_2)$ is not true. We then say that d can be applied to K with t-homomorphism h. We add $h(x_1 \theta x_2)$ to K, and output K'.

Stage II: Check K' for consistency. We distinguish between two cases.

(1) If K' is not consistent, we say that the result of applying d to K with h is "failure," and write $K \xrightarrow{d,h} \bot$.

(2) Otherwise, we say that the result of applying d to K with h is K', denoted $K \xrightarrow{d,h} K'$.

Stage III: Return all the induced t-instances $K'_1, \ldots, K'_n$ of K' in compact form, and denote this step $K \xrightarrow{d,h} \{K'_1, \ldots, K'_n\}$.

We now define the AC-chase tree, the finite AC-chase, and the successful AC-chase.

Definition 6.11 (AC-chase tree)
Let Σ be a set of tgd-ACs and acgds, and J be an instance. An *AC-chase tree* of J with Σ is a tree (finite or infinite) such that:

- the root is a dummy node with children all t-instances induced by J; and

- for each node K in the tree, let $\{K'_1, \ldots, K'_l\}$ be the set of its children. There must exist a tgd-AC or an acgd d in Σ, a t-homomorphism h from the lhs of d to K, and an instance K', such that $K \xrightarrow{d,h} K'$, and $K'_1, \ldots, K'_l$ are all the t-instances induced by K'.

A *finite AC-chase* of J with Σ is a finite chase tree such that each leaf is either $\perp$ or satisfies Σ. The *result of a finite AC-chase* is the union of all the leaf nodes that are not $\perp$. If the result is not empty, we refer to it as the result of a *finite successful AC-chase*.

Example 6.12   Suppose we have the following set Σ of dependencies:
$$d_1 : a(X, Y) \rightarrow b(X, Y, Z), Z \leq X.$$
$$d_2 : b(X, Y, Z), Z < X \rightarrow c(X, W), W \leq X.$$
$$d_3 : c(X, X) \rightarrow d(X).$$
$$d_4 : c(X, W), W < X \rightarrow e(X).$$
Let $I = \{a(1, 2)\}$ be a ground instance on which we apply AC-chase using the dependencies in Σ. The AC-chase tree has depth six, and is as follows.

1. The root is $I = \{a(1, 2)\}$.

2. Applying d_1 to the root yields (a child of the root that is) $I_1 = \{a(1, 2), b(1, 2, Z), Z \leq 1\}$; this is the second level of the tree.

3. The child of the root has a partial order, so we construct two nodes in the third level of the tree, as the only possible total orderings are $Z < 1$ and $Z = 1$. These are the two total orderings that are induced by $Z \leq 1$ in the instance $I_1 = \{a(1, 2), b(1, 2, Z), Z \leq 1\}$ that resulted from the above application of d_1. The instances $I_{21} = \{a(1, 2), b(1, 2, 1)\}$ and $I_{22} = \{a(1, 2), b(1, 2, Z), Z < 1\}$ are the children of I_1.

4. Applying d_2 to I_{22} yields $I_{31} = \{a(1, 2), b(1, 2, 1), c(1, W), W \leq 1\}$ as the child of I_{22}.

5. We create two children of I_{31}, I_{41} and I_{42}, for the two total orderings induced by the partial order: $I_{41} = \{a(1,2), b(1,2,1), c(1,1)\}$ and $I_{42} = \{a(1,2), b(1,2,1), c(1,W), W < 1\}$.

6. Applying d_3 to I_{41} yields $I_{51} = \{a(1,2), b(1,2,1), c(1,1), d(1)\}$. Applying d_4 to I_{42} yields $I_{52} = \{a(1,2), b(1,2,1), c(1,W), e(1), W < 1\}$.

The output of the AC-chase is the set of the three leaves

$$\{I_{21}, I_{51}, I_{52}\}.$$

The following result is analogous to Theorem 5.7.

Theorem 6.13   *Let Σ be a set of tgds and egds. Suppose D is a ground database instance that satisfies the dependencies in Σ. Let K be a t-instance such that there is a t-homomorphism h from K to D. Let K_Σ be the result of a successful finite AC-chase on K with the set of dependencies Σ. Then there is a t-instance, K_Σ^t, in K_Σ such that t-homomorphism h can be extended to a t-homomoprhism h' from K_Σ^t to D.*

Proof. While the proof is generally along the lines of the proof of Theorem 5.7, here we have the additional task of deciding which child on the chase tree to follow. We choose the one whose t-instance restricted to the newly added labeled nulls conforms with (i.e., is the same as) the total order on the structure (D) that we are considering, as follows. Based on extending h through the previous AC-chase steps, we construct an intermediate h_i. Via this h_i, in the current AC-chase step that considers dependency d, we map by mapping μ the left-hand side of d to D, then find the extension of μ that satisfies d. (Such an extension always exists, since D satisfies the dependencies.) The variables in D that are involved in this extension of μ have a certain total order, which is the total order that we use to choose the child on the AC-chase tree of the current AC-chase step. $\square$

We now discuss termination conditions for the AC-chase. We define weak acyclicity for a set of AC-tgds by first dropping the ACs from the AC-tgds; we call the outcome the derived set of tgds. We say that *a set of AC-tgds is weakly acyclic* if the derived set of tgds is weakly acyclic. The following result can be proven either using the proof of Theorem 5.6, or by observing that each path on the AC-chase tree can produce a chase sequence if we use the derived set of tgds. The lengths of the resulting paths are only a fraction shorter than the input path on the AC-chase tree. The value of the fraction can be computed by observing that dropping the ACs from multiple tgd-ACs could result in the same tgd; the number of tgd-ACs resulting in the same tgd is at most equal to the total number of tgd-ACs in the given set of dependencies.

Theorem 6.14   *If a set of AC-tgds and acgds is weakly acyclic ,then the AC-chase using the set terminates on every instance.*

6.2.3 SOLUTIONS AND UNIVERSAL SOLUTIONS

We now define the concepts of *solution* and *universal solution* in a DEAC setting. Not surprisingly, both definitions share similarities with the corresponding definitions in simple data-exchange settings (i.e., settings without arithmetic comparisons).

Definition 6.15   (Solution and universal solution)
Let $\mathbf{M} = (\mathbf{S}, \mathbf{T}, \Sigma_{st}, \Sigma_t)$ be a DEAC setting, and I be a source instance.

- We call an instance J over $\mathbf{T}$ a *t-solution for I under $\mathbf{M}$* (or simply *t-solution*, in case I and $\mathbf{M}$ are understood from the context) if J is a t-instance that satisfies the dependencies Σ_t, and the instance $I \cup J$ satisfies the dependencies $\Sigma_{st} \cup \Sigma_t$. A t-solution that is a ground instance is called a *ground solution*.

- We call an instance J of $\mathbf{T}$ a *solution for I under $\mathbf{M}$* (or simply *solution*, in case I and $\mathbf{M}$ are understood from the context) if every t-instance induced by J is a t-solution.

- A *universal solution* for I under $\mathbf{M}$ (or simply *universal solution*, in case I and $\mathbf{M}$ are understood from the context) is a *set* $\mathcal{J} = \{J_1, \ldots, J_m\}$ of solutions for I, such that for every ground solution K, there is a solution $J_i \in \mathcal{J}$ that t-homomorphically maps to K. A *universal t-solution* is a universal solution that consists solely of t-solutions.

The following example illustrates the concepts of solution and universal solution in DEAC settings.

Example 6.16   Let $\mathbf{M} = (\mathbf{S}, \mathbf{T}, \Sigma_{st}, \Sigma_t)$ be a DEAC setting in which $\mathbf{S}$ has a single binary relation E, $\mathbf{T}$ has a single binary relation H, $\Sigma_t = \emptyset$, and
$$\Sigma_{st} = \{ d : E(X, Y), X < Y \to \exists Z (H(X, Z), H(Z, Y), Z < X \}.$$
Let $\mathrm{I} = \{E(2, 5), E(4, 7)\}$ be a ground instance defined over the source schema $\mathbf{S}$. Consider the following instances over the target schema $\mathbf{T}$:

$$J_1 = \{H(2, z_1), H(z_1, 5), H(4, z_2), H(z_2, 7), z_2 < z_1 < 2\};$$
$$J_2 = \{H(2, z_1), H(z_1, 5), H(4, z_2), H(z_2, 7), z_1 = z_2 < 2\};$$
$$J_3 = \{H(2, z_1), H(z_1, 5), H(4, z_2), H(z_2, 7), z_1 < z_2 < 2\};$$
$$J_4 = \{H(2, z_1), H(z_1, 5), H(4, z_2), H(z_2, 7), z_1 < 2 = z_2\};$$
$$J_5 = \{H(2, z_1), H(z_1, 5), H(4, z_2), H(z_2, 7), z_1 < 2 < z_2 < 4\};$$
$$J_6 = \{H(2, z_1), H(z_1, 5), H(4, z_2), H(z_2, 7), z_1 < 2, z_2 > 7\};$$
$$J_7 = \{H(2, z_1), H(z_1, 5), H(4, z_2), H(z_2, 7), z_2 < z_1 < 3\};$$
$$J_8 = \{H(2, z_1), H(z_1, 5), H(4, z_2), H(z_2, 7), z_1 < 2, z_2 \le 2\};$$
$$J_9 = \{H(2, z_1), H(z_1, 5), H(4, z_2), H(z_2, 7), z_1 < 2, z_2 < 4\};$$
$$J_{10} = \{H(2, 1), H(1, 5), H(4, 0), H(0, 7)\};$$
$$J_{11} = \{H(2, 2), H(2, 5), H(4, 0), H(0, 7), H(8, 7)\}.$$

Note that in all instances above we omitted the trivial total order $2 < 4 < 5 < 7$. For instance, the total order in J_1 should be $z_2 < z_1 < 2 < 4 < 5 < 7$. J_1 is a t-instance, since its arithmetic comparisons define a total order of its labeled nulls (z_1 and z_2) and its constants in I. (There is no constant in the tgd-AC.) Similarly, J_2, J_3, J_4, J_5, and J_6 are all t-instances.

J_1 is a t-solution, because the dependency d in Σ_{st} is satisfied on $I \cap J_1$. Indeed, there are two homomorphism from the left-hand side of d to $I \cap J_1$, the homomorphism h_1 that maps X to 2 and Y to 5 and the homomorphism h_2 that maps X to 4 and Y to 7. In $I \cap J_1$, h_1 can be extended to a homomorphism h'_1 that maps the right-hand side of d to $I \cap J_1$ (the extended homomorphism maps Z to z_1) and the images of the arithmetic comparisons in d under h'_1 are also satisfied, hence h'_1 is a t-homomorphism. Similarly, J_2–J_5 are t-solutions. J_6 is not a t-solution, because the arithmetic comparison $z_2 > 7$ ruins the possibility of the dependency d being satisfied on $I \cap J_6$.

J_7, J_8, and J_9 are instances but not t-instances. Indeed, in each instance two different total orderings are possible. In J_7, we have at least the following two total orderings: $z_2 < z_1 < 2 < 3 < 4 < 5 < 7$ or $z_2 < 2 < z_1 < 3 < 4 < 5 < 7$. (Recall that we have to take into account the constants 2, 4, 5, and 7.)

In J_8, we have at least the following two total orderings: $z_2 < z_1 < 2 < 3 < 4 < 5 < 7$ and $z_1 < z_2 < 2 < 3 < 4 < 5 < 7$. In J_9, we have at least the following two total orderings: $z_2 < z_1 < 2 < 3 < 4 < 5 < 7$ and $z_1 < z_2 < 2 < 3 < 4 < 5 < 7$.

J_1–J_5 are all the t-instances induced by J_9; J_9 is a solution but not a t-solution, because it is not a t-instance. Similarly, J_7 and J_8 are solutions.

Both J_{10} and J_{11} are ground instances, since they do not contain labeled nulls. J_{10} is a ground solution, because the two homomorphisms from the left-hand side of d to $I \cap J_{10}$ can be extended by mapping the variable Z of d to the constant 1 for the extension of one of the homomorphisms, and by mapping Z to the constant 0 for the extension of the other homomorphism. The images of the arithmetic comparisons of d are also satisfied, since $1 < 2$ and $0 < 4$. J_{11} is not a solution.

There is a t-homomorphism h from J_7 to J_1, where h is the identity mapping from $\underline{\text{Const}}(J_7) \cup \underline{\text{Var}}(J_7)$ to $\underline{\text{Const}}(J_1) \cup \underline{\text{Var}}(J_1)$. In particular, the mapping turns $z_2 < z_1 < 3$ into $z_2 < z_1 < 3$, which is implied by $z_2 < z_1 < 2$. Similarly, J_1 t-homomorphically maps to the ground instance J_{10}. However, there is no t-homomorphism from J_6 to J_1, because the identity mapping from the variables of J_6 to the variables of J_1 is the only homomorphism, provided that we ignore the arithmetic comparisons; this is not a t-homomorphism, because the ACs in J_1 do not imply the ACs in J_6. In other words, $z_2 < z_1 < 3$ does not imply $z_1 < 2$ and $z_2 > 7$.

Finally, J_1, J_2, J_3, and J_4 are all the t-instances induced by J_8.

The following result is analogous to Theorem 6.5 for the CDE settings discussed in Section 6.1.

Theorem 6.17   *Given a DEAC setting* $\mathbf{M} = (\mathbf{S}, \mathbf{T}, \Sigma_{st}, \Sigma_t)$ *with source instance I, the AC-chase on I with dependencies* $\Sigma_{st} \cup \Sigma_t$ *yields a universal solution for I under* $\mathbf{M}$.

Example 6.18   (Continued from Example 6.16)
The set $\mathcal{J}_1 = \{J_1, \ldots, J_5\}$ is a universal t-solution computed by the AC-chase as follows: In the first step, we add the following relational atoms and ACs:

$$\{H(2, z_1), H(z_1, 5), H(4, z_2), H(z_2, 7), z_1 < 2, z_2 < 4\}.$$

The second step produces the induced t-instances, which yield the set $\mathcal{J}_1 = \{J_1, \ldots, J_5\}$.

$\mathcal{J}_3 = \{J_9\}$ is a universal solution, since all the induced t-solutions of J_9 comprise the universal t-solution computed above. The set $\mathcal{J}_2 = \{J_5, J_8\}$ is a universal solution, because all the induced t-solutions of J_8 comprise the universal t-solution computed above, except J_5.

We now contrast solutions in DEAC settings with solutions in simple data-exchange settings (i.e., in settings without arithmetic comparisons). For example, consider instance $K : a(5, N_1), b(5, N_2)$ and tgd $d : a(5, N), b(5, N) \rightarrow c(X, N)$. Observe that K is a solution in simple data-exchange settings, since there is no homomorphism from the lhs of d to K. However, K is not a solution in a DEAC setting, because a ground instance of K is $K' : a(5, 8), b(5, 8)$, and there exists a homomorphism from the lhs of d to K' that cannot be extended. This observation should not come as a surprise.

6.2.4   SOLUTIONS AND CONJUNCTIVE QUERIES

We now discuss how solutions for a DEAC setting can be connected to CQAC queries, and how solutions for a CDE setting can be connected to CQ queries. First, with every instance K we associate a Boolean conjunctive query with arithmetic comparisons q^K, such that the body of q^K contains exactly all the facts in K as subgoals (with labeled nulls replaced by variables), and the (possibly partial) order of K is added to q^K as arithmetic-comparison predicates. We use a fresh predicate name for the predicate in the head of q^K. We call q^K the *corresponding Boolean query* of K. We also associate a Boolean query with a set of instances, by creating for each instance a Boolean query with the same head predicate and by then taking the union of the resulting queries. Proposition 6.19 states that a universal solution contains any solution as a query. Its proof is a rather straightforward consequence of Theorem 6.13. Moreover, we also provide here for completeness Proposition 6.20, which holds for CDE settings; the proof is immediate from the definition of universal solution in CDE settings.

Proposition 6.19   *Let* $\mathbf{M} = (\mathbf{S}, \mathbf{T}, \Sigma_{st}, \Sigma_t)$ *be a DEAC setting. If* $\mathcal{J}$ *is a universal solution of* $(\mathbf{M}, I)$, *then for each* $K \in SOL(\mathbf{M}, I)$, *we have that* $q^{\mathcal{J}}$ *contains* q^K.

Similarly, for the CDE setting we have the following result, in which q^J and q^K are CQs without arithmetic comparisons.

Proposition 6.20   *Let* $M = (S, T, \Sigma_{st}, \Sigma_t)$ *be a CDE setting. If* J *is a universal solution of* (M, I), *then for each* $K \in SOL(M, I)$, *we have that* q^J *contains* q^K.

6.2.5 QUERY ANSWERING

In this section we study the *query-answering problem* in DEAC settings, for queries posed over the target schema that belong to the class of *unions of conjunctive queries with arithmetic comparisons* (unions of CQACs).

Certain answers in a DEAC setting are defined over all ground solutions, because CQAC queries should be computed over domains that are totally ordered. (Recall that we restrict ourselves to ground instances over totally ordered domains.)

Definition 6.21   (Certain answers in DEAC settings)
Let $M = (S, T, \Sigma_{st}, \Sigma_t)$ be a DEAC setting, I be a source instance, and q be a CQAC query posed over the target schema T. Then,

$$certain_M(q, I) = \cap \{q(J) : J \in GS(M, I)\},$$

where $GS(M, I)$ is the set of all the ground solutions for I under M, and $q(J)$ is the result of evaluating q on J.

In DEAC settings and for CQAC queries, some challenges may arise from the fact that the query may contain constants that do not appear in the t-instance. Therefore, the order of the t-instance, even if it is a total order on the instance itself, may no longer be a total order with respect to the additional constants in the query. For this reason, we introduce the concept of a *qt-instance*, defined as an instance that forms a total order with respect to also the constants of the query.

Qt-instances
The following example illustrates that the concept of qt-instance may prove to be necessary.

Example 6.22   Consider the following CQAC query:

$$q : \text{ans}(A) :\!- R(A), A < 3.$$

Let $J = \{R(X), X < 7\}$ be a t-instance. If we substitute the constant 2 for the labeled null $X \in J$, the answer to the query would be $\{2\}$. However, if we substitute the constant 5 for X, the answer to the query becomes *empty*. Observe that, although J defines a total order with respect to its own constants and labeled nulls, the query may introduce fresh constants (e.g., the constant 3 in this case). Consequently, J may no longer form a total order w.r.t. the labeled nulls, the constants in the t-instance, and the fresh constants of the query.

Formally, let $\mathbf{M} = (\mathbf{S}, \mathbf{T}, \Sigma_{st}, \Sigma_t)$ be a DEAC setting, q be a CQAC query, and J be an instance over $\mathbf{T}$. Let $\mathcal{C} = \underline{\text{Const}}(J) \cup \underline{\text{Const}}(\Sigma_{st} \cup \Sigma_t) \cup \underline{\text{Const}}(q)$. An instance K is called a *qt-instance with respect to q and J under* $\mathbf{M}$ if it is a t-instance with respect to $\mathcal{C}$ and the labeled nulls of K. For simplicity, we say that K is a *qt-instance induced by* J whenever clear from the context.

Evaluating a CQAC Query on an Instance

We now show how the concept of qt-instance can be used to evaluate a CQAC query q on a given t-instance J. Let J_q denote the *set of qt-instances of J w.r.t. q*, which we define to be all the qt-instances J_i such that there is a t-homomorphism from J to J_i. Definition 6.23 formalizes the evaluation of a CQAC query on a t-instance. We evaluate a query q on a qt-instance K by treating the labeled nulls in K as distinct constants, and by removing from the output the tuples containing labeled nulls. (The latter is denoted by the operator "$\downarrow$".)

Definition 6.23   Let J be an instance and q be a CQAC query. Let J_q be the set of qt-instances of J w.r.t. q. The result of evaluating q on J, denoted $q(J)$, is defined as:

$$q(J) = \cap\{q(K)_\downarrow : K \in J_q\},$$

where $q(K)$ is the set of answers of q on qt-instance K.

Computing Certain Answers

The following result is analogous to Theorem 6.6.

Theorem 6.24   *Let J be a universal solution for a given DEAC setting and source instance. Then for any query q in the language of unions of CQACs, J can be used to compute the certain answers to q, as follows:*

$$certain_M(q, I) = \cap_{J \in \mathcal{J}} q(J).$$

Here, $q(J)$ is computed as in Definition 6.23.

The following example uses Definition 6.23 to compute certain answers of a query on an instance.

Example 6.25

Consider the following query Q and t-instance J:

$$\begin{aligned} &\text{Q:} \quad q() \text{ :- } R(A, B), A > 3, B < 5; \\ &\text{J:} \quad \{R(x, y), R(y, z), 3 < x < z < 4 < y\}. \end{aligned}$$

To test if the query Q is true on the instance J, we need to find a homomorphism from the single subgoal of the query to one of the two facts in J, such that the arithmetic comparisons in the query would be satisfied. Consider homomorphism μ_1, which maps A to x and B to y. The homomorphism μ_1 maps the subgoal $R(A, B)$ to the fact $R(x, y)$. We also require that $\mu_1(A) > 3$ and $\mu_1(B) < 5$, i.e., we require that x > 3 and y < 5. The comparison x > 3 is true in J, but we know nothing about the comparison y < 5. However, we know that there are two cases for y: Either y < 5 or y ≥ 5. In the first case, μ_1 suffices to answer the query. In the second case, consider μ_2 that maps A to y and B to z. Now we require that $\mu_2(A) > 3$ and $\mu_2(B) < 5$, that is, that y > 3 and z < 5. Since y ≥ 5, the first requirement is satisfied. The second requirement is also satisfied, because z < 4. Thus, the answer to Q on J is true. To compute the answers, we used the following qt-instances that are induced by the instance J:

$$J_1: \quad \{R(x, y), R(y, z), 3 < x < z < 4 < y < 5\}.$$
$$J_2: \quad \{R(x, y), R(y, z), 3 < x < z < 4 < y = 5\}.$$
$$J_3: \quad \{R(x, y), R(y, z), 3 < x < z < 4 < 5 < y\}.$$

The Algorithm for Computing Certain Answers of a CQAC Query

The main goal of this section is to show how we can use a universal solution to compute the certain answers of a CQAC query posed over the target schema of a DEAC setting. By Theorem 6.24, the following algorithm computes the certain answers.

1. Compute the universal solution J of the DEAC setting by applying AC-chase.

2. For each leaf of the universal solution, take its qt-instance.

3. For each leaf of the universal solution and for each qt-instance J_i induced by this leaf, compute $q(J_i)$.

4. Compute the intersection of all the $q(J_i)$ computed in Step 3. Keep in the intersection only those tuples that do not involve variables. The resulting set is the set of certain answers.

DEAC setting: $M = (S, T, \Sigma_{st}, \Sigma_t)$
Σ_{st}: set of tgd-ACs
Σ_t : set of acgds and egd-ACs.
A **universal solution** is computed by applying the **AC-chase** algorithm on the input I, which is an instance on the source schema **S**.

Let q be a union of conjunctive queries with arithmetic comparisons posed over the target schema **T**, and I be a source instance. The set of **certain answers** of q for the input I and setting **M**, denoted by $certain_M(q, I)$, is computed by evaluating q on the universal solution.

6.2.6   WHEN THE HOMOMORPHISM PROPERTY HOLDS—PRELIMINARIES

Similarly to what we saw in previous chapters in this book, when we reason about homomorphisms in presence of arithmetic comparisons, there could be special cases that allow for simpler algorithms. In particular, the homomorphism property that we discussed earlier can be useful in simplifying the AC-chase for special kinds of tgd-ACs and acgds. We now provide the definition: If $(\mathcal{B}_1, \mathcal{B}_2)$ is a pair of sets of ACs that enables the homomorphism property (see page 35) and Σ is a set of tgd-ACs and acgds such that (i) all the ACs on the left-hand sides of all the dependencies in Σ belong to the class $\mathcal{B}_1$, and (ii) all the ACs on the right-hand sides belong to $\mathcal{B}_2$, then we say that Σ *has the homomorphism property for AC-chase.*

Recall that we call a tgd or a tgd-AC *full* if it does not have existential variables. (That is, all the variables on the right-hand side of a tgd or tgd-AC also appear on the left-hand side.) Whenever we use full tgd-ACs in a set of source-to-target dependencies, we will require that they have ACs only on the left-hand side.

Before we formally introduce a version of AC-chase applicable to the cases in which the homomorphism property holds, we will provide some intuition, by presenting simple cases in which we do not need the chase tree to provide answers to queries. We will be using the abbreviation UCQAC for the query language of unions of CQACs.

- Case I: Σ_{st} comprises full tgd-ACs; Σ_t comprises full tgd-ACs and acgds; queries: UCQAC.

  It is straightforward to show that no labeled nulls are produced during the AC-chase in this case. Indeed, labeled nulls are the only reason for AC-chase to produce a tree instead of a sequence, because in every step it has to create one or more descendant t-instances. Thus, in this special case we have only one ground solution.

- Case II: The dependencies are tgds and egds, and queries are unions of CQs.

  While this case is covered by the CDE setting, let us discuss it in a little more detail. In this case, AC-chase will actually create a tree. It turns out that the tree is not necessary for the purpose of answering CQs, because there are no ACs either in the dependencies or in the query. Hence, we can show that in this case we can use regular chase, rather than AC-chase, and then find the certain answers by evaluating the query on the outcome.

  For the general case of answering CQAC queries in presence of tgd and egd dependencies, we need AC-chase. While this case will not be formally discussed further in this book, we note that the way to approach it is to do postprocessing on the results of AC-chase, as all the total orderings need to be considered. That is, we use AC-chase on an input I, and then produce all the t-instances induced by the outcome J. We then obtain the certain answers to the given CQAC query by evaluating the query on each of theses t-instances and taking the intersection of the answers. The following example shows that we cannot do better than considering all total orderings, because one homomorphism is not enough to evaluate a CQAC query.

Example 6.26   We are given a single source-to-target tgd d and no target dependencies:

$$d :$$
$$r(Z, Z', W) \rightarrow s(W), p(X, Y, Z', Z, U, U), p(Z, Z', X, Y, U, U), p(Z, Z', Z', Z, X, Y).$$

On input instance $I = \{r(1, 2, 3)\}$, the output of AC-chase is

$$J = \{s(3), p(X, Y, 2, 1, U, U), p(1, 2, X, Y, U, U), p(1, 2, 2, 1, X, Y)\}.$$

Consider CQAC query Q:

$$q(W) :\text{-} \ s(W), p(X, Y, Z, Z', U, U), X < Y, Z > Z'.$$

Evaluating this query on all the t-instances induced by J and taking the intersection of the answers yields the final answer $\{(3)\}$. That is, although J is derived by AC-chase and can on its own represent all the t-solutions that are necessary to answer the query, to answer the query we still need to perform another step that produces all the t-solutions induced by J.

Notice the relationship of this case here with the setting of Example 2.17. Indeed, the intuition is the same in both cases. In this current example, we have to consider all the total orderings of the variables X, Y, and U, with constants 1 and 2 added, to make sure that there is a way to satisfy the dependencies using J. While we know we will not get any query answer other than (3), it is conceivable that we could get the empty answer if the arithmetic comparisons in the query q are not satisfied when q is computed on J. The only way to ensure that the arithmetic comparisons of q are satisfied is to consider more than one homomorphism from the query subgoals to J.

- Case III: The dependencies are tgds and egds, and queries belong to the language UCQAC-LSI with closed LSIs.

This is an extension of the case above in which queries are CQs. In this case, we can use chase to produce a universal solution J, and then evaluate the query using a single homomorphism from the query to J. This approach is correct because of the homomorphism property.

- Case IV: Σ_{st} comprises tgd-ACs; Σ_t is empty; queries are unions of CQs.

  Here, when we use AC-chase, in each chase step the left-hand side of any tgd in Σ_{st} can map to constants only. Thus, we do not need the t-instances, and hence do not need the tree produced by AC-chase.

- Case V: Σ_{st} comprises tgd-ACs; Σ_t is empty; queries are UCQAC with the homomorphism property.

  This case is an extension of the previous case.

  The succinct AC-chase introduced in the following section builds on the intuition of these cases.

6.2.7   SUCCINCT AC-CHASE

We introduce a new chase procedure called *succinct AC-chase (SAC-chase)*. In SAC-chase, we obtain chase sequences, rather than trees as in the case of AC-chase.

For ease of reference, as we did with t-homomorphism, we define the concept of *p-homomorphism*. This notion extends naturally the notion of *t-homomorphism*, by allowing a mapping from an instance with arithmetic comparisons to an instance with *partial*, rather than total, order. (Those instances are thus not necessarily t-instances.) The formal definition follows.

Definition 6.27   (p-homomorphism)
Let $F(\mathbf{x}) = F_0(\mathbf{x}) + \beta_F(\mathbf{x})$ be a instance and $K(\mathbf{x}) = K_0(\mathbf{x}) + \beta_K(\mathbf{x})$ be an instance in compact form. A *p-homomorphism* h from F to K is a mapping from $\underline{\text{Const}}(F) \cup \underline{\text{Var}}(F)$ to $\underline{\text{Const}}(K) \cup \underline{\text{Var}}(K)$ with the following properties.
- Each constant in F is mapped to itself in K.
- Whenever $R(x_1, \ldots, x_k)$ holds in F, $R(h(x_1), \ldots, h(x_k))$ holds in K.
- $\beta_K(\mathbf{x}) \Rightarrow \beta_F(h(\mathbf{x}))$.

We say that F *p-homomorphically maps to* K if there is a p-homomorphism from F to K. A p-homomorphism h from F to K implies a homomorphism h_0 from F_0 to K_0. We call h_0 the *underlying homomorphism* of h.

Informally, a p-homomorphism is a homomorphism h from F_0 to K_0, such that the ACs in K imply the image under h of the ACs in F.

The following result relates a p-homomorphism to t-homomorphisms. Recall that we use the term "instance" to refer to sets of relational atoms associated with a set of ACs on the variables appearing in the atoms.

Proposition 6.28   *Let F and K be two instances, with K in compact form. If there exists a p-homomorphism from F to K, then there exists a t-homomorphism from F to each induced t-instance of K.*

Proof. Let h be the p-homomorphism from F to K, and let K_i be the t-instance induced by K. By definition of induced t-instance, there exists a t-homomorphism h_i from K to K_i. The composition $h_i \circ h$ is a t-homomorphism from F to K_i. ☐

Let d_1 be a tgd-AC, d_2 be an acgd, and K be an instance, possibly with partial order. Similarly to the case of instances with total order, we say that K *p-satisfies* d_1 if, whenever there is a p-homomorphism h from the lhs of d_1 to K, there exists an extension h' of h, where h' is a p-homomorphism from the conjunction of the lhs and rhs of d_1 to K. We say that K *p-satisfies* d_2 if, whenever there is a p-homomorphism h from the lhs of d_2 to K, then the image of the rhs of d_2 under h is true. Whenever clear from context, we say simply "satisfies."

We proceed to the definition of SAC-chase. Technically, a SAC-chase step comprises the first two stages of an AC-chase step (Definition 6.10), while using a p-homomorphism rather than a t-homomorphism. A SAC-chase step does not decompose instances into their induced t-instances. (See Stage III in Definition 6.10.) As a result, every node in the SAC-chase step yields a single child instance, rather than multiple children. Notice that, since the instance considered in each SAC-chase step may contain a partial order, rather than total order, we consider p-homomorphisms rather than t-homomorphisms. The formal definition follows.

Definition 6.29 (SAC-chase Step)
Let $K = K_0 + \beta_K$ be an instance. A *SAC-chase step* consists of two stages.
Stage I: Constructing an instance K' by adding relational facts and arithmetic comparisons to K:

(a) **(tgd-AC):** Let $d : \phi(\mathbf{x}) \wedge \beta_\phi(\mathbf{x}) \to \psi(\mathbf{x}, \mathbf{y}) \wedge \beta_\psi(\mathbf{x}, \mathbf{y})$ be a tgd-AC. Let h be a p-homomorphism from $\phi(\mathbf{x}) \wedge \beta_\phi(\mathbf{x})$ to K, such that it is not possible to extend h to a p-homomorphism from $\phi(\mathbf{x}) \wedge \beta_\phi(\mathbf{x}) \wedge \psi(\mathbf{x}, \mathbf{y}) \wedge \beta_\psi(\mathbf{x}, \mathbf{y})$ to K. We say that d can be applied to K with p-homomorphism h. Let h_0 be the underlying homomorphism of h, and let K'_0 be the union of K_0 with the set of facts obtained by:

  (i) extending h_0 to a homomorphism h'_0 such that each variable in $\mathbf{y}$ is assigned a fresh labeled null, followed by

  (ii) taking the image of the atoms in the rhs of d under h'_0.

  For each arithmetic comparison $x_1 \theta x_2$ in $\beta_\psi(\mathbf{x})$, we add $h'_0(x_1 \theta x_2)$ to K'_0, which gives rise to K' in compact form.

(b) **(acgd):** Let d be an acgd $\phi(\mathbf{x}) \wedge \beta_\phi(\mathbf{x}) \to (x_1 \theta x_2)$, and let h be a p-homomorphism from $\phi(\mathbf{x}) \wedge \beta_\phi(\mathbf{x})$ to K such that $h(x_1 \theta x_2)$ is not true. We say that d can be applied to K with p-homomorphism h. We add $h(x_1 \theta x_2)$ to K, which gives rise to K'.

Stage II: Checking K' for consistency. We distinguish two cases:

(i) We say that K' is not consistent if either $h'_0(\beta_\psi(\mathbf{x}, \mathbf{y})) \wedge \beta_K$ (the tgd-AC case) or $h'_0(x_1 \theta x_2) \wedge \beta_K$ (the acgd case) is not consistent. If K' is not consistent, we say that the result of applying d to K with h is "failure," and write $K \xrightarrow{d,h} \perp$.

(ii) Otherwise, we say that the result of applying d to K with h is K', denoted $K \xrightarrow{d,h} K'$.

We continue with the definition of the SAC-chase, whose structure follows that of regular chase.

Definition 6.30   (SAC-Chase)
Let Σ be a set of tgds and egds, and K be a database instance.
- A *SAC-chase sequence* of K with Σ is a sequence (finite or infinite) of SAC-chase steps $K_i \xrightarrow{d,h} K'_{i+1}$, with $i = 0, 1, \ldots$, where $K = K_0$ and d is a dependency in Σ.
- A *finite SAC-chase* of K with Σ is a finite chase sequence $K_i \xrightarrow{d,h} K'_{i+1}$, $0 \le i < m$, with $K = K_0$, such that either *(a)* $K_m = \perp$, or *(b)* there is no dependency d of Σ and there is no homomorphism h such that d can be applied to K_m with h. We say that K_m is the result of the finite SAC-chase. We refer to the case *(a)* as *failing* finite SAC-chase, and to the case *(b)* as *successful* finite SAC-chase.

Example 6.31 shows how SAC-chase can be used to compute the singleton universal solution $\mathcal{J}_3$ of Example 6.18.

Example 6.31   (Continued from Example 6.18)
We start with applying the source-to-target dependency

$$d : E(X, Y), X < Y \to \exists Z\, (H(X, Z), H(Z, Y), Z < X$$

to the source instance

$$I = \{E(2, 5), E(4, 7)\}$$

with p-homomorphism $X \to 2, Y \to 5$. The result of this SAC-chase step is the instance

$$\{E(2, 5), E(4, 7), H(2, z_1), H(z_1, 5), z_1 < 2\}.$$

Applying to this instance d with p-homomorphism $X \to 4, Y \to 7$ produces the universal solution $\mathcal{J}_3 = \{J_9\}$, where $J_9 = \{H(2, z_1), H(z_1, 5), H(4, z_2), H(z_2, 7), z_1 < 2, z_2 < 4\}$; $\mathcal{J}_3 = \{J_9\}$ is a singleton set. The SAC-chase stops here, because $I \cup J_9$ satisfies all the dependencies.

The following result parallels those of Theorem 5.7 and Theorem 6.13. The proof follows the lines of the proof of Theorem 5.7.

Theorem 6.32   *Let Σ be a set of tgds and egds, such that the homomorphism property for chase holds. Suppose that D is a ground database instance that satisfies the dependencies in Σ, and K is a ground* *database instance such that there is a homomorphism h from K to D. Let K_Σ be the result of a successful finite SAC-chase on K with set of dependencies Σ. Then the homomorphism h can be extended to a homomoprhism h' from K_Σ to D.*

We now discuss termination conditions for SAC-chase. When introducing AC-chase, we defined weak acyclicity for sets of AC-tgds. The proof of the next result follows from Theorem 6.14, after we observe that a SAC-chase sequence produces an AC-chase tree. Hence, if the AC-chase terminates, then the SAC-chase terminates too.

Theorem 6.33   *If the given set Σ of AC-tgds and acgds is weakly acyclic, then SAC-chase with Σ terminates on every instance.*

Notice that in those cases where there are no target dependencies (even if the source-to-target dependencies are simple tgds), AC-chase can still produce a tree. This is precisely the reason why SAC-chase is a useful tool: in certain well-behaving cases it avoids the unnecessary complexities of AC-chase. Consider an illustration.

Example 6.34   Consider the DEAC setting $\mathbf{M} = (\mathbf{S}, \mathbf{T}, \Sigma_{st}, \Sigma_t)$, in which $\Sigma_t = \emptyset$ and
$$\Sigma_{st} = \{\, d_1 : \ E(X, Y), \ X < Y \rightarrow \exists Z \ F(X, Z, 8)\}.$$
Consider the source instance $I = \{E(2, 5)\}$. The result of SAC-chase on I is the instance $J = \{E(2, 5), F(2, Z_1, 8)\}$. Note that AC-chase would continue, by considering all the t-instances (7 in total) induced by J. For instance, for the instances where $2 < Z_1$, *Stage III* of the AC-chase step would consider five instances, with the respective total orders $2 < 5 < Z_1 < 8$, $2 < 5 = Z_1 < 8$, $2 < Z_1 < 5 < 8$, $2 < 5 < Z_1 = 8$, and $2 < 5 < 8 < Z_1$. We observe that, while the universal solutions produced by SAC-chase and AC-chase are homomorphically equivalent, SAC-chase is more efficient.

The following result is analogous to Propositions 6.19 and 6.20.

Proposition 6.35   *Let $\mathbf{M} = (\mathbf{S}, \mathbf{T}, \Sigma_{st}, \Sigma_t)$ be a DEAC setting in which the homomorphism property for chase holds on the dependencies. For a source instance I, let J be the result of SAC-chase on I. Then for each instance K in $SOL(\mathbf{M}, I)$, we have that q^J contains q^K.*

6.2.8   COMPUTING CERTAIN ANSWERS USING SUCCINCT AC-CHASE

We now discuss how to compute certain answers using the result of SAC-chase. We focus on the case in which:

- the dependencies use closed LSI comparisons (recall that LSI stands for left semi-interval arithmetic comparisons); and

- the query is a CQAC-LSI that uses closed LSI comparisons.

Definition 6.36   Given a source instance I and a CQAC query q in a DEAC setting, let J be the result of SAC-chase on I. We say that *a tuple t belongs to $q(J)$* for a query q if there is a p-homomorphism from q to J that maps the head of q to t.

Theorem 6.37   *Let $M = (S, T, \Sigma_{st}, \Sigma_t)$ be a DEAC setting in which Σ_{st} and Σ_t use only closed LSI arithmetics comparisons. Let I be a source instance, and J the result of SAC-chase on I with the dependencies $\Sigma_{st} \cup \Sigma_t$. Let q be a query in the language of unions of CQACs that uses only closed LSIs. Then we can compute certain answers to q by using J, as follows:*

$$certain_M(q, I) = q(J)_\downarrow.$$

Here, $q(J)$ is evaluated as in Definition 6.36.

Proof. The difficult direction is to prove that $q(J)_\downarrow$ computes all the certain answers. To show that, we will prove that there is a t-solution K such that $q(K)_\downarrow = q(J)_\downarrow$. (Recall that $q(K)_\downarrow$ includes only those tuples from $q(K)$ that do not involve variables.)

We now show how to construct K from J. First, replace all the variables in J with distinct constants in the following way. Let *Const* be the set of all those constants that appear in I, in the dependencies $\Sigma_{st} \cup \Sigma_t$, or in the arithmetic comparisons of the query q. If a variable x is not used in any arithmetic comparison in J, then we replace x with a constant whose value is larger than any constant in *Const*. If a variable x is used in an arithmetic comparison in J, then let c be the smallest constant among the constants c_i that appear in the ACs in J as $x \leq c_i$. Let c' be a constant that is smaller than c and, at the same time, larger than any of the constants in *Const* that are smaller than c. We replace x with any constant c_x such that $c' < c_x < c$. Observe that by doing so, we make sure that the following claim is true.

Claim: If there is a homomorphism h from the body of the query q to K that satisfies the ACs of q, then there is a p-homomorphism from the body of q to J.

To prove the claim, we observe that in our replacing the variable x with c_x, if a closed LSI comparison $x' \leq c_q$ of the query q is satisfied when the homomorphism h maps x' to c_x, then $c_x \leq c_q$ also holds. From the way we have chosen c_x we can derive that $c \leq c_q$, where c is as defined above. Hence, $x \leq c$ implies $x \leq c_q$. Thus, since the relational atoms in J and K are isomorphic, the homomorphism h becomes a p-homomorphism from the query body to J. It follows that all the tuples computed in $q(K)_\downarrow$ are also computed in $q(J)_\downarrow$.

The other direction is to prove that all the tuples computed in $q(J)_\downarrow$ are certain answers, i.e., they can be computed on any ground solution. This is shown by arguing as follows. The p-homomorphism that computes a tuple t in $q(J)_\downarrow$ can be composed with the homomorphism from J to any ground solution K, to derive a homomorphism that computes the tuple t in $q(K)_\downarrow$. $\square$

> **DEAC setting—the homomorphism property**
> $\mathbf{M} = (\mathbf{S}, \mathbf{T}, \Sigma_{st}, \Sigma_t)$;
> Σ_{st}: set of tgd-ACs;
> Σ_t : set of acgds and egd-ACs.
> While this is the same setting as the DEAC setting, we additionally require that all the given **dependencies are such that the homomorphism property holds**.
> Let q be a union of conjunctive queries with arithmetic comparisons posed over the target schema $\mathbf{T}$, and I be a source instance.
>
> Suppose all the given dependencies and the query use only closed LSI (RSI respectively) ACs. Then **Succinct AC-chase** applied on I computes an instance J, such that the **certain answers** to q can be obtained by computing $q(J)_\downarrow$.

The following example shows a scenario in which succinct AC-chase cannot be used to compute certain answers.

Example 6.38   Consider a DEAC setting with the following target dependencies:

$$d_1 : \quad a(x, y), x < y \rightarrow b(x),$$

$$d_2 : \quad a(x, y), x > y \rightarrow b(x),$$

$$d_3 : \quad a(x, y), x = y \rightarrow b(x),$$

and with the following source-to-target dependency:

$$d : \quad e(x, y) \rightarrow e'(y, z), a(z, w).$$

Suppose the input instance is $I = \{e(1, 2)\}$, and the query is $Q() \text{ :- } b(x)$.

The first step of SAC chase, which applies to I the dependency d, yields $J_1 = \{e(1, 2), e'(2, x), a(x, y)\}$. No other step of SAC chase can be applied, because the left-hand side of any of the three target dependencies does not p-homomorphically map to J_1. (That is, there is no homomorphism such that the ACs in J_1 would imply the image of the ACs of d_i.) Hence, J_1 is the result of SAC chase in this case. The answer to Q on J_1 is empty (i.e., false), which yields the empty set of answer tuples.

This empty-set answer to Q is an incorrect set of certain answer to Q. Indeed, consider the three t-instances induced by J_1:

$$J_{11} : \{a(x, y), x < y\}; \quad J_{12} : \{a(x, y), x > y\}; \quad J_{13} : \{a(x, y), x = y\}.$$

(Each of the three instances also includes the two facts $e(1, 2)$ and $e'(2, x)$. As these facts do not participate in any further application of SAC chase steps, we do not refer to these tuples any further in the rest of the example.)

On the instance J_{11} we can apply the tgd-AC d_1, on the instance J_{12} we can apply the tgd-AC d_2, and on the instance J_{13} we can apply the tgd-AC d_3, to obtain, respectively, the following t-instances:

$$J'_{11} : \{a(x, y), x < y, b(x)\}; \quad J'_{12} : \{a(x, y), x > y, b(x)\}; \quad J'_{13} : \{a(x, y), x = y, b(x)\}.$$

On each of J'_{11}, J'_{12}, and J'_{13}, the query Q evaluates to the empty tuple (i.e., to true), and the set $\{()\}$ is the correct set of certain answers to Q in this case.

6.3 INCOMPLETE DATA EXCHANGE

In this section we consider a data-exchange setting in which the input source instance is not complete, in that there are missing atoms, and the given atoms may involve unknown values represented by nulls. We consider dependencies that are regular tgds and egds (that is, the types without arithmetic comparisons), and discuss the problem of evaluating conjunctive queries (without arithmetic comparisons) over the target schema. We call this setting the *incomplete data-exchange setting (IDE)*.

6.3.1 INCOMPLETE INSTANCES

Each incomplete instance $\mathcal{I}$ represents a set, $Rep(\mathcal{I})$ (possibly of infinite size), of complete (i.e., ground) intances I_j, $j = 1, 2, \ldots$, defined as follows. For each $j = 1, 2, \ldots$, I_j is such that there exists a homomorphism from $\mathcal{I}$ to I_j. That is, each I_j contains all the tuples in $\mathcal{I}$, with their null values replaced by constants. Consider the following example.

Example 6.39 Consider incomplete instance $\mathcal{I} : \{a(11, 1, p)\}$, where p is a null value. $\mathcal{I}$ represents infinitely many complete instances, including the following instances I_1—I_4:

$$I_1 : \{a(11, 1, 1), a(15, 2, 1)\};$$
$$I_2 : \{a(11, 1, 2)\};$$
$$I_3 : \{a(11, 1, 1), a(15, 2, 2)\};$$
$$I_4 : \{a(11, 1, 2), a(15, 2, 3), b(1, 2)\}.$$

The set $Rep(\mathcal{I})$ of all the complete instances represented by $\mathcal{I}$ comprises all the instances containing the tuple $a(11, 1, p)$ for some constant value p, as well as potentially a finite set of any other tuples. For each $I \in Rep(\mathcal{I})$, there is a homomorphism from $\mathcal{I}$ to I. In particular, for $i = 1, 2, 3, 4$, there is a homomorphism from $\mathcal{I}$ to the instance I_i shown above.

We can require that a set Σ of dependencies be satisfied on an incomplete instance. We denote by $Sat(\Sigma)$ the set of all the ground instances that satisfy Σ. Given a (possibly incomplete) instance $\mathcal{I}$ and a set of dependencies Σ_s, the set $Rep(\mathcal{I}) \cap Sat(\Sigma_s)$ is the set of those complete instances represented by $\mathcal{I}$ that also satisfy Σ_s. Consider the following example.

Example 6.40 To the setting of Example 6.39, we add the following dependency d:

$$d : a(Z, X, Y) \rightarrow X = Y.$$

The instance I_1 of Example 6.39 does not satisfy the dependency d. Indeed, for the tuple $a(15, 2, 1)$ in I_1, the dependency d requires that the constants 2 and 1 in the second and third positions of the atom be the same (which they are not). The only complete instance of Example 6.39 that satisfies the dependency d is I_3. Hence, if we denote by Σ_s the set $\{ d \}$, the instance I_3 of Example 6.39 is the only ground instance provided in that example that is an element of the set $Rep(\mathcal{I}) \cap Sat(\Sigma_s)$.

6.3.2 THE IDE SETTING AND THE CORRESPONDING CDE SETTINGS

The following definition formalizes an incomplete data-exchange setting.

Definition 6.41 (Incomplete data-exchange setting)
An *incomplete data-exchange setting (IDE)* is a quintuple $\mathbf{M} = (\mathbf{S}, \mathbf{T}, \Sigma_s, \Sigma_{st}, \Sigma_t)$, where:
- $\mathbf{S}$ is a source schema and $\mathbf{T}$ is a target schema;
- Σ_s is a finite set of source tgds and source egds;
- Σ_{st} is a finite set of source-to-target tgds; and
- Σ_t is a finite set of target tgds and target egds.

Let $(\mathcal{I}, \mathbf{M})$ be a pair where

$$\mathbf{M} = (\mathbf{S}, \mathbf{T}, \Sigma_s, \Sigma_{st}, \Sigma_t)$$

is an IDE setting and $\mathcal{I}$ is an incomplete instance of schema $\mathbf{S}$. An *IDE problem* $(\mathcal{I}, \mathbf{M})$ is the problem of defining certain answers for $(\mathcal{I}, \mathbf{M})$ for a given CQ query.

Corresponding CDE Settings
We saw in Section 6.3.1 how an incomplete instance $\mathcal{I}$ and a set of dependencies Σ_s represent a set of complete instances $Rep(\mathcal{I}) \cap Sat(\Sigma_s)$.

Let $\mathbf{M} = (\mathbf{S}, \mathbf{T}, \Sigma_s, \Sigma_{st}, \Sigma_t)$ be an IDE setting. We call the CDE setting $\mathbf{M}' = (\mathbf{S}, \mathbf{T}, \Sigma_{st}, \Sigma_t)$ *the CDE setting that corresponds to* $\mathbf{M}$ *(CCDE setting)*.

Example 6.42 We revisit Examples 6.39 and 6.40, in which we discussed the incomplete instance $\mathcal{I} = \{a(11, 1, p)\}$, with p a null value. For the instance $\mathcal{I}$ and the set Σ_s of dependencies given in Example 6.40, all the complete instances in $Rep(\mathcal{I}) \cap Sat(\Sigma_s)$ must contain $a(11, 1, 1)$. We saw in Example 6.40 that the instance I_3 of Example 6.39 is an element of the set $Rep(\mathcal{I}) \cap Sat(\Sigma_s)$.

Now assume an IDE setting $\mathbf{M}$, whose set Σ_s of source dependencies comprises the dependency d of Example 6.40, which we reproduce here for convenience:

$$d : a(Z, X, Y) \rightarrow X = Y.$$

Let $\mathbf{M}$ have fixed source and target schemata, $\mathbf{S}$ and $\mathbf{T}$, respectively, a fixed set of source-to-target dependencies Σ_{st}, and a fixed set of target dependencies Σ_t. The corresponding CDE setting is $\mathbf{M}' = (\mathbf{S}, \mathbf{T}, \Sigma_{st}, \Sigma_t)$; note that $\mathbf{M}'$ includes the source-to-target and target dependencies of $\mathbf{M}$, but not its source dependencies.

Semantics of Query Answering in IDE Settings

For a given IDE setting $\mathbf{M}$, let $\mathbf{M}'$ be the corresponding CDE setting. Let $\mathcal{I}$ be an incomplete instance of schema $\mathbf{S}$. Let $I_i \in Rep(\mathcal{I}) \cap Sat(\Sigma_s)$ for $i = 1, 2, \ldots$, and let SOL_i be the set of solutions for each $(I_i, \mathbf{M}')$. Let $SOL = \cup_i SOL_i$. We define certain answers for $(\mathcal{I}, \mathbf{M})$ as follows.

Definition 6.43   (*Certain^B* answers)
Let $\mathbf{M} = (\mathbf{S}, \mathbf{T}, \Sigma_s, \Sigma_{st}, \Sigma_t)$ be an IDE setting, $\mathcal{I}$ be an incomplete source instance, and q a CQ. Then,
$$certain_{\mathbf{M}}^B(q, I) = \cap_{J_i \in SOL} q(J_i).$$
Here, SOL is as defined above for the corresponding CDE setting $\mathbf{M}'$ for $\mathbf{M}$.

Recall that in the CDE setting, the target instance may contain incomplete data, while in the IDE setting both the source instance and the target instance may be incomplete. In the CDE setting, we use labeled nulls to model unknown values in the target instances. In the IDE setting, for the sake of clarity of presentation we use nulls to represent unknown values in the source and labeled nulls to represent unknown values in the target.

Similarly to complete data-exchange settings, we assume here an infinite domain of constants $\underline{\text{Const}}$ and an infinite set $\underline{\text{Var}}$ of variables, called *labeled nulls*, such that $\underline{\text{Const}}$ and $\underline{\text{Var}}$ are disjoint. We also assume an infinite domain $\underline{\text{Null}}$ of nulls, which is pairwise disjoint from $\underline{\text{Const}}$ and $\underline{\text{Var}}$. An *incomplete instance* over a schema consists of relational facts with constants from $\underline{\text{Const}}$, nulls from $\underline{\text{Null}}$, and labeled nulls from $\underline{\text{Var}}$. An incomplete source instance in an IDE setting contains only constants from $\underline{\text{Const}}$ and nulls from $\underline{\text{Null}}$.

6.3.3   COMPUTING CERTAIN ANSWERS IN IDE SETTINGS

Given an IDE setting $\mathbf{M} = (\mathbf{S}, \mathbf{T}, \Sigma_s, \Sigma_{st}, \Sigma_t)$ and a source instance $\mathcal{I}$, we rename the nulls in $\mathcal{I}$ into labeled nulls and apply on the outcome chase with the dependencies $\Sigma_s \cup \Sigma_{st} \cup \Sigma_t$. We refer to the outcome of the chase projected on the target schema as *universal instance*.

Computing Certain^B Answers

We now show that the result of chase, i.e., the universal instance, can be used to compute certain^B answers to unions of conjunctive queries, by evaluating the query on the universal instance. The following result states it formally.

Theorem 6.44   *Let* $\mathbf{M} = (\mathbf{S}, \mathbf{T}, \Sigma_s, \Sigma_{st}, \Sigma_t)$ *be an IDE setting, and q be a union of conjunctive queries posed over the target schema $\mathbf{T}$. For every (possibly incomplete) source instance $\mathcal{I}$, we have that* $certain^B(q, \mathcal{I}) = q(J)_{\downarrow}$, *where J is the result of chase on $\mathcal{I}$ with the dependencies* $\Sigma_s \cup \Sigma_{st} \cup \Sigma_t$.

Proof. The proof of Theorem 6.44 is a consequence of the property of the chase stated in Theorem 5.7 (Chapter 5). Essentially, we would like to prove that for each I_i in $Rep(\mathcal{I}) \cap Sat(\Sigma_s)$ for which the CDE problem $(I_i, \mathbf{M}')$ has a solution, we have that $\cap\{q(J_i)_{\downarrow}\} = q(J)_{\downarrow}$, where $J_1, \ldots, J_k$ are universal solutions to the CCDE problems for $\mathbf{M}$.

J_i satisfy the dependencies, hence, according to Theorem 5.7, there is a homomorphism from J to J_i. Hence, $q(J)_{\downarrow} \subseteq \cap\{q(J_i)\}$. Moreover, J is a universal solution to one of the CCDE problems. Hence, $\cap\{q(J_i)_{\downarrow}\} = q(J)_{\downarrow}$. $\square$

The following example shows how the result of the chase can be used to compute certain answers.

Example 6.45   We revisit Example 6.42, in which we were considering the incomplete source instance $\mathcal{I} = \{a(11, 1, p)\}$, with p a null value. Let us also have the following dependencies.

- One source dependency:
$$d_s : a(Z, X, Y) \rightarrow X = Y.$$

- One source-to-target dependency:
$$d_{st} : a(X, Y, Z) \rightarrow b(X, Y, Z); \text{ and}$$

- No target dependencies.

Let the query be $Q_1 : q(Y) :\!\!- b(Y, Z, X)$.

We first illustrate how to compute the certain answers to the query in this setting by using the definition of certain answers, and then how to compute the answers by using the chase. In both cases we arrive at the same result.

Computing the certain answers using the definition: As mentioned in Example 6.42, for the source instance $\mathcal{I}$ there is one CCDE problem $(I_1, \mathbf{M}')$ and infinitely many CCDE problems $(I_{2i}, \mathbf{M}')$. Observe that only the CDE problem $(I_1, \mathbf{M}')$ has a solution according to the definition of solution for the CDE setting. Thus, $certain_{M'}(q, I_{2i}) = \emptyset$. To compute $certain_{M'}(q, I_1)$, we apply the theory for CDE settings, i.e., we apply chase on $I_1 = \{a(11, 1, 1)\}$ with the union of the sets of dependencies given in Example 6.39, to obtain universal solution $J_1 = $

$\{b(11, 1, 1)\}$. We then compute the query on this universal solution. Hence, $certain_{M'}(q, I_1) = q(\{b(11, 1, 1)\}) = \{11\}$.

Thus,

$$certain^B_M(q, \mathcal{I}) = certain_{M'}(q, I_1) = q(\{b(11, 1, 1)\}) = \{(11)\}.$$

Computing the certain answers using the chase: The universal instance of $\mathcal{I} = \{a(11, 1, N)\}$ under $\mathbf{M}$ is $J = \{b(11, 1, 1)\}$. We compute $certain^B$ for $Q_1 : q(X) :\!\text{-} b(X, Y, Z)$, which yields $q(J) = \{(11)\}$.

IDE setting: M $= (\mathbf{S}, \mathbf{T}, \Sigma_s, \Sigma_{st}, \Sigma_t)$
Σ_s: set of tgds and egds;
Σ_{st}: set of tgds; and
Σ_t : set of tgds and egds.

Let q be a union of conjunctive queries posed over the target schema $\mathbf{T}$, and $\mathcal{I}$ be a source instance. The **certain**^{B} **answers** of q for the input $\mathcal{I}$ and setting $\mathbf{M}$, denoted by $certain^B_M(q, \mathcal{I})$, are computed by evaluating q on the outcome of the **chase** algorithm applied on $\mathcal{I}$.

6.4   EXERCISES

6.1. Prove that for the query language of unions of conjunctive queries with inequalities, the following two definitions of certain answers coincide: (a) the definition based on solutions in complete data-exchange settings, and (b) the definition of certain answers based on ground solutions in DEAC settings. That is, prove the following result.

Proposition 6.46   *Let* $\mathbf{M} = (\mathbf{S}, \mathbf{T}, \Sigma_{st}, \Sigma_t)$ *be a complete data-exchange setting (without arithmetic comparisons). Let q be a union of conjunctive queries with inequalities. Then* $certain^{DE}_M(q, I) = certain_M(q, I)$ *for each input I.*

6.2. Let $\mathbf{M} = (\mathbf{S}, \mathbf{T}, \Sigma_{st}, \Sigma_t)$ be a DEAC setting with $\Sigma_{st} = \{\mathtt{d} : \mathtt{E(Y)} \to \mathtt{A(Y, Z)}, \mathtt{Y} \leq \mathtt{Z}\}$ and $\Sigma_t = \emptyset$. Let $\mathtt{I} = \{\mathtt{E(5)}\}$ be the source instance.

Find the result of the AC-chase on I and the SAC-chase on I, and compare the two results.

6.3. Given the following instance I of the source schema $\{ P \}$ and the following dependencies σ and τ, compute the certain answers to the given query Q on the target schema $\{ T \}$.

$I = \{\, p(1,2),\ p(1,3),\ p(3,2),\ p(3,1)\,\}.$

$\sigma:\ p(X,Y) \rightarrow t(X,Y), t(Y,Y).$

$\tau:\ t(X,Y) \rightarrow t(Y,X).$

$Q(X,Y) \text{:- } T(X,Y), T(Y,X), T(X,X).$

6.4. Given the following instance I of the source schema $\{\, P\,\}$ and the following dependencies σ and τ, compute the certain answers to the given query Q on the target schema $\{\, S, T\,\}$.

$I = \{\, p(1,2),\ p(1,3),\ p(3,2),\ p(3,1)\,\}.$

$\sigma:\ p(X,Y) \wedge p(Y,W) \rightarrow t(X,Z), t(Y,Z), s(Z).$

$\tau:\ t(X,Y) \wedge t(X,Z) \rightarrow Y = Z.$

$Q(X,Y) \text{:- } T(X,Y), S(Y).$

CHAPTER 7

Answering Queries Using Views

The problem of answering queries using views suggests several theoretical questions. In this chapter we discuss some of these questions.

7.1 CERTAIN ANSWERS FOR QUERIES IN PRESENCE OF VIEW INSTANCES

In this section, we first define the notion of certain answers for a query Q in presence of a view instance $\mathcal{I}$, under both the closed and open world assumptions. Then, in Section 7.1.2, for a CQ query Q, set of views $\mathcal{V}$, and MCR R in the language of unions of CQs, we study the question of whether $certain(Q, \mathcal{I})$ equals $R(\mathcal{I})$ under the open world assumption.

7.1.1 CLOSED VS. OPEN WORLD ASSUMPTION

The definition of certain answers depends on the assumptions, *closed world* vs. *open world*, that we make about views. Given a view instance $\mathcal{I}$, under the *closed world assumption* (CWA), $\mathcal{I}$ stores *all* the tuples that satisfy the view definitions in $\mathcal{V}$, i.e., $\mathcal{I} = \mathcal{V}(D)$. Under the *open world assumption* (OWA), instance $\mathcal{I}$ is possibly incomplete and might store only *some* of the tuples that satisfy the view definitions in $\mathcal{V}$, i.e., $\mathcal{I} \subseteq \mathcal{V}(D)$. In data integration we usually take the OWA, while in query optimization we focus on the CWA.

Definition 7.1 For a query Q and view instance $\mathcal{I}$, we define the certain answers of $(Q, \mathcal{I})$ with respect to a set of view definitions $\mathcal{V}$ as follows.

- Under the closed world assumption:

$$certain(Q, \mathcal{I}) = \bigcap\{Q(D) : D \text{ such that } \mathcal{I} = \mathcal{V}(D)\}.$$

- Under the open world assumption:

$$certain(Q, \mathcal{I}) = \bigcap\{Q(D) : D \text{ such that } \mathcal{I} \subseteq \mathcal{V}(D)\}.$$

In presence of a set of dependencies Σ, we also require that all the databases D used for computing $certain(Q, \mathcal{I})$ satisfy Σ.

Example 7.2   Consider CQ queries and views that are path queries. Let Q be path query P_{13}; the two views are as follows. V_1 is P_{15}, and V_2 is P_{14}. Consider a database D that is a simple path with nodes along the path $1, 2, 3, \ldots, 16$, i.e., the facts in D are $\{(1, 2), (2, 3), \ldots, (14, 15), (15, 16)\}$. The result of computing the views on D comprises the tuples $V_1(1, 16)$, $V_2(1, 15)$, and $V_2(2, 16)$. If we are given only the view instance $\mathcal{I} = \{V_1(1, 16), V_2(1, 15), V_2(2, 16)\}$, under the closed world assumption we know that there is a path of length 13 from node 2 to node 15. Hence, $(2, 15)$ is among the certain answers to the query Q. However, under the open world assumption, since all the tuples in $\mathcal{V}(D)$ are not necessarily in the view instance, we cannot reason that there is a path in D from node 2 to node 15.

To prove that the set of certain answers to Q is empty under the OWA, we need to reason that there is a database D' such that $\mathcal{I} \subseteq \mathcal{V}(D')$ and there is no path of length 13 connecting nodes 2 and 15. Such a database would represent a graph that consists of (a) a path of length 15 from node 1 to node 16, with nodes $n_0 = 1, n_1, n_2, \ldots, n_{15} = 16$; (b) a path of length 14 from node 1 to node 15, with nodes $n_0 = 1, n'_1, n'_2, \ldots, n'_{14} = 15$; and (c) a path of length 14 from node 2 to node 16, with nodes $n''_0 = 2, n''_1, n''_2, \ldots, n''_{14} = 16$. On such a database, there is no path from node 2 to node 15. Hence, the set of certain answers to Q is empty under the OWA.

7.1.2   CERTAIN ANSWERS VS. MCRS

We now prove that for CQ views, a maximally contained rewriting $\mathcal{P}$ with respect to the language UCQ of a UCQ query Q computes the certain answers of Q under the OWA. That is, we prove the following result.

Theorem 7.3   *Let Q be a UCQ query, V a set of CQ views, and $\mathcal{P}$ an MCR of Q with respect to UCQ. Let $\mathcal{I}$ be a view instance such that there exists a database instance D for which $\mathcal{I} \subseteq \mathcal{V}(D)$ (equivalently, such that $certain(Q, \mathcal{I}) \neq \emptyset$). Then, under the open world assumption $\mathcal{P}$ computes all the certain answers of Q in any view instance $\mathcal{I}$, i.e., $\mathcal{P}(\mathcal{I}) = certain(Q, \mathcal{I})$.*

We begin by pointing out an interesting case, which is essentially a technicality that we need to consider for the proof of Theorem 7.3. The point in question is the part of the statement of the theorem that requires the existence of a database instance D for which $\mathcal{I} \subseteq \mathcal{V}(D)$. We illustrate with an example. Under the open world assumption, if $\mathcal{I} \not\subseteq \mathcal{V}(D)$ for all databases D, and R is an MCR of a query Q using the views with respect to a query language $\mathcal{L}$, then it is possible for $certain(Q, \mathcal{I}) = \emptyset$ and $R(\mathcal{I}) \neq \emptyset$ to hold at the same time.

Example 7.4   Consider a query $Q(x, y) :- a(x, y)$, view $v(x, x, y) :- a(x, y)$, and view instance $\mathcal{I} = \{v(1, 2, 3), v(4, 4, 5)\}$. Since $v(1, 2, 3) \in \mathcal{I}$ and $v(1, 2, 3) \notin \mathcal{V}(D)$ for any database D, we have that $\mathcal{I} \not\subseteq \mathcal{V}(D)$ for all databases D.

There is only one rewriting $R(x, y) :- V(x, x, y)$. Then $R(\mathcal{I}) = \{(4, 5)\}$, and we have that

$$\text{certain}(Q, \mathcal{I}) = \bigcap_{D \ s.t. \ \mathcal{I} \subseteq V(D)} Q(D) = \emptyset, \ \text{because} \ \nexists D \ \text{such that} \ \mathcal{I} \subseteq V(D).$$

Before we proceed, it is convenient to define for a given view instance $\mathcal{I}$ a canonical database instance $D_{\mathcal{I}}$ that has the property $\mathcal{I} \subseteq V(D_{\mathcal{I}})$. First, we construct from the views a set of tgds (we will refer to them as the *view tgds*): for each view definition, the left-hand side of the tgd is the head of the rule that defines the view, and the right-hand side is the body of the rule.

Definition 7.5 (Canonical database instance of $\mathcal{I}$)
Let $\mathcal{I}$ be a view instance for a set of views V. We chase $\mathcal{I}$ with the set of the view tgds for V, to obtain $\mathcal{I} \cup D_{\mathcal{I}}$. The database $D_{\mathcal{I}}$ is called the *canonical database instance of* $\mathcal{I}$, provided that $\mathcal{I} \subseteq V(D_{\mathcal{I}})$.

Observe that for a given set of views V, view instance $\mathcal{I}$, and database D, the following statements are equivalent.

- $\mathcal{I} \subseteq V(D)$; and

- $\mathcal{I} \cup D$ satisfies the view tgds.

Proposition 7.7, which we are about to formulate, states a condition for $\mathcal{I} \subseteq V(D_{\mathcal{I}})$ to hold for *any* $\mathcal{I}$, while Proposition 7.8 states that, whenever for a given view instance $\mathcal{I}$ there exists a database D such that $\mathcal{I} \subseteq V(D)$, then $\mathcal{I} \subseteq V(D_{\mathcal{I}})$. Notice that given a query and a set of views, for some view instance $\mathcal{I}$ there may exist a database D such that $\mathcal{I} \subseteq V(D)$. However, there may exist another view instance $\mathcal{I}_1$, such that there is not database D for which $\mathcal{I}_1 \subseteq V(D)$.

As an illustration, consider the following example, where a view definition has repeated variables; still, in this example, there is a view instance $\mathcal{I}_1$ such that there is a database D for which $\mathcal{I} \subseteq V(D)$, but this is not true for view instance $\mathcal{I}_2$.

Example 7.6 Let a view V be defined as

$$V : v(X, X) :- a(X, Y), b(Y, Z).$$

Consider two view instances: $\mathcal{I}_1 = \{(5, 5)\}$ and $\mathcal{I}_2 = \{(5, 6)\}$. It is not hard to see that there exists a database D such that $\mathcal{I}_1 \subseteq V(D)$. However, there is no D such that $\mathcal{I}_2 \subseteq V(D)$; indeed, by definition of the view, there are no view instances that include a tuple with two different values in its two positions.

Proposition 7.7 *Given a set V of CQ views, the following statements are equivalent.*

1. *None of the view definitions in $\mathcal{V}$ has repeated variables in the head.*

2. *For every instance $\mathcal{I}$ of $\mathcal{V}$, there exists a database instance D such that $\mathcal{I} \subseteq \mathcal{V}(D)$.*

Proof. (1) $\Longrightarrow$ (2): Consider the canonical database instance $D_\mathcal{I}$ of $\mathcal{I}$. Since the head of any view V_i does not contain repeated variables, during the construction of $D_\mathcal{I}$ by chase, there is a homomorphism from the left-hand side of the view tgd for V_i to the head of any tuple $V_i(t)$ in $\mathcal{I}$. This chase step will create all the atoms used to prove that $V_i(t)$ is in $\mathcal{V}(D_\mathcal{I})$.

(2) $\Longrightarrow$ (1): Suppose that for every view instance $\mathcal{I}$ there exists a database instance D such that $\mathcal{I} \subseteq \mathcal{V}(D)$. Toward a contradiction, let $V_0 \in \mathcal{V}$ be such that V_0 has repeated variables in the head. Without loss of generality, assume that the head of V_0 has two repeated variables and is defined as $V_0(x, x, x_3 \ldots, x_n)$.

Let $\mathcal{I}_0$ be the view instance $\mathcal{I}_0 = \{t\}$, where $t = v_0(c_1, c_2, c_3, \ldots, c_n)$, $c_1 \neq c_2$, and $c_1, c_2, c_3, \ldots, c_n \in Const(\mathcal{I})$. From our hypothesis we have that there is a database instance D_0 such that $\mathcal{I} \subseteq \mathcal{V}(D_0)$, so $t \in \mathcal{V}(D_0)$. Thus, there is a homomorphism $h : Var(V_0) \longrightarrow Const(\mathcal{V}(D))$, so that $t = v_0(h(x), h(x), h(x_3), \ldots, h(x_n))$. Since it also holds that $t = v_0(c_1, c_2, c_3, \ldots, c_n)$, we have that $c_1 = h(x) = c_2$, which is a contradiction, because we assumed that $c_1 \neq c_2$. $\qquad \square$

Proposition 7.8 *Let $\mathcal{V}$ be a set of CQ views and $\mathcal{I}$ a view instance such that there exists a database instance D for which $\mathcal{I} \subseteq \mathcal{V}(D)$. Then the canonical database instance $D_\mathcal{I}$ of $\mathcal{I}$ is such that $\mathcal{I} \subseteq \mathcal{V}(D_\mathcal{I})$.*

Proof. By Theorem 5.7, $\mathcal{I} \cup D_\mathcal{I}$ maps to every database $\mathcal{I} \cup D$ such that $\mathcal{I} \subseteq \mathcal{V}(D)$. (Recall that $\mathcal{I} \cup \mathcal{V}(D)$ satisfies the view tgds.) $\qquad \square$

Proposition 7.9 *Let $\mathcal{V}$ be a set of CQ views and $\mathcal{I}$ a view instance, such that there exists a database instance D for which $\mathcal{I} \subseteq \mathcal{V}(D)$. Let Q be a CQ query. Then $Q(D_\mathcal{I})$ is equal to the set of certain answers of $(Q, \mathcal{I})$ with respect to $\mathcal{V}$.*

Proof. We know from Proposition 7.8 that $\mathcal{I} \subseteq \mathcal{V}(D_\mathcal{I})$. Hence, the set of certain answers of $(Q, \mathcal{I})$ with respect to $\mathcal{V}$ is a subset of $Q(D_\mathcal{I})$. Now for all database instances D such that $\mathcal{I} \subseteq \mathcal{V}(D)$, the following holds: $\mathcal{I}$ homomorphically maps to $D \cup \mathcal{I}$, and $D \cup \mathcal{I}$ satisfies the dependencies of the view tgds. Hence, by Theorem 5.7, there is a homomorphism from $D_\mathcal{I} \cup \mathcal{I}$ to $D \cup \mathcal{I}$. Thus, any answer tuple t to Q on $D_\mathcal{I} \cup \mathcal{I}$ is an answer on $D \cup \mathcal{I}$. It follows that t is an answer to Q on any database D such that $\mathcal{I} \subseteq \mathcal{V}(D)$. Thus, t is in the set of certain answers of $(Q, \mathcal{I})$ with respect to $\mathcal{V}$. Thus, the set of certain answers of $(Q, \mathcal{I})$ with respect to $\mathcal{V}$ can be computed on $D_\mathcal{I}$. $\qquad \square$

Proposition 7.10   *Let Q be a CQ query, V a set of CQ views, R a contained CQ rewriting of Q, and $\mathcal{I}$ a view instance such that there exists a database instance D for which $\mathcal{I} \subseteq V(D)$. Then $R(\mathcal{I}) \subseteq$ certain$(Q, \mathcal{I})$.*

Proof. For the contained rewriting R of Q, suppose the body of R produces a tuple t when mapped to $\mathcal{I}$; we prove that t is a certain answer to Q. The expansion R^{exp} homomorphically maps to $D_{\mathcal{I}}$ by construction of $D_{\mathcal{I}}$. There is a containment mapping from Q to R^{exp}, hence Q maps to $D_{\mathcal{I}}$ to yield t. By Proposition 7.9, $Q(D_{\mathcal{I}})$ computes exactly the certain answers. Thus, t is in the set of certain answers of $(Q, \mathcal{I})$ with respect to V. $\square$

Proposition 7.11   *Let Q be a CQ query and V ba set of CQ views. Let $\mathcal{I}$ be a view instance for which there exists a database instance D satisfying $\mathcal{I} \subseteq V(D)$. Then there is a space S of CQ contained rewritings of Q using V such that S is finite and is of size that is a function of the sizes of only the views and the query, for which the following holds: For each tuple $t_0 \in$ certain$(Q, \mathcal{I})$, there is a contained CQ rewriting (of Q), R in S, such that $t_0 \in R(\mathcal{I})$.*

Proof. We construct a contained rewriting R that computes t_0 on $\mathcal{I}$, as follows. First we construct $D_{\mathcal{I}}$, for which we know that $\mathcal{I} \subseteq V(D_{\mathcal{I}})$ holds. Hence, if $t_0 \in$ certain$(Q, \mathcal{I})$, then $t_0 \in Q(D_{\mathcal{I}})$. Let h be a homomorphism that computes t_0 in $Q(D_{\mathcal{I}})$. If Q has m subgoals, then h has at most m targets in $D_{\mathcal{I}}$. These targets were constructed from at most m tuples in $\mathcal{I}$; let these tuples in $\mathcal{I}$ be the only elements of the set S_t. We use the tuples in S_t to construct R, as follows: The head of R is t_0 with the constants replaced with variables (same constants to same variables and distinct constants to distinct variables), and the body of R comprises all the tuples in S_t in which constants are replaced by variables (same constants to same variables and distinct constants to distinct variables).

Now we prove that R is a contained rewriting. Observe that R^{exp} is isomorphic to the part of $D_{\mathcal{I}}$ that is created by the tuples in S_t. Hence, the homomorphism h maps Q to R^{exp}. We conclude that Q contains R^{exp}. $\square$

We now give a proof of Theorem 7.3.

Proof. (**Theorem 7.3**) We show the following:

1. $\mathcal{P}(\mathcal{I}) \subseteq$ certain$(Q, \mathcal{I})$; and

2. certain$(Q, \mathcal{I}) \subseteq \mathcal{P}(\mathcal{I})$.

Since $\mathcal{P}$ is a contained rewriting of Q, the first claim above is a direct consequence of Proposition 7.10. To prove the second claim, we first consider the case in which $\mathcal{I} = \emptyset$. Then $\mathcal{P}(\mathcal{I}) = \emptyset$, and we have that

$$\text{certain}(Q, \mathcal{I}) = \bigcap_{D \text{ s.t. } \mathcal{I} \subseteq V(D)} Q(D) = \bigcap_{D \text{ s.t. } \emptyset \subseteq V(D)} Q(D) = \bigcap_{\text{for all } D} Q(D) = \emptyset.$$

Thus, $certain(Q,\mathcal{I}) = \emptyset \subseteq \emptyset = \mathcal{P}(\mathcal{I})$.

Suppose now that $\mathcal{I} \neq \emptyset$. We consider the following two cases. (Recall the space $\mathcal{S}$ of contained rewritings defined in Proposition 7.11).

1. There exists a contained rewriting $R \in \mathcal{S}$ such that $R(\mathcal{I}) \not\subseteq \mathcal{P}(\mathcal{I})$. Here we obtain a contradiction, because R is a contained rewriting of Q, and we assumed that $\mathcal{P}$ is an MCR of Q using $\mathcal{V}$ with respect to UCQ.

2. There is no contained rewriting $R \in \mathcal{S}$ such that $R(\mathcal{I}) \not\subseteq \mathcal{P}(\mathcal{I})$. That is, $\forall R \in \mathcal{S} : R(\mathcal{I}) \subseteq \mathcal{P}(\mathcal{I})$. Suppose that $t_0 \in certain(Q,\mathcal{I})$. By Proposition 7.11, there is a rewriting in $\mathcal{S}$ that computes t_0, i.e., $t_0 \in R(\mathcal{I})$. Hence, $t_0 \in \mathcal{P}(\mathcal{I})$.

□

7.2 DETERMINACY

A query Q can be thought of as defining a partition of the set of all databases, in the sense that the databases on which the query produces the same set of answer tuples belong to the same equivalence class. A set of views defines a partition of the set of all databases in the same sense. The definition that follows considers a setting where the view-induced partition is a refinement of the partition defined by the query. Thus, an equivalence class of $\mathcal{V}(D)$ can be used to find the corresponding equivalence class of $Q(D)$.

For databases D_1 and D_2, we use the notation $\mathcal{V}(D_1) = \mathcal{V}(D_2)$ to represent the statement that $V_i(D_1) = V_i(D_2)$ holds for each $V_i \in \mathcal{V}$.

Definition 7.12   (Views determine query)
Given a query Q and views $\mathcal{V}$, we say that $\mathcal{V}$ *determines* Q if the following is true: for any pair of databases D_1 and D_2, if $\mathcal{V}(D_1) = \mathcal{V}(D_2)$ then $Q(D_1) = Q(D_2)$.

Here, a natural question to ask is the following: Given that a set of views determines a query, is there an equivalent rewriting of the query using the views and, if so, then in which language? We discuss this question in this section.

7.2.1 DEFINITIONS AND PRELIMINARIES

Let $\mathcal{L}$ be a query language. We say that a subset $\mathcal{L}_1$ of $\mathcal{L}$ *contains almost all* the queries in $\mathcal{L}$ if the following holds. We represent $\mathcal{L}$ as a disjoint union of sets of queries, called *eq-sets*, such that each eq-set contains exactly all the queries in $\mathcal{L}$ that are equivalent to each other (i.e., for every pair of queries coming from a particular eq-set, the queries are equivalent). Then $\mathcal{L}_1$ contains all the queries in $\mathcal{L}$, except those queries that are contained in a finite number of eq-sets.

Definition 7.13   Let $\mathcal{L}_Q$ be a set of queries and $\mathcal{V}$ a set of views. Let $\mathcal{L}$ be a query language. We say that $\mathcal{L}$ is *complete for $\mathcal{V}$-to-$\mathcal{L}_Q$ rewriting* if the following is true for any query Q in $\mathcal{L}_Q$: if $\mathcal{V}$ determines Q, then there is an equivalent rewriting of Q using $\mathcal{V}$ in the language $\mathcal{L}$.

   We say that $\mathcal{L}$ is *almost complete for $\mathcal{V}$-to-$\mathcal{L}_Q$ rewriting* if there exists a subset $\mathcal{L}_{Q1}$ of $\mathcal{L}_Q$ that contains almost all the queries in $\mathcal{L}_Q$ for which $\mathcal{L}$ is complete for $\mathcal{V}$-to-$\mathcal{L}_{Q1}$ rewriting.

Definition 7.14   ((Almost) complete language for rewriting)
Let $\mathcal{L}_Q$, $\mathcal{L}_V$, and $\mathcal{L}$ be query languages. We say that $\mathcal{L}$ is *complete for $\mathcal{L}_V$-to-$\mathcal{L}_Q$ rewriting* if the following is true for any query Q in $\mathcal{L}_Q$ and any set of views $\mathcal{V}$ in $\mathcal{L}_V$: If $\mathcal{V}$ determines Q, then there is an equivalent rewriting in $\mathcal{L}$ of Q using $\mathcal{V}$ (or, in other words, $\mathcal{L}$ is complete for $\mathcal{V}$-to-$\mathcal{L}_Q$ rewriting).

   We say that $\mathcal{L}$ is *almost complete for $\mathcal{L}_V$-to-$\mathcal{L}_Q$ rewriting* if for every set $\mathcal{V}_1$ of views from $\mathcal{L}_V$, $\mathcal{L}$ is complete for $\mathcal{V}_1$-to-$\mathcal{L}_Q$ rewriting.

   The following easy result is a good introduction to the concept of determinacy.

Theorem 7.15   *If there is an equivalent rewriting of a query Q given a set of views $\mathcal{V}$, then $\mathcal{V}$ determines Q.*

   Let us denote by CQ_{path} the language of path queries, with the exception of the path query P_1. The proof of the following result sets the stage for Definitions 7.13 and 7.14.

Theorem 7.16
   1. *CQ is complete for $\{P_2, P_3\}$-to-CQ_{path} rewriting.*
   2. *CQ is complete for $\{P_3, P_4\}$-to-CQ_{path1} rewriting, where $CQ_{path1} = (CQ_{path} - \{P_5\})$.*
   3. *CQ is amost complete for $\{P_3, P_4\}$-to-CQ_{path} rewriting.*

Proof. We provide a detailed proof of part (1). The reasoning is based on the observation that any path query P_n, $n \geq 2$, has an equivalent chain-CQ rewriting using the views in the set $\{P_2, P_3\}$. Indeed, the rewriting is constructed as follows: If n is an even integer, then the equivalent rewriting will use the view P_2 $n/2$ times, and if n is odd, then the equivalent rewriting will use the view P_3 once and the view P_2 $(n-3)/2$ times.

   The statement "CQ is complete for $\{P_2, P_3\}$-to-CQ_{path} rewriting" means that whenever the set $\{P_2, P_3\}$ determines a query in CQ_{path}, then there is an equivalent rewriting in the language of CQ_{path} of this path query using this view set. We have proved that for any path query, there is an equivalent CQ_{path} rewriting. Now, it should be easy to work out the proof of part (2). Part (3) is a direct consequence of part (2). □

It is interesting to note that the set of views $\{P_3, P_4\}$ determines the query P_5. Indeed, the following formula is an equivalent rewriting of $P_5(X, Y)$:

$$\phi(X, Y) : \exists Z[P_4(X, Z) \wedge \forall W((P_3(W, Z) \rightarrow P_4(W, Y)))].$$

Note that this formula is not in the language of CQ. Further, there is no CQ equivalent rewriting of P_5 using $\{P_3, P_4\}$, as will be discussed in Proposition 7.21. In the next subsection, we consider the case in which the set of views is a singleton set, and both the view and the query are path queries.

7.2.2   PATH QUERIES—SINGLE VIEW

In this subsection we consider the case in which the set of views is a singleton set. We say that a language $\mathcal{L}$ is *almost s-complete for $\mathcal{L}_V$-to-$\mathcal{L}_Q$ rewriting* if for every view set $\mathcal{V}_1$ that contains a single view from $\mathcal{L}_V$, there exists a subset $\mathcal{L}_{Q1}$ of $\mathcal{L}_Q$ that contains almost all the queries in $\mathcal{L}_Q$, and such that $\mathcal{L}$ is s-complete for $\mathcal{V}_1$-to-$\mathcal{L}_{Q1}$ rewriting. The definition of a language $\mathcal{L}$ being s-complete for $\mathcal{V}_1$-to-$\mathcal{L}_{Q1}$ rewriting is analogous; it only allows one view in the set of views.

We now set the stage for Theorem 7.17. Let Q be a CQ query with two distinguished variables that uses only binary relations in its subgoals. Then the set of the query subgoals can be viewed as a labeled graph. By ignoring the labels and the direction of the edges in this graph, we obtain an undirected graph $G_Q^{undirected}$. We say that a binary query Q is *connected* (or *is not disjoint*) if there is a path in $G_Q^{undirected}$ from one of its distinguished variables to the other.

Theorem 7.17   *CQ_{path} is s-complete for CQ_{path}-to-CQ_{path} rewriting.*

Proof. For a query Q in CQ_{path}, either $G_Q^{undirected}$ is disjoint or it is not. If it is not disjoint, then the canonical rewriting is an equivalent rewriting. If $G_Q^{undirected}$ is disjoint, then $\mathcal{V}$ does not determine P_n. This is a consequence of the following lemma.

Lemma 7.18   *Let query Q and views $\mathcal{V}$ be CQ chain queries. If the canonical rewriting of Q using $\mathcal{V}$ is disjoint, then $\mathcal{V}$ does not determine Q.*

Proof. Let database D_Q be the canonical database of the query Q. We consider in the set $\mathcal{V}(D_Q)$ (from which the canonical rewriting is constructed) the connected components of $G_{\mathcal{V}(D_Q)}^{undirected}$. We refer to any one of those connected components as the connected component that contains a certain constant from D_Q.

Suppose the canonical rewriting of Q using $\mathcal{V}$ is disjoint. We construct two databases D' and D'', such that $\mathcal{V}(D') = \mathcal{V}(D'')$ and $Q(D') \neq Q(D'')$. We begin by constructing databases D_1, D_2, and D_3, each of which is isomorphic to D_Q (but see the details below). Then we construct (a) D' as the union of D_Q and D_1, and (b) D'' as the union of D_2 and D_3.

The database D_1 is a copy of D_Q in which all the constants are replaced by fresh constants. For ease of reference, we assume that each constant of D_Q is replaced in D_1 by its primed version, e.g., c in D_Q is replaced in D_1 by c'.

Suppose D_Q is a simple path from a to b. We construct the database D_2 as follows. Consider an isomorphic image of D_Q, with the constants being the same as the corresponding constants in D_Q, except that the constants in the connected component of b are replaced by their corresponding primed versions used in D_1. Finally, D_3 is the reverse image of D_2, in terms of which constants are used, i.e., if a constant is used in its non-primed version in D_2, then it is used in its primed version in D_3, and vice versa. Consider an illustration for query P_7 and view P_2. (In this example, node a is represented by node 0 and node b by node 7.)

$$D_Q = \{(0,1),(1,2),(2,3),(3,4),(4,5),(5,6),(6,7)\}.$$
$$D_1 = \{(0',1'),(1',2'),(2',3'),(3',4'),(4',5'),(5',6'),(6',7')\}.$$
$$D_2 = \{(0,1'),(1',2),(2,3'),(3',4),(4,5'),(5',6),(6,7')\}.$$
$$D_3 = \{(0',1),(1,2'),(2',3),(3,4'),(4',5),(5,6'),(6',7)\}.$$

Consider another illustration, this time for query P_7 and view P_3:

$$D_Q = \{(0,1),(1,2),(2,3),(3,4),(4,5),(5,6),(6,7)\}.$$
$$D_1 = \{(0',1'),(1',2'),(2',3'),(3',4'),(4',5'),(5',6'),(6',7')\}.$$
$$D_2 = \{(0,1'),(1',2),(2,3),(3,4'),(4',5),(5,6),(6,7')\}.$$
$$D_3 = \{(0',1),(1,2'),(2',3'),(3',4),(4,5'),(5',6'),(6',7)\}.$$

We now prove that this construction is correct, i.e., that $\mathcal{V}(D') = \mathcal{V}(D'')$. Observe that $\mathcal{V}(D_Q) \cap \mathcal{V}(D_1) = \emptyset$ and $\mathcal{V}(D_2) \cap \mathcal{V}(D_3) = \emptyset$. The latter claim is not obvious; to prove it, recall that $\mathcal{V}(D_Q)$ is disjoint. This means that the primed versions of constants in D_2 appear in facts in $\mathcal{V}(D_2)$ together with other primed versions of constants; the same holds for unprimed versions of constants in the facts in $\mathcal{V}(D_2)$. Indeed, suppose there is a fact that contains a primed and unprimed version of a constant. This means that the connected component in $\mathcal{V}(D_Q)$ that contains b (which is node 7 in our example above) is connected to another connected component in $\mathcal{V}(D_Q)$. This is a contradiction, as it means that the component is not a connected component.

The same observation holds for $\mathcal{V}(D_3)$. Since each of $\mathcal{V}(D')$ and $\mathcal{V}(D'')$ computes the same number of facts, we have that $\mathcal{V}(D') = \mathcal{V}(D'')$, where D' is the union of D_Q and D_1, and D'' is the union of D_2 and D_3. Finally, observe that the fact $(0,7)$ is in $Q(D')$ but not in $Q(D'')$. Thus, this set of views does not determine the query. □

□

7.2.3 PATH QUERIES—CQ IS ALMOST COMPLETE FOR REWRITING

Theorem 7.19 *CQ is almost complete for CQ_{path}-to-CQ_{path} rewriting.*

This result is a consequence of Lemma 7.20.

Lemma 7.20   *Consider query P_n and set of views $\mathcal{V}=\{P_{k_1}, P_{k_2}, \ldots, P_{k_K}\}$. Then there is a positive integer n_0 that is a function of $k_1, k_2, \ldots, k_K$, such that for any $n \geq n_0$, the following statements are equivalent.*

1. There is no equivalent rewriting in CQ of P_n using $\mathcal{V}$.
2. The canonical rewriting of P_n using $\mathcal{V}$ is disjoint.
3. $\mathcal{V}$ does not determine P_n.

Proof. We prove (3) $\Rightarrow$ (1) first; this is straightforward, as the existence of an equivalent rewriting is a witness to determinacy.

The direction (2) $\Rightarrow$ (3) follows the proof of Lemma 7.18.

The remaining direction is that of (1) $\Rightarrow$ (2). The proof provided below generalizes the proof of Theorem 7.16, in the following sense: Since the canonical rewriting R is connected, there is a path in $G_R^{undirected}$ from one distinguished variable to the other. We show that this path can be used to construct a directed path on the canonical rewriting from one distinguished variable to the other. Hence, the canonical rewriting is an equivalent rewriting. Note that there is a finite number of path queries for which this construction is not possible; these queries are the queries P_n for all $n < n_0$, where n_0 is a positive integer that depends only on the sizes of the views.

We now prove the direction (1) $\Rightarrow$ (2), by showing correctness of the following equivalent statement: If the canonical rewriting is not disjoint, then there exists an equivalent CQ rewriting of the query.

Because the canonical rewriting is not disjoint, by definition there is an undirected path from its start node to its end node. Therefore, $\Sigma_{i=1}^{K} x_i k_i = n$ has an integer solution. The x_i's are positive integers if the undirected path in the canonical rewriting is traveling toward the end node, and the solutions are negative otherwise. Here, x_i is equal to the number of times that we consider the path P_{k_i} in the canonical rewriting. In the rest of the proof we show that $\Sigma_{i=1}^{K} x_i k_i = n$ has a positive integer solution for $n > n_0$, where

$$n_0 > \sum_{i \neq q; i,q=1,\ldots,j} k_i k_q.$$

This is sufficient for constructing a chain CQ rewriting, in which view P_{k_i} is used x_i' times, provided that x_i' is in the positive-integer solution of the above equation. We thus obtain a CQ_{path} rewriting.

Since $\Sigma_{i=1}^{K} x_i k_i = n$ has an integer solution, the greatest common divisor (GCD) of $k_1, \ldots k_K$ divides n. (Indeed, if both sides of $\Sigma_{i=1}^{K} x_i k_i = n$ are divided by the GCD, the left-hand side of the resulting equation is an integer, hence the right-hand side is an integer too, hence the GCD divides n.) We prove that for $n > \Sigma_{i \neq q; i,q=1,\ldots,K} k_i k_q$, if the GCD of $k_1, \ldots k_K$

divides n, then $\Sigma_{i=1}^{K} x_i k_i = n$ has a nonnegative integer solution. We prove it inductively on the number of k_i's.

Inductive hypothesis: For any positive integers $k_1, \ldots k_j$ and for any positive integer m, if the GCD of $k_1, \ldots k_j$ divides m and

$$m > \sum_{i \neq q; i, q = 1, \ldots, j} k_i k_q, \tag{7.1}$$

then the equation $\Sigma_{i=1}^{j} x_i k_i = m$ has a nonnegative integer solution $x_1^0, \ldots, x_j^0$, such that for any d in $\{1, 2, \ldots, j\}$ we have that

$$x_d^0 k_d > m - \sum_{i \neq q; i, q = 1, \ldots, j} k_i k_q. \tag{7.2}$$

Proof of the inductive hypothesis:

Base Step. For positive integers a_1, a_2, and b_0 such that $b_0 > a_1 a_2$, the Diophantine equation $a_1 x_1 + a_2 x_2 = b_0$ is known to have a nonnegative integer solution x_1^0, x_2^0 that satisfies $a_1 x_1^0 > b_0 - a_1 a_2$.

Inductive step. Suppose that the inductive hypothesis holds for $j - 1 \to j$. We prove that it also holds for $j \to j + 1$. I.e., we prove that for any positive integers $k_1, \ldots k_{j+1}$ and any positive integer p such that the GCD of $k_1, \ldots k_{j+1}$ divides p and such that

$$p > \sum_{i \neq q; i, q = 1, \ldots, j+1} k_i k_q \tag{7.3}$$

holds, then the equation $\Sigma_{i=1}^{j+1} x_i k_i = p$ has a nonnegative integer solution $x_1^0, \ldots, x_{j+1}^0$, such that for any d in $\{1, 2, \ldots, j + 1\}$, we have that

$$x_d^0 k_d > p - \sum_{i \neq q; i, q = 1, \ldots, j+1} k_i k_q. \tag{7.4}$$

Without loss of generality, suppose that $d = 1$. From here on, we assume that $k_1 = a_1$ and $k_2 = a_2$. We rewrite the equation as $a_1 x_1 + a_2 x_2 = p - \Sigma_{i=3}^{j+1} x_i k_i$. Denoting by b the GCD of a_1 and a_2, we obtain $(a_1/b) x_1 + (a_2/b) x_2 = (p - \Sigma_{i=3}^{j+1} x_i k_i)/b$. We now look for solutions of $p = \Sigma_{i=3}^{j+1} x_i k_i + bx$. Solutions must exist, because the GCD of $k_3, \ldots k_{j+1}, b$ equals the GCD of $k_1, \ldots k_{j+1}$. (Observe that any common divisor of a_1 and a_2 must divide b.) Hence, the GCD divides p. We also have

$$p > a_1 a_2 + \sum_{i \neq q; i, q = 3, \ldots, j+1} k_i k_q + b \sum_{i = 3, \ldots, j+1} k_i. \tag{7.5}$$

(This is due to $b < a_1$ and $b < a_2$.) Hence, according to the inductive hypothesis, $p = \Sigma_{i=3}^{j+1} x_i k_i + bx$ has a nonnegative integer solution $x_3^0, \ldots, x_{j+1}^0, x^0$, such that

$$bx^0 > p - \sum_{i \neq q; i, q = 3, \ldots, j+1} k_i k_q - b \sum_{i = 3, \ldots, j+1} k_i > a_1 a_2. \tag{7.6}$$

The last inequality holds due to

$$p > a_1a_2 + \sum_{i \neq q; i,q=3,\ldots,j+1} k_ik_q + b \sum_{i=3,\ldots,j+1} k_i. \tag{7.7}$$

We thus obtain $(p - \Sigma_{i=3}^{j+1}x_i^0k_i)/b = x^0$. It now suffices to show that the equation $a_1x_1 + a_2x_2 = bx^0$ has a nonnegative integer solution x_1^0, x_2^0, such that $a_1x_1^0 > bx^0 - a_1a_2$. Observe that $bx^0 > a_1a_2$. Further, the GCD of a_1, a_2 (i.e., b) divides bx^0. Hence, $a_1x_1 + a_2x_2 = bx^0$ has a nonnegative integer solution x_1^0, x_2^0, such that $a_1x_1^0 > bx^0 - a_1a_2$. Hence, $a_1x_1^0 + a_2x_2^0 = bx^0$, and by replacing bx^0 we have that $a_1x_1^0 + a_2x_2^0 = p - \Sigma_{i=3}^{j+1}x_i^0k_i$. Finally, we show that x_1^0 satisfies the inequality required in the inductive hypothesis. Indeed, since $a_1x_1^0 > bx^0 - a_1a_2$, we obtain

$$a_1x_1^0 > bx^0 - a_1a_2 >$$

$$p - \sum_{i \neq q; i,q=3,\ldots,j+1} k_ik_q - b \sum_{i=3,\ldots,j+1} k_i - a_1a_2 > p - \sum_{i \neq q; i,q=1,\ldots,j+1} k_ik_q. \tag{7.8}$$

□

7.2.4 CHAIN QUERIES

The following result gives a simple example of a case in which CQ is not complete for rewriting a query using a set consisting of two views.

Proposition 7.21 *The set of views $\{P_3, P_4\}$ determines the query P_5. At the same time, there is no CQ rewriting of P_5 using $\{P_3, P_4\}$.*

Proof. Let $P_5(X, Y) :- e(X, Z_1), e(Z_1, Z_2), e(Z_2, Z_3), e(Z_3, Z_4), e(Z_4, Y)$.
The following formula is an equivalent rewriting of P_5:

$$\phi(X, Y) : \exists Z[P_4(X, Z) \wedge \forall W((P_3(W, Z) \rightarrow P_4(W, Y)))].$$

The proof that this is an equivalent rewriting of P_5 follows from Theorem 7.22. To see that there is no CQ rewriting, consider the canonical rewriting

$$R_c(X, Y) :- P_3(X, Z_3), P_3(Z_1, Z_4), P_3(Z_2, Y), P_4(X, Z_4), P_4(Z_1, Y)$$

of P_5. The expansion of R_c is not equivalent to P_5. □

Theorem 7.22 *For the chain conjunctive query*

$$Q(X_1, Y) :- r_1(X_1, X_2), \ldots r_{i-1}(X_{i-1}, X_i), \ldots, r_{j-1}(X_{j-1}, X_j), \ldots r_{n-1}(X_{n-1}, Y).$$

and set of chain views $\mathcal{V} = \{R_2, R_3, R_4\}$, *where*

$$R_2(X_1, X_i) :\text{-} r_1(X_1, X_2), \dots r_{i-1}(X_{i-1}, X_i), \dots, r_{j-1}(X_{j-1}, X_j).$$
$$R_3(X_i, X_j) :\text{-} r_i(X_i, X_{i+1}), \dots, r_{j-1}(X_{j-1}, X_j).$$
$$R_4(X_i, Y) :\text{-} r_i(X_i, X_{i+1}), \dots, r_{j-1}(X_{j-1}, X_j), \dots r_{n-1}(X_{n-1}, Y).$$

The following first-order formula is an equivalent rewriting of Q using $\mathcal{V}$:

$$\phi(X, Y) : \exists Z [R_2(X, Z) \wedge \forall W((R_3(W, Z) \rightarrow R_4(W, Y)))].$$

Proof. Suppose $(a, b) \in Q(D)$ for database D. By definition of Q, there must exist a homomorphism h from the variables of Q to the constants of D, such that $h(X_1) = a$ and $h(Y) = b$, and the facts

$$r_1(h(X_1), h(X_2)), \dots, r_{i-1}(h(X_{i-1}), h(X_i)), \dots,$$

$$r_{j-1}(h(X_{j-1}), h(X_j)), \dots, r_{n-1}(h(X_{n-1}), h(Y))$$

are true in D. Hence, $(a, h(X_j)) \in R_2(D)$ holds. Moreover, whenever there exists a homomorphism h' from the variables of R_3 to D such that $h'(X_j) = h(X_j)$ and $(h'(X_i), h'(X_j)) \in R_3(D)$, define the homomorphism h'' that (a) coincides with h' for the variables $X_i, \dots X_j$, and (b) coincides with h for the rest of the variables in the body of R_4. Thus, $(h''(X_i), h''(Y)) \in R_4(D)$. Hence, the formula $\phi(a, b)$ is true on $\mathcal{V}(D)$.

For the other direction, suppose $\phi(a, b)$ holds on $\mathcal{V}(D)$; let c be the witness for Z. This means that $R_2(a, c)$ holds on $\mathcal{V}(D)$. Thus, there exists a homomorphism h from the variables of R_2 to the constants in D, such that the facts

$$r_1(h(X_1), h(X_2)), \dots, r_{i-1}(h(X_{i-1}), h(X_i)), \dots, r_{j-1}(h(X_{j-1}), h(X_j))$$

are true in D. Hence, $R_3(h(X_i), h(X_j))$ is true. Then, according to ϕ, there exists a homomorphism h' such that $h'(X_i) = h(X_i)$, so that $R_4(h'(X_i), h'(Y))$. We define h'' to coincide with h for variables $X_1, \dots, X_i$ and to coincide with h' for the variables $X_{i+1}, \dots, X_{n-1}, Y$. This yields (a, b) in $Q(D)$.   □

CHAPTER 8

XPath Queries and Views

For tree-structured data, such as XML documents, query languages are used that have a similar tree structure. In this chapter we present the most popular fragment of XPath, which is such a query language. This is the fragment that includes wildcard, descendant, and branching. In this chapter, we present efficient query containment tests and define and discuss equivalent rewritings.

8.1 XML DATABASES AND XPATH QUERIES

In this section, we define XML trees and patterns that define XPath queries. They are both defined in terms of labeled trees.

Consider a directed, rooted, labeled tree t, where its labels come from an infinite set Σ. We denote $N(t)$ and $E(t)$, the set of nodes and edges, respectively, of t, and we write $label(n)$ to denote the label of a node n of t. The number d of edges of the unique path through which node n is reachable from the root of t is said to be the *depth* of n. By convention, the direction of all edges are toward the node which is the farthest away from the root. A *leaf* of a tree is a node without outgoing edges. The *height* of a tree is the maximum depth of the tree. We define *children* and *descendants* of a node n to be those nodes farther from the root than n and which have an edge or a path to n, respectively.

We consider two types of trees—those that represent XML documents and those that represent XPath queries. An XML document is represented by a tree (also called *XML tree*) that has labels from Σ on its nodes. XPath queries are different from XML trees in three aspects. First, the labels of a query come from the set $\Sigma \cup \{*\}$, where $*$ is the "wildcard" symbol. Second, a query Q has two types of edges: $CE_/(Q)$ is the set of child edges (represented by a single line) and $DE_{//}(Q)$ is the set of descendant edges (represented by a double line). Third, a non-Boolean query Q has an *output node*, denoted by $out(Q)$, and is represented by a circled node. A *Boolean XPath query* does not have any output node. We also refer to a tree that represents an XPath query as a *pattern* and denote by P.[1] The *selection path* of a non-Boolean query Q is the path from the root to the output node. Given a tree pattern P, consider a tree which consists of a subset of the nodes of P and a subset of the edges of P. Then this tree is called a *subtree* of P.

---

[1]We use the notation Q or P interchangebly.

The result of applying a query Q on an XML tree t is based on a mapping from the nodes of Q to the nodes of t, called embedding.

Definition 8.1   An *embedding* from Q to t is a mapping $e : N(Q) \rightarrow N(t)$ with the following properties.
(1) Root preserving: $e(root(Q)) = root(t)$.
(2) Label preserving: For all nodes $n \in N(Q)$, either $label(n) = *$ or $label(n) = label(e(n))$.
(3) Child preserving: For all edges $(n_1, n_2) \in CE(Q)$, we have that $(e(n_1), e(n_2)) \in E(t)$.
(4) Descendant preserving: For all edges $(n_1, n_2) \in DE(Q)$, the node $e(n_2)$ is a proper descendant of the node $e(n_1)$.

Given an embedding $e : N(Q) \rightarrow N(t)$, we usually denote by o the image of the output node, i.e., $o = e(out(Q))$. The embedding e *produces* the tree t^o, that is, the subtree of t that is rooted at o. We denote by $Q(t)$ the *result* of applying the pattern for query Q to the tree t. It is naturally defined as the set of subtrees produced by all embeddings from Q to t, i.e., the result $Q(t)$, of applying a non-Boolean query Q on a tree t is:

$$Q(t) = \left\{ t^{e(out(Q))} | e \text{ is an embedding from } Q \text{ to } t \right\}.$$

If Q is a Boolean query then the result $Q(t)$ is "*true*," only if there is an embedding from Q to t.

Example 8.2   Figure 8.1 contains an example of an XML document. The XML document in Figure 8.1 is a tree with root *Products* and lists the products of two companies, Sony and Samsung, which are on the label of the two children of the root. The tree also uses more nodes to describe characteristics of each product, e.g., the size of the screen of a TV set. We have an XPath query shown in the pattern in Figure 8.2. This query asks for a listing of all companies together with their products that sell "something" (the wildcard says that any product can be considered) with a screen of size 32 inches and this company also sells a TV set and provides information on the XML tree about the model and the screen of this TV set.

Now, let us compute the output of this query as defined above using embeddings. There are two embeddings. One embedding, e_1, maps the output node to *Samsung* and the other embedding, e_2, maps the output node to *Sony*. In detail, e_1 maps both nodes u_2 and u_4 of the query pattern to the node labeled with *TV* which is a child of the node labeled *Samsung* and the rest of the nodes as mapped according to e_1 in the obvious manner on descendants of *Samsung* on the XML tree. In detail, e_2 maps both nodes u_2 and u_4 of the query pattern to node labeled with *TV* which is a child of the node labeled *Sony*. Thus, we have two outputs: because of embedding e_1 we obtain the subtree rooted at the node labeled *Samsung* and because of embedding e_2 we obtain the subtree rooted at the node labeled *Sony*.

Recall that the wildcard $*$ may appear in P, but is not in Σ. Thus, we can choose not to include in the labels of the query pattern. Similarly, we may choose only patterns where each

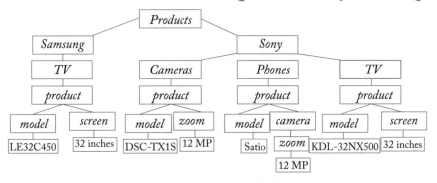

Figure 8.1: Tree representation of an XML document.

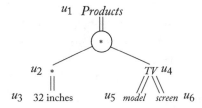

Figure 8.2: XPath query in tree-like form.

node has a single child or zero children; we say, then, that the pattern does not use branching. In this chapter by XPath queries, we mean this fragment of XPath queries which uses descendant, wildcard, and branching, and is denoted as $XP^{\{//,*,[]\}}$. We also consider subfragments of $XP^{\{//,*,[]\}}$ by choosing not to include either wildcard or descendant edges or branching in the definition. We denote those fragments by $XP^{\{//,[]\}}$, $XP^{\{[],*\}}$, and $XP^{\{//,*\}}$, respectively.

8.2   XPATH QUERIES VS. CONJUNCTIVE QUERIES

The remark in this section concerns the subfragment $XP^{\{[],*\}}$ and provides some intuition as regards the connection between embeddings and homomorphisms. We can view the XML document as a relational database and, specifically, we use one binary relation (the edges of the tree) and several unary relations, one for each label. We consider the fragment $XP^{\{[],*\}}$. This fragment has no descendant which is the only part that introduces recursion into an XPath query. For this fragment, we can also view an XPath query as a conjunctive query over the same database schema (i.e., one binary relation and several unary relations). Then an $XP^{\{[],*\}}$ query pattern can be written as a conjunctive query with the binary relation describing the tree of the pattern and with the unary relations denoting the labels on the pattern and a special unary relation to denote the root. Of corce, if there is a star then we simply do not add a unary relation for this node/variable. In the head of the query we put the output node of the pattern. Now, an embedding from the $XP^{\{[],*\}}$ query pattern to the XML tree can be viewed as a homomorphism from the conjunctive query to the database and vice versa.

8.3   XPATH QUERY CONTAINMENT AND EQUIVALENCE

Containment and equivalence of XPath queries are defined in an analogous way as for conjunctive queries.

Definition 8.3   Containment/Equivalence.   A pattern P_1 is *contained* in a pattern P_2 if $P_1(t) \subseteq P_2(t)$ for all XML trees t. The patterns P_1 and P_2 are *equivalent* if $P_1 \sqsubseteq P_2$ and $P_2 \sqsubseteq P_1$, that is, $P_1(t) = P_2(t)$ for all XML trees.

Containment of P_1 in P_2 means that if a subtree t_{sub} of t is produced by some embedding of P_1 in t, then t_{sub} is also produced by an embedding of P_2 in t. We can define containment for queries where each query is a union (set) of patterns.

Let Q_1, Q_2 be two sets of patterns in $XP^{\{//,[],*\}}$. We denote by $Q_1(t)$ the union of the outputs for patterns in Q_1, i.e.,

$$Q_1(t) = \bigcup_{P_1 \in Q_1} P_1(t).$$

We denote by $Q_2(t)$ the union of the outputs for patterns in Q_2, i.e.,

$$Q_2(t) = \bigcup_{P_2 \in Q_1} P_2(t).$$

Then Q_2 is *contained* in Q_1, denoted $Q_2 \sqsubseteq Q_1$, if $Q_2(t) \subseteq Q_1(t)$ for all trees $t \in \mathbf{T}_\Sigma$. Q_1 and Q_2 are *equivalent*, denoted $Q_2 \equiv Q_1$, if $Q_2 \sqsubseteq Q_1$ and $Q_1 \sqsubseteq Q_2$.

From an XPath pattern, we can form an XML document by turning the descendant edges into child edges and turning each wildcard into a distinct fresh label. We call this document the *primal canonical document* of the pattern.

Theorem 8.4   *If a pattern P is contained in a pattern P' then the height of P is at least equal to the height of P'. If two patterns are equivalent then they have the same height.*

Proof. If the height of P' is less than the height of P, then take the primal canonical XML document of P'; there must be an embedding from P to this model. However, the existence of an embedding means that pattern P has height at least equal to the height of the XML document.   □

8.4   DEFINITION OF EXTENDED EMBEDDING BETWEEN PATTERNS

We have defined an embedding from a pattern to an XML tree. Now we will define an extended embedding between two patterns. We will use this for containment test.

Considering two patterns P_1, P_2 in $XP^{\{//,[],*\}}$, an *extended embedding* from P_1 to P_2 is a mapping $h : \mathcal{N}(P_1) \to \mathcal{N}(P_2)$ with the following properties.

1. Root preserving: $h(root(P_1)) = root(P_2)$.

2. Output preserving: $h(out(P_1)) = out(P_2)$.

3. Label preserving: For all nodes $n \in \mathcal{N}(P_1)$, either $label(n) = *$ or $label(n) = label(h(n))$.

4. Child preserving: For all edges $(n_1, n_2) \in \mathcal{E}_/(P_1)$, we have that $(h(n_1), h(n_2)) \in \mathcal{E}_/(P_2)$.

5. Descendant preserving: For all edges $(n_1, n_2) \in \mathcal{E}_{//}(P_1)$, then node $h(n_2)$ is a proper descendant of the node $h(n_1)$.

8.5   CONTAINMENT TEST FOR $XP^{\{//,[]\}}$ AND $XP^{\{[],*\}}$

The existence of an extended embedding from one pattern to another constitutes a sufficient condition for deciding containment of patterns in $XP^{\{//,[],*\}}$. However it does not also constitute a necessary condition. For patterns either in $XP^{\{//,[]\}}$ or $XP^{\{[],*\}}$, the existence of an extended embedding constitutes both a necessary and sufficient condition for deciding containment of single patterns.

For patterns in $XP^{\{//,*\}}$, however, an extended embedding does not suffice in order to decide containment. For deciding containment in this fragment we define a new mapping between patterns, called *d-homomorphism* ("d" from adorned), by relaxing the concept of extended embedding. The formal definition of the d-homomorphism will be given in Section 8.9.1.

Theorem 8.5   *Let Q_1 and Q_2 be queries from $XP^{\{[],*\}}$. Query Q_2 is contained in query Q_1 iff there is an extended embedding from Q_1 to Q_2.*

Proof. Suppose there is a extended embedding from Q_1 to Q_2. Let D be an XML document. We will show that for each output t of Q_2 on D there is the same output t of Q_1 on D. Let e be the embedding of Q_2 to D that computes t. Then we compose the extended embedding from Q_1 to Q_2 with the embedding e and we produce an embedding e' that computes t when we apply Q_1 to D.

Suppose Q_2 is contained in query Q_1. We consider an XML document that is produced from Q_2 after replacing in the tree pattern of Q_2 the wildcard with a fresh symbol not appearing in other symbols. Then the output of Q_1 on D is computed from an embedding that is indeed a extended embedding from Q_1 to Q_2.   □

Theorem 8.6 *Let Q_1 and Q_2 be queries from $XP^{\{//,[]\}}$. Query Q_2 is contained in query Q_1 iff there is an extended embedding from Q_1 to Q_2.*

Proof. Suppose there is an extended embedding from Q_1 to Q_2. Let D be an XML document. We will show that for each output t of Q_2 on D there is the same output t of Q_1 on D. Let e be the embedding of Q_2 to D that computes t. Then we compose the extended embedding from Q_1 to Q_2 with the embedding e and we produce an embedding e' that computes t when we apply Q_1 to D.

Suppose Q_2 is contained in query Q_1. We consider an XML document that is produced from Q_2 after replacing in the tree pattern of Q_2 the descendants with child edges. Then the output of Q_1 on D is computed from an embedding that is indeed an extended embedding from Q_1 to Q_2. □

8.6 EXTENDED EMBEDDING IS NOT ENOUGH TO PROVE CONTAINMENT

First, we define and discuss redundant and minimal patterns.

Definition 8.7 A pattern P is *redundant* if and only if P has a proper subtree P' which is equivalent to P.

Theorem 8.8 *A pattern is redundant if and only if it has a redundant leaf.*

The problem of *minimizing* a pattern P is to find an equivalent pattern that has the minimum size. This is called a *minimal* pattern. By definition, a minimal pattern is non-redundant. Actually, all the patterns without branches are minimal (see Exercise 8.2 in this chapter).

Example 8.9
In Figure 8.3a and 8.3b we see two patterns that differ only in that pattern that expresses query (b) is constructed from pattern (a) (in Figure 8.3) by adding a descendant edge on the top of pattern (a). However, pattern (a) is minimal whereas pattern (b) is not minimal because it is equivalent to pattern in Figure 8.3c.
Figure 8.3 proves:

1. that a subpattern may be minimal but the pattern is not minimal. Pattern (a) is a subpattern of (b) and (a) is minimal but (b) is not minimal, and

2. that extended embedding is not enough to check containment. Patterns (b) and (c) are equivalent but there is no extended embedding from (b) to (c).

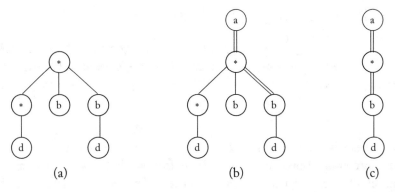

Figure 8.3: Query (a) is a minimal pattern. Query (b) is not a minimal pattern. Pattern (c) is minimal and is equivalent to the pattern of (b).

8.7   CANONICAL MODELS

From a pattern we can construct several XML documents. As for conjunctive queries, the main property of a canonical model is that, in order to find a witness t that p is not contained in p', it suffices to restrict the search to certain canonical models.

Let us start with a pattern without descendant nodes. Then the tree of the XML, which we call, in this case, the *canonical XML document* of the pattern (also called a canonical model), is the same as the tree of the pattern. The labels are the same too, except for the wildcards which are replaced with fresh labels that do not appear anywhere else.

Canonical models for a specific XPath expression are like canonical databases for a conjunctive query. They are formed as follows.

First, given a query Q, we define what *unfolding* a descedant edge r times means. We replace this descendant edge by a path of length r with labels on the nodes of this path being * (here the meaning of * is different but we keep the same symbol to show the intuition). (In fact, the labels of nodes along the paths we unfold are z but z denotes here that they are different.)

Definition 8.10   Suppose query Q uses a pattern with child, wildcard, branching, and descendant. Suppose the pattern of Q uses j descendant edges, the edges $e_1, e_2, \ldots, e_i$. A canonical model of Q of rank $r_1, r_2, \ldots r_j$ is an XML document where we unfold each descendant edge as follows: edge e_i, $i = 1, 2, \ldots, j$ is unfolded r_i times.

8.8   CONTAINMENT FOR GENERAL CASE

We show that, in order to test containment (and equivalence) of patterns, it is enough to consider only certain canonical models.

Now the following theorem gives the containment test.

Theorem 8.11   *Let Q_1 and Q_2 be queries from the XPath fragment that uses only child, wildcard, branching, and descendant. Suppose Q_1 uses s nodes. Query Q_2 is contained in query Q_1 iff there is a embedding from Q_1 to every canonical model of Q_2 of rank $r_1, r_2, \ldots r_j$ for any combination where $r_i \leq s$.*

Proof. Suppose there is an embedding from Q_1 to every canonical model of Q_2 of rank $r_1, r_2, \ldots r_j$ for any combination where $r_i \leq s$. Then, for any XML document of rank $r_1, r_2, \ldots r_j$ for a combination where $r_i \leq s$, this embedding is used in combosition with the embedding that produces output t in $Q_1(D)$ if t is in output of $Q_2(D)$. Now, suppose D is such that there is at least one path p of length greater than s. Then any embedding from Q_1 to D uses a descendant edge to map on this specific path. Since in the canonical models there is one model where everything is the same as in D except that the path p is replaced by a shorter path, but still long enough so descendant edge is used in the embedding to map on p. Thus, the same embedding can be used for D.

Suppose Q_2 is contained in query Q_1. We consider an XML document that is produced from Q_2 after replacing in the tree pattern of any canonical model of Q_2 the wildcard with a fresh symbol not appearing in other symbols. Then the output of Q_1 on D is computed from an embedding that is indeed a extended embedding from Q_1 to Q_2.   □

8.9   CONTAINMENT AND EQUIVALENCE OF UNION OF XPATH QUERIES

For unions of XPath queries, the canonical models can be used, according to the following theorem.

Theorem 8.12   *Let Q_1, Q_2 be two sets of patterns in $XP^{\{//,[\,],*\}}$. Suppose Q_1 includes only patterns with at most s nodes. $Q_2 \sqsubseteq Q_1$ if and only if for each canonical model of rank $r_1, r_2 \ldots, r_i \leq s$ for each query in Q_2, there is a pattern P in Q_1 such that there is an embedding from P to this canonical model.*

In relational databases, deciding containment of unions of conjunctive queries is reduced to checking containment of single conjunctive queries. However, this method cannot be used for deciding containment between union of patterns in $XP^{\{//,[\,],*\}}$. The following theorem says that this method can be used for $XP^{\{[\,],*\}}$ queries.

Theorem 8.13   *Let Q_1, Q_2 be two sets of patterns in $XP^{\{[\,],*\}}$. $Q_2 \sqsubseteq Q_1$ if and only if for each pattern $P_2 \in Q_2$ there is pattern $P_1 \in Q_1$ such that $P_2 \sqsubseteq P_1$.*

8.9.1 CONTAINMENT TEST FOR $XP^{\{//,*\}}$ FOR SINGLE-PATTERN QUERY

We present an efficient algorithm to test containment for the subfragment $XP^{\{//,*\}}$.

Let P be a pattern in $XP^{\{//,*\}}$. We say that a node u of P is a *core node* if at least one of the following holds:

- u is the root of P (i.e., $u = root(P)$),

- the label of u is not a wildcard (i.e., $label(u) \neq *$), or

- u is an output node (i.e., $u = out(P)$).

We use $\widehat{\mathcal{N}}(P)$ to denote the set of core nodes of P. We say that a path $p = u, z_1, \ldots, z_n, v$ of P is a *core path*, where $n \geq 0$, if $z_1, \ldots, z_n \in (\mathcal{N}(P) - \widehat{\mathcal{N}}(P))$ and $u, v \in \widehat{\mathcal{N}}(P)$.

The *core pattern* of P, denoted $\widehat{P}$, is the pattern obtained from P by replacing each core path $u, z_1, \ldots, z_n, v$ of P, where $n \geq 0$, with a descendant edge. For example, the set $\widehat{\mathcal{N}}(P)$ of the pattern P, illustrated in Figure 8.4, is $\{n_1, n_2, n_4\}$ (the first two nodes are labeled by a non-wildcard and the last is the output). Moreover, the paths from n_1 to n_2 and from n_2 to n_4 are the core paths of P. The core pattern $\widehat{P}$, now, of P is also illustrated in Figure 8.4.

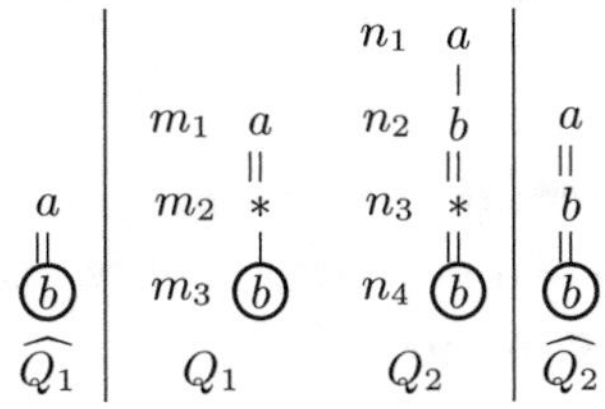

Figure 8.4: d-homomorphism.

Definition 8.14 Let P_1 and P_2 be two patterns in $XP^{\{//,*\}}$. We say that a homomorphism h from $\widehat{P_1}$ to $\widehat{P_2}$ is a *d-homomorphism* from P_1 to P_2 if for each edge (u, v) in $\mathcal{E}_{//}(\widehat{P_1})$, the following hold:

1. the length of the core path $u, \ldots, v$ in P_1 is less than or equal to the length of the path $h(u), \ldots, h(v)$ in P_2; and

2. if $u, \ldots, v$ in P_1 has only child edges then $h(u), \ldots, h(v)$ in P_2 has only child edges and its length is equal to the length of $u, \ldots, v$.

Example 8.15 Consider the patterns Q_1, Q_2 and their core patterns $\widehat{Q_1}$, $\widehat{Q_2}$, respectively, which are illustrated in Figure 8.4. Notice that there exists a homomorphism from $\widehat{Q_1}$ to $\widehat{Q_2}$, which is also a d-homomorphism from Q_1 to Q_2. On the other hand, there is not any d-homomorphism from Q_2 to Q_1. □

Notice that an extended embedding between two patterns in $XP^{\{//,*\}}$ is also a d-homomorphism. The following proposition formally shows that d-homomorphism suffices for deciding containment for patterns in $XP^{\{//,*\}}$.

Theorem 8.16   *Let P_1 and P_2 be two patterns in $XP^{\{//,*\}}$. $P_2 \sqsubseteq P_1$ if and only if there is an d-homomorphism from P_1 to P_2.*

8.9.2   DESCENDANT UNROLLINGS

Example 8.20 (that we explain in the next subsection) shows that deciding containment of unions of patterns in $XP^{\{//,*\}}$ cannot be reduced to checking containment between single patterns. For this case, we need to develop a tool called descendant unrollings.

Definition 8.17   Let P be a pattern in $XP^{\{//,[],*\}}$, (u, v) be an edge in $\mathcal{E}_{//}(P)$ and k be a positive integer. The k-*unrolling* of (u, v), denoted $Unroll^k_{(u,v)}(P)$, is the set of patterns $\{Q_1, \ldots, Q_{k+1}\}$, where

- for each $i = 1, \ldots, k$, the pattern Q_i is obtained from P by replacing (u, v) with a path p whose length is i, its start node is u, its end node is v, all intermediate nodes are labeled by $*$, and all edges are child edges; and

- the pattern Q_{k+1} is obtained from Q_k by replacing the last edge (z, v) of p with a path z, x, v such that $label(x) = *$, (z, x) is a child edge and (x, v) is a descendant edge.

Now, consider a positive integer k, we refer to a core path which has a descendant edge and its length is less than k as k-*unrollable*. Instead, we say that a pattern in $XP^{\{//,*\}}$ is k-*unrolled* if it has not any k-unrollable core path.

Example 8.18   Consider the 2-unrollable pattern P which is illustrated in Figure 8.5. By applying 2-unrolling to the descendant edge (n_1, n_2) of P, we get the set $Unroll^2_{(n_1,n_2)}(P)$ (also illustrated in Figure 8.5). More specifically, the patterns Q_1 and Q_2 are obtained from P by replacing (n_1, n_2) with core path which have only child edges and whose lengths are 1 and 2, respectively, while Q_3 is obtained from Q_2 by replacing the last edge of the first core path with a core path of length 2 whose last edge is a descendant edge (the other edge is child edge). Notice, now, that each pattern in $Unroll^2_{(n_1,n_2)}(P)$ is 2-unrolled. □

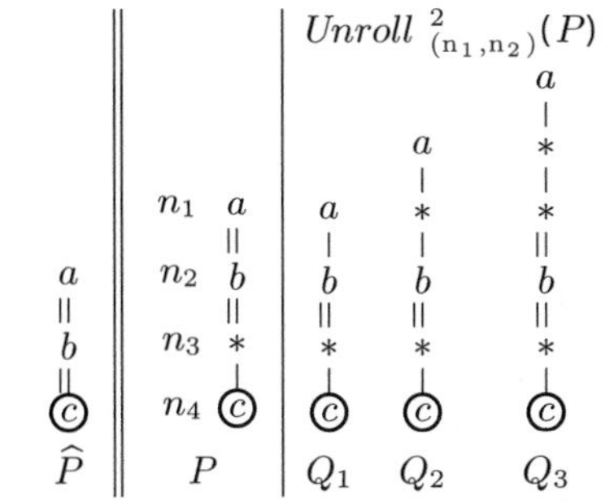

Figure 8.5: Descendant unrolling.

8.9.3 CONTAINMENT TEST FOR $XP^{\{//,*\}}$ FOR UNION-OF-PATTERNS QUERY

In this section, we show that constructing the unroll set of a set of patterns in $XP^{\{//,*\}}$ and then finding d-homomorphisms from another set of patterns in $XP^{\{//,*\}}$ to the unroll set, we can decide containment of two union of patterns in $XP^{\{//,*\}}$.

Consider a set $\mathcal{Q}$ of patterns in $XP^{\{//,*\}}$ and the length k_{max} of the longest core path appearing in the patterns of $\mathcal{Q}$. Constructing the $Unroll^{k_{max}}(\mathcal{Q})$ it is easy to see that the descendant edges appear only in the core paths of length k_{max}. However, there may be core paths of length k_{max} which do not have any descendant edges. If we construct, now, the $Unroll^{k_{max}+1}(\mathcal{Q})$ we both force descendant edges to appear only in core paths of length $k_{max} + 1$ and guarantee that every core path of such length has a descendant edge. All other core paths have only child edges. This observation provides the key for deciding containment of two sets of patterns in $XP^{\{//,*\}}$. The following theorem formally gives a necessary and sufficient condition for containment of unions of patterns in $XP^{\{//,*\}}$.

Theorem 8.19   *Let $\mathcal{Q}_1$, $\mathcal{Q}_2$ be the sets of patterns in $XP^{\{//,*\}}$ and $k = k_{max} + 1$ be an integer, where k_{max} is the length of the longest core path appearing in a pattern in either $\mathcal{Q}_1$ or $\mathcal{Q}_2$. Then $\mathcal{Q}_2 \sqsubseteq \mathcal{Q}_1$ if and only if for each pattern $P_2 \in Unroll^k(\mathcal{Q}_2)$ there is a pattern $P_1 \in \mathcal{Q}_1$ such that there is a d-homomorphism from P_1 to P_2.*

The following example shows that, unlike conjunctive queries, for this case, we cannot check for the existence of d-homomorphism between patterns and use this test to decide query containment. So d-homomorphism is not sufficient and using unrollings is necessary in order to decide containment.

Example 8.20   Consider the patterns P_1, P_2, P_3, and P_4 in Figure 8.6. On checking whether or not the set $\mathcal{Q}_2 = \{P_3, P_4\}$ is contained in the set $\mathcal{Q}_1 = \{P_1, P_2\}$, we notice that there is a d-homomorphism from P_2 to P_3 but there is not any from either P_1 or P_2 to P_4. Hence, $P_3 \sqsubseteq P_2$ but $P_4 \not\sqsubseteq P_1$ and $P_4 \not\sqsubseteq P_2$. However, we prove that $P_4 \sqsubseteq P_1 \cup P_2$.

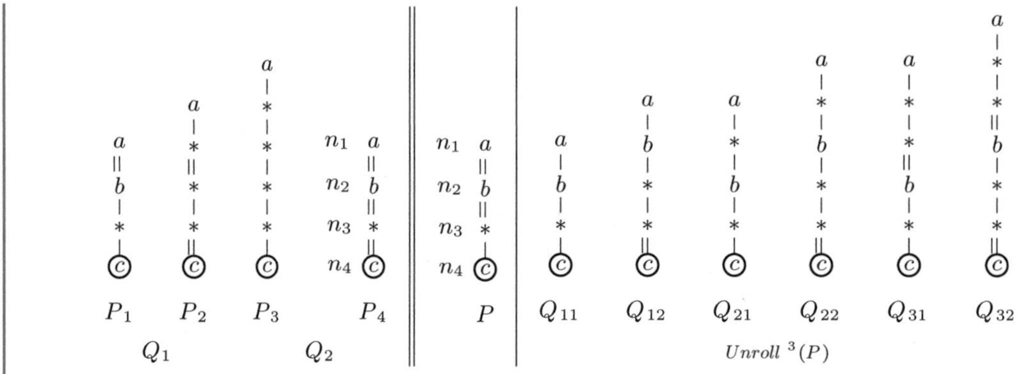

Figure 8.6: $Q_2 \sqsubseteq Q_1$.

We give the intuitive explanation. Let t be the XML document. Let e be the embedding from P_4 to t that produce, as output node n of t, i.e., $e(n_4) = n$. We have two cases. First case: suppose the distance from $e(n_1)$ to $e(n_4)$ is equal to 3. Then, there is an embedding e' from P_1 to t ther produces again n. Second case: suppose the distance from $e(n_1)$ to $e(n_4)$ is greater than 3. Then, there is an embedding e'' from P_2 to t ther produces again n.

Hence, for every tree t we have that $P_3(t) \cup P_4(t) \subseteq P_1(t) \cup P_2(t)$, which implies the containment $Q_2 \sqsubseteq Q_1$. □

The following example demonstrates how the unrollings can be used to decide query containment.

Example 8.21   Consider the pattern P in Figure 8.6. P is contained in P_4, thus, we expect that P is contained to the union of $P_!$ and P_2. We form the unrollings for pattern P. We have six unrollings, the $Q_{11}, Q_{12}, Q_{21}, Q_{22}, Q_{31}$, and Q_{32}. There is a d-homomorphism from P_1 to Q_{11} and there is a d-homomorphism from P_1 to each of $Q_{12}, Q_{21}, Q_{22}, Q_{31}$, and Q_{32}. Hence, according to Theorem 8.19 P is contained in the union of P_1 and P_2.

8.10 REWRITINGS

We have the same scenario as for conjunctive queries. We describe in terms of XML documents and XPath queries.

A *view* is the result of precomputing a query pattern V; that is, V has already been applied to a tree t and the result $V(t)$ is available. When a new pattern P has to be applied to t, we sometimes want to use $V(t)$, rather than t, as the input (due to efficiency considerations or when t itself is not available). Thus, the problem at hand is to find a pattern R, such that applying R to $V(t)$ produces the same result as applying P to t, i.e., $R(V(t)) = P(t)$. This equality must hold for any XML document t, since we do not know t in advance. If this equality holds, then we call R a *rewriting (or single-view rewriting) of P using V*.[2]

Now, starting to look for techniques to find whether or not, given a query pattern P and a view V, the new pattern R is indeed a rewriting according to the above definition, we need to define the concept of pattern composition.

8.10.1 PATTERN COMPOSITION

The *composition* of a pattern R with a pattern V, denoted by $R \circ V$, is obtained as follows. Let l_R^r be the label of the root of R and let l_V^o be the label of the output node of V. If $l_R^r, l_V^o \in \Sigma$, and $l_R^r \neq l_V^o$, then $R \circ V = \ empty$ (the empty pattern). Otherwise, $R \circ V$ is obtained by merging the output node of V with the root of R and assigning the label $l_R^r = l_V^o$ to the merged node if $l_R^r = l_V^o$, otherwise assign one of the non-star labels. The children of the merged node are all those of $out(V)$ and $root(R)$. The pattern $R \circ V$ has the same root as V and the same output node as R.

As an example, Figure 8.7 shows three patterns: R, V, and their composition $R \circ V$. Note that the merged node of $R \circ V$ is marked as m and its label is $*$, since both the output node of V and the root of R are labeled with $*$. Had one of these two nodes been labeled with $l \neq *$ and the other with either $*$ or l, then l would have been the label of m.

The following theorem says that applying $R \circ V$ to a tree is the same as first applying V and then applying R.

Theorem 8.22 $R \circ V(t) = R(V(t))$ *holds for all trees t.*

By Proposition 8.22, the problem can be reformulated as follows. We say that R is an *equivalent rewriting* (or just *rewriting*) of P using V if $R \circ V \equiv P$. As an example, consider the patterns V, P, and R of Figure 8.7. It is easy to verify that the composition $R \circ V$ is equivalent to P. Thus, R is a rewriting of P using V.

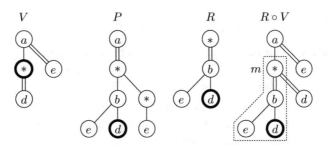

Figure 8.7: Pattern composition.

---

[2]We only discuss equivalent rewritings for XPath queries and views, thus we refer to them as simply "rewritings."

8.10.2 REWRITINGS FOR QUERY AND VIEW IN $XP^{\{[\ ],*\}}$

Starting from the remarks of Section 8.2, we can prove the following theorem.

Theorem 8.23 *Let P and V be query and view from $XP^{\{[\ ],*\}}$. Let R be the subtree rooted at the k node of P where k is depth of the output node of V. Then, if there is a rewriting, the composition $R \circ V$ is such a rewriting.*

8.10.3 REWRITINGS THAT ARE UNIONS OF XPATH QUERIES

We define a multiple view rewriting to be a union of rewritings as follows: Let P be a query patterns and $V_1, V_2, \ldots$ be a set of views. A set of patterns $R_1, R_2, \ldots$ is a union-rewriting of P using $V_1, V_2, \ldots$ if the union of $R_1 \circ V_1, R_2 \circ V_2, \ldots$ is equivalent to P.

The following example describes a case in which a single-view rewriting does not suffice in order to equivalently rewrite a pattern in $XP^{\{//,*\}}$. Then, based on Theorem 8.19, we construct a union-rewriting.

Example 8.24 Let P and $\mathcal{V}$ be the pattern and the set of views, respectively, illustrated in Figure 8.8. Notice that there is no pattern R in $XP^{\{//,*\}}$ such that for a view V in $\mathcal{V}$ we have $R \circ V \equiv P$.

However, constructing the patterns $R_1 \circ V_1, R_2 \circ V_2, R_3 \circ V_3, R_4 \circ V_4$, and $R_5 \circ V_4$ we can see (using Theorem 8.19) that for every tree t, we have $R_1(V_1(t)) \cup R_2(V_2(t)) \cup R_3(V_3(t))$ $\cup R_5(V_4(t)) \cup R_3(V_4(t)) = P(t)$. To verify this we unroll three times the first descendant of P (the resulted set, denoted as $\mathcal{P}$, is illustrated in the bottom-right corner of Figure 8.8). Notice, now, that Q_1 is equivalent to both $R_1 \circ V_1$ and $R_2 \circ V_2$. Moreover, $R_3 \circ V_3$ and $R_4 \circ V_4$ are equivalent to Q_2 and Q_3. Finally, the pattern $R_5 \circ V_4$ is equivalent to Q_5. Now, according to Theorem 8.19, the union of Q_1, Q_2, Q_3, and Q_4 is equivalent to P, because they cover all the unrollings of P. □

8.11 CONCLUSION AND BIBLIOGRAPHICAL NOTES

XPath query containment has been studied in a reries of works, including [11, 113, 138, 176] (this one studies also minimization). Also, containment is studied in [180] and [173]. Containment for the fragments $XP^{\{//,[\ ]\}}$, $XP^{\{[\ ],*\}}$, and $XP^{\{//,*\}}$ can be decided in PTIME, while for $XP^{\{//,[\ ],*\}}$ is coNP-complete [176]. Bag equivalence for XPath queries is studied in [61]. The material in this chapter is from the above works. A comprehensive recent work for XPath query containment is in [66]. Other work on containment includes [73].

More specifically, concerning containment tests, the existence of a homomorphism (here refered to as extended embedding) from one pattern to another constitutes a sufficient condition for deciding containment of patterns in $XP^{\{//,[\ ],*\}}$ [138]. The existence, however, of a homomorphism does not also constitute a necessary condition. For patterns either in $XP^{\{//,[\ ]\}}$ or

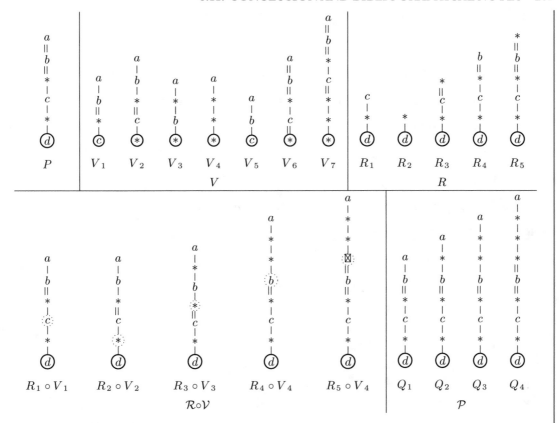

Figure 8.8: Union rewriting of a pattern.

$XP^{\{[\,],*\}}$ the existence of a homomorphism constitutes both a necessary and sufficient condition for deciding containment of single patterns [21, 138, 175, 177].

Concerning minimality, in [65] an interesting question is answered: a nonredundant tree pattern is given which, however, has an equivalent tree pattern that is of smaller size.

Little work has been about query rewriting and finding equivalent rewritings. This includes [9, 50, 121]. For multiple views rewriting, see [11, 49, 172]. [162] focuses on view selection for query rewriting.

The *rewriting-existence problem* is that of determining, for a pattern P and a view V, whether there is an equivalent rewriting R of P using V. It is proven in [9] that this problem for XP is decidable.

8.12   EXERCISES

8.1.   Prove Theorem 8.8.

8.2.   Prove that all the patterns without branches are minimal.

8.3.   Consider Figure 8.3 and prove that patterns (b) and (c) are equivalent.

8.4.   Prove Theorem 8.13.

8.5.   Prove Theorem 8.16.

8.6.   Prove Theorem 8.22.

8.7.   Consider Figure 8.7 and prove that $R \circ V \equiv P$.

8.8.   Prove Theorem 8.23.

CHAPTER 9

Tree-Structured Records Queried with SQL Dialect

Query languages like XPath are fundamentally navigation languages on trees. A more recent approach to query languages attempts to be more SQL-like, and to think of the instances of a tree data type as if they were tuples of a relation. We present in this chapter a data model which is defined by neither a standard relation (like the relational model) nor by a tree (like an XML document), but it is a "combination" of both. Thus, it enables the use of an SQL-like query language.

We first present the data model informally. The schema in this case is not a list (or vector) of attributes but a tree of attributes. Accordingly, a tuple instance of such a schema is a tree with basic values in the leaves of the tree. The data is stored in a relation which is a collection of tree tuples with the same schema. The second important difference is that, for some attributes, we allow for multiple values. Let us see an example in an informal way, before we give the formal definition. We give a toy example in Figure 9.1; we will give a more complex real-life example in the next section. In Figure 9.1, we present a schema tree (in the bottom of the figure) and an instance of this schema (in the top of the figure). First, let us discuss informally the schema. If we compare to a schema of a regular relation, there are two main differences:

- the attributes in the schema are arranged on a tree instead of being a list; and

- there are some attributes (the ones marked by a star) that are allowed to have multiple values.

Thus, this schema tree, says that we have a leaf attribute C which may have more than one value, and there are two leaf attributes A and B which, however, are arranged as children of an internal attribute M. Attribute M is a sibling of the attribute C. (Internal attributes are also allowed to have multiple instances but we keep it simple here since we will present a more complex example later.) The attribute B is labeled by an asterisk in the schema tree and this means that B may have multiple values. The attribute A has no label and this means that it should have exactly one value. Now let us see the instance we have depicted in the top on Figure 9.1. There we have four tuples, each tuple according to the given schema in the bottom of the figure. In each tuple, values are given to the leaf attributes of the schema tree. The first tuple, $t1$, has two values for the attribute C, the values $a1$ and $a3$ which are children of the root of the tuples $t1$. Also, the first tuple has the unique value for attribute A, the value $d1$ and two values for the attribute B, the values $b2$ and $b3$. The second tuple, $t2$, has: a) two values for attribute C, the values $a2$ and $a1$, b) a unique value for attribute A, the value $d4$, and c) a unique value for attribute B, the value $b3$. Now it is obvious how to read the other two tuples, $t3$ and $t4$. Since values of sibling attributes in the schema tree are also siblings in the instance data tree, in the rest of this chapter we will make explicit (by the notation) which values correspond to what attributes. In Figure 9.1, this was not necessary because we did not have two starred attributes that are siblings. Still we have used the letter a for the values of attribute C, the letter d for the values of attribute A, and the letter b for attribute B.

We continue with the formal definitions for schema tree and instance data tree in Section 9.1.

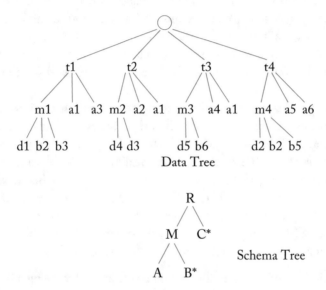

Figure 9.1: A relation with four tuples, t_1, t_2, t_3, and t_4 (top) and its schema (bottom).

9.1   TREES AS DATA AND AS DATA TYPES

A schema is defined as a data type. We define data types recursively as follows.

1. The *type of an attribute* is either a *basic type* (integer, real, string, etc.) or a tuple type. Further, attributes within a tuple type can be either *required* (one occurrence), *optional* (zero or one occurrence), *repeated* (zero, one, or more occurrences), or *required and repeated* (one or more occurrences).

2. A *tuple type* is a list of attribute names and a (previously defined) type for each attribute.

3. A *relation type* is a repeated tuple type.

We shall refer to the type of tuples (unrepeated) as the *schema* of the relation.

9.1.1 REPRESENTING DATA TYPES AND SCHEMAS AS TREES

We use the conventional notation for types. For example, *int* and *string* will denote the basic types integer and string. A tuple type T with attributes $A_1, \ldots, A_n$ whose types are $T_1, \ldots, T_n,$[1] respectively, will be denoted

$$T = \{A_1 : T_1, \ldots, A_n : T_n\}.$$

The repeated type T will be denoted T^* and the optional type T will be denoted $T?$; we also use T^+ to denote "one or more occurrences."

We shall use trees to represent schemas. The following rules define how a tree is constructed from a data type. Each node represents either the entire type (if the node is the root) or one of the subtypes used to define that type.

1. A node that represents a tuple type has children for each attribute of that tuple type, in order from the left.

2. The children are labeled by their corresponding attribute names.

3. In addition, each attribute has a *repetition constraint*. An attribute that is *required* has no label on it. An attribute that is repeated is labeled with a *; an optional attribute is labeled with a ?, and an attribute that is required and repeated is labeled by a +.[2]

4. The root itself is labeled by the name of the type. Typically, the root type is starred, since it is the type of a relation and the relation consists of zero or more tuples of the root type.

5. Leaf nodes are of basic type.

Technically, we should attach the type of each leaf to the leaf itself, but in examples these types will all be integers, reals, or strings, and the choice among these will be both obvious and irrelevant to the points we are trying to make.

Example 9.1 In Figure 9.2, we see the tree schema for a hypothetical data type that represents advertisers at a search engine. The root is labeled Advertiser, the name of the type. In queries, we shall also use Advertiser as the name of a relation containing tuples of this type. Advertiser is a tuple type, with three attributes: required attributes Name (of the advertiser) and Email (of the advertiser) and a repeated attribute Campaign. Each advertiser can thus have any number of Campaigns, including zero.

A Campaign comprises CID, a unique identifier for the Campaign, a Budget, zero or more WordSets, and zero or more Clicks. A WordSet is a tuple type consisting of a required

---

[1]All attributes are distinct.

[2]In the rest of this chapter, we will pretend that we only have required and repeated attributes because the others do not add extra complexity but they are cumbersome to carry around.

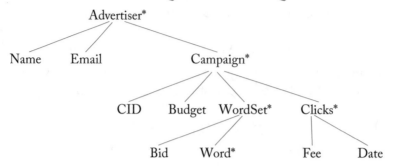

Figure 9.2: A relation schema represented as a tree.

Bid and a set of Words. The subtype Click is a tuple type with two required attributes: the Fee collected for the click and the Date of the click.

9.1.2 INSTANCES OF A SCHEMA (REPRESENTING DATA AS TREES)

An instance of a data type or schema consists of replacement of each subtype by an appropriate number of instances of that subtype. More formally, we have the following.

1. An instance of a basic type is any single value of the appropriate type.

2. An instance of a tuple type is a node whose children are each instances of one of the types of one of its attributes. The nodes for the attributes are sorted in the same order as the attributes themselves. However, there can be zero or more instances for each attribute, depending on its repetition constraint, as follows.

    a) A required attribute must have exactly one occurrence.

    b) An optional attribute can have zero or one occurrence.

    c) A repeated attribute can have any number of occurrences.

    d) An attribute that is both required and repeated can have one or more instances.

Thus, when we depict the data on a tree, each node that corresponds to an attribute A may have two kinds of siblings: a) those that are instances of different attribute than A and b) those that are instance of attribute A (if A is a repeated attribute). The distinction on our examples will be made clear because usually, we use lowercase letters for instance of each attribute that are the same with the letter used for the attribute in uppercase letter. Thus, for attribute A, we will use node names for its instances $a1, a2$, etc.

Example 9.2

Figure 9.3 suggests a possible instance of the relation that is described by the schema of Figure 9.2. The root, labeled *o*, represents the relation with this type. For all other instance nodes, we use a naming scheme that indicates to which schema node it belongs.

The root has two children *a1* and *a2*, representing two Advertiser tuples. The second of these is just sketched, so let us concentrate on *a1*. The node for *a1* has children *n1* and *e1*, the Name and Email for the first Advertiser.

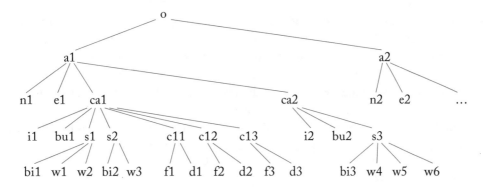

Figure 9.3: An instance of the schema of Figure 9.2.

Then we see two instances of the Campaign attribute, represented by nodes *ca1* and *ca2*. The first of these, *ca1*, has two instances of Wordset and three instances of Clicks, whereas the second, *ca2*, has one instance of WordSet and zero instance of Clicks.

9.2   QUERYING TREE-STRUCTURED DATA

As we explained, we think of the instances of a tree data type as if they were tuples of a relation. Now, we use an SQL-like language to query them. In particular, the syntax is the same as SQL. Before we give formal definitions, we discuss informally. Suppose we have an SQL SELECT query, with an inequality constraint on one of the leaf-attributes of the schema of Figure 9.3.[3] We apply all the queries on Figure 9.3. First, suppose we have the constraint *Name* ≠ *n1*. Then we should delete the whole tuple *a1* because the query says that we do not care about information when *Name* = *n1*. Now, suppose we have a second query with constraint *CID* ≠ *i2*. Then, we should not discard the whole tuple *a1* because the instance for *ca1* in still useful. Thus, this query returns part of the tuple *a1* and in particular, the part that includes everything except the subtree rooted at *ca2*.

---

[3]We will discuss the constraint on various attributes of the schema of Figure 9.3 and see how a difference is made depending on the presence or not of a star (which denotes whether an attribute is repeated or not).

How does the algorithm decide that this subtree should be deleted? It does that recursively as follows. After the algorithm deletes the node $i2$ (remember we work on the Figure 9.3), it visits its parent on Figure 9.3, which is $ca2$. Since on the schema tree (Figure 9.2) CID is a required attribute, the algorithm also deletes the whole subtree rooted at $ca2$. However, after visiting the parent of $ca2$, the algorithm observes that the attribute Campaign is a repeated attribute for the attribute Advertiser, so it does not need to process the instance $s1$ and it stops.

Now, imagine a third query with filter $Fee \neq f1$. Now required attributes should have exactly one instance, thus if we delete the leaf node $f1$ on the Figure 9.3, its parent (the node $cl1$) lacks one required attribute from its children; hence, it should be deleted too together with all the subtree rooted at $cl1$. The intuitive reason is that the Fee defines each instance of the Clicks attribute and if it is missing then we do not have a definition of the Clicks attribute as the designer of the schema intended to be. If the designer of the schema wanted the definition of the Clicks to have the flexibility of missing the Fee altoghter but still wanted to allow only one instance for Clicks, then he had the option to label the attribute Fee with ?, which means that the attribute has either one instance or is missing. This intuition gives rise to the tree-pruning algorithm for filter queries that we present formally in the rest of this section.

9.2.1   FILTER QUERIES

A *filter* is a conjunction of comparisons $A\theta B$ where A is an attribute of basic type, B is an attribute of basic type or a constant and θ can be any comparison for which, given two values, the outcome is "true" or "false." This include inequality, $\neq$, and arithmetic comparisons in $\{\leq, < , \geq, >\}$. A *filter query* is an SQL SELECT query which refers to the attributes at the leaves of the schema tree and uses such filters.

In the beginning of this section we gave the intuition of a tree-pruning algorithm that answers filter queries. However, there is another subtlety that we did not explain there. The problem appears when we compare two attributes (in the example we gave in the beginning of this section we imagined that we were comparing an attribute with a constant). We will start the explanation with the following example.

Example 9.3   Let us consider two queries on the schema of Figure 9.2 that look almost the same, but in fact behave quite differently.

Query Q_1 is:

```
SELECT CID
FROM Advertiser
WHERE Budget < Fee;
```

Query Q_2 is:

```
SELECT CID
FROM Advertiser
WHERE Bid < Fee;
```

Now, considering query Q_1, if a pair of Budget and Fee does not satisfy the inequality, it makes sense to delete the Fee value and leave the Budget value in tact because the Budget value is "more important" than the Fee value. It is more important because each Fee value will be compared with a single Budget value, while each Budget value will be compared with many Fee values, thus in essence Budget "dominates" Fee. We will make the dominance relation formal in the next subsection.

9.2.2   DOMINANCE RELATION

Informally, a leaf node V in a tree schema is dominated by another leaf node U if, in all instances of this schema, we have: if W is the attribute that is the LCA (lowest common ancestor) of U and V on the scheme tree, then the following is true: for any instance/node w of attribute W, the subtree rooted at w contains only one value of U while it may contain multiple values of V. We now give the formal definition.

Definition 9.4   A path in a schema tree from a node A to a descendant of A, D, is *star free* if none of the nodes on the path, with the possible exception of A, is repeated or required-and-repeated.

Definition 9.5   An attribute A *dominates* another attribute B if, in the schema tree, the path from A to the lowest common ancestor (*LCA*) of A and B is star free.

Example 9.6   Consider the schema of Figure 9.2. The lowest common ancestor of Budget and Fee is Campaign. The path from Budget to Campaign has no stars, except for the star at Campaign. Since Campaign itself is the LCA, its star is not considered part of the path. Thus, we say that Budget dominates Fee. Fee does not dominate Budget. The reason is that the path from Fee to the LCA includes the node Clicks, which is starred. Now, consider the two attributes Bid and Fee involved in query Q_2. Again, the LCA is Campaign. But now, Bid and Fee each have a star on their paths to the LCA, namely the nodes WordSet and Clicks, respectively. Therefore, neither dominates the other.

For a final example, consider nodes Fee and Date. Their LCA is Clicks. Neither has a star on their path to the LCA; again, the star at the LCA itself does not matter. Therefore, Fee and Date each dominate the other.

The key observation to be made from Example 9.6 is: in any instance of the schema in Figure 9.2, there is only one Budget node in any subtree rooted at an instance of Campaign, the LCA of Budget, and Fee. This fact makes query Q_1 implementable by tree pruning. But for Q_2 a single instance of Campaign, which is also the LCA of Bid and Fee, can have multiple Bid descendants and also multiple Fee descendants. Since awkward combinations of the Bid and

Fee descendants can survive the filtering, it is impossible, in general, to implement Q_2 by tree pruning.[4]

9.2.3   TREE-PRUNING ALGORITHM FOR FILTER QUERIES

We can now give the algorithm for modifying the tree in the way suggested by Example 9.6 in order to provide an answer to a filter query. The algorithm works only for legitmate filter queries as defined below. In the rest of this chapter, by filter queries we will always mean legitimate filter queries.

Definition 9.7   A filter query is a *legitimate filter query* if each comparison either compares an attribute to a constant or compares two attributes where one dominates the other.

The tree-pruning algorithm proceeds as follows: There is a node-deletion step followed by a recursive deletion process for ancestors of the deleted nodes. We shall start with the initial deletion.

Case 1: If the comparison involves only one leaf attribute A, delete all leaves in the instance tree that are instances of A and that do not satisfy the predicate.

Case 2: If the comparison involves leaf attributes A and B, where A dominates B, let C be the LCA of A and B in the schema tree. In the instance tree, look at all occurrences of A and B such that the LCA of these nodes in the instance tree is an occurrence of C. If the values of the A- and B-nodes in the instance tree are such that the comparison is not satisfied, then delete the B-node from the instance tree.

Now, having deleted certain nodes from the instance tree, we need to propagate these deletions up the tree. In particular, if we delete a required node, then we have to delete the entire subtree rooted at its parent. Also, suppose n is a node in the instance tree, and it has some children that are occurrences of some attribute A, which is of kind required-and-repeated. If all these children have been deleted, then n must also be deleted. These rules can propagate up the instance tree indefinitely.

Example 9.8   Consider the query Q_1 from Example 9.3.

```
SELECT CID
FROM Advertiser
WHERE Budget < Fee;
```

For example, suppose that *f2* is greater than *bu1*, but *f1* and *f3* are not. The effect on the instance of Figure 9.3 is that the subtrees rooted at *cl1* and *cl3* are removed, but other than that, the tree remains the same and the result after applying the algorithm is shown in Figure 9.4.

A more complex example follows.

---

[4]This will be illustrated in more examples later.

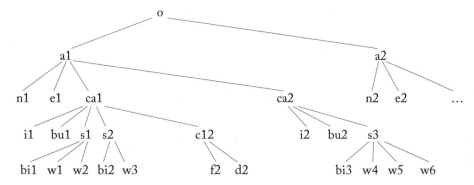

Figure 9.4: Result of eliminating Fees that are not greater than the Budget for their Campaign.

Example 9.9   Let us consider the schema tree of Figure 9.2 and the instance tree of Figure 9.3. Suppose the comparison involves Fee and Date, and we have chosen to regard Fee as dominating Date (note that in this case, either could have been chosen as the dominating attribute). The LCA of these attributes is Clicks. In Figure 9.3, the pairs of Fee and Date that have a Clicks node as LCA are $(f1, d1)$, $(f2, d2)$, and $(f3, d3)$. Note, for example, that $f1$ and $d2$ are not compared, because their LCA is $ca1$, which is not a Clicks instance. Suppose further that the first two pairs satisfy the comparison, but $(f3, d3)$ does not. Then, because we have chosen to regard Fee as dominating, we delete the $d3$ node. Now, we must propagate the deletion upward. Because Date is a required child of Clicks, we must delete its Clicks parent, $cl3$, and its entire subtree. That deletion causes $f3$ to be deleted as well.[5] We next need to consider the parent of the newly deleted node $cl3$. That parent is the campaign occurrence $ca1$. However, Clicks is a repeated child of Campaign, thus, the deletion of $cl3$ has does not cause the deleting of $ca1$. The latter simply has one fewer Clicks child in the instance tree.

If we have the AND of two or more comparisons of these types, we can apply one comparison at a time. As long as each comparison can be implemented by tree pruning, the cascade of pruning steps will result in a tree that satisfies all of the comparisons.

9.3   FLATTENING

In this section, we define flattening the data tree and show how to compute filter queries in an equivalent fashion as tree-pruning but using the flattened data and standard SQL computing algorithm.

Informally, we flatten an instance of a tree data type by selecting one from each repeated group of values in all possible ways. This selection is made independently at all levels. If an

---

[5]Note that had we chosen to regard Date as dominating Fee, we would have deleted $f3$ first, but then would have deleted $cl3$ and $d3$, leading to the same tree.

attribute at any level is repeated and has zero values, or an optional attribute is not present, then the attribute's value is taken to be the dummy instance; that is, all its descendant leaves are taken to be NULL. This expansion using NULL's is necessary to avoid losing information. The formal definition follows.

Definition 9.10   If I is an instance of some schema, we define the (ordinary) relation flatten(I) recursively as follows.

1. If I is a single element of basic type, then flatten(I) is the tuple with a single component; that component is the value of I.

2. If I is an instance of some tuple type with attributes $A_1, \ldots, A_n$: divide the children of the root of I into n groups, such that the first group is all the nodes that are occurrences of A_1, the second group is all the occurrences of A_2, and so on. For the ith group, construct a relation R_i that has attributes for all the leaves of the schema tree rooted at A_i, as follows.

   a) Recursively apply the flatten operation to the instance represented by each node in the group for A_i. However, if A_i is repeated or optional, include the dummy instance in this set of instances.

   b) Take the union of the relation produced for each instance. The union is the relation R_i.

3. Finally, to get the relation flatten(I), take the Cartesian product $R_1 \times R_2 \times \cdots \times R_n$.

   The result is the *full flattening* of the given instance.

Example 9.11   Let us see how to flatten the instance in Figure 9.3, whose schema we saw in Figure 9.2. First, let us observe that the relation schema for the flattened relation is

$$(Name, Email, CID, Budget, Bid, Word, Fee, Date)$$

since these are the attribute names of the leaves of the schema, from the left. In Table 9.1, we present the flattening of the part of the instance with root *a1*. The entire result is the union of the relation we get from *a1* with the relations we get from all the other instances of Advertiser.

The relation for *ca1* is the Cartesian product of the relation for *i1* (which is $\{(i1)\}$), the relation for *bu*1, the union of the relations for *s*1 and *s*2 and, the union of the relations for *cl*1, *cl*2, and *cl*3. The result appears in rows 1 through 25 of Table 9.1. Similarly, for *ca2*, the result appears in rows 26–30 of Table 9.1.

Finally, to construct the relation for *a1*, we take the product of the relations $\{(n1)\}$, $\{(e1)\}$, and the relation of Table 9.1. The result looks similar to Table 9.1, but there are two new attributes at the left, Name and Email, and the value of each of the 21 tuples of Table 9.1 has values *n1* and *e1* in those new columns.

Table 9.1: Tuples of resulting from the full flattening of the dummy Campaign (row 1), *ca1* (rows 2–25), and *ca2* (rows 26–30)

	CID	Budget	Bid	Word	Fee	Date
1	NULL	NULL	NULL	NULL	NULL	NULL
2	i1	bu1	NULL	NULL	NULL	NULL
3	i1	bu1	NULL	NULL	f1	d1
4	i1	bu1	NULL	NULL	f2	d2
5	i1	bu1	NULL	NULL	f3	d3
6	i1	bu1	bi1	NULL	NULL	NULL
7	i1	bu1	bi1	NULL	f1	d1
8	i1	bu1	bi1	NULL	f2	d2
9	i1	bu1	bi1	NULL	f3	d3
10	i1	bu1	bi1	w1	NULL	NULL
11	i1	bu1	bi1	w1	f1	d1
12	i1	bu1	bi1	w1	f2	d2
13	i1	bu1	bi1	w1	f3	d3
14	i1	bu1	bi1	w2	NULL	NULL
15	i1	bu1	bi1	w2	f1	d1
16	i1	bu1	bi1	w2	f2	d2
17	i1	bu1	bi1	w2	f3	d3
18	i1	bu1	bi2	NULL	NULL	NULL
19	i1	bu1	bi2	NULL	f1	d1
20	i1	bu1	bi2	NULL	f2	d2
21	i1	bu1	bi2	NULL	f3	d3
22	i1	bu1	bi2	w3	NULL	NULL
23	i1	bu1	bi2	w3	f1	d1
24	i1	bu1	bi2	w3	f2	d2
25	i1	bu1	bi2	w3	f3	d3
26	i2	bu2	NULL	NULL	NULL	NULL
27	i2	bu2	bi3	NULL	NULL	NULL
28	i2	bu2	bi3	w4	NULL	NULL
29	i2	bu2	bi3	w5	NULL	NULL
30	i2	bu2	bi3	w6	NULL	NULL

9.3.1 USING FLATTENED DATA TO ANSWER FILTER QUERIES

If we have the tree-structured tuples flattened, then we can alternatively process legitimate SQL-like queries as follows: flatten the tuples and apply the query to the ordinary relation that results. We will discuss later that this is not true for queries that are not legitimate (see Definition 9.7). Before we state the Theorem 9.12 below, we need to specify how we evaluate an flter/inequality if a NULL occurs.

- If a NULL occurs in either or both parts of an inequality then the inequality evaluates to true.

Theorem 9.12 *Let I be an instance tree and let* flatten(I) *be the flattened relation of I. Then, for any query Q which uses a filter such that one attribute in a comparison dominates the other, the following holds:*

$$\text{flatten}(Q(I)) = Q(\text{flatten}(I)).$$

Before we contiue with the proof of the theorem we give the intuition arguing on Table 9.1 in the following example.

Example 9.13 We continue from Example 9.8. Let us apply the SQL query Q_1 using the ordinary SQL semantics on the flattened data of Table 9.1. The rows that contain $f1$ and $f3$ will be deleted, i.e., the following rows will be deleted: 3, 5, 7, 9, 11, 13, 15, 17, 19, 21, 23, and 25. The rest of the rows will survive because the value of *Fee* in those rows in NULL, and we have adopted the convention (as we already mentioned) that rows with value UNKNOWN for a filter condition pass the filter.

Now observe that what remains after this deletion is the flattening of Figure 9.4.

Example 9.14 We continue from Example 9.9. Let us apply the SQL query using the ordinary SQL semantics on the flattened data of Table 9.1. Then we remove the following rows: 5, 9 ,13, 17, 21, and 25 because the pair ($f3, d3$) does not satisfy the filter (as we assumed in Example 9.9).

The proof of Theorem 9.12 follows.

Proof. Let T_i be the input data tree and F_i be the full flattening of T_i. Let A be a leaf attribute of the schema tree. Let v_A be a leaf node of the instance data tree that corresponds to attribute A. We denote by F_{v_A} the set of rows in F_i in which the node (the value of) v_A appears. Let u_A be a sibling node of v_A on attribute A in the instance data tree. We can prove the following.

- F_{v_A} and F_{u_A} are disjoint and each tuple of F_{v_A} comes from F_{u_A} by changing the value of the node u_A to the value of the node v_A.

- Let $T_i(v_A)$ be the tree T_i in which we have applied the tree-pruning algorithm with respect to the node v_A (i.e., we delete v_A and then recursively delete its ancestors nodes according to the algorithm). Then the flattening of $T_i(v_A)$ is F_i after deleting the rows in F_{v_A}.

Useful note: The way we evaluate NULLs on inequalities guarantees that when all values of a repeated attribute are gone (on the flattened data), the value of their sibling attributes still remain in the result.

The proof of the first bullet is an easy consquerice of the definition of flattening. For the proof of the second bullet, notice the subtlety that after deleting the rows in F_{v_A} we may have no more rows left with nodes/values of attribute A. But we have one row with null in this attribute. If there are nulls in other attributes as well in this row, then the original tree will be pruned recursively till the lowest common ancestor of all the leaf attributes with nulls which has the property: all its required children have non-NULL values (including the trees rooted in these children, in which case non-NULL value means that there is a non-all-NULL tree rooted on them after the tree-pruning).

Now, in order to prove the theorem, it suffices to observe that a filter on attribute A and attribute B (where B dominates A) either deletes all nodes in F_{v_A} (if the filter is not satisfied) or leaves them all in tact (when the fillter is satisfied). This is so, because a certain (same) value/node of B appears in all rows in F_{v_A}. Hence, the filter either deletes all rows in F_{v_A} or leaves them all in tact.   □

9.4   DISCUSSION: TREE-PRUNING VS. FLATTENING

First, we discuss the following situation: Suppose we obtain from data tree T the flattened relation R and then we apply any filter query Q on R (in the standard SQL-processing manner) and get R'.

- The question is: can we get back from R' to a tree T' that is of the same schema as the schema of tree T?

The answer is "not always" and this is known fact from the study of nested relations. This answers also the question why we limit ourselves to legitimate queries. We discuss on the following example.

Example 9.15   Consider the schema in Figure 9.5(a) and an instance of that schema in Figure 9.5(b). The values of B and C are integers, but we give each occurrence of a B-value or C-value a name, such as b_1, to make clear which attribute, B or C, each integer comes from. Suppose we apply to the instance of Figure 9.5 the query:

    SELECT B, C FROM A WHERE B<C.

We may view this query as applying to the flattened version of Figure 9.5(b), which is shown in Figure 9.6(a). Note that this relation does not include the tuples where one or both of B and C are NULL. However, in this particular example, the result would not change if

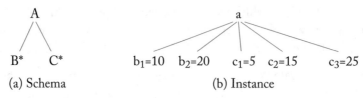

(a) Schema   (b) Instance

Figure 9.5: A schema and an instance.

we considered the full flattening (shown in Figure 9.6(b)) and it is simpler to argue on this relation (i.e., of Figure 9.6(a)) instead of the relation in Figure 9.6(b). We shall see shortly, in Example 9.16, how the NULLs play an important role and, therefore, in the general case, it becomes essential to use the full flattening.

	B	C
1	10	5
2	10	15
3	10	25
4	20	5
5	20	15
6	20	25

	B	C
1	10	5
2	10	15
3	10	25
4	20	5
5	20	15
6	20	25
7	NULL	NULL
8	10	NULL
9	20	NULL
10	NULL	5
11	NULL	15
12	NULL	25

(a) Flattening without usings NULLs   (b) Full Flattening

Figure 9.6: Flattening without using NULLs and full flattening of Figure 9.5b.

Notice that, in Figure 9.6a, the second, third, and sixth tuples satisfy the filter, while the others do not. Thus, the result of this query is shown in Figure 9.7. However, this relation is not the flattening of any tuple with the schema of Figure 9.5a. To see why, notice that such a tree-structured tuple would have B-values 10 and 20 and also have C-values 15 and 25. But then the flattening of the tree would also yield the tuple (20, 15), which is not included in Figure 9.7. We conclude that this SQL query cannot be executed on tree-structured tuples; it can only be

	B	C
2	10	15
3	10	25
6	20	25

Figure 9.7: Result of SELECT B, C FROM A WHERE B<C.

executed on the flattened version of the tree, and the result has a schema different from the schema of the input tuples.

There is an additional interesting observation in Example 9.15: the fact that Figure 9.7 cannot be the flattening of any instance of the given schema may depend on a simple change: If the schema of Figure 9.5(a) had a * on the A, then we could view Figure 9.7 as an instance of such a schema: this instance would have three occurrences of A, one for each of the three rows in Figure 9.7.

However, even in the more common case where the schema has a * at the root and represents a relation with an arbitrary number of tree-structured tuples, we want to rule out the possibility of using more than one tuple to represent the result of a query applied to a single tuple.

This strategy (of applying filter queries only on single tuples) is efficient, simple, and avoids explosion in the size of the data (imagine if the tree of Figure 9.5(b) were actually part of some much larger tree, which would have to be replicated for each of the three rows in the result).

9.4.1 THE ROLE OF NULLS FOR COMPUTING LEGITIMATE QUERIES

We can use the schema and instance of Figures 9.5a and 9.5b, respectively, to show that NULLs are needed in flattening even in the case we have legitimate queries (e.g., in Example 9.16, all filters/inequalities have one side being a constant, hence the query is legitimate).

Example 9.16

Now, using the same schema and instance, Figure 9.5, suppose we have the query

```
SELECT *
FROM A
WHERE B = 10 AND C = 35;
```

According to the tree-pruning algorithm, the data leaves that do not satisfy the filter will be deleted. The "AND" is interpreted as two filters $B = 10$ and $C = 35$ Thus, the first component of the filter is checked on attribute B and the second component on attribute C The first component deletes $b2$ and leaves only $b1$. The second component deletes all leaves on attribute C. Thus, the output data tree has only one leaf for attribute B and no leaves for attribute

C. The flattening, thus, contains only the row (10 NULL), and this is the row we get when if we apply on the relation of Figure 9.6(b) the query, because row (8) t survives the filtering, since it represents the one remaining B-value, paired with the NULL that represents the lack of any C-children.

9.5 FLATTENING FOR LINEAR SCHEMAS

In this section we will talk about cases where the number of rows in flattening is linear on the size of the instance data tree. These are the cases where the schema is linear.

Definition 9.17 Call a schema *linear* if there is a path p from the root to a leaf u such that the following is true: If a node is labeled with a star then this node is a node of p. We call the leaf u the *primary leaf.*

Lemma 9.18 *For any data tree on a linear schema, full flattening has a number of rows which is equal at most to the size of the data tree plus the total number of repetitions of the repeated attributes in the instance data tree.*

Proof. The proof is done by induction on the number of stars on the path p. The basic step is straightforward: All attributes except one are non-repeated, hence they have only one value which appears in all the rows. We have a number of rows equal to the number of values of the single repeated attribute in the schema. We also have an extra row with a NULL as the value of the repeated attribute.

Suppose the inductive assertion is true for $n = k$ stars on the path p. We will prove that it is true for $n = k + 1$ stars on the path p. For each sub-instance corresponding to the last (i.e., toward the leaf) k stars the inductive assertion is true. Now, we construct the flattening of the whole instance by doing the following for the uppermost (in p, i.e., the one closer to the root) repeated attribute A_{k+1}: Suppose A_{k+1} has a_{k+1} repetitions. For each of its repetitions, we add a number of rows that is equal to the number of rows of the sub-instance with k repeated attributes in its schema plus one in order to accommodate the NULLs. Thus, in total we have the number of rows as in the statement of the lemma. □

Motivated by the good properties of a linear schema, we define below what a subschema is and when a subschema is linear.

Definition 9.19 Given a schema S and a set A of leaf attributes, then the following construction obtains a subschema S_A of S for this set of attributes: We keep (in the tree of S) only those nodes and edges that lie on paths from the root to attributes in A.

A subschema can be viewed as a schema for the attributes in A, so we can define a *linear subschema* by carrying over the definition of a linear schema.[6]

Flattening may explode in size. Hence, linear subschemas are of use. The idea of linear subschema can be extended to define the concept of *semi-flattening* which offers enough information for legitimate filter queries. It is outside the scope of this chapter to discuss in detail semi-flattening but we will discuss briefly on an example how flattening is offering too much information that is not necessary to answer legitimate filter queries. For this, let us look closer at the flattened data of Table 9.1. We will observe that if we only have legitimate filter queries then some rows may be deleted without affecting the result of answering those queries by considering only the rest of the rows. Thus, rows 3, 4, and 5 contain NULLs that are useful as we explained earlier here. Rows 11, 12, and 13 are useful for answering legitimate queries regarding the first tuple for i1 (and bu1); we will not talk about the first tuple for i2 because it is a similar story. We need two more rows, the 14 and 23, to answer queries that comapre Bid to Word. Hence, 24 and 25 row are completely useless because they does not contain NUlls or values that can be compared by legitimate queries which are not contained in the rows we discussed before.

9.6   AGGREGATE QUERIES

Now we have all the necessary components (from previous sections) to use to explain how to answer aggregate queries on a linear schema (or subschema).

The aggregate functions we consider are SUM, MAX, MIN, COUNT, AVG, and COUNT-DISTINCT. We consider queries with one aggregated attribute. Moreover, we have the following constraints:

(a) the aggregated attribute should be dominated by all grouping attributes; and

(b) the SELECT clause should include only the grouping attributes and the aggregation(s).

When these constraints are met in queries, we call them *legitimate aggregate queries*.

We give the algorithm to compute an aggregate query with one grouping attribute. Suppose we have a query with grouping attribute $A1$ and aggregated attribute $A0$, where $A1$ dominates $A0$. The output will be a normal relation with two attributes; one attribute is the grouping attribute $A1$ and the other is a new attribute A_{agg} which stores the result of applying the aggregate function on bags, one bag for each value of $A1$. This is the description of the *tree-aggregating algorithm* that does the computation.

1. Suppose the attribute that is the lowest common ancestor of $A1$ and $A0$ in the schema tree is $A01$. For each value u of $A1$, let $\{v1, v2, \ldots, \}$ be the nodes in the data tree with value u, and let $\{v01, v02, \ldots, \}$ be the corresponding values of attribute $A01$ (i.e., $v1$ has ancestor $v01$, $v2$ has ancestor $v02$, and so on).

---

[6]Some refer to a linear subschema as the "repetition context" of its single-dominated attribute, i.e., the primary leaf. We find this term rendundant and we do not use it here.

2. For each value u of $A1$, we form a bag of values of the aggregated attribute $A0$. This bag stores all values for each data leaf which is (a) an occurrence of $A0$ and (b) is a descendant of a node in $\{v01, v02, \ldots, \}$.

3. Then we aggregate over the values in each bag (which corresponds to a value of $A0$) and store the result in the new attribute A_{agg}.

Of course, we need not form bags explicitly. We compute the aggregation function on the fly, except for the average function, where we need to compute both count and sum on the fly and divide at the end and the count-distinct function where we need to compute a set instead of a bag.

Example 9.20   We refer to the data tree in Figure 9.3 and we consider the query:

```
SELECT Budget, SUM(Bid)
FROM Advertiser
GROUP BY Budget;
```

If $bu1 \neq bu2$, the answer to this query is on the left below. However, if $bu1 = bu2$ then the answer to the query is on the right (it contains only one row):

Budget	SUM (Bid)
bu1	bi1 + bi2
bu2	bi3

Budget	SUM (Bid)
bu1	bi1 +bi2 + bi3

When there is more than one grouping attribute, there is at least one grouping attribute that is dominated by all other grouping attributes; call one of them arbitrarily the *most dominated attribute*.[7] We form one bag for each tuple of values of the grouping attributes. In this case, the computation is led by the most dominated attribute as to which subtrees we consider for all their aggregated attribute values.

Legitimate aggregate queries can be answered by flattening or semi-flattening but we should consider the subschema of all the attributes involved in the query and form the flattening for this subschema only (which is linear). Then we can apply standard SQL computation techniques. The proof of the following theorem is a straightforward consequence of the definition of aggregate SQL queries and Theorem 9.12.

Theorem 9.21   *Let Q be a legitimate aggregate query with one aggregated attribute and let S_Q be the subschema for the attributes in Q of the given schema S for the data. Let I be an instance tree of S_Q and let* flatten(I) *be the flattened relation of I. Then, the following holds:*

$$Q(I) = Q(\text{flatten}(I)).$$

---

[7]It can be shown that if there are more than one, then all have the same LCA with a specific aggregated attribute, so the computation is not affected by which one we choose to call.

9.7 CONCLUSION AND BIBLIOGRAPHICAL NOTES

After presenting the data model and the language for tree-like data, we presented the following in this chapter.

(a) We gave an algorithm to perform the filtering on the tree itself, whenever it is possible to do so.

(b) We gave an algorithm to compute aggregate queries.

(c) We have shown when the result of filter queries on a flattened relation is what we get by pruning the tree and then flattening (i.e., when do pruning and flattening commute).

(d) We have shown when the result of aggregate queries on a flattened relation is what we get by running the tree-aggregating algorithm on the data tree.

We defined the conditions for queries to be legitimate, introducing, for this purpose, the dominance relation

Examples of the data model and the query language presented here include the SQL variants used in Dremel (BigQuery)[12, 137] and F1 [135, 159]. On a more generic level, two important examples of such models are the JSON data format [1] and Google's protocol buffers [2]. Dremel was first discussed in [137] where the focus was on the systems part of the engine. A theoretical presentation is done later in [12] where the material presented here is from. The schema and the data in Dremel are described as trees (the syntax is protocol buffers). The data tree is stored in columnar storage associating with each data value two other values that are called "levels." These levels are used to define exactly the position of the data value on the data tree. When a query is issued, the data of the relevant (to the query) columns are retrieved in semi-flattening format, and a standard SQL evaluation algorithm is applied to compute the query. Thus, the syntax of the Dremel language is SQL syntax, the evaluation algorithm on the data tree is the tree-pruning and the tree-aggregating algorithm, but the actual computation is carried out as standard SQL computation on the semi-flattened data.

Flattening can expand greatly the amount of space needed to hold a tuple. For example, instances of the schema of Figure 9.2 could have campaigns with hundreds of Words among its WordSets, and many thousands of Clicks. The flattened relation for a tree-structured tuple would then be hundreds of times larger than the original tuple. Thus, Semi-flattening is the appropriate model for how Dremel processes tree-structured tuples.

9.7.1 DISCUSSION ON RELATED WORK

Similar models have been studied many years ago as *nested relations* [64, 157]. Flattening has always been regarded as a fundamental algebraic operation on nested relations [64, 147].

Rather recently, there has been a large body of work about tree-like structures, storing and querying them. Much of it stems from XML documents, and the query languages examined are fragments of XQuery, not SQL. A flattening technique is proposed in [90] to map XML data into relational tables. [163] builds on [90] and proposes three approaches to map efficiently an XML document to a relational database. Other approaches have been used, e.g., [146] is native algebraic based. In [42], a formal data model for JSON is proposed. As concerns columnar storage, [43] supports a uniform interface for querying efficiently both the structure and the data values for highly regular data and techniques to avoid storing NULLs are developed.

CHAPTER 10

Bibliographical Notes for Chapters 1–7

We begin this chapter by presenting the sources for the original results that have been covered in detail in this book. We then discuss the related work that either precedes or follows the development of the results presented in this book; the aims of the discussion include covering seminal papers that started some of the lines of work, as well as outlining major recent activity on the topic.

The structure of the rest of this chapter is as follows. In Section 10.1, we discuss the work focused on investigating the computational complexity of containment tests, for CQs under both set and bag semantics, as well as for CQACs, CQNs, and aggregate queries. In Section 10.2, we discuss the papers on query rewritings that originated in the 1990's, as well as some of the more recent papers on the topic. In Section 10.3, we first mention the papers that pioneered the dependency theory and the chase algorithm, and then, some recent developments. In Section 10.4, we cite work that has focused on data exchange, the topic that has enjoyed much recent activity; we discuss in detail some recent and current lines of work. Finally, in Section 10.5, we list recent work on determinacy, and present the published sources for other theoretical considerations around the problem of answering queries using views. While our presentation in Sections 10.1–10.5 is not exhaustive, we make an effort to be representative and to provide pointers to the papers that showcase major lines of work.

We now initiate the discussion of the published sources of the results that have been discussed in detail in this book. In reference to the results presented in Section 2.1 on CQ queries, Chandra and Merlin defined in their 1977 publication [51] the class of conjunctive queries on relational databases, showed that the containment problem for conjunctive queries is NP complete, and proved that each conjunctive query has a unique minimal equivalent query. They also showed that containment mappings can be used for testing containment for this class of queries.

Some of the algorithms [106, 179] for testing containment for CQAC queries that were covered in Section 2.2 begin by normalizing the given queries. The containment is then tested by checking logical implication using multiple containment mappings. Another containment test, covered in Section 2.2, is based on canonical databases [114, 123]. The homomorphism property was formally defined in [13], but already observed back in [114].

The test for checking containment between two CQNs, as discussed in Section 2.3, is described in [165].

Sara Cohen's thesis [54] studied containment and equivalence tests for conjunctive aggregate queries. Section 2.4 presents some of the results of [54].

Acyclic schemas were studied in a series of papers in early work by Beeri and colleagues, Fagin, and Fagin and colleagues [33, 34, 80, 87]. The containment test presented in Section 2.5 originates from the work [53] by Chekuri and colleagues. It is shown in [53] that testing for query containment can be done in polynomial time in those cases where the containing query is acyclic. Algorithms for efficient computation of acyclic joins using semijoins appeared in [40, 178]; the results show that acyclic queries can be evaluated in polynomial time in the sizes of the input database, of the query, and of the query answer.

The results presented in Section 3.2 are drawn primarily from the work by Levy and colleagues [124]. By the results of [124] and [154], for a given query Q there exists a maximally contained UCQ rewriting, such that each CQ component of the rewriting can have at most as many subgoals as Q.

The results presented in Section 3.2.3 follow the work of [17]. The results presented in Section 3.3 follow the work of [53].

In reference to the results presented in Section 3.4, Afrati and colleagues [13] studied the problem of answering queries using views, where the queries and views are conjunctive queries with arithmetic comparisons over dense orders. It is shown in [13] that obtaining equivalent rewritings for conjunctive queries with arithmetic comparisons is decidable.

In reference to the results presented in Section 3.5, Example 3.24 originates from [174]. Further, Afrati and Pavlaki addressed in [18] the problem of rewriting queries using views, for the case where the queries and views are conjunctive queries with safe negation (CQNs). As shown in [18], in the case of CQN queries and CQN views without nondistinguished (a.k.a. existential) variables, finding equivalent rewritings is decidable in those scenarios where the rewriting is in the language of CQNs or of unions of CQNs.

The results of Section 3.6 follow Sara Cohen's work in [54]. The presentation of central rewritings is from [8].

Section 4.2 presents the results developed in [152] (the MiniCon algorithm) and in [140] (the SharedVariable algorithm). The earlier bucket algorithm [102, 125] shares the same intuition.

In [13], Afrati and colleagues studied the problem of answering queries using views in the scenario where the queries and views are conjunctive queries with arithmetic comparisons over dense orders. The results presented in [13] include a containment test that can be performed in NP for a special case of CQACs; this test is a reduction to checking for containment of a CQ query in a Datalog query, where neither query has arithmetic comparisons. Based on this result, it can be shown that the Datalog query in Example 4.40 is an MCR of the input query in the language of Datalog. We follow [13] in the presentation of AC-containment in Section 4.3, as well as in the presentation of the bucket/MS algorithm for the case where the homomorphism property holds. The results of Section 4.4.3 follow the work [77] by Duschka and Genesereth.

Section 5.3 focuses on the problem of finding equivalent rewritings for the case where the database schema includes a set of dependencies. Weakly acyclic sets of constraints are introduced in the work by Fagin and colleagues [83]. The concept of a weakly acyclic set of target dependencies is broad enough to contain as special cases sets of full tuple-generating dependencies (full tgds), as well as acyclic sets of inclusion dependencies. Chase [35, 101, 133] is a useful tool for reasoning about dependencies, which can also be used for finding rewritings in presence of dependencies. That problem was studied in [149], [150], [71], and, [74], as well as in the work [72] by Deutsch and colleagues.

In Section 5.3 we outlined an algorithm for finding equivalent rewritings for the case where the database schema includes a set of dependencies. In Chapter 3 we used the tuple-core techniques of [16] and [17] to obtain an efficient algorithm for finding equivalent rewritings in presence of weakly acyclic sets of local-as-view tuple-generating dependencies. In addition to the notion of tuple cores, the works [16] and [17] introduced a number of other techniques for reducing the number of combinations to be considered.

Section 5.4.2 presents work [78] by Duschka and colleagues. The intuition offered in Example 5.18 is provided by Jeff Ullman.

The results presented in Section 6.1 follow the work [82, 83] by Fagin and colleagues. [82, 83] formalized the data-exchange setting, and proved that a canonical universal solution can be computed (if a solution exist) in polynomial time by using the chase procedure [35], provided the set of target tgds is weakly acyclic. In general, universal solutions may not be unique. Fagin, Kolaitis, and Popa [84] used the notion of core of a graph or data structure [108], and showed that the core is also a universal solution, which is in addition the smallest universal solution. The above setting was generalized by Afrati et al. [14] to include arithmetic comparisons in the query, as well as in the tgds and egds; these results, presented in Section 6.2, include two chase algorithms suitable for dealing with arithmetic comparisons: the AC-chase and, for the case where the homomorphism property holds, the SAC-chase. Section 6.3 presents the work by Afrati et al. [15] on treating incomplete data.

In presence of incompleteness in the data, it is natural to look for certain answers, that is, for those query answers that do not depend on the interpretation of the unknown data; this is discussed in Section 7.1. The concept was first formally defined in [132]. Certain answers were used in [101, 168] as standard semantics in presence of incomplete databases. It then became the standard semantics of query answering in data integration [122] and data exchange [82]. The first observation about the connection between MCRs and certain answers appeared in [3].

Section 7.2 presents some of the work by Afrati [7] on the topic of determinacy. We continue the discussion of determinacy later in this current chapter.

Now that we have referenced the works whose results are presented in detail in the first seven chapters of this book, we begin a discussion of the related bibliography and further contributions (to the best of our ability) to the topics discussed in this book. Before we start discussing the bibliography, let us mention overviews of work in the area, as presented in the survey by Halevy [107] and tutorial by Lenzerini [122], as well as in the book by Doan and colleagues [76] on principles of data integration. Reference books and textbooks on databases include [4] and [94].

10.1   QUERY CONTAINMENT

Query evaluation and query containment are related in terms of their complexity results. Barceló et al. [31] ask the question of whether query-evaluation tractability can help query containment. Concerning complexity of query evaluation, Vardi in [169] introduced the notions of "data complexity," "query complexity," and "combined complexity." He defined data complexity as the complexity of evaluating a fixed query on a database instance, expressed as a function of the size of the database. Combined complexity considers both the query and the database instance as input variables, and is expressed as a function of their sizes. In this book, unless explicitly specified otherwise, we use the term "complexity" to refer to "data complexity."

10.1.1   QUERY CONTAINMENT—SET SEMANTICS

Chandra and Merlin showed in [51] that the problems of containment, minimization, and equivalence of conjunctive queries are NP complete. They also presented the containment test using homomorphisms. For conjunctive queries, restricted classes of queries are known for which the containment-checking problem is polynomial. For instance, if each database predicate occurs in the contained query at most twice, then the problem can be solved in linear time [158], but is NP complete if each database predicate occurs at least three times in the body of the contained query. If the containing query is acyclic, then the containment-checking problem is polynomial [153].

An efficient algorithm for checking containment between CQNs and unions of CQNs is given in [174].

Klug [114] showed that the containment-checking problem for the class of conjunctive queries with arithmetic comparisons is in Π_2^P. In the same work, it was also shown that when only left (or right) semi-interval comparisons are used, the containment-checking problem is in NP. In a more recent work, Afrati and colleagues [6] showed more classes of conjunctive queries with arithmetic comparisons for which the problem of query-containment checking is in NP. Van der Meyden [166] proved Klug's conjecture that containment for conjunctive queries with inequality arithmetic comparisons is Π_2^P complete; the reductions use only $\neq$ comparisons. This result is extended in [118] to use only one $\neq$ comparison and at most three occurrences of the same predicate name in the contained query. The same reduction shows that the problem remains Π_2^P complete even in the case where the containing query is acyclic. In fact, Kolaitis and colleagues [118] proved that the complexity of the containment-checking problem for safe conjunctive queries with inequalities ranges between coNP and Π_2^P completeness, depending on how many times the name of each database predicate occurs in the body of the contained query. They also showed that when one of the two queries is fixed, the problem can be DB-complete, where DB is the class of all decision problems that are the conjunction of a problem in NP and a problem in coNP. Koutris and colleagues [120] consider CQ queries with $\neq$ and study combined complexity.

A problem that is related to that of query containment is the problem of the size of a join, for the case of CQs without nondistinguished variables. This problem has been studied recently in work by Atserias and colleagues [26, 27].

Van der Meyden [167] addresses complexity of evaluating queries in logical databases that contain potentially incomplete information about orderings among data points. It is shown in [167] that, in general, even the data complexity for queries in this setting is intractable; at the same time, the results include several polynomial-time special cases.

10.1.2 QUERY CONTAINMENT—BAG SEMANTICS, AGGREGATION

The classic foundational work by Chaudhuri and Vardi [52] provides equivalence tests for CQ bag and bag-set queries; correctness of the tests follows from the results of [57]. Please also see [56, 62, 63]. Chaudhuri and Vardi [52] also provide a well-known sufficient containment condition for CQ bag queries.

Definitive results on containment between CQ queries under bag and bag-set semantics have not been obtained so far. Please see Jayram, Kolaitis, and Vee [112] for original undecidability results on containment of CQ queries with inequalities under bag semantics. The authors point out that it is not known whether the problem of bag containment for CQ queries is even decidable. For the case of bag-set semantics, sufficient conditions for containment of two CQ queries can be expressed via containment of (the suitable) aggregate queries with aggregate function count(*). The latter containment problem can be solved using the methods proposed in [58]. Please see [10, 52] for other results on bag and bag-set containment of CQ queries. The general problems of containment for CQ bag and bag-set queries remain open.

In her papers [56, 57], Cohen provided an elegant and powerful formalism for treating queries evaluated under each of set, bag, and bag-set semantics uniformly as special cases of the more general "combined semantics." The latter semantics captures user-specified elimination of duplicates at intermediate stages of query processing. The papers [56, 57] contain a general sufficient condition for combined-semantics equivalence of CQ queries with disjunction, negation, and arithmetic comparisons, as well as necessary and sufficient equivalence conditions for special cases. The proof in [57] of its general sufficient condition for equivalence of queries is in terms of containment between the queries under combined semantics. That (implicit) sufficient query-containment condition is proved in [57] for the case where the two queries have the same number of multiset variables. Also, [57] contains an excellent overview of the literature on query equivalence and containment for query languages that properly contain the language of CQ queries.

Kolaitis [117] presents a comprehensive overview of results on the complexity of the query-containment problem for conjunctive queries and their variants, under both set semantics and bag semantics.

Bag containment of unions of conjunctive queries (UCQs) is shown to be undecidable by Ioannidis and Ramakrishan [111]. The Π_2^P hardness result for checking bag containment of CQs is reported in [52], but the decidability of the problem remains open.

Bag equivalence of UCQs was shown to be decidable (and, similarly to the case of CQs, was shown to have the same complexity as isomorphism checking) by Cohen et al. [60]; see also [144].

For aggregate queries, it seems that characterizing query equivalence may be easier than characterizing query containment. In particular, almost all known results on query containment for aggregate queries are derived by reduction from query equivalence.

One of the earliest studies of aggregation was by Klug [115], who extended relational algebra and relational calculus to allow aggregate functions and showed the equivalence of these two languages.

A survey of the containment and equivalence problems for aggregate queries, containing references to most works on this topic, appears in [55].

The peculiarities of individual aggregate functions make finding a general solution for the equivalence and containment problems very difficult. Thus, characterizations for equivalence of aggregate queries often are defined separately for each aggregate function.

Characterizations have been presented for equivalence of conjunctive queries with the aggregate functions count, sum, max, and count-distinct [59], and these were extended in [60] to queries with disjunctive bodies. Equivalence of conjunctive queries with aggregate functions avg and percent were characterized in [103].

Srivastava and colleagues [160] consider the problem of answering queries with aggregation using views.

10.1.3 ACYCLICITY

Papadimitriou et al. [145] show lower complexity upper bounds for query evaluation for the extension of conjunctive acyclic queries with $\neq$ (but not $<$) inequalities.

Maier et al. [134] show that it is NP complete to determine whether the result of a join (CQ) is nonempty.

[91] and [97] consider evaluation based on tree decomposition, in ways similar to decomposition for acyclic queries.

Barceló and colleagues [32] study semantic acyclicity on graph databases.

10.2 QUERY REWRITING

The problem of determining whether there exists an equivalent rewriting of a query using views was first studied by Halevy and colleagues [124]. It is shown in this work that it is NP complete to decide whether a given CQ has an equivalent rewriting that is a conjunctive query using a given set of CQ views. This problem was further investigated in many works, including [17, 100, 124].

In [100], the notion of tuple core is extended to tuple coverage, with the objective of finding a minimal (rather than maximal) cover of the query's subgoals when using view tuples to find equivalent rewritings of a conjunctive query using CQ views. In addition, the notion of tuple coverage is used in [100] for finding equivalent rewritings for conjunctive queries with aggregation using views that are also conjunctive queries with aggregation.

[5, 13, 140, 152] present algorithms for finding maximally contained rewritings for queries and views that are conjunctive queries with or without arithmetic comparisons. [77, 79] presents the inverse-rule algorithm for the problem of finding maximally contained rewritings in the absence of dependencies. [78] presents a modification of the inverse-rule algorithm to address the same problem in presence of functional or full dependencies. The algorithm creates a Datalog program, similarly to the case in which no dependencies are present, and then adds extra rules that simulate chasing the query with the dependencies. It is noted in [78] that this particular extension of the inverse-rule algorithm would not work in settings that involve inclusion dependencies that are not full. The reason is, the existential variables introduced by the algorithm may create new skolem terms recursively, which could lead to nontermination of the semi-naive evaluation of the resulting Datalog program. Fan and colleagues [88] study equivalent query rewritings for queries with inequalities.

Koch [116] presents an algorithm that finds maximally contained rewritings in presence of dependencies belonging to the class of conjunctive inclusion dependencies. Dependencies in this class are essentially GLAV mappings viewed as dependencies. The algorithm introduced in [116] is sound but not complete, and can be seen as an extension of the inverse-rule algorithm of [78].

Calì and colleagues [45] study the problem of creating maximally contained rewritings in global-as-view data-integration systems in presence of inclusion dependencies and key constraints. It is shown in [45] that the problem is undecidable both in the general case and in the case where inclusion dependencies are present together with key constraints. [45] also introduces a sound and complete algorithm for the case of inclusion dependencies and in presence of key constraints together with inclusion dependencies, belonging to the class that the authors call "non key conflicting inclusion dependencies." The main idea of the algorithm is extended in [44] to GLAV data-integration systems in presence of tuple-generating dependencies.

Additional work on related problems includes [28, 105]. Bai and colleagues [28] propose a modification of the MiniCon algorithm for the problem of finding contained rewritings in presence of inclusion dependencies. The algorithm chases the query and the views with the dependencies, and then applies a version of MiniCon that utilizes the new view and query subgoals. Gryz [105] proposes an algorithm that finds equivalent rewritings in presence of inclusion dependencies. The algorithm first undoes all the chase steps that may have been applied to the query, and then uses the inclusion dependencies in finding for each atom in the query equivalent replacement atoms. [105] also presents a modification of the algorithm that finds all the contained rewritings.

Other related work includes the paper [126] by Levy and colleagues, which considers CQ queries in presence of infinite sets of views. Deutsch and colleagues [72] consider the problem in presence of dependencies. The problem in presence of binding patterns is considered in [154].

10.2.1 BINDING PATTERNS

A setting related to that of answering queries using views is the setting in which views are expressed by restrictions on the access possibilities of the relations, instead of being expressed by queries. These restrictions are usually given by *access (binding) patterns*, which specify which positions in a retrieved relational tuple are free and which are bound. A solution is then a query plan, which specifies an order in which relations should be accessed, so that the previously accessed relations offer the bindings to the attributes for the relations to be accessed later. Work on this topic was started by Rajaraman and colleagues [154], and was followed by Li and colleagues [127, 129, 130]. More recent work on this subject has been done by Benedikt and colleagues [29, 36, 37, 37–39], as well as by Deutsch and colleagues [68].

Work by Duschka and colleagues [78] on recursive plans for data integration presents the inverse-rule method for the case of answering views in presence of dependencies and access patterns.

The work by Barcelo and colleagues [30] focuses on approximations of conjunctive queries that are guaranteed to return correct answers. The results in the paper focus on acyclic approximations, due to acyclic CQs having good complexity properties for various related problems.

Containment of pattern-based queries is studied by David and colleagues in [67]. Fan and colleagues [89] study answering pattern queries using views.

Ileana and colleagues [109] apply the Chase-Backchase (CB) algorithm to query rewriting under dependencies, using the concepts of canonical rewriting and universal solution or plan. This work improves on inspecting all possible minimal rewritings by using provenance.

The recent book by Benedikt and colleagues [36] provides an interpolation-based perspective on query reformulation.

10.3 DEPENDENCIES—THE CHASE

Chase was first defined and used to address the problem of checking whether a given dependency is implied by other dependencies [134, 170]; early chase algorithms address this problem. Algorithms that are precursors to chase appear in [19, 20]. The term "chase" appeared first in [133]. The work [35] unified the theory of the implication problem for various dependency classes, by introducing chase for tuple-generating and equality-generating dependencies. Extensions of chase, including extensions to XML, are discussed in [69, 70, 75].

10.4 DATA EXCHANGE

The problem of data exchange is the problem of exchanging data between databases with different schemas, in such a way that all the dependencies specified in the setting are satisfied. The data-exchange problem is related to the data-integration problem. In data exchange, however, the focus is on materializing a target instance (i.e., a solution) that reflects the source data as accurately as possible. In contrast, in data integration the focus is on answering queries posed over the target schema using views that express the relationship between the target and source schemas.

A book on foundations of data exchange Arenas and colleagues [22] contains extensive examples, exposition on data exchange for relational and XML data, as well as recent work on mapping compositions and inverting schema mappings.

Kolaitis and colleagues show [119] that relaxing the weak-acyclicity assumption for dependencies, even in a minimal way, leads to the existence-of-solution problem becoming undecidable.

Systems supporting data exchange have been developed, such as Clio by IBM Almaden [139, 151].

Gottlob and colleagues [96, 98] extended results on the core produced by chase in a data-exchange setting. [164] uses concepts and intuition from data exchange with arithmetic comparisons to study the problem of data exchange with arithmetic operations. In this setting, dependencies may include arithmetic formulas; the study covers the complexity of the existence-of-solutions problem for several cases of the setting, as well as the data complexity of computing certain answers for CQ queries with arithmetic operations. Libkin [131] studies data-exchange solutions under the closed-world assumption (CWA). Work that studies combined complexity of data exchange appears in [119], schema-mapping composition is studied in [85, 141], and schema-mapping inversion is considered in [25, 81].

Other work on settings that are similar to data exchange is done by Bernstein and Melnik [41]. Extensions of the data-exchange setting to XML data exchange have been studied in, e.g., [23, 75]. Extensions to peer data exchange are discussed in [93]. Universal solutions, which are the preferred solutions to materialize in data exchange, are closely related to strongly-universal models [70].

The seminal work by Imielinski and Lipski [110] on incomplete data is highly cited and has often been an inspiration. Many of the subsequent work, including the results presented in this book, can be seen as extensions of that work. Recent work on incomplete data includes the papers [24, 86] on data exchange, as well as the work by Sundarmurthy and colleagues [161] on the complexity of computing certain answers and possible answers on m-tables, which are extensions of conditional tables in [110].

10.5   OTHER RELATED WORK

We first present work about determinacy, and then highlight some considerations, most of which have been discussed in recent work.

10.5.1   DETERMINACY

The definition of determinacy in this book is as it first appears in Nash and colleagues [143]. Determinacy and related notions have also been investigated in [46, 47, 104]. Grumbach and colleagues introduce in [104] the notion of subsumption and use it to define complete rewritings. Calvanese and colleagues introduce in [46, 47] the concept of lossless view with respect to a query; this notion is investigated in [46, 47] for regular-path queries, under both the sound-view assumption and the exact-view assumption. Losslessness under the exact-view assumption is identical to determinacy.

Afrati and colleagues show [7] that for chain queries and views, the views determine the query if and only if the canonical rewriting is connected. In this case, there is a first-order equivalent rewriting of the query using the views. Afrati [7] shows that the language for chain CQs is almost complete for CQ_{path}-to-CQ_{path} rewriting and that the language of first-order logic is complete for CQ_{chain}-to-CQ_{chain} rewriting, where CQ_{chain} is the language of chain CQs. [7] also shows that in the cases where the set of views is a singleton set, CQ_{chain} is complete for CQ_{chain}-to-CQ_{chain} rewriting. Pasaila [148] extended the work [7] beyond chain queries, to include more general queries that can be represented by graphs over binary relational schemas. The work by Francis [92] extended the results presented in Section 7.2 by allowing disjunction.

Work done by Nash and colleagues [142, 143] includes the following results. First-order logic (FO) is not complete for FO-to-FO rewriting, in fact, any language complete for FO-to-FO rewriting must express all computable queries. FO is not complete for ∃FO-to-FO rewriting, but both ∃SO and ∀SO are complete for such rewriting. Datalog$\neq$ is not complete for UCQ-to-UCQ rewriting, where UCQ stands for the language of finite unions of conjunctive queries. This also holds for CQ$\neq$-to-CQ rewriting. No monotonic language is complete for CQ-to-CQ rewriting. (Each of CQ$\neq$, UCQ, and Datalog$\neq$ is a monotonic language.) Determinacy is undecidable for UCQ views and queries. Marx in [136] identifies a language, called packed fragment of FO (PackedFO), that is complete for rewriting for views and queries in the same language. PackedFO is a generalization of the guarded fragment of FO. The guarded CQs are exactly the acyclic CQs.

Gogacz and Marcinkowski [95] prove that conjunctive-query determinacy is undecidable both in the finite and infinite cases.

10.5.2 MORE RECENT RELATED WORK

A significant number of results have been obtained in the direction of understanding various challenges in the problem of answering queries using views. We present some of these results, which focus on defining notions and concepts toward addressing the challenges.

The work by Li and colleagues [128] considers the problem of minimizing the number of given views in ways that would retain the query-answering power enabled by the views.

Rosati [155] provides decidability, undecidability, and complexity results for query answering in description logics. Rosati [156] studies query answering in presence of dependencies under the open-world assumption (OWA), to isolate cases in which OWA query answering over finite databases coincides with OWA query answering over infinite databases—such cases are referred to as *finitely controllable*. The paper establishes finite controllability for containment of conjunctive queries under arbitrary inclusion dependencies, as well as under key and foreign-key dependencies. The results are based on chase, including a modification called canonical chase.

Cao and colleagues [48] consider view-based "bounded" rewritings, which are rewritings that are allowed to access a small fraction of the original database in addition to the view instance. In [48], the problem is considered for data sets that satisfy access constraints.

Gottlob and colleagues [99] consider the problems of query rewriting and query optimization for ontological queries. Such queries are evaluated against knowledge bases, which consist of extensional databases and associated ontologies represented by assertions and dependencies.

Regular queries and rewritings for them have been studied in the past two decades; see [171] and references therein. Intuitively, regular queries can be thought of as regular-language queries on graphs. Unlike general queries, regular queries have decidable query-containment properties.

CHAPTER 11

Conclusion for Chapters 1–7

What we covered in this book can be arranged along the following four axes that cut across chapters.

A. (*Existence of rewritings in various query languages*) This book began by giving basic definitions for the notions of query containment, equivalent rewriting, contained rewriting, and maximally contained rewriting (MCR). Existence of equivalent rewritings and of MCRs depends on the language of the rewriting. In particular, we saw the following.

- For CQ queries and views, equivalent rewritings may not exist in the language of unions of CQs, but could still be found in first-order logic. In contrast, this setting always allows for existence of MCRs in the language of unions of CQs.

- For CQAC queries and views, there exist MCRs in the language of unions of CQACs in all the cases in which the homomorphism property holds. In those cases where the homomorphism property does not hold, finding MCRs may require a query language with the power of recursion. That is, MCRs in these scenarios may not always exist in the language of unions of CQACs.

- For CQ queries and views that are unions of CQs, finding MCRs may require a query language with the power of recursion.

- For Datalog queries and CQ views, MCRs always exist in the language of Datalog.

- In presence of constraints on data that are tuple-generating and equality-generating dependencies, finding MCRs may require recursion even in the case of CQ queries and views, and even if all the constraints are equality-generating dependencies.

B. (*Certain answers*) We define certain answers, a concept independent of the language of the rewritings. Certain answers are defined both under the open and closed world assumptions (OWA and CWA, respectively). We showed that CQ contained rewritings for CQ queries and views coincide under the OWA and the CWA. At the same time, a contained rewriting in a non-monotone query language (e.g., first-order logic) under the CWA is not always a contained rewriting under the OWA. We showed that for CQ queries and views, MCRs in the language of unions of CQs can find all the certain answers under the OWA.

The data-exchange setting uses tuple-generating and equality-generating dependencies, rather than queries as views, to define the relationship between the source instance and the target instance. Rather than being done via rewritings, certain answers are computed by applying the query on the target instance that is produced from the source instance using the dependencies.

  C. (*Algorithms*) This book provided efficient algorithms for the following problems.

- Testing query containment for CQ, CQAC, CQN, and aggregate queries, as well as for a subclass of CQs called acyclic queries. Algorithms for containment tests are based on **homomorphisms, containment mappings**, and **canonical databases**.

- Finding equivalent rewritings for queries using views for CQs, CQACs, and aggregate queries. The algorithms are based on query containment and on the concept of **expansion of a rewriting**. We discussed CQN queries, including the concept of expansion in this case.

- Finding maximally contained rewritings for queries using views for CQs, CQACs, as well as for the case of Datalog queries and CQ views. The algorithms are based on **expansions** and their properties. We presented the MS algorithm for the cases of CQs and of CQACs with the **homomorphism property**. We also presented the inverse-rule algorithm for Datalog queries. Further, we observed that in the case of CQ queries and of views that are unions of CQs, as well as in the case of CQAC queries, finding MCRs requires **recursion**.

- We revisited the above three problems, and provided algorithms, for the cases in which the data satisfy constraints that are tuple-generating and equality-generating dependencies. Considering the concept of **the chase** and its properties was central in the presentation here.

- In the data-exchange setting, algorithms for finding certain answers were presented for three cases.

  (a) The case in which the constraints are tuple-generating and equality-generating dependencies. The chase is central in this case.

  (b) The case in which the constraints are tuple-generating and equality-generating dependencies with arithmetic comparisons. The AC-chase and SAC-chase are central in this case.

  (c) The case in which the constraints are tuple-generating and equality-generating dependencies, and the input data are incomplete. The chase is central in this case.

  D. (*Advanced topics*) In the context of further exploring the subject of answering queries using views, we studied determinacy and proved various noteworthy and insightful results.

Bibliography

[1] JSON. http://www.json.org/ 221

[2] Protocol Buffers. https://code.google.com/p/protobuf/ 221

[3] S. Abiteboul and O. M. Duschka. Complexity of answering queries using materialized views. In *Proc. of the 17th ACM SIGACT-SIGMOD-SIGART Symposium on Principles of Database Systems*, pages 254–263, Seattle, WA, June 1–3, 1998. DOI: 10.1145/275487.275516 225

[4] S. Abiteboul, R. Hull, and V. Vianu. *Foundations of Databases*. Addison-Wesley, 1995. 226

[5] F. Afrati, C. Li, and P. Mitra. Answering queries using views with arithmetic comparisons. In *Proc. of the 21st ACM SIGMOD-SIGACT-SIGART Symposium on Principles of Database Systems (PODS)*, pages 209–220, New York, 2002. DOI: 10.1145/543613.543641 229

[6] F. Afrati, C. Li, and P. Mitra. On containment of conjunctive queries with arithmetic comparisons. In *EDBT*, 2004. DOI: 10.1007/978-3-540-24741-8_27 226

[7] F. N. Afrati. Determinacy and query rewriting for conjunctive queries and views. *Theoretical Computer Science*, 412(11):1005–1021, 2011. DOI: 10.1016/j.tcs.2010.12.031 225, 232

[8] F. N. Afrati and R. Chirkova. Selecting and using views to compute aggregate queries. *Journal of Computer and System Sciences*, 77(6):1079–1107, 2011. DOI: 10.1007/978-3-540-30570-5_26 224

[9] F. N. Afrati, R. Chirkova, M. Gergatsoulis, B. Kimelfeld, V. Pavlaki, and Y. Sagiv. On rewriting XPath queries using views. In *EDBT*, pages 168–179, 2009. DOI: 10.1145/1516360.1516381 201

[10] F. N. Afrati, M. Damigos, and M. Gergatsoulis. Query containment under bag and bag-set semantics. *Information Processing Letters*, 110(10):360–369, 2010. DOI: 10.1016/j.ipl.2010.02.017 227

[11] F. N. Afrati, M. Damigos, and M. Gergatsoulis. Union rewritings for XPath fragments. In *15th International Database Engineering and Applications Symposium (IDEAS)*, pages 43–51, Lisbon, Portugal, September 21–27, 2011. DOI: 10.1145/2076623.2076630 200, 201

[12] F. N. Afrati, D. Delorey, M. Pasumansky, and J. D. Ullman. Storing and querying tree-structured records in Dremel. *PVLDB*, 7(12):1131–1142, 2014. DOI: 10.14778/2732977.2732987 221

[13] F. N. Afrati, C. Li, and P. Mitra. Rewriting queries using views in the presence of arithmetic comparisons. *Theoretical Computer Science*, 368(1–2):88–123, 2006. DOI: 10.1016/j.tcs.2006.08.020 223, 224, 229

[14] F. N. Afrati, C. Li, and V. Pavlaki. Data exchange in the presence of arithmetic comparisons. In *Proc. of the 11th International Conference on Extending Database Technology (EDBT)*, pages 487–498, Nantes, France, March 25–29, 2008. DOI: 10.1145/1353343.1353403 225

[15] F. N. Afrati, C. Li, and V. Pavlaki. Data exchange: Query answering for incomplete data sources. In *3rd International ICST Conference on Scalable Information Systems, (INFOSCALE)*, page 6, Vico Equense, Italy, June 4–6, 2008. DOI: 10.4108/icst.infoscale2008.3476 225

[16] F. N. Afrati, C. Li, and J. D. Ullman. Generating efficient plans for queries using views. In *Proc. of the ACM SIGMOD International Conference on Management of Data*, pages 319–330, New York, 2001. 225 DOI: 10.1145/376284.375705

[17] F. N. Afrati, C. Li, and J. D. Ullman. Using views to generate efficient evaluation plans for queries. *Journal of Computer and System Sciences*, 73(5):703–724, 2007. DOI: 10.1016/j.jcss.2006.10.019 224, 225, 229

[18] F. N. Afrati and V. Pavlaki. Rewriting queries using views with negation. *AI Communications*, 19(3):229–237, 2006. 224

[19] A. V. Aho, C. Beeri, and J. D. Ullman. The theory of joins in relational databases. *ACM Transactions on Database Systems*, 4(3):297–314, 1979. DOI: 10.1109/sfcs.1977.33 230

[20] A. V. Aho, Y. Sagiv, and J. D. Ullman. Efficient optimization of a class of relational expressions. *ACM Transactions on Database Systems*, 4(4):435–454, 1979. DOI: 10.1145/320107.320112 230

[21] S. Amer-Yahia, S. Cho, L. V. S. Lakshmanan, and D. Srivastava. Minimization of tree pattern queries. In *SIGMOD*, pages 497–508, ACM, 2001. DOI: 10.1145/376284.375730 201

[22] M. Arenas, P. Barceló, L. Libkin, and F. Murlak. *Foundations of Data Exchange*. Cambridge University Press, 2014. DOI: 10.1017/cbo9781139060158 231

[23] M. Arenas and L. Libkin. XML data exchange: Consistency and query answering. *Journal of the ACM*, 55(2):7:1–7:72, 2008. DOI: 10.1145/1346330.1346332 231

[24] M. Arenas, J. Pérez, and J. L. Reutter. Data exchange beyond complete data. *Journal of the ACM*, 60(4):28:1–28:59, 2013. DOI: 10.1145/2508028.2505985 231

[25] M. Arenas, J. Pérez, J. L. Reutter, and C. Riveros. Inverting schema mappings: Bridging the gap between theory and practice. *Proc. of the VLDB Endowment*, 2(1):1018–1029, 2009. DOI: 10.14778/1687627.1687742 231

[26] A. Atserias, M. Grohe, and D. Marx. Size bounds and query plans for relational joins. In *49th Annual IEEE Symposium on Foundations of Computer Science, (FOCS)*, pages 739–748, Philadelphia, PA, October 25–28, 2008. DOI: 10.1109/focs.2008.43 227

[27] A. Atserias, M. Grohe, and D. Marx. Size bounds and query plans for relational joins. *SIAM Journal on Computing*, 42(4):1737–1767, 2013. DOI: 10.1109/focs.2008.43 227

[28] Q. Bai, J. Hong, and M. F. McTear. Query rewriting using views in the presence of inclusion dependencies. In *Proc. of the 5th ACM International Workshop on Web Information and Data Management (WIDM)*, pages 134–138, New York, 2003. DOI: 10.1145/956728.956729 229

[29] V. Bárány, M. Benedikt, and P. Bourhis. Access patterns and integrity constraints revisited. In *Joint EDBT/ICDT Conferences, Proceedings*, pages 213–224, Genoa, Italy, March 18–22, 2013. DOI: 10.1145/2448496.2448522 230

[30] P. Barceló, L. Libkin, and M. Romero. Efficient approximations of conjunctive queries. *SIAM Journal on Computing*, 43(3):1085–1130, 2014. DOI: 10.1137/130911731 230

[31] P. Barceló, M. Romero, and M. Y. Vardi. Does query evaluation tractability help query containment? In *Proc. of the 33rd ACM SIGMOD-SIGACT-SIGART Symposium on Principles of Database Systems, (PODS)*, pages 188–199, Snowbird, UT, June 22–27, 2014. DOI: 10.1145/2594538.2594553 226

[32] P. Barceló, M. Romero, and M. Y. Vardi. Semantic acyclicity on graph databases. *SIAM Journal on Computing*, 45(4):1339–1376, 2016. DOI: 10.1137/15m1034714 228

[33] C. Beeri, R. Fagin, D. Maier, A. Mendelzon, J. Ullman, and M. Yannakakis. Properties of acyclic database schemes. In *Proc. of the 13th Annual ACM Symposium on Theory of Computing, (STOC)*, pages 355–362, New York, 1981. DOI: 10.1145/800076.802489 224

[34] C. Beeri, R. Fagin, D. Maier, and M. Yannakakis. On the desirability of acyclic database schemes. *Journal of the ACM*, 30(3):479–513, 1983. DOI: 10.1145/2402.322389 224

[35] C. Beeri and M. Y. Vardi. A proof procedure for data dependencies. *Journal of the ACM*, 31(4):718–741, 1984. DOI: 10.1145/1634.1636 225, 230

[36] M. Benedikt, J. Leblay, B. ten Cate, and E. Tsamoura. *Generating Plans from Proofs: The Interpolation-based Approach to Query Reformulation.* Synthesis Lectures on Data Management. Morgan & Claypool Publishers, 2016. DOI: 10.2200/s00703ed1v01y201602dtm043 230

[37] M. Benedikt, J. Leblay, and E. Tsamoura. Querying with access patterns and integrity constraints. *PVLDB*, 8(6):690–701, 2015. DOI: 10.14778/2735703.2735708 230

[38] M. Benedikt, B. ten Cate, and E. Tsamoura. Generating low-cost plans from proofs. In *Proc. of the 33rd ACM SIGMOD-SIGACT-SIGART Symposium on Principles of Database Systems, (PODS)*, pages 200–211, Snowbird, UT, June 22–27, 2014. DOI: 10.1145/2594538.2594550

[39] M. Benedikt, B. ten Cate, and E. Tsamoura. Generating plans from proofs. *ACM Transactions on Database Systems*, 40(4):22:1–22:45, 2016. DOI: 10.1145/2847523 230

[40] P. A. Bernstein and D. W. Chiu. Using semi-joins to solve relational queries. *Journal of the ACM*, 28(1):25–40, 1981. DOI: 10.1145/322234.322238 224

[41] P. A. Bernstein and S. Melnik. Model management 2.0: Manipulating richer mappings. In *Proc. of the ACM SIGMOD International Conference on Management of Data*, pages 1–12, Beijing, China, June 12–14, 2007. DOI: 10.1145/1247480.1247482 231

[42] P. Bourhis, J. L. Reutter, F. Suárez, and D. Vrgoc. JSON: Data model, query languages and schema specification. In *Proc. of the 36th ACM SIGMOD-SIGACT-SIGAI Symposium on Principles of Database Systems, (PODS)*, pages 123–135, Chicago, IL, May 14–19, 2017. DOI: 10.1145/3034786.3056120 222

[43] P. Buneman, B. Choi, W. Fan, R. Hutchison, R. Mann, and S. Viglas. Vectorizing and querying large XML repositories. In *ICDE*, pages 261–272, 2005. DOI: 10.1109/icde.2005.150 222

[44] A. Calì. Query answering by rewriting in GLAV data integration systems under constraints. In *SWDB*, pages 167–184, 2004. DOI: 10.1007/978-3-540-31839-2_13 229

[45] A. Calì, D. Lembo, and R. Rosati. Query rewriting and answering under constraints in data integration systems. In *IJCAI*, pages 16–21, MK, 2003. 229

[46] D. Calvanese, G. D. Giacomo, M. Lenzerini, and M. Y. Vardi. Lossless regular views. In *PODS*, pages 99–108, ACM, 2002. DOI: 10.1145/543613.543646 232

[47] D. Calvanese, G. D. Giacomo, M. Lenzerini, and M. Y. Vardi. View-based query query processing: On the relationship between rewriting, answering and losslessness. In *International Conference on Database Theory (ICDT)*, pages 321–336, 2005. DOI: 10.1016/j.tcs.2006.11.006 232

[48] Y. Cao, W. Fan, F. Geerts, and P. Lu. Bounded query rewriting using views. In *Proc. of the 35th ACM SIGMOD-SIGACT-SIGAI Symposium on Principles of Database Systems, (PODS)*, pages 107–119, San Francisco, CA, June 26–July 01, 2016. DOI: 10.1145/3183673 233

[49] B. Cautis, A. Deutsch, and N. Onose. XPath rewriting using multiple views: Achieving completeness and efficiency. In *WebDB*, 2008. 201

[50] B. Cautis, A. Deutsch, N. Onose, and V. Vassalos. Efficient rewriting of XPath queries using query set specifications. *PVLDB*, 2(1):301–312, 2009. DOI: 10.14778/1687627.1687662 201

[51] A. K. Chandra and P. M. Merlin. Optimal implementation of conjunctive queries in relational data bases. In *Proc. of the 9th Annual ACM Symposium on Theory of Computing*, pages 77–90, Boulder, CO, May 4–6, 1977. DOI: 10.1145/800105.803397 223, 226

[52] S. Chaudhuri and M. Y. Vardi. Optimization of *Real* conjunctive queries. In *Proc. of the 12th ACM SIGACT-SIGMOD-SIGART Symposium on Principles of Database Systems*, pages 59–70, Washington, DC, May 25–28, 1993. DOI: 10.1145/153850.153856 227, 228

[53] C. Chekuri and A. Rajaraman. Conjunctive query containment revisited. In *Database Theory (ICDT), 6th International Conference, Proceedings*, pages 56–70, Delphi, Greece, January 8–10, 1997. DOI: 10.1016/s0304-3975(99)00220-0 224

[54] S. Cohen. Equivalence, containment and rewriting of aggregate queries. Ph.D. thesis, Hebrew University, 2004. 224

[55] S. Cohen. Containment of aggregate queries. *SIGMOD Record*, 34(1):77–85, 2005. DOI: 10.1145/1058150.1058170 228

[56] S. Cohen. Equivalence of queries combining set and bag-set semantics. In *Proc. of the 25th ACM SIGACT-SIGMOD-SIGART Symposium on Principles of Database Systems*, pages 70–79, Chicago, IL, June 26–28, 2006. DOI: 10.1145/1142351.1142362 227

[57] S. Cohen. Equivalence of queries that are sensitive to multiplicities. *VLDB Journal*, 18(3):765–785, 2009. DOI: 10.1007/s00778-008-0122-1 227

[58] S. Cohen, W. Nutt, and Y. Sagiv. Containment of aggregate queries. In *Database Theory (ICDT), 9th International Conference, Proceedings*, pages 111–125, Siena, Italy, January 8–10, 2003. DOI: 10.1007/3-540-36285-1_8 227

[59] S. Cohen, W. Nutt, and Y. Sagiv. Deciding equivalences among conjunctive aggregate queries. *Journal of the ACM*, 54(2):5, 2007. DOI: 10.1145/1219092.1219093 228

[60] S. Cohen, W. Nutt, and A. Serebrenik. Rewriting aggregate queries using views. In *Proc. of the 18th ACM SIGACT-SIGMOD-SIGART Symposium on Principles of Database Systems*, pages 155–166, Philadelphia, PA, May 31–June 2, 1999. DOI: 10.1145/303976.303992 228

[61] S. Cohen and Y. Y. Weiss. Bag equivalence of XPath queries. In *ICDT*, 2010. DOI: 10.1145/1804669.1804685 200

[62] S. Cohen and Y. Y. Weiss. Bag equivalence of XPath queries. In *Database Theory (ICDT), 13th International Conference, Proceedings*, pages 116–128, Lausanne, Switzerland, March 23–25, 2010. DOI: 10.1145/1804669.1804685 227

[63] S. Cohen and Y. Y. Weiss. Bag equivalence of tree patterns. *ACM Transactions on Database Systems*, 36(4):24, 2011. DOI: 10.1145/2043652.2043657 227

[64] L. S. Colby. A recursive algebra and query optimization for nested relations. In *SIGMOD Conference*, pages 273–283, 1989. DOI: 10.1145/66926.66952 221

[65] W. Czerwinski, W. Martens, M. Niewerth, and P. Parys. Minimization of tree pattern queries. In *Proc. of the 35th ACM SIGMOD-SIGACT-SIGAI Symposium on Principles of Database Systems, (PODS)*, pages 43–54, San Francisco, CA, June 26–July 01, 2016. DOI: 10.1145/2902251.2902295 201

[66] W. Czerwinski, W. Martens, P. Parys, and M. Przybylko. The (almost) complete guide to tree pattern containment. In *Proc. of the 34th ACM Symposium on Principles of Database Systems, (PODS)*, pages 117–130, Melbourne, Victoria, Australia, May 31–June 4, 2015. DOI: 10.1145/2745754.2745766 200

[67] C. David, A. Gheerbrant, L. Libkin, and W. Martens. Containment of pattern-based queries over data trees. In *Joint EDBT/ICDT Conferences, (ICDT) Proceedings*, pages 201–212, Genoa, Italy, March 18–22, 2013. DOI: 10.1145/2448496.2448521 230

[68] A. Deutsch, B. Ludäscher, and A. Nash. Rewriting queries using views with access patterns under integrity constraints. In *Database Theory (ICDT), 10th International Conference, Proceedings*, pages 352–367, Edinburgh, UK, January 5–7, 2005. DOI: 10.1007/978-3-540-30570-5_24 230

[69] A. Deutsch, B. Ludäscher, and A. Nash. Rewriting queries using views with access patterns under integrity constraints. *Theoretical Computer Science*, 371(3):200–226, 2007. DOI: 10.1007/978-3-540-30570-5_24 230

[70] A. Deutsch, A. Nash, and J. B. Remmel. The chase revisited. In *Proc. of the 27th ACM SIGMOD-SIGACT-SIGART Symposium on Principles of Database Systems, (PODS)*, pages 149–158, Vancouver, BC, Canada, June 9–11, 2008. DOI: 10.1145/1376916.1376938 230, 231

[71] A. Deutsch, L. Popa, and V. Tannen. Physical data independence, constraints, and optimization with universal plans. In *Proc. of 25th International Conference on Very Large Data Bases, (VLDB)*, pages 459–470, Edinburgh, Scotland, UK, September 7–10, 1999. 225

[72] A. Deutsch, L. Popa, and V. Tannen. Query reformulation with constraints. *SIGMOD Record*, 35(1):65–73, 2006. DOI: 10.1145/1121995.1122010 225, 230

[73] A. Deutsch and V. Tannen. Containment and integrity constraints for XPath fragments. In *KRDB*, 2001. 200

[74] A. Deutsch and V. Tannen. Reformulation of XML queries and constraints. In *ICDT*, pages 225–241, 2003. DOI: 10.1007/3-540-36285-1_15 225

[75] A. Deutsch and V. Tannen. XML queries and constraints, containment and reformulation. *Theoretical Computer Science*, 336(1):57–87, 2005. DOI: 10.1016/j.tcs.2004.10.032 230, 231

[76] A. Doan, A. Y. Halevy, and Z. G. Ives. *Principles of Data Integration*. Morgan Kaufmann, 2012. 226

[77] O. M. Duschka and M. R. Genesereth. Answering recursive queries using views. In *Proc. of the 16th ACM SIGACT-SIGMOD-SIGART Symposium on Principles of Database Systems*, pages 109–116, Tucson, Arizona, May 12–14, 1997. DOI: 10.1145/263661.263674 225, 229

[78] O. M. Duschka, M. R. Genesereth, and A. Y. Levy. Recursive query plans for data integration. *Journal of Logic Programming*, 43(1):49–73, 2000. DOI: 10.1016/s0743-1066(99)00025-4 225, 229, 230

[79] O. M. Duschka and A. Y. Levy. Recursive plans for information gathering. In *IJCAI (1)*, pages 778–784, 1997. 229

[80] R. Fagin. Degrees of acyclicity for hypergraphs and relational database schemes. *Journal of the ACM*, 30(3):514–550, July 1983. DOI: 10.1145/2402.322390 224

[81] R. Fagin. Inverting schema mappings. *ACM Transactions on Database Systems*, 32(4):25, 2007. DOI: 10.1145/1292609.1292615 231

[82] R. Fagin, P. G. Kolaitis, R. J. Miller, and L. Popa. Data exchange: Semantics and query answering. In *International Conference on Database Theory (ICDT)*, pages 207–224, 2003. DOI: 10.1007/3-540-36285-1_14 225

[83] R. Fagin, P. G. Kolaitis, R. J. Miller, and L. Popa. Data exchange: Semantics and query answering. *Theoretical Computer Science*, 336(1):89–124, 2005. DOI: 10.1007/3-540-36285-1_14 225

[84] R. Fagin, P. G. Kolaitis, and L. Popa. Data exchange: Getting to the core. *ACM Transactions on Database Systems*, 30(1):174–210, 2005. DOI: 10.1145/1061318.1061323 225

[85] R. Fagin, P. G. Kolaitis, L. Popa, and W. C. Tan. Composing schema mappings: Second-order dependencies to the rescue. *ACM Transactions on Database Systems*, 30(4):994–1055, 2005. DOI: 10.1145/1114244.1114249 231

[86] R. Fagin, P. G. Kolaitis, L. Popa, and W. C. Tan. Reverse data exchange: Coping with nulls. In *Proc. of the 28th ACM SIGMOD-SIGACT-SIGART Symposium on Principles of Database Systems, (PODS)*, pages 23–32, Providence, Rhode Island, June 19–July 1, 2009. DOI: 10.1145/1966385.1966389 231

[87] R. Fagin, A. O. Mendelzon, and J. D. Ullman. A simplified universal relation assumption and its properties. *ACM Transactions on Database Systems*, 7(3):343–360, 1982. DOI: 10.1145/319732.319735 224

[88] W. Fan, F. Geerts, W. Gelade, F. Neven, and A. Poggi. Complexity and composition of synthesized web services. In *Proc. of the 27th ACM SIGMOD-SIGACT-SIGART Symposium on Principles of Database Systems, (PODS)*, pages 231–240, Vancouver, BC, Canada, June 9–11, 2008. DOI: 10.1145/1376916.1376949 229

[89] W. Fan, X. Wang, and Y. Wu. Answering pattern queries using views. *IEEE Transactions on Knowledge Data Engineering*, 28(2):326–341, 2016. DOI: 10.1109/icde.2014.6816650 230

[90] D. Florescu and D. Kossmann. Storing and querying XML data using an RDMBS. *IEEE Data Engineering Bulletin*, 22(3):27–34, 1999. 222

[91] J. Flum, M. Frick, and M. Grohe. Query evaluation via tree-decompositions. *Journal of the ACM*, 49(6):716–752, 2002. DOI: 10.1145/602220.602222 228

[92] N. Francis. Asymptotic determinacy of path queries using union-of-paths views. In *18th International Conference on Database Theory, (ICDT)*, pages 44–59, Brussels, Belgium, March 23–27, 2015. DOI: 10.1007/s00224-016-9697-x 232

[93] A. Fuxman, P. G. Kolaitis, R. J. Miller, and W. C. Tan. Peer data exchange. *ACM Transactions on Database Systems*, 31(4):1454–1498, 2006. DOI: 10.1145/1189769.1189778 231

[94] H. Garcia-Molina, J. D. Ullman, and J. Widom. *Database Systems—The Complete Book*, 2nd ed., Pearson Education, 2009. 226

[95] T. Gogacz and J. Marcinkowski. Red spider meets a rainworm: Conjunctive query finite determinacy is undecidable. In *Proc. of the 35th ACM SIGMOD-SIGACT-SIGAI Symposium on Principles of Database Systems, (PODS)*, pages 121–134, San Francisco, CA, June 26–July 01, 2016. DOI: 10.1145/2902251.2902288 232

[96] G. Gottlob. Computing cores for data exchange: New algorithms and practical solutions. In *Proc. of the 24th ACM SIGACT-SIGMOD-SIGART Symposium on Principles of Database Systems*, pages 148–159, Baltimore, MD, June 13–15, 2005. DOI: 10.1145/1065167.1065187 231

[97] G. Gottlob, N. Leone, and F. Scarcello. Hypertree decompositions and tractable queries. In *Proc. of the 18th ACM SIGACT-SIGMOD-SIGART Symposium on Principles of Database Systems*, pages 21–32, Philadelphia, PA, May 31–June 2, 1999. DOI: 10.1145/303976.303979 228

[98] G. Gottlob and A. Nash. Data exchange: Computing cores in polynomial time. In *Proc. of the 25th ACM SIGACT-SIGMOD-SIGART Symposium on Principles of Database Systems*, pages 40–49, Chicago, IL, June 26–28, 2006. DOI: 10.1145/1142351.1142358 231

[99] G. Gottlob, G. Orsi, and A. Pieris. Query rewriting and optimization for ontological databases. *ACM Transactions on Database Systems*, 39(3):25:1–25:46, 2014. DOI: 10.1145/2638546 233

[100] G. Gou, M. Kormilitsin, and R. Chirkova. Query evaluation using overlapping views: Completeness and efficiency. In *Proc. of the ACM SIGMOD International Conference on Management of Data*, pages 37–48, New York, 2006. 229
DOI: 10.1145/1142473.1142479

[101] G. Grahne. *The Problem of Incomplete Information in Relational Databases*, vol. 554 of *Lecture Notes in Computer Science*. Springer, 1991. DOI: 10.1007/3-540-54919-6 225

[102] G. Grahne and A. O. Mendelzon. Tableau techniques for querying information sources through global schemas. In *Database Theory (ICDT), 7th International Conference, Proceedings*, pages 332–347, Jerusalem, Israel, January 10–12, 1999. DOI: 10.1007/3-540-49257-7_21 224

[103] S. Grumbach, M. Rafanelli, and L. Tininini. On the equivalence and rewriting of aggregate queries. *Acta Informatica*, 40(8):529–584, 2004. DOI: 10.1007/s00236-004-0101-y 228

[104] S. Grumbach and L. Tininini. On the content of materialized aggregate views. In *PODS*, pages 47–57, 2000. DOI: 10.1016/s0022-0000(02)00033-8 232

[105] J. Gryz. Query rewriting using views in the presence of functional and inclusion dependencies. *Information Systems*, 24(7):597–612, 1999. DOI: 10.1016/s0306-4379(99)00034-4 229, 230

[106] A. Gupta, Y. Sagiv, J. D. Ullman, and J. Widom. Constraint checking with partial information. In *PODS*, pages 45–55, 1994. DOI: 10.1145/182591.182597 223

[107] A. Y. Halevy. Answering queries using views: A survey. *VLDB Journal*, 10(4):270–294, 2001. DOI: 10.1007/s007780100054 226

[108] P. Hell and J. Nesetril. The core of a graph. *Discrete Mathematics*, 109(1–3):117–126, 1992. DOI: 10.1016/0012-365x(92)90282-k 225

[109] I. Ileana, B. Cautis, A. Deutsch, and Y. Katsis. Complete yet practical search for minimal query reformulations under constraints. In *International Conference on Management of Data, (SIGMOD)*, pages 1015–1026, Snowbird, UT, June 22–27, 2014. DOI: 10.1145/2588555.2593683 230

[110] T. Imielinski and W. Lipski. Incomplete information in relational databases. *Journal of the ACM*, 31(4):761–791, 1984. DOI: 10.1016/b978-0-934613-53-8.50027-3 231

[111] Y. E. Ioannidis and R. Ramakrishnan. Containment of conjunctive queries: Beyond relations as sets. *ACM Transactions on Database Systems*, 20(3):288–324, 1995. DOI: 10.1145/211414.211419 228

[112] T. S. Jayram, P. G. Kolaitis, and E. Vee. The containment problem for REAL conjunctive queries with inequalities. In *Proc. of the 25th ACM SIGACT-SIGMOD-SIGART Symposium on Principles of Database Systems*, pages 80–89, Chicago, IL, June 26–28, 2006. DOI: 10.1145/1142351.1142363 227

[113] B. Kimelfeld and Y. Sagiv. Revisiting redundancy and minimization in an XPath fragment. In *EDBT*, pages 61–72, 2008. DOI: 10.1145/1353343.1353355 200

[114] A. Klug. On conjunctive queries containing inequalities. *Journal of the ACM*, 35(1), 1988. DOI: 10.1145/42267.42273 223, 226

[115] A. C. Klug. Equivalence of relational algebra and relational calculus query languages having aggregate functions. *Journal of the ACM*, 29(3):699–717, 1982. DOI: 10.1145/322326.322332 228

[116] C. Koch. Query rewriting with symmetric constraints. In *Proc. of the 2nd International Symposium on Foundations of Information and Knowledge Systems (FoIKS)*, pages 130–147, Springer-Verlag, London, UK, 2002. DOI: 10.1007/3-540-45758-5_9 229

[117] P. G. Kolaitis. The query containment problem: Set semantics vs. bag semantics. In *Proc. of the 7th Alberto Mendelzon International Workshop on Foundations of Data Management*, Puebla/Cholula, Mexico, May 21–23, 2013. 228

[118] P. G. Kolaitis, D. L. Martin, and M. N. Thakur. On the complexity of the containment problem for conjunctive queries with built-in predicates. In *PODS*, pages 197–204, 1998. DOI: 10.1145/275487.275510 226

[119] P. G. Kolaitis, J. Panttaja, and W. C. Tan. The complexity of data exchange. In *Proc. of the 25th ACM SIGACT-SIGMOD-SIGART Symposium on Principles of Database Systems*, pages 30–39, Chicago, IL, June 26–28, 2006. DOI: 10.1145/1142351.1142357 231

[120] P. Koutris, T. Milo, S. Roy, and D. Suciu. Answering conjunctive queries with inequalities. In *18th International Conference on Database Theory, (ICDT)*, pages 76–93, Brussels, Belgium, March 23–27, 2015. DOI: 10.1007/s00224-016-9684-2 227

[121] L. V. S. Lakshmanan, H. Wang, and Z. J. Zhao. Answering tree pattern queries using views. In *VLDB*, pages 571–582, 2006. DOI: 10.1145/1951365.1951386 201

[122] M. Lenzerini. Data integration: A theoretical perspective. In *Proc. of the 21st ACM SIGACT-SIGMOD-SIGART Symposium on Principles of Database Systems*, pages 233–246, Madison, WI, June 3–5, 2002. DOI: 10.1145/543643.543644 225, 226

[123] A. Levy and Y. Sagiv. Queries independent of updates. In *VLDB*, pages 171–181, 1993. 223

[124] A. Y. Levy, A. O. Mendelzon, Y. Sagiv, and D. Srivastava. Answering queries using views. In *Proc. of the 14th ACM SIGACT-SIGMOD-SIGART Symposium on Principles of Database Systems*, pages 95–104, San Jose, CA, May 22–25, 1995. DOI: 10.1007/978-1-4899-7993-3_849-2 224, 228, 229

[125] A. Y. Levy, A. Rajaraman, and J. J. Ordille. Querying heterogeneous information sources using source descriptions. In *Proc. of 22th International Conference on Very Large Data Bases, (VLDB)*, pages 251–262, Mumbai (Bombay), India, September 3–6, 1996. 224

[126] A. Y. Levy, A. Rajaraman, and J. D. Ullman. Answering queries using limited external query processors. *Journal of Computer and System Sciences*, 58(1):69–82, 1999. DOI: 10.1006/jcss.1998.1599 230

[127] C. Li. Computing complete answers to queries in the presence of limited access patterns. *VLDB Journal*, 12(3):211–227, 2003. DOI: 10.1007/s00778-002-0085-6 230

[128] C. Li, M. Bawa, and J. D. Ullman. Minimizing view sets without losing query-answering power. In *Database Theory (ICDT), 8th International Conference, Proceedings*, pages 99–113, London, UK, January 4–6, 2001. DOI: 10.1007/3-540-44503-x_7 233

[129] C. Li and E. Y. Chang. Answering queries with useful bindings. *ACM Transactions on Database Systems*, 26(3):313–343, 2001. DOI: 10.1145/502030.502032 230

[130] C. Li and E. Y. Chang. On answering queries in the presence of limited access patterns. In *Database Theory (ICDT), 8th International Conference, Proceedings*, pages 219–233, London, UK, January 4–6, 2001. DOI: 10.1007/3-540-44503-x_15 230

[131] L. Libkin. Data exchange and incomplete information. In *Proc. of the 25th ACM SIGACT-SIGMOD-SIGART Symposium on Principles of Database Systems*, pages 60–69, Chicago, IL, June 26–28, 2006. DOI: 10.1145/1142351.1142360 231

[132] W. Lipski. On semantic issues connected with incomplete information databases. *ACM Transactions on Database Systems*, 4(3):262–296, 1979. DOI: 10.1145/320083.320088 225

[133] D. Maier, A. O. Mendelzon, and Y. Sagiv. Testing implications of data dependencies. *ACM Transactions on Database Systems*, 4(4):455–469, 1979. DOI: 10.1145/582095.582119 225, 230

[134] D. Maier, Y. Sagiv, and M. Yannakakis. On the complexity of testing implications of functional and join dependencies. *Journal of the ACM*, 28(4):680–695, 1981. DOI: 10.1145/322276.322280 228, 230

[135] G. N. B. Manoharan, S. Ellner, K. Schnaitter, S. Chegu, A. Estrella-Balderrama, S. Gudmundson, A. Gupta, B. Handy, B. Samwel, C. Whipkey, L. Aharkava, H. Apte, N. Gangahar, J. Xu, S. Venkataraman, D. Agrawal, and J. D. Ullman. Shasta: Interactive reporting at scale. In *Proc. of the International Conference on Management of Data, SIGMOD*, pages 1393–1404, San Francisco, CA, June 26–July 01, 2016. DOI: 10.1145/2882903.2904444 221

[136] M. Marx. Queries determined by views: Pack your views. In *Proc. of the 26th ACM SIGACT-SIGMOD-SIGART Symposium on Principles of Database Systems*, pages 23–30, Beijing, China, June 11–13, 2007. DOI: 10.1145/1265530.1265534 232

[137] S. Melnik, A. Gubarev, J. J. Long, G. Romer, S. Shivakumar, M. Tolton, and T. Vassilakis. Dremel: Interactive analysis of web-scale datasets. *PVLDB*, 3(1):330–339, 2010. DOI: 10.1145/1953122.1953148 221

[138] G. Miklau and D. Suciu. Containment and equivalence for a fragment of XPath. *Journal of the ACM*, 51(1):2–45, 2004. DOI: 10.1145/962446.962448 200, 201

[139] R. J. Miller, L. M. Haas, and M. A. Hernández. Schema mapping as query discovery. In *Proc. of 26th International Conference on Very Large Data Bases, (VLDB)*, pages 77–88, Cairo, Egypt, September 10–14, 2000. 231

[140] P. Mitra. An algorithm for answering queries efficiently using views. In *12th Australasian Database Conference, (ADC)*, pages 99–106, Bond University, Queensland, Australia, January 29–February 1, 2001. DOI: 10.1109/adc.2001.904470 224, 229

[141] A. Nash, P. A. Bernstein, and S. Melnik. Composition of mappings given by embedded dependencies. *ACM Transactions on Database Systems*, 32(1):4, 2007. DOI: 10.1145/1206049.1206053 231

[142] A. Nash, L. Segoufin, and V. Vianu. Determinacy and rewriting of conjunctive queries using views: A progress report. In *International Conference on Database Theory (ICDT)*, page 207–224, 2007. DOI: 10.1007/11965893_5 232

[143] A. Nash, L. Segoufin, and V. Vianu. Views and queries: Determinacy and rewriting. *ACM Transactions on Database Systems*, 35(3):21:1–21:41, 2010. DOI: 10.1145/1806907.1806913 232

[144] W. Nutt, Y. Sagiv, and S. Shurin. Deciding equivalences among aggregate queries. In *Proc. of the 17th ACM SIGACT-SIGMOD-SIGART Symposium on Principles of Database Systems*, pages 214–223, Seattle, WA, June 1–3, 1998. DOI: 10.1145/275487.275512 228

[145] C. H. Papadimitriou and M. Yannakakis. On the complexity of database queries. *Journal of Computer and System Sciences*, 58(3):407–427, 1999. DOI: 10.1006/jcss.1999.1626 228

[146] S. Paparizos, Y. Wu, L. V. S. Lakshmanan, and H. V. Jagadish. Tree logical classes for efficient evaluation of Xquery. In *SIGMOD Conference*, pages 71–82, 2004. DOI: 10.1145/1007568.1007579 222

[147] J. Paredaens and D. V. Gucht. Possibilities and limitations of using flat operators in nested algebra expressions. In *PODS*, pages 29–38, 1988. DOI: 10.1145/308386.308402 221

[148] D. Pasaila. Conjunctive queries determinacy and rewriting. In *Database Theory (ICDT), 14th International Conference, Proceedings*, pages 220–231, Uppsala, Sweden, March 21–24, 2011. DOI: 10.1145/1938551.1938580 232

[149] L. Popa, A. Deutsch, A. Sahuguet, and V. Tannen. A chase too far? In *Proc. of the ACM SIGMOD Conference*, pages 273–284, 2000. DOI: 10.1145/335191.335421 225

[150] L. Popa and V. Tannen. An equational chase for path-conjunctive queries, constraints, and views. In *Database Theory (ICDT), 7th International Conference, Proceedings*, pages 39–57, Jerusalem, Israel, January 10–12, 1999. DOI: 10.1007/3-540-49257-7_4 225

[151] L. Popa, Y. Velegrakis, R. J. Miller, M. A. Hernández, and R. Fagin. Translating web data. In *Proc. of 28th International Conference on Very Large Data Bases, (VLDB)*, pages 598–609, Hong Kong, China, August 20–23, 2002. DOI: 10.1016/b978-155860869-6/50059-7 231

[152] R. Pottinger and A. Y. Halevy. Minicon: A scalable algorithm for answering queries using views. *VLDB Journal*, 10(2–3):182–198, 2001. 224, 229

[153] X. Qian. Query folding. In *ICDE*, pages 48–55, 1996. DOI: 10.1109/icde.1996.492088 226

[154] A. Rajaraman, Y. Sagiv, and J. D. Ullman. Answering queries using templates with binding patterns. In *Proc. of the 14th ACM SIGACT-SIGMOD-SIGART Symposium on Principles of Database Systems*, pages 105–112, San Jose, CA, May 22–25, 1995. DOI: 10.1145/212433.220199 224, 230

[155] R. Rosati. The limits of querying ontologies. In *Database Theory (ICDT), 11th International Conference, Proceedings*, pages 164–178, Barcelona, Spain, January 10–12, 2007. DOI: 10.1007/11965893_12 233

[156] R. Rosati. On the finite controllability of conjunctive query answering in databases under open-world assumption. *Journal of Computer and System Sciences*, 77(3):572–594, 2011. DOI: 10.1016/j.jcss.2010.04.011 233

[157] M. A. Roth, H. F. Korth, and A. Silberschatz. Extended algebra and calculus for nested relational databases. *ACM Transactions on Database Systems*, 13(4):389–417, 1988. DOI: 10.1145/49346.49347 221

[158] Y. Saraiya. Subtree elimination algorithms in deductive databases. Ph.D. thesis, Department of Computer Science, Stanford University, 1991. 226

[159] J. Shute, R. Vingralek, B. Samwel, B. Handy, C. Whipkey, E. Rollins, M. Oancea, K. Littlefield, D. Menestrina, S. Ellner, J. Cieslewicz, I. Rae, T. Stancescu, and H. Apte. F1: A distributed SQL database that scales. *PVLDB*, 6(11):1068–1079, 2013. DOI: 10.14778/2536222.2536232 221

[160] D. Srivastava, S. Dar, H. V. Jagadish, and A. Y. Levy. Answering queries with aggregation using views. In *Proc. of 22th International Conference on Very Large Data Bases, (VLDB)*, pages 318–329, Mumbai (Bombay), India, September 3–6, 1996. 228

[161] B. Sundarmurthy, P. Koutris, W. Lang, J. F. Naughton, and V. Tannen. M-tables: Representing missing data. In *20th International Conference on Database Theory, (ICDT)*, pages 21:1–21:20, Venice, Italy, March 21–24, 2017. 231

[162] N. Tang, J. X. Yu, M. T. Özsu, B. Choi, and K.-F. Wong. Multiple materialized view selection for XPath query rewriting. In *ICDE*, pages 873–882, 2008. DOI: 10.1109/icde.2008.4497496 201

[163] I. Tatarinov, S. Viglas, K. S. Beyer, J. Shanmugasundaram, E. J. Shekita, and C. Zhang. Storing and querying ordered XML using a relational database system. In *SIGMOD Conference*, pages 204–215, 2002. DOI: 10.1145/564691.564715 222

[164] B. ten Cate, P. G. Kolaitis, and W. Othman. Data exchange with arithmetic operations. In *Joint EDBT/ICDT Conferences, Proceedings*, pages 537–548, Genoa, Italy, March 18–22, 2013. DOI: 10.1145/2452376.2452439 231

[165] J. D. Ullman. Information integration using logical views. *Theoretical Computer Science*, 239(2):189–210, 2000. DOI: 10.1016/s0304-3975(99)00219-4 224

[166] R. van der Meyden. The complexity of querying indefinite data about linearly ordered domains. In *PODS*, 1992. DOI: 10.1145/137097.137902 226

[167] R. van der Meyden. The complexity of querying indefinite data about linearly ordered domains. *Journal of Computer and System Sciences*, 54(1):113–135, 1997. DOI: 10.1145/137097.137902 227

[168] R. van der Meyden. Logical approaches to incomplete information: A survey. In *Logics for Databases and Information Systems (the book grow out of the Dagstuhl Seminar 9529: Role of Logics in Information Systems, 1995)*, pages 307–356, 1998. DOI: 10.1007/978-1-4615-5643-5_10 225

[169] M. Y. Vardi. The complexity of relational query languages. In *Proc. 14th ACM Symposium on Theory of Computing*, page 137–146, 1982. DOI: 10.1145/800070.802186 226

[170] M. Y. Vardi. Inferring multivalued dependencies from functional and join dependencies. *Acta Informatica*, 19:305–324, 1983. DOI: 10.1007/bf00290729 230

[171] M. Y. Vardi. A theory of regular queries. In *Proc. of the 35th ACM SIGMOD-SIGACT-SIGAI Symposium on Principles of Database Systems, (PODS)*, pages 1–9, San Francisco, CA, June 26–July 01, 2016. DOI: 10.1145/2902251.2902305 233

[172] J. Wang and J. X. Yu. XPath rewriting using multiple views. In *DEXA*, pages 493–507, 2008. DOI: 10.1007/978-3-540-85654-2_43 201

[173] J. Wang, J. X. Yu, and C. Liu. Independence of containing patterns property and its application in tree pattern query rewriting using views. *World Wide Web*, 12(1):87–105, 2009. DOI: 10.1007/s11280-008-0057-x 200

[174] F. Wei and G. Lausen. Containment of conjunctive queries with safe negation. In *Database Theory (ICDT), 9th International Conference, Proceedings*, pages 343–357, Siena, Italy, January 8–10, 2003. DOI: 10.1007/3-540-36285-1_23 224, 226

[175] P. T. Wood. Minimising simple XPath expressions. In *WebDB*, pages 13–18, 2001. 201

[176] W. Xu and Z. M. Özsoyoglu. Rewriting XPath queries using materialized views. In *VLDB*, pages 121–132, 2005. DOI: 10.1016/j.jcss.2011.12.001 200

[177] M. Yannakakis. Algorithms for acyclic database schemes. In *VLDB*, pages 82–94, 1981. 201

[178] M. Yannakakis. Algorithms for acyclic database schemes. In *Very Large Data Bases, 7th International Conference, Proceedings*, pages 82–94, Cannes, France, September 9–11, 1981. 224

[179] X. Zhang and M. Z. Ozsoyoglu. On efficient reasoning with implication constraints. In *DOOD*, pages 236–252, 1993. DOI: 10.1007/3-540-57530-8_15 223

[180] R. Zhou, C. Liu, J. Wang, and J. Li. Containment between unions of XPath queries. In *DASFAA*, pages 405–420, Springer-Verlag, 2009. DOI: 10.1007/978-3-642-00887-0_36 200

Authors' Biographies

FOTO N. AFRATI

Foto N. Afrati is a professor in the Electrical and Computing Engineering Department of the NTUA, Greece. She received a B.S. degree from the Mechanical and Electrical Engineering Department of National Technical University of Athens (NTUA) and a Ph.D. from Imperial College of the University of London. She is a Fellow of ACM. She has received the ACM Recognition for Service Award in 2005 and the best-paper award in ICDT 2009. She has been the program-committee chair for the Conference on Principles of Databases (PODS) 2005, and for the International Conference on Database Theory (ICDT) 1997, for which she was the organizing committee chair as well. She currently serves as associate editor of the IEEE *TKDE* journal. In 2012–2013, she spent her sabbatical leave visiting Google at Mountain View. She has published over 100 papers in the areas of databases, algorithms, and distributed computing. Her research interests are in the area of database theory, recent research interests are mainly in the area of big data, including query optimization for MapReduce and other distributed platforms.

RADA Y. CHIRKOVA

Rada Y. Chirkova is an associate professor of Computer Science at North Carolina State University. She has received a B.Sc. and a M.Sc., both in Applied Mathematics, from Moscow State University (Moscow, Russia), and an M.Sc. and a Ph.D., both in Computer Science, from Stanford University. She is a senior member of the Association for Computing Machinery, and served in 2017 as General Co-Chair of the ACM International Conference on Management of Data (SIGMOD). She is associate editor of the *SIGMOD Record* journal and of *The Computer Journal* (Oxford). She has co-authored 3 books (including this book), and has over 60 peer-reviewed publications on topics ranging from query containment and equivalence, query processing, view-based reformulation of data and queries, information security and leakage, to applications of policies to agent behaviors. She has received the National Science Foundation (NSF) CAREER Award, as well as numerous IBM Faculty and University Partnership Program Awards. Her research interests span information and knowledge management, algorithms and theory of computation, and data sciences and analytics, with applications including data wrangling, cyber security, and healthcare information technology.

Printed in the United States
by Baker & Taylor Publisher Services